Paradise Under the Shades of Swords

A Short Encyclopedia of Islam to Understand
Quran and Hadiths
Through 786 Textual Questions

Dr. Umesh Patri

Paradise Under
the Shades of Swords
by Dr Umesh Patri,PhD.

© Umesh Patri

ISBN: **978-1-926800-07-3**

Printed in USA

About the Author

Umesh Patri earned his MA degree in British and American Literature from Gurukul University, Hardwar and in 1982 he was awarded PhD on Comparative Literature from Utkal University, Odisha.

Patri has a long and distinguished teaching career in different University colleges including Ravenshaw and BJB. As a part of his Post-doctoral project he has visited 57 libraries abroad that include Harvard University library, Cambridge; British library, London; and the Library of Congress, Washington, D.C. Besides he had an extensive lecture tour in USA, Canada, England, Germany, Israel, Jordan, Egypt and a part of Arab.

Because of exemplary performance he is listed in the most selective directories of International Organisations for Good Temperance (IOGT) England; Asian Admirable Achievers in Rifacimento International. He is referred to as a writer in the Norwegian and British Humanist Journals and the Thoreau Society Bulletin, N.Y.

His books in English and in Oriya include *Hindu Scriptures and American Transcendentalists*, prefaced by Walter Harding, Distinguished Professor of American Literature Emeritus, State University of New York; *Problems in Paradise,* Prefaced by Jim Herrick, Literary Editor of the New Humanist, London and Introduction by Dr. Bill Cooke, School of Visual Arts, University of Auckland. His article : "A Fresh Interpretation of Emerson's 'Brahma' in the light of Bhagawat Gita", has been included in the compilation of Indian Contribution to American Studies, Somiya Publications and won the Olive I. Reddick Award by the American Studies Research Centre for the best paper presented at the IAAS annual conference for the year 1994-1995. He is retired but not tired. As an animal activist he has associated himself with many philanthropic organisations.

Acknowledgements

I am very grateful to Dr. K.V. Paliwal, a renowned Orientalist and a master of comparative religious studies for inspiring me to write this book.

My special thanks to the following for quoting them in the question series. They are : Warraq Ibn, Benjamin Walker, Abdallah Al-Fadi, Sujit Das and others.

Though I do not remember their names whom I met on my way to the Middle-East but they have helped me to enrich my practical knowledge on Islam. They deserve my thanks. I cannot claim my book is free from errors and lapses. I sincerely apologize to my readers if they feel anything offending as my intention is not to cast aspiration rather while asking questions I have become more impersonal, text based and friendly. However all the mistakes that the reader points out will be taken care of in the further edition.

Dedicated
to
Brindaban Patri & Saraswati Devi
My beloved Parents
Who initiated me to study the
Holy Quran & Hadiths
So that I could be a Practising Muslim

Umesh

Abbreviations

Quran	=	Used only reference number such as 12 : 10; 18 : 98, etc.
Buk	=	Sahih Bukhari
Mus	=	Sahih Muslim
Daw	=	Sunan Abu Dawud
Tir	=	Jame Tirmizi
Tab	=	Tabari
Ish	=	Ishaq
Mal	=	Muwalta of Imam Malik
Maj	=	Sunan ibn Majah
Mis	=	Mishkat ul Masabih
Nas	=	Sunanal Nasai
Gn	=	Genesis (Bible)
Ex	=	Exodus (Bible)
Jn	=	St.John (Bible)
Qtd	=	Quoted by
CQV	=	Comments on Quranic Verses

Preface

The famous Odia writer Dr Umesh Patri needs no introduction. Many of his books are being published from time to time. One of his fundamental characteristics is to initiate an innovative wave of thought process through his investigative and insightful research. Islam and Quran is always much discussed throughout the world. Each writer and philosopher has studied and interpreted Quran according to their perception. The Holy Quran is the most debated document in the world.

Since Quran is basically in Arabic, linguistically it can be translated into different languages, nevertheless its essence has been interpreted and analysed very differently depending on the perception of the readers. Quran has been translated into 97 languages. There are innumerable themes in Quran. So some writers deal with the thematic aspect of the Quran whereas many others look at the material content while few others interpret the Holy Quran from a spiritual point of view.

Quran is so diverse in its approach that it not only fascinates writers and poets alike but also cognitively challenges the knowledge and understanding of scientists and philosophers. Each thinker tries to create something original and innovative in their respective field through their individual perception and insight. That is why Dr Patri feels the need to understand and explicate the essence of this divine scripture. Dr Patri does not delimit the Holy Scripture to its religiosity only. He explores its relevance in the present day materialistic society. He also raises some pertinent issues to understand the Holy Quran. He believes that a dialogic form helps for better understanding of any text.

Dr Patri has presented a vast series of questions on Quran so that an ordinary reader easily understands the scripture and even if someone is unable to comprehend any revealed message they always know what exactly to ask so that the subject expert can explain them with ease. The Arabic language has an extensive lexicon and each lexicon comes with multiple levels of meaning such that one word is used in different places in Quran with very different meanings. And Dr Patri, being a successful teacher, has very rightly pointed these issues and has also very meticulously provided their answers too.

In the chapter "Miracle of Miracles" he states that there wasn't much of a syntactic difference with the linguistic structure of the Holy Quran and that of the other verses written during that time. This implies that the Holy Quran was available in a language which was readily accepted by the society at large. Initially the writer presents some information on the Holy Quran in this chapter but as we move on the writer shocks us when he asks that when other divinely inspired scriptures were available what was the need of another divinely revealed scripture in the form of Holy Quran? This question seems relevant because Islam respects and acknowledges all the earlier prophets. The wise writer Umesh Patri has asked about 786 questions in his book. The book revolves round these questions.

Although it is quite difficult to answer the intellectual and academic questions asked on Quran and Islam the author seems to have suggested their answers within the framework of the questions. Besides, the questions are designed and answers suggested in such a manner that each answer gives rise to a set of new questions. Some interesting questions can be quoted here. For example the writer asks in question 227 : "For whom was the Quran written?" and goes on to ask "is Quran only for the Arabs?" In question 232 the writer asks "is Quran a complete book?

Besides these questions, the writer gives us some important information regarding the other religions that were prevalent during those times. He also tries to satisfy the quest of his readers by asking queries on previous prophets like Moses and Jesus, the predecessors of Prophet Muhammad. The writer also tries to find the points of contact between Quran and other scriptures of that time. Dr Patri has given a comprehensive list of the Suras and Aayats of the Holy Quran. He has also recorded the chronological history of Islam.

The book is entitled "Paradise Under the Shades of Sword" and any reader who reads this book will be compelled to conclude that the book is actually "The Reflection of Saraswati in the Shades of Pen".

Padmashree Dr Muzaffer Hussain
Mumbai
March 16, 2012

Contents

Introduction

Islam, though practised by the Muslims the world over was in deep dark like the African forests until it was discovered by Dr. David Livingstone. After 1400 years of inaccessibility and reticence Dr. Umesh Patri penetrated deep into the multi-faceted Quran and revealed minutely all its aspects with the light of Hadith and other commentaries made by renowned scholars of Europe and the USA like the Vedas, which came to light and the parameter of analytical study after it was revealed by the German Professor of Oxford MaxMuller, Dr. Patri also has catered to all the concepts of the Quran from different perspectives minutely for the contemplation of enthusiastic scholars indiscriminate of any religions and schools of thoughts.

After the demolition of World Trade Centre, people of America for the first time encountered the brunt of Islamic terrorism and thereafter they began to grope to find out the epicenter of its eruption. They suspected over Islam and its key source Quran. But even after a thorough search of Quran through the trail trodden by Dr. Patri, I could not trace a single flash of militancy in the Quran and Islam. Rather it reveals the life style of a great man, the monotheist and polygamist Muhammad whose philosophy and outlook has created and shaped the exogamous Islamic cloud that has overshadowed all the nations of the world. It is surprising that within a short span of fourteen hundred years, a majority section of the world population consisting of more that one billion people are imbibed by Islam which has its profoundly distinct economy, literature, culture, history, art of warfare (popularly known as Jihad) marriage system, language and a code of conduct to be followed by the followers of Islam in their daily routine life.

Hence everyone has the right to know, to study and to ponder over this marvelous contribution of a single great man Muhammad and his brainchild Allah, a nascent and formless being who appears in his mind whenever he needs to arrive at a decision and also positively suggests whenever Muhammad determines to change in his policy dictated to him by Allah, (who is acknowledged by Muhammad as Omniscient, Omnipotent and all Merciful) who framed the character of Muhammad to become an uncompromising leader to erect the infrastructure of a militant religion admixed with sex and violence that would bring the entire nations of the world under the banner of Islamic nation, the own nation of Muhammad, with Universal followers like him who unmistakably wish to follow his path without any deviation and deflection and take delight by prefixing or suffixing his violence and sex crazy name Muhammad in every Islamic nomenclature.

I would like to compare this book with Uncle Tom's Cabin written by Mrs. Harriet Elizabeth Beecher Stowe which had a great impact on the humanitarian institutions and leaders of the world that impelled for the emancipation of millions of Blacks of the USA from their century long slavery.

This book would also act as a beacon light for the emancipation of more than half a billion women of the world who are suffering from involuntary divorce, honour killing, stoning to death and a life of slavery under polygamous husbands. The system of castration is still in vogue in many Islamic countries. The worst sufferers of the modern world would certainly get a solace by observing the reflection of their sufferings in the mirror of this book and raise their last voice for freedom.

I thank Dr. Patri for his great contribution, the presentation of analytical study of Islam, as a first and foremost manifestation of its kind in the world literature of ethics.

Anwar Sheikh
LIBERTY
Cardiff, Great Britain
24.11.2004

Know Your Quran and Hadiths

Quran: It is the central religious text of Islam which Muslims consider the verbatim word of God. It is regarded widely as the finest piece of literature in the Arabic language. The Quran is divided into 114 *suras* of unequal length which are classified either as Meccan or Medinan depending upon their place and time of revelation. Muslims believe the Quran to be verbally revealed through angel Gabriel from God to Muhammad gradually over a period of approximately twentythree years beginning in 610 CE, when Muhammad was 40, and concluding in 632 CE, the year of his death.

Hadith: It refers to reports of statements or actions of Muhammad or of his tacit approval of something said or done in his presence. The two major aspects of hadith are the text of the report (*Matn*), which contains the actual narrative, and the chain of narrators (*isnad*) which documents the route by which the report has been transmitted. Muslims consider hadith to be essential supplements to and clarifications of the Quran, as well as in clarifying issues pertaining to Islamic jurisprudence. But it is very much said that these Hadiths actually contain materials from Pre-Islamic time : much was added to it after Muhammad's death, and it was augmented with fresh material as the Islamic empire grew (Walker 1999 : 171).

Sunni and Shia hadith collections differ because scholars from the two traditions differ as to the reliability of the narrators and transmitters. Besides these six Hadiths Shias have 4 others and Sufis have their own Hadiths too... Sunni Muslims view six major Hadith collections as most important whereas Shias have four hadith collections. In order of authenticity, the six Hadith collections of the Sunnis are :

1. **Al-Bukhari** (810-870) the author is known as Imam Bukhari, born in Bukhara, present day Uzbekistan, on July 21, 810. He began his study of the Hadith at the early age of ten. It is said that Bukhari retained in his memory one million Hadith of the Prophet Muhammad with all the details of their sources. Out of the million Hadith which he had learnt from some 80,000 reporters he selected 7,275 Hadith.

2. **Sahih Muslim** (819-875) compiled by Abdul Hussain Muslim-b-al-Hajjaj al-Nishapuri. It is one of the six most authentic collections of the traditions of the holy prophet. He had selected 9,200, out of 300,000 hadiths. His collection is somewhat superior to Bukhari's work in the detail of arrangement of tradition and in freedom (Karim 2001 : 39).

3. **Sunan Abu Daud al-Sijistani** (817-889) Out of 500,000 tradition it contains 4, 800 traditions relating to Jurisprudence.

4. **Sunan Al-Nasai-**(828-915) by Abu Abdur Rahman Ahmad-b-Shu'aib-Al Nasai. This Hadith was recognised best of his times. Out of 5,000,000 traditions 5270 traditions were selected as authentic.

5. **Sunanibn Majah-** (823-887) compiled by Muhammad-b-yezid. He compiled only 4341 Hadiths in 32 books divided into 1500 chapters.

6. **Jame' Tirmizi-** (825-892) by Imam Tirmizi. While compiling the Hadiths he was the first to identify the names, surnames and titles of the narrators and tried to evaluate the reliability of each Hadith (Paliwal nd.6).

As all the Hadiths were compiled under the rule of the Abbasid Caliphs, so reports on praise of the Umayyads were excluded. Ibn Hanbal made a collection, which he called Musnad, more on the lines of the earliest collections and in it are preserved references to the Umayyads which were excluded from the Six Books. Ibn Hanbal may have been an impossible person but he had the courage of his convictions.

Al-Sira: It is a collection of various traditional Muslim biographies of Muhammad from which, in addition to the Quran and Hadiths, most historical information about his life and the early period of Islam is derived. The earliest form of *Sira* was that of the storytellers who told stories of Muhammad. One of the popular teachers of Sira was Muhammad ibn Ishaq who collected oral traditions that formed the basis of an important extant biography of the Prophet. His work survived through that of his editors, most notably Ibn Jarir al-Tabari. al-Tabari's two main books are *History of the Prophets and Kings* and *The Commentary on the Quran.* The first one is generally known as the *Annals.* This is a universal history from the time of Quranic creation to 915 AD and is renowned for its detail and accuracy concerning Muslim history. The second book was the commentary on the Quran, which was marked by the same fullness of detail as the *Annals.*

Shia Hadith is a collection of four books called *Nahj al-Balagha* or *The Four Books* the sermons of which are attributed to Ali. The three authors who have written these hadiths are known as the "Three Muhammads." The Shia hadiths are:

Kitab al-Kafi : by Muhammad ibn al-Razi. It is divided into three sections : *Usul-al Kafi,* which is concerned with the principle of religion, *Furu al-Kafi,* which is concerned with the details of religious law, and *Rawdat al-Kafi,* which is concerned with various religious aspects.

Man la yahduruhu al-Faqih : by Abu Jafar al-Qummi. This book is meant to be a reference book to help ordinary Shia Muslims in the practice of the legal requirements of Islam.

Tahdhib al-Ahkam : by Abu Jafar al-Tusi. It is concerned with the practical regulations for carrying out the *Sharia*, the holy Law of Islam.

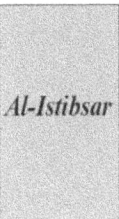

Al-Istibsar : by Abu Jafar al-Tusi. It is concerned with Islamic jurisprudential decrees and injunctions.

Section

I

The Prophet of Arabia

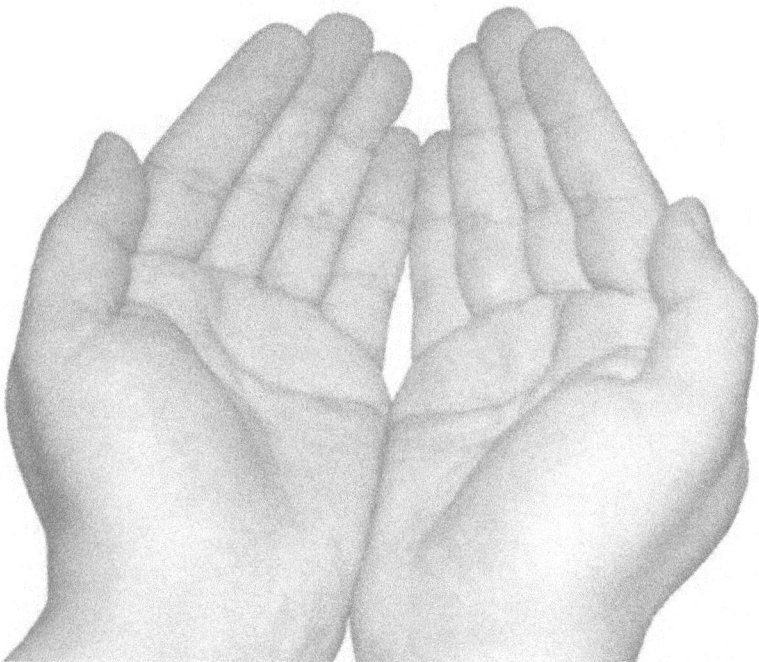

1- Muhammad the Ideal Role Model

I

The desert of Arab covers about 2.6 million square kilometres with a range of mountains running parallel to the Red Sea coast. Its constituent countries are Bahrain, Kuwait, Oman, Qatar, United Arab Emirates, Yemen and the largest South Arabia. The inhabitants were mainly the Bedouins, a wandering tribe who with their flocks and herds searched the water holes and pasturage. Rivers there are none, the streams that gather from the rainfall are scarcely formed but they sink into the thirsty desert. Climb hill after hill, one will meet barren and sunburnt rocks and the rare green valleys, inhospitable to all but the Arabs. They lived with dates, milk and meat of the camel and their tents were made of camel hair. For transportation they had their horses who were used to gain booty.

The two major cities of Arab were Mecca and Medina. Compared to the forbidding deserts and arid steppes of Mecca, Medina was not that barren. It had oasis in which date palms flourished and cereals grew. Fruits and vegetables were plenty in some parts of the Jewish areas of Medina.

Midway between Yemen and Egypt there were no trees except some low brushwood and layers of rocks and a valley. In the centre of the valley a wonderful well of unusually cool and sweet water affords an inexhaustible supply, probably fed by a perennial stream below. The name of the well is Zamzam. Wind Wood Read remarks : This valley, on account of its well, was made the halting-place of the Indian caravans, and there the goods changed carriers-- the south developed them over to the north (1972 : 94).

Though at times the North did not cooperate with South but they agreed to maintain peace and took the solemn oaths for the protection of the trade. It was long before the advent of Islam that there was a classless society where the country ran without police or court. So there were no problems for the travellers or tradesmen.

Very soon the sanctuary near the Zamzam well brought its fame for Kaaba. In the last month of each year people came to Zamzam and eventually they established a shrine in Kaaba. Each tribe either found or introduced in the Kaaba their domestic worship; the temple was adorned with 360 idols of men, eagles, lions and antelopes, and the most conspicuous was the statue of Hubal, of red agate, holding in his hand seven arrows without heads or feathers. Most of the deities of the Arab tribes were sky gods, associaed with heavenly bodies such as the Sun and Moon. The Southern Arabian pantheon was Athtar, god of thunderstorms and rain. In northern Arabia they included a wall enclosed altar where animal sacricifies, and other offerings were made to the gods, and priests interpreted oracles (*Britannica* 2006 : 119). Edward Gibbon thus said : "The rocks of the desert were hewn into gods or altars in imitation of the black stone of Mecca, which is deeply tainted with the reproach of an idolatrous origin...Naturally the religion of Arabs, as well as of

2

the Indians, consisted in the worship of the sun, the moon and the fixed stars"(1941: 71-72). In the campus of Kaaba shrine the poets met during Ramadan in a great national gathering week with their compositions at Okaz.

II

Early in the seventh century, when the Arabians were engaged in religious rituals and rites, a new faith emerged in Arabian Peninsula. That new faith was not only different from the Jewish and the Christian faith, but it grew indigenously and independently to cater to the needs of the people of Arabia. Little more than twenty years, this desert-borne fastest growing faith spreaded swiftly throughout the Middle East, North Africa and South Asia within a century. Islam controlled an empire more vast than that of Rome or Alexander the Great. It was an empire-building agenda from day one. It became the youngest of the world's major religions, founded six centuries after Jesus and nearly twelve centuries after Buddha. This movement was called Islam.

It is not easy to say anything about Prophet Muhammad, the founder of Islam, as there was no biography available until more than a century after his death. We know very little about his childhood. But it is certain that he was born in an environment that was less civilized than ancient Judaea.

Like every year in the month of Rajab, Muhammad would go to Mount Hira to meditate and fast. In 610, when he was 40, he had a vision of a majestic being and heard voices which instructed him to "Read." Muhammad answered "I cannot read !" Again and again he heard the same :

> *Read : In the name of thy lord who created*
> *Created man from a clot*
> *Read : And it is thy lord the most bountiful*
> *Who teacheth by the pen*
> *Teacheth each man that which he knew not.*

When the spirit disappeared, Muhammad came back home and told everything to his wife Khadijah. Khadijah saw her husband's fear and covered him with a cloak to sleep. Again the spirit made him restless and shouted :

> *O thou that are cloaked, arise and warn !*
> *Thy lord Magnify ! Thy Raiment Purify !*
> *And from Iniquity get thee away.*

Later he identified the voice as the voice of angel Gabriel. The revelation was made on one Monday in the month of Ramadhan.

Muhammad woke up and told Khadijah that the spirit made him restless to call men to God. But to whom should he tell and call to believe such incident ? Khadijah promptly responded "Call me the first, for I believe in thee." Muhammad began to have additional revelations and Gabriel told Muhammad that he was chosen as the Messenger of God. He gained a small number of converts to his belief. After Khadijah, Ali, his cousin and son-in-law, Abu Bakr, and the freed slave Zayd ibn Haritha, were among the first. The early converts came from young men of influential families, young men of weaker families and a few foreigners.

3

Thereafter Muhammad the caravan leader became Muhammad the Messenger of God. He took a long route from an orphan to a merchant, from merchant to a messenger and from a messenger to a politician. He made a collection of his confused sayings in trance and called them revelations which were in Arabi and his local dialect Hidjaaz. J. Mecabe opined that most experts agree that he was neuropathic, many say epileptic (p. 396).

During his time Arab was in a conflicting and difficult situation and was prepared for a great revolution through the revelation of Muhammad. Muhammad compelled the obstinate Arabs to surrender to Islam which meant acceptance, submission and commitment to the only God called Allah. But the prophet feared that the Arabians may not accept him as a Prophet so he kept his station as a Messenger of Allah. Therefore Muhammad did not like to call his religion as "Muhammadanism" in the sense they call Christianity for worshipping Christ, or Buddhism for worshipping the Buddha. He did not force his people to worship him in Islam as Christ in Christianity or Buddha in Buddhism. However, Muhammad politely proclaimed that he should be considered the last of a series of Prophets.

Unhesitatingly he confesses : "I am but a man like you" (18 : 110), "I am not your guardian" (10 : 108), "I am not sent to "watch over your doings" (6 : 104). He did not claim that "with him are the treasures of heaven" nor does he know the secret things (6 : 59) as God alone knows the unseen (27 : 26; 7 : 186) and he neither knows what will be done with me or you (46 : 9).

During his time a group called the Hanifs claimed spiritual descent from Ibrahim and were gaining popularity for their virtue and deep religiousness and monotheism. Muhammad claimed himself a Hanif for the safer side (Parrinder 1971 : 465).

The dearest wife of Muhammad, Ayesha, commented on his habits : The Prophet loved three things, women, perfume and food, and the first two he had his heart's desire." Loving women, prefume and food was never bad. He was allowed by Allah who told him : Apart from the women you have married, you can take as wives to whom you like among the slaves you capture in the war and also those offered from the daughters of your father's brother and your father's sister and your mother's brother and your mother's sister. This special privilege is exclusively to you only but not for other believers.

The Western critics were never favourable to Muhammad, his love for women and hatred for heathens. So they always gave a partial view denying him a rightful place in history. The mass media do not leave any stone unturned, when they talk about Muhammad or Muslims be it the cartoons or Hollywood portrayals. They portrayed Muhammad as a camel-thief, a Rake, sorcerer, a brigand chief (*Year Book of Muslim*), the bandit, the invader, the robber and the women hunter (Malabari, p. 8).

For Voltaire, the French Philosopher, Muhammad was a theocratic tyrant (Qtd. Esposits 1993 : 48). Voltaire had immense hatred for Islam, particularly Prophet Muhammad, the founder of Islam. He wrote a play entitled "Mahomet" where Muhammad was presented as an imposter who enslaved men's souls. This play was performed in 1742 (Spencer 2005 : 20). Voltaire dedicated the play to Pope Benedict XIV. The play is a study of religious fanaticism and self-serving manipulation based on an episode in the traditional biography of Muhammad in

4

which he orders the murder of his critics. Voltaire described the play as, "... written in opposition to the founder of a false and barbarous sect to whom could I with more propriety inscribe a satire on the cruelty and errors of a false Prophet."

Explaining the comment of Voltaire, Sujit Das remarks : "Today, with the development of psychology and personality studies, thanks to Freud, Kohut, Kernberg, Vaknin, Masterson, Hotchkiss and many others, we know how true Voltaire was in his thinking. Muslim's perpetual mental slavery is repugnant and awful and because of this perpetual mental slavery, Muslims cannot write an honest biography of their Prophet that does not shun the truth. Muslims have to defend Islam's foolishness (2010 : 196).

Muhammad was termed as a bandit, an invader, a robber, women hunter, hypocrite and an agent of evil and was branded as a sower of discard, a sensualist by the Western critics. They said, Muhammad was merciless and fanatical. He introduced religious hatred into large parts of the world that lived in religious harmony before. He curtailed the freedom of women, endorsed slavery and broke up families. He ordered cruel punishments. The world would have been a better place if he had not succeeded in spreading his religion (Colin 1985 : 16).

The Truth Seeker magazine writes : He was one of the most vicious, murderous, irrational, religious fanatics who ever lived. His followers are of a similar type. He told his murderous gang of soldiers and supporters to kill anyone who refused to accept his ideas or his orders. Millions of innocent people have been killed by his followers and many now suffer death at their hands. Moslem leaders are dangerous, murderous fanatics, worse than the Jewish and Christian religious promoters (Nov-1983 : 339).

Whatever the people might say about Muhammad but everybody will have to accept one thing about him that he could achieve what Moses and Jesus could not in their life time. Moses talked about the promised land through out his life but could not enter into it. Jesus talked about the kingdom of his father but before establishing it he was crucified. Whereas an orphan Muhammad who was not a great prophet like Moses neither the only son of God, died as a sovereign, a conqueror and the head of a state.

At times his simplicity was amazing. For example, when a man offered him money he refused, saying : "I have a goat to give us milk and a beast to ride; what more do I want" (Tritton 1957 : 89) ?

Muhammad is "the only one of the world's Prophets to be born within the full light of history", says the eminent historian Philip K. HiHi (2001, p. III). Whereas there is no such historical document available for Buddha, Zoroaster, Moses and Jesus.

Not only the western critics but the Muslim critics like Ali Dashti, the Iranian writer of *Twenty-three Years* (1937) ridicules the Prophet for political assassinations, murder, and the elimination of all opponents as the "services to Islam." Regarding the God of the Quran the author established Allah as a cruel, angry and a proud God.

A Sudanese theologian Mahamud Muhammad Taha tried to minimize the role of the Quran as a source of law. He advocated for new laws for the new age.

But religious authorities in Khartoum did not agree with his ideas and declared him guilty of apostasy in 1968. His writings were burned. Taha himself managed to escape execution for seventeen years. He was tried again and was publicly hanged at 76 years in Khartoum in January 1985 (Reddy 2004 : 213).

Mu'ammar Al Gaddafi whose public statements on Muhammad, the Quran, and Islam amount to blasphemy far greater than anything discussed so far. Gaddafi confined Sharia to private matters. He changed the Islamic calendar, mocked Meccan pilgrims as "guileful and foolish", criticized the Prophet, and claimed that his own achievements were greater than those of the Prophet. Though religious leaders found Gaddafi anti-Islamic and deviant and condemned his "perjury and lies," he was the only author who was not executed because he was a Libyan leader, nor were any of his writings banned (Ready 2004 : 213).

According to Gustav Weil, Muhammad was suffering from epilepsy. For Franz Buhl, Muhammad revealed the unattractive side of his character : Cruelty, slyness, dishonesty, untrustworthiness; someone whose leading principle was 'the end justifies the means' (Qtd. Das 2010 : 15).

Muhammad at last died in Ayesha's apartment, presumably was poisoned by one of his Jewish female slaves and was buried right there. There is no proof whatsoever that he ever uttered the famous line, "Not tonight, honey, I have got a headache." Before he died, he had sent forces to attack Syria, beginning a struggle that would not end until a major part of the civilized world was subject to Arab and to his new religion.

I have a series of doubts on Islam and its last Prophet. These are all my personal queries. Can you help ?

Top among the Hundred

1. How far is Michael Hart justified to place Prophet Muhammad at the very top of the list in his "The 100 : A Ranking of the Most Influential Persons in History" ? Did he ever mention whether the influence was positive or negative ?

Did not Muhammad, the Prophet, exploit the God-fearing Arabians and control the psyche of his followers to follow him as an excellent example (33:21) in eating, drinking, walking, talking, sleeping, dressing etc. ?

A Magnificant Man for Mankind

2. Did not the Prophet demand "none of you is a believer till I am dearer to you than your child, your father and the whole of mankind (*Mus* 1 : 71) ?

Did he not proclaim himself as the anointed Messenger of God and the Seal of the Prophets (33.40); this megalomaniac regarded himself as *Khayru-l-Khalq* (the best of creation), an "excellent example" (33.21), and gave us a hint that he is "exalted above other Prophets in degrees" (2.253), "the preferred one" (17.55), and sent as a "Mercy to the worlds" (21.107), to have been risen "to a praised estate" (17.79)?

God's Chosen Tribe

3. Did Muhammad not establish himself and his tribe, the Quresh, among the best tribes in Arab ? Did he not say : "Of the two tribes that God chose as the best were the descendents of Ishmael and Isaac. God preferred the children of Ishmael for the Arabs and the children of Isaac for the Jews. Then God created Muhammad in the chosen tribe--- the Quresh, the descendants of Ishmael and then He chose his family as the best among the Qureish families, and created Muhammad as the best of all men" (*Tir* vol.2; Paliwal, *Jihad in the Way of Allah,* p.47) ? At times does Muhammad not declare : "May Allah humiliate those who seek to humiliate the Quresh" (his tribe) [*Tir* 2 : p.835] ?

The Only Prophet from Quresh Tribe

4. Is it not a fact that Muhammad wanted to be the one and the only prophet of Arabia ? He did not want more than one prophet for Arab, that too from the Quresh tribe who could add a sense of pride, dignity and self respect for Arab as a Nation. Therefore he arranged to kill Musailma, who wanted to share prophethood with Muhammad, at the battle of Yemama ; Aswad Ansi of Yeman was killed and Jajah escaped but also died because they too claimed prophethood along with Muhammad.

Arabic : the Lingua-franca for Muslims

5. Why did Allah dictate the Quran in Arabic and how did Arabic become the lingua-franca of the Muslim Paradise (*Mis* 3 : 5751; Shaikh, 1999 : 177) ?

Direction of the Prayer from Jerusalem to Mecca

6. Why did Muhammad change the direction of the prayer from Jerusalem to Mecca ? Did he not pray facing towards Jerusalem initially for some 17 months to gain the favour of the Jews after migrating to Medina ? When he found that the Jews did not favour him or accept him as their prophet did he not change his direction to Kaaba as his *qibla* ?

Anwar Shaikh, an eminent Muslim scholar, aptly commented : "The Kaaba serves a much greater national purpose of the Arabs than Zion or Jerusalem rendered to the Jews. It is the guardian of the Arab nationalism at the expense of the national conscience of the non-Arab Muslims who believe that they have no individual nationality of their own, and prefer to be called Muslims" (1995 : 78-80).

Allah is Everywhere or at Kaaba ?

7. While changing the *qibla* from Jerusalem to Mecca did Muhammad not give the message of Allah to the Jews : "Allah belongs to the East and the West, whithersoever you turn, there is Allah's Face" (2 : 115) ? Does he not mean that Allah is everywhere ?

In the words of Abd al-Fadi : If the *qibla* was a law and a pillar of prayer, why should it change ? Or was it merely a political scheme to win the Arabs over at one time, and the Jews at another ? While Muhammad was with the Arabs in Mecca, he faced the Kaaba, and when he emigrated to Medina, where there were many Jews, he faced Jerusalem. But when the Jews opposed him, he made the Kaaba his *qibla* once again ! The change of the *qibla* actually had a rebounding

7

effect on the people, in that many of the Muslims embraced Judaism and said, "Muhammad has returned to the religion of his forefathers, and has turned away from the true *qibla* of the Jews !" The Jews taunted the Muslims, for Huyay Ibn Ahtab and his Jewish friends said : "Tell us about your prayer towards Jerusalem. If it was the true guidance, then why did you leave it ? And if it was by error, you have worshipped God by it, and those of you who died have died in error !" Among those who died before the *qibla* was changed to Kaaba were Ahmad Ibn Zurara of the family of Najjar and al-Bara Ibn Marur of the family of Salama, both of whom were chiefs of their people. The families of these people rushed to Muhammad, and he calmed them down by saying : "The fools among the people will say, 'What has turned them from the direction they were facing in their prayers aforetime ?' Say : 'To God belong the East and the West.' But why did Muhammad accuse those who objected to his shifting the *qibla* of being fools (1997 : 211) ?

Mosque with a Difference

8. Why did Muhammad say : "A prayer in my Mosque-in-Medina is a thousand times more excellent than a prayer in any other mosques except the Masjid-al-Haram of Kaaba (*Mus* 2 : 3209-3211) ? Is it because the Masjid-al-Haram is in the birth place of Muhammad and like the last of the Apostles, that was his last of the mosques and that mosque invokes 100,000 benedictions compared to a similar worship in other mosque (*Maj* 1463; Shaikh 1999 : 177) ?

Paradise through the Graveyard of Arab

9. Why should a Muslim's head who dies in a country other than Arab, be kept at the direction of the Arabian graveyard known as Jannat-ul-Mualla and Jannat-ul-Baquee ? Is it a fact that any one who is buried at Mualla and Baquee shall enter Paradise and be privileged to intercede among the seventy thousand people (Shaikh 1999 : 178) ?

Hajj : A Perennial Income Source for the Arabs

10. By insisting on Hajj for all Muslims of the world does Muhammad not bring back the old pre-Islamic Arab rite and create an everlasting source of income for the Arabs ?

Quran Manifests Arab Nationalism

11. Is it not a fact that the Quran has been revised a number of times by a number of people after the Prophet's death ? The early Caliphs Abu Bakr, Umar and Othman made the changes for personal and doctrinal reasons. But the later changes made by the Omayyad Caliph were for political, dynastic and imperialist ends. The unalterable Quran became the manifesto of Arab nationalism propagating the Arabs as the best people ever created (3 : 110) and Arabia as the holy land. Does this kind of a propaganda by the Quran not justify the Arab chauvinism and the conquest and domination ?

The Last Words of the Last Prophet

12. Did not the Prophet say three things as his last orders :

First order : Turn the pagans out of the Arabian Peninsula.

Second order : Respect and give gifts to the foreign delegations as you have seen me dealing with them.

Third order : "I forgot it."

Are not the above two orders for the benefit of the entire Arabian Peninsula ?

Muhammad seems to be much worried about his Arab. Does he not declare : "I will not intercede for those or love them who are not fair with the Arabs" and said to Sulaiman Farsee : "If you bear odium against the Arabs, who will bear odium against me" ? (*Tir* 2 : p. 840).

The Property List of Prophet Muhammad

13. Can a poor man maintain a large family ?

Can he marry nine wives, each wife having her independent house, a number of maids and slaves to look after ?

Can he give a lavish party to the residents of Medina for the whole week by slaughtering hundreds of goats on the occasion of his wedding with his daughter-in-law, Zaynab (Das 2010 : 204) ?

Can a person be called poor when he has good number of slaves, servants, slave girls, personal assistants, bodyguards and a large number of mules, horses, donkeys, goats and camels ?

Source of Income for Prophet Muhammad

14. Is not it a fact that Muhammad used to take one-fifth share of the booty in Allah's name?

In the battle of Honein, which was fought on February 1, 630 AD, Muslims captured the following booty :

"24,000 camels, 40,000 sheep and goats, 4,000 ounces of silver and 6,000 prisoners. They were removed to the neighbouring valley of Al-jirana and sheltered there" (*Shaikh* 1999 : 20).

The Apostle held a large number of captives. There were 6,000 women and children prisoners. He had captured so many sheep and camels they could not be counted (*Ish* 592).

When Muhammad suddenly attacked Banu Mustaliq, he captured the following :

"600 were taken prisoners by the Muslims. Among the booty there were 2,000 camels and 5,000 goats" (*Buk* 3.46.717).

9

That Property was not sufficient for his needs so he grasped the property of other Muslims who had no heir (*Daw* 18 : 2895).

Was not the Prophet greedy enough to obtain the hidden property of Kinana of Khaibar and gave the order "Torture him until you extract what he has" ?

Sujit Das remarks : Muhammad lived a parasitic life without ever being engaged in any meaningful employment. He had an evil eye for all the wealth that the Jews and Christians had earned by their hard work. His fanatic greed motivated him to attack the Jews and Christian tribes and steal their property (2010 : 233).

Property of the Prophet's Family

15. Is not it a fact that Muhammad's cousin Zubair was found to be having estates worth of fifty million and two hundred thousand *dirhams* ? A son of the pious Omar had 1000 slaves at the time of his death (Das 2010 : 205).

2- Diamond in a Heap of Stones

The Arab as a nation and people, true to their Semitic tradition, never bother for any other art other than the art of saying. The unmatched eloquence of the Quran as a testimony of Muhammad's full use of linguistic feature can be seen expressed in a single short sentence : "*La illaha illa-l-llah; Muhammadan rasulu-l-Llah*" or no god whatsoever but God; Muhammad is the messenger of God.

The Holy Quran tells that Muhammad was an *Ummi*, the illiterate or the unlettered Prophet (*7 : 157*). Does *Ummi* mean ignorance of reading, and writing or some one who does not have a divinely inspired Book ? There were two sons of Ibrahim--- Isaac and Ishmael. The descendants of Issac became Jews and are called *Kitabiyyan* or "people of the Book" and the descendants of Ishmael are called *Ummiyyan* or "People without a Book." The Quran invites both people of the Book and people without Book of Islam (*3 : 20*). People those who know not the book are usually called, "illiterates" (*2 : 78*). The Arabs were proud that Allah sent Muhammad as a messenger to those who were unlettered (*62 : 2*). If people who had no Book earlier are called *Ummiyyan* then to call Muhammad an *Ummi* is justified. This is clear that Muhammad was not unlettered but was sent without any Book.

Iqra has a Meaning

16. If Allah "knoweth all things" why did He examine the illiterate Muhammad through Gabriel, saying "Iqra" or to "recite" ? Why did He say to him : "by the pen and by the record which men write" (68 : 1)? Because Allah knew that Muhammad was not uneducated. Muhammad knew the difference between educated and being illiterate and asked can they be the same (39 : 9) ? Out of his modesty he could tell that the calculation of months are confusing, sometimes 29 days and sometimes 30 days. So he said : "We are an illiterate nation, we neither write, nor know accounts" (*Buk* 3 : 137). Where did he say that they do not know reading ?

Prophet of the Illiterates

17. When an early enemy, Ibn Siyad was asked by Muhammad : "Do you bear witness that I am the prophet of God ?" Ibn Siyad replied : "I bear witness that you are a prophet of the illiterate." Can we accept the comment of an enemy that Muhammad was illiterate (Walker 1999 : 97) ? Let the wise decide.

The Holy Quran tells about Muhammad that he was an *ummi*, the illiterate or the unlettered Prophet (7 : 157). Does *ummi* mean ignorant of reading, writing or the one who does not have a divinely inspired Book ?

The Arabs were proud that Allah sent Muhammad as a messenger to them, who are unlettered (62 : 2). Is not it clear that Muhammad was not unlettered but was sent without any Book ?

Can an Illiterate be a Business Manager ?

18. Can you prove that Muhammad was illiterate though his paternal grandfather Abd al-Muttalib and uncle Abu Talib were reputed poets ? Can an uneducated person be an accountant and maintain commercial office of an intelligent lady like Khadija?

Did Khadija ever insist Muhammad to Learn Writing ?

19. Is it not a fact that a great successful business woman like Khadija was so influenced by Muhammad for his skilful work that she proposed to marry him to which Muhammad agreed ? Did she ask him that he should learn how to read and write?

Can an Illiterate change Words in a Treaty ?

20. If Muhammad was illiterate how did he alter certain words in his own handwriting in the drafting of the treaty of Al-Hudaibiya (Walker 1.999 : 97; *Buk* 3 : 891)?

Was Muhammad a Kahin?

21. Is it not a fact that many Meccans considered Muhammad a *Kahin*, soothsayer or fortune-teller (*69 : 42*) ? When the Meccans could not understand the confused personality of Muhammad did not they call him a *shair* or a poet (*37 : 36*) who will bring some calamity hatched by time (*52 : 30*)?

Who said Muhammad was Illiterate?

22. Is it not a fact that Muhammad was never an illiterate? When he had suffered from grievous ailment due to the food he ate at Khaiber and he felt as if his aorta is being cut from that poison (*Buk* 5 : 713) did he not ask : "Bring for me (writing) paper and I will write for you a statement after which you will not go astray"? The people present there differed in this matter. Umar said : "The Prophet is seriously ill, and we have got Allah's Book with us and that is sufficient for us." There was a hue and cry. On that the Prophet said to them : "Go away and leave me alone. It is not right that you should quarrel in front of me." Ibn Abbas came out saying : "It was most unfortunate that Allah's Messenger was prevented from writing that statement for them because of their disagreement and noise (*Buk* 1 : 114; 5 : 716).

Was Muhammad a Narcissist?

23. Is not it a fact that Muhammad used the narcissist method of projection on his followers to hide his own inferiority and declared himself the guardian of illiterates

11

sent by Allah? Does it not mean Allah loves the illiterates and hates the educated? This way Muhammad glorified his shortcomings by saying the following words :

"O Prophet! We have sent you as a witness (for Allah's True regulation) and a giver of glad tidings (to the faithful believers), and a warner (to the unbelievers) and guardian of the illiterates. You are My slave and My Messenger" (*Buk* 3.34.335).

Ibn 'Abbas reported that the Holy Prophet of Allah said : "We are the last umma to (come) and the first umma who will be reckoned. It will be said, 'Where is the unlettered umma and its Prophet?' We are the last (umma) and the first (umma) to be reckoned and admitted in the Paradise" (*Maj* 5.4290).

In the Quran it is said: "Those who follow the Apostle, the unlettered Prophet, whom they find mentioned in their own (Scriptures), - in the Law and the Gospel... so believe in God and his Apostle, the unlettered Prophet" (7 : 157, 158).

3- Fear and Phobia

The defenders of Islam boldly claim that Prophet Muhammad was a hero of his time. He feared nothing, dared everything. If so why was he afraid of strong wind, afraid of evil spirits, suffering from bewitchment and afraid of the whisper of evil? Very often he looked perturbed and asked to be covered with a sheet or blanket.

He was afraid of everything because he was suffering from neurological disorder caused by paroxysmal malfunction of neurons in the brain. Whether he was really affected with epilepsy or not let us verify from the Hadith and the Holy Quran.

It is characterized by strength, movements or sensations in parts of the body, odd behaviours, emotional disturbances, and sometimes convulsion and momentary lapses of consciousness. Here is the proof :

Did the Prophet Suffer from Epilepsy ?
24. Is it not a fact that others in Mecca claimed that Muhammad was a *mashur* bewitched and controlled by evil spirits (*44 : 13; 81 : 25*) and when he claimed he received revelation from angel Gabriel he actually had Narcissistic Personality Disorder :

1. Muhammad experienced the ringing sound in his ears as if he were hearing bells (*Buk* 1 :1; 4 : 438).

2. His heart would beat rapidly (*Buk* 1 : 3).

3. His face would turn red (*Buk* 2 : 16; 5 : 618; 6 : 508).

4. He would breathe heavily (*Buk* 6 : 508).

5. His lips would tremble as he lay on the ground (*Buk* 1 : 4).

6. He heard and saw things that none else heard or saw

(*Buk* 1 : 2-3; 4 : 458, 461; 6 : 447).

7.   He would sweat profusely (*Buk* 1 :2; 2 : 544 ; 3 : 829; 4 : 95;   5 : 462).

8.   He would ask to be covered with a sheet or blanket (*Buk* 1 : 3; 2 : 16; 3 : 17; 4 : 461; 5 : 170).

9.   He would sometimes suddenly fall down (*Buk* 2 : 16; 4 : 461; 5 : 170) unconscious with both his eyes (open) towards the sky (*Buk* 6 : 448).

10. He would sometimes snore like a camel (*Buk* 2 : 16; 3 : 17).

11. He would sometimes dream (*Buk*1 :3; 5 : 659; 6 : 478).

12. When he came to his senses, he said : "My waist sheet ! My waist sheet !" (*Buk* 6 : 447-448, 468, 481).

Do not these above symptoms indicate that the Prophet was suffering from the *Grand Mal Epilepsy* which is followed by loud scream and stiffening and jerking movements of the body, that made him totally disoriented, confused and sleepy and which also led to some unusual pattern of E.E.G. associated with visual hallucinations ?

Robert Morey remarked that the above symptoms are found in someone who has epilepsy or some other brain disorder (1992 : 191-192). It seems Prophet Muhammad was not suffering from symptomatic or acquired epilepsy where convulsions and seizures occur in quite a number of brain syndromes like neuro syphilis but he was suffering from idiopathic epilepsy where it had no relation with the toxic condition of the brain. Were not the vision that Muhammad received from the unknown the result of a combination of epileptic seizures and an overactive imagination (Morey 1992 : 71; Mc Clintock 1981 : I : 339) ?

Why Words in the Quran are Obscure and Meaningless ?
25. What sort of revelation is it that renders a man unconscious, where his body would begin to jerk, eyes would roll backward and would make him perspire profusely ? According to al-Masih : he went into a semi-coma, changed from the normal state and looked like a drunkard... a noise like the humming of bees could be heard around his face (1993 : 15-16). Is it not a neurological disorder caused by paroxymal malfunction of neurons, the brain seizures ? When his lips trembled (*Buk* 1 :4) he would babble some meaningless words which are kept in the opening of 29 suras in the Quran such as :

Alif Lam Ra : Yunus 10, Hud 11, Yusuf 12, Ibrahim 14, Al-Hijr 15; *Alif Lam Mim* : Al-Baqara 2, Al Imran 3, Al-'Ankabut 29, Al-Rum 30, Luqman 31, Al-Sajda 32; *Alif Lam Mim Ra* : Al-- Ra'd 13; *Alif Lam Mim Sad* : Al-A'raf 37; *Ha Mim* : Al-Mu'minun 40, Fussilat 41, al-Zukhruf 43, al-Dukhan 44, al-Jathiya 45, Al-Ahqaf 46;   *Ha Mim 'Ain Sin Qaf* : Al-Shura 42; *Sad* : Sad 38; *Ta Sin* : al-Naml 27; *Ta Sin Mim* : Al-Shu'ara' 26, Al-Qasas 28; *Ta Ha* : Ta Ha 20; *Qaf* : Qaf 50; *Kaf Ha Ya 'Ain Sad* : Maryam 19; *Nun* : Al-Qalam 68; *Ya Sin* : Ya Sin 36.

The Muslim scholars claim that only Allah knows the meaning of the above words. If there is Allah can He speak to His messenger meaningless words? He is supposed to tell the truth with clear and meaningful words.

Was Muhammad a Madjnun ?

26. Is not it a fact that the people of Mecca before they believed Muhammad, called him *Madjnun,* mad or possessed *(68 :2)*?

Was the Prophet suffering from Bewitchment ?

27. Did Muhammad not believe that a Jewish man bewitched him by hiding some of his hairs and a few teeth of his comb under a rock in a well for which he was suffering ? The story begins like this...

One day two persons came to Muhammad in his dream. One of them asked the other, "What is the ailment of this man ?" "He has been bewitched. He is under the spell of magic." "Who cast the magic spell ?" "A Jew" . "What material did he use ?" "A comb, the hair knotted on it, and the outer skin of the pollen of the male date palm" (*Buk* 4. 54. 490, 7.71. 658).

Now the story in detail. A Jewish male servant was serving Muhammad, to whom the Jews came, persuading him to give them Muhammad's fallen hair and several teeth of his comb, which they wanted to use to cast a spell on Muhammad. It was Lubaid b. al-A'sam the Jew who undertook this job. He hid Muhammad's belongings in a well called Zarwan, which was owned by the clan of Zuraiq. Muhammad fell ill, his hair fell out and he began to imagine he was having intercourse with his wives. He kept on going about not knowing what had come over him and started to imagine he did things which he did not do. While he was asleep one day, two angels came to him. One of them sat at his head, and the other at his feet. The one at his head asked : 'What is the matter with the man ?' 'A spell', the other one answered : 'Who cast it on him ?' he asked. The other one answered : 'Lubaid b. al-A'sam, the Jew.' He asked : 'What did he use ?' 'A comb and fallen hair,' the other one answered. The first one asked : 'Where are they ?' 'In a *pollen hull* under a stone at the bottom of the well of the clan of Zuraiq,' the other one answered. At that Muhammad woke up and sent Ali, al-Zubair, and Ammar b. Yasir, who drained the well and found its water as red as *henna* dye. They lifted the stone and got the hull out, where they found Muhammad's fallen hair and comb teeth together with a knotted string that had eleven knots stitched in it with a needle. Therefore, he recited two suras (al-Falaq 113, al-Nas 114) which had eleven verses. With each verse he recited, the knots were loosened one by one, like one who was freed from his shackles. And Gabriel began to say : 'In the name of Allah, I charm you against whatever harms you and against the evil eye. Allah's eye heals you.' Muhammad's companions asked him : 'O prophet of Allah, shall we not take the malicious one and kill him ?' He answered : 'As for me, Allah has healed me, and I hate to provoke evil upon people' (*Buk* 7 : 660; *CQV* 1994 : 267).

Symtoms of Paranoid

28. Was not Muhammad suffering from paranoia for which he used to see conspiracies every where ? Ibn Ishaq mentioned :

"(Ayesha recalls) Muhammad never failed to come by our house every day at the two ends of the day. ... Once he came during the heat of the day so we knew that it was because of something special. When he came in dad(Abu Bakr) rose from his bed, and the Messenger sat down. Muhammad said, 'Send out those who are with you.' My father said, 'Prophet, these are my daughters (one of which is now your wife); they can do you no harm, may my father and mother be your ransom'" (*Isha*

223). Abu Bakr had to swear by his parent's name to remove Muhammad's paranoid fear.

Prophet's Fear and Superstitions

29. Is not it a fact that Muhammad was afraid of strong wind blowing (*Buk* 2 : 144) ?

Was not the Prophet suffering from superstitions such as the power of the evil eye and told people to recite the Quran to fight against it (*Buk* 7 : 636) ?

Did he not believe in good and bad omens such as the appearance of certain birds and certain other animals (*Buk* 4 : 110, 111; 7 : 648-650) ?

Was he not afraid that evil spirits might enter his body whenever he would urinate or defecate and had his special prayer (*Buk* 1 : 144) ?

Did he not believe that if a green palm leaf was placed on the grave of those suffering, their pain would be lessened as it dried (*Buk* 2 : 443) ?

Did he not stipulate that an odd number of stones be used whoever cleans private parts (*Buk* 1 : 162) ? The fear complex was so much with the Prophet that though he mentioned Maryam, the mother of Jesus , many times in the Holy Quran he did not dare to mention his only mother--Amina, his beloved wives Khadija and Ayesha and his loving daughter Fatima.

Does Quran End with the Fear of Muhammad ?

30. Is it not a fact that Muhammad had no peace of mind, he was frightened on every side, and saw himself under attack from man, Satan and demons ? In the Quran it is said : "from the mischief of the whisperer of Evil, who withdraws after his whisper", who whispers into the hearts of mankind, among Jinns and among men" (114 : 4-6) ? Does it not reflect the mental condition of Muhammad ? That may be the reason for which every Muslim while uttering the name of Muhammad suffix it by saying "may peace be upon him. "

4- When Habit Becomes Hobby

It is universally accepted that Prophet Muhammad was well-known for his cleanliness and orderliness. He was fond of perfumes and spent more on buying perfumes than on food. His nice pleasant smell filled the air of any place he passed, so that whosoever passed there, knew that the holy Prophet of Islam had passed that way.

He used to brush his teeth a lot and washed his blessed hands both before and after meals. Whenever the Holy Prophet of Islam was about to come out of his house, he would look into a mirror or into water and always left home with a clean pleasant appearance (*Teheran Times* Nov. 21. 1989 : 7). He dyed his hair in red. He became more furious when someone else prolonged prayers. He did not like questions and at times refused to answer. He behaved extraordinarily and showed kindness to men of dignity and might but was indifferent to the poor and the oppressed. His habit became hobby and hobby became habit. Here are a few examples of how it happened :

What the Prophet Loved
31. Is not it a fact that the Prophet loved pillow, perfume and milk (*Tir* 3 : 176) ?

Did not the Prophet dye his Hair Red ?
32. Is it not a fact that Muhammad dyed his hair (*Buk* 1 : 167) in red and failed to keep it free from lice (*Buk* 9 : 130) and after his death, some of his red hair was kept and shown to others (*Buk*4 : 747; 7 : 785) ?

Appeasement to Friends
33. Is it not a fact that Muhammad, unlike the other prophets, at times, shifted his position and presented his message to satisfy and please his audience ? Salman al-Farisi, a friend of Muhammad was an idol-worshiper, on whom Muhammad said, "they are in fire". When Salman was disappointed on hearing this, did Muhammad not say the following verse, to please his friend : Those who believe in the Quran, and those who follow the Jewish scriptures, and the Christians and the Sabians, -- any who believe in Allah and the last day, and work righteousness, shall have their reward with their Lord on them shall have no fear, nor shall they grieve *(2 : 62)*. Was not Salman happy on hearing this ?

Prophet's Partiality
34. Is it not a fact that in the early days of Islam, Muslim men were refrained from sexual activity with their wives after waking up in the morning ? But Umar broke this restriction. Later he wept and went to Muhammad and apologized and said, "Is there hope for me ?" Muhammad told him, "You should not have done this Umar," and uttered the following verse which, he claimed, was revealed to him immediately : "Permitted to you, upon the night of the Fast, is to go into your wives; they are a vestment for you, and you are a vestment for them. God knows that you have been betraying yourselves, and has turned to you and pardoned you. So now lie with them, and seek what God has prescribed for you" (Tabari's Commentary on Sura *The Cow* 2 : 183). Can we deny then that Muhammad was partial to his own people and made concessions to them to make them happy ?

The Disregard for his Mother and Relatives
35. Is not it a fact that when Muhammad requested Allah to forgive his mother after her death Allah stopped him, this made him weep bitterly ? If he could not help his own mother how can we hope that he will help us during the judgement day? Is not it strange for Prophet Muhammad to insult his pre-Islamic past and his uncle Abu Talib and his own mother because his uncle refused to accept Islam and his mother did not happen to be a Muslim ?

Love Me, My Daughter and My Wife
36. Is it not a fact that Muhammad was much worried about his family mainly about his daughter Fatima and child wife Ayesha? He did not hesitate to say : "Fatima is the chief mistress of the women in Paradise." "Fatima is a part of me, and whoever makes her angry, makes me angry" (*Buk* 5 : 110-111). Did he not say about Ayesha : "The superiority of Ayesha over other women is like the superiority of Tharid to other meals" (*Buk* 5 : 114).

Short Tempered
37. Is it not a fact that when Muhammad heard of someone leading in prolonged prayers he became more furious (*Buk* 1 : 90) and when a man asked him where to find his lost camel, the prophet got angry and his cheeks and his face became red (*Buk* 1 : 91)?

No Appreciation for Questions

38. Is it not a fact that Muhammad did not like to answer questions, he felt it offending ? When he was asked about things which he did not like, and when the questioner insisted, the prophet got angry and his cheeks or his face became red (*Buk* 1 : 91). He was scared to answer the disputed religious questions (*Buk* 2 : 555; 3 : 591) and cursed the questioner with : "Allah has hated you" (*Buk* 2 : 555). Does not Allah say to the believers, "Ask not questions about things which, if made plain to you, may cause you trouble (*Buk* 9 : 391). Because some people before you did ask such questions, and on that account lost their faith" (*5 : 101-102*).

Angry with the Jews

39. Why did the Jews not accept Muhammad as a prophet though he claimed so ? Did he not cite the Torah that there was prophecy for his prophethood ? But to be a prophet for the Jews is it not necessary to come in the line of David ? They did not even accept the Quran as the Divine Revelation because it was not in the sacred tongues like Hebrew or Syriac and he performed no miracles like their prophets. These are the causes for which he became outrageous and rebuked the Jews that, "they shall be companions of Hell-fire (*5 : 86*), and changed the Hebrew term for prophet as *nabi* into the Arabic term as *rasul* or apostle and changed the direction of prayer from Jerusalem to Mecca (*2 : 144*) and changed Saturday as sabbath to Friday as special day (*Walker* 1999 : 183-184).

Cursed the Mudar Tribe

40. Is it not a fact that Muhammad cursed the Mudar tribe to suffer from drought and famine for seven years and within a year they were reduced to eating hides, carcasses, and rotten dead animals (*Buk* 2 : 120-121) ?

Indecent Behaviour towards Uqba

41. When Uqba was imprisoned after the battle of Boar and was taken away to be executed, did he not pray to Muhammad : "What will become of my little children ?" In return Muhammad replied : "Hell fire." Is it the word of a prophet (Maine 1979 : 16) ?

Unitarian in Theology but Trinitarian in Practice

42. Is it not a fact that Muhammad was a Unitarian in theology but a Trinitarian in his ablution ? Regarding performance of his ablution he washed his hands thrice. He then rinsed his mouth and cleaned his nose three times. He then washed his face three times, washed his right arm up to the elbow three times, washed his left arm like that, wiped his head, washed his right foot up to the ankle three times, then washed his left foot, and so on. Muhammad said : "he who performs ablution like this ablution of mine... all his previous sins are expiated." This became the standard ablution. According to Muslim canon scholars, this is the most complete of the ablutions performed for prayer. There are twenty-one *ahaadis* repeating Muhammad's practice and thought on the subject as given above (*Mus* 436-457).

Example of Cleanliness

43. Is it a fact that when Muhammad was at Ayesha's house he had discharged and found mark of fluid on his cloth. Her maid-servant saw him while he was dipping his clothes in water. When the Hanafite school of Fiqh insist for a wash in case of passing urine for male and female how did Ayesha dare to scrape the dried up semen on the garment of the Prophet with her nails (*Mus* 572) ?

Yes by Allah No by Allah

44. Why do the Muslims use Allah's name unnecessarily by using oath like phrases : "Yes, by Allah!", "No, by Allah!" How can offering a sacrifice (*Kaffarah*) help a Muslim to avoid the serious consequences of breaking an oath ?

Can Oath be Revoked ?

45. Can an oath always be binding when Muhammad himself revoked it (66 : 2) ?

Substitute for Oath-breaking

46. Is not it easy, for a Muslim to break an oath by offering *Kaffarah* (consist of food and clothes for ten poor people) or by releasing a Muslim slave or by a three-day fast for those who are not rich enough for this (5 : 89) ?

Between Words and Work

47. Did not Muhammad command everyone to have a will when he himself failed to have one (*Buk* 4 : 3-4) ?

Indifferent to the Poor

48. Was not Muhammad indifferent to the poor and the oppressed and showed kindness to men of dignity and might ? Did he not frown at a blind man and ignore him though the blind man came to him to learn Islam (80 : 1-10; 6 : 52) ? When Muhammad realized that his action was improper, did he not say that God reprimanded him ?

5- Pagan Practices in Islam

A pagan became a Prophet. Though Muhammad was well-known as an Iconoclast but he himself was not free from pagan practices. Influenced by his uncle Abbas he carried stone for reconstruction of the pagan shrine Kaaba. All these forty years before his Prophethood he was a pagan that too a devotee of Hubal. Can it be denied that Muhammad was not aware of the Ibrahimic religion which preached against the worship of graven images, and is one of the commandments given in the Ten commandments (*Ex* 2 : 17) ? Even Muhammad could not forget his pagan custom to visit Safa and Marwa. Here are some evidences :

Pagan Grandfather's Muslim Grandson

49. Being the last Prophet Muhammad changed the world but how could he fail to convince his grandfather who lived and died a pagan ?

Is the Word Rahman of Pagan Origin ?

50. Is not it a fact that the term "Rahman" which was used as Merciful in the early pagan inscriptions and subsequently used as a Christian quality (19 : 21; 57 : 27) was later adopted by Muhammad who used the terms 'Rahman' and 'Allah' as the titles of God (20 : 4) ?

Reconstructing the Pagan Shrine

51. Why did Muhammad take off the lower garment and keep on his shoulder under the influence of his uncle Abbas to carry stone when Kaaba was reconstructed (*Mus* 1 : 670-672) ? When he took it off did he not fall on the ground with his eyes open towards the sky with the words "Give me my waist sheet" and he covered himself with it (*Buk* 2 : 652) ? Why did Allah not give him a mild warning as to not to be naked while carrying stone to the Kaaba ?

For whom did Muhammad carry Stone ?

52. There were 360 deities worshipped in Kaaba shrine. Among them were Hadad, a Syrian God; Elh, Alh or Allah; Hubal; the goddesses Allat, Ozza and Manat; Kayis; Aziz; Nasr; Wadd; Sowa; Dhu Ghabat, 'He of the Thicket'; Dhu Shara, 'He of the Highlands', worshipped in the form of a Black Stone; Shay al Kaum; Ara; Baal Shamim; and Rahmar honoured in conjuction with Rahim. Can we say that Muhammad was carrying the stones for all the deities of the shrine (Walker 1999 : 22) ?

Five Gods in Arab Remembered

53. Is not it a fact that the five idols of gods : Wadd, Suwa, Yughuth, Ya' uq and Nasr (71 : 23) were worshipped by Noah's people earlier to Muhammad ? It is likely that they were transferred by means of the flood to the Arabian Peninsula. I agree with al-Razi the commentator of Quran that if Noah himself transferred the idols with flood we have to prove that these idols were made of a substance insoluble in water, for they were submerged for a long period of time. Even if we grant that they were transferred by means of the flood, how could the Arabs know the names of these idols ? Was every idol's name written in the Arabic language ? So it is clear that these five gods were aboriginal and were associated with the Arabs and their culture (*CQV* 1994 : 262).

Were the Five Gods Adam's Sons ?

54. When Allah said in the Quran "Abandon not your gods; abandon neither Wadd nor Suwa; neither Yaguth nor Ya'uq nor Nasr", does He mean these five gods were sons of Adam ? Al-Qurtubi, on the strength of *Muhammad b.Ka'b*, told another story about these idols : "Adam had five sons, whose names were Wadd, Suwa, Yaghuth, Ya'uq and Nasr, who were worshipers (of Allah). They were sad when one of them died, so that Satan said to them : "I will fashion for you a likeness of him. Whenever you look to it you will remember him." They said to him : "Do (what you say)." He fashioned it of brass and lead in the worship place. Another one died, so they fashioned his likeness. By the time then they all died, they all had their likeness fashioned. With the passage of time they fell into oblivion, and the people forsook the worship of Allah. So Satan said to them : "Why are you not worshipping anything ?" "What could we possibly worship ?" they answered back. He said : "Your gods and the gods of your fathers. Do you not see them in your temple ?" So they worshipped them apart from Allah, and said to one another when Allah sent Noah : "Do not leave your gods, and do not leave Wadd" (*CQV* 1994 : 263). It may be possible, but the great objection to al-Qurtubi is that Adam did not have five sons but three : Cain, Abel and Seth.

Muhammad's Devotion for Hubal

55. Is it not a fact that in the Pre-Islamic period Allah was personified in the God Hubal ? In semitic language "Hu" means "He" or "He is" with the suffix El, means God. Did not Muhammad, in his youth, help with the preparations being made for the ceremonial installation of Hubal in the Kaaba (Walker 1998 : 42) ?

Muhammad's Pagan Past

56. What was Muhammad's religion prior to his prophethood ? Did he not spend his forty years in paganism ? When Allah found him "wandering away from His

19

knowledge and laws" He gave him guidance and taught him by revelation and inspiration (Baidawi's Commentary on Sura 93 : 7-8) ?

Retain the Pagan Rituals

57. Is it not a fact that after he seized the shrine, Muhammad preserved most of the pagan rituals, such as the pilgrimage (hajj), the circumambulation round the Kaaba (tawaf), the ritual consecration (ihram), the minor pilgrimage ('umra), the throwing of the seven pebbles (rejm) at Jumra-e- Aqba into the valley of Mina to kill the devil, making seven rounds between the hills of Safa and Marwa (Saie), kissing the black stone (taqbil), and making sacrifices (nahr), which he inherited from the pagan because he had no option ?

Decorated Canopy : a Pagan Practice

58. Is it not a pagan practice to drape the Kaaba in a richly decorated "canopy" (*kiswa*) every year which was started by Asad Abu Karib (AD 415) more than three centuries before the birth of Muhammad (Walker 1998 : 38) ?

Pagan Custom to Visit Safa and Marwa

59. In the *Jahiliyya* period demons visited their idols on the top of Mounts Safa and Marwa. There were two idols Asaf on Safa and Nalia on Marwa. During the pre-Islamic period people used to visit the area of the mountains out of reverence for the two idols. When Islam came and idols were broken, Muslims refrained themselves from visiting the mountains. Why did Muhammad later allow the Hajjis to visit these mountains by the permission of Allah (2 : 158) ?

Image talks to Image

60. Are the stories that Allah told through Muhammad regarding the images of Ibrahim not contradictory ? If among the images there were Ibrahim and Ishmael in Kaaba, why did Ibrahim quarrel with his father ?

6- Last Man and End of History

At the age of 40 when Muhammad was in the cave of Hira, the angel Gabriel came to him with some written messages and asked him to read. But very politely Muhammad replied : "I do not know how to read." Thrice Muhammad denied to show his ability to read the message but by the order of Allah Gabriel anyhow gave the message, that was the first revelation of Quran : "Read (Muhammad) in the name of the Lord who created man, out of Leech like clot : Read, your Lord is the most Generous, who taught the use of the pen, taught the human, what he did not know" (96 : 1-5; *Buk* 1 : 3).

There are sharp differences between Sanatani and Semitic religions. Gita and Gospels, Puran and Quran have different views on the concept of creation, the forbidden fruit of knowledge, the Devil and the original sin. The former is all inclusive and the latter is exclusive. One believes in impersonal eternal theory of Divinity, the other rests on historical personality of God. One believes in independent investigation of truth, the other in infallibility of their religious text. One believes in destiny is character, the other character is destiny. One believes in

20

human centered Universe the other believes in evil centric Universe. So without Christ, there is no Christianity and without Muhammad no Islam, whereas Hinduism stands with God, without God, with priest or without priest. There are thousands of living Avatars and nobody questions their Godhood in Hinduism, whereas Kaab, son of Ashraf and Asma, daughter of Marwan were put to death because they disagreed with the concept of the last Prophet. Inspite of these differences Hindus generously accept the semitic Prophets as one of their own. Prophethood is a process, let it grow into the eternity. If it is stopped from flowing it will be a dirty pond.

Khatm al-nubuwwa (finality of Prophethood) is derived from Quran (33 : 40) which states that, "Muhammad is not the father of any one of your men, but the messenger of God (rasul'u'llah) and the Seal of the Prophets (Khatam al-nabiyyin)... (Meaning of Khatm here is "last") and Muhammad substantiates his statement on behalf of Allah. He has compared the relationship between himself and the prophets who preceded him to a man who had almost finished the construction of a beautiful house, leaving a space for only one brick at a corner. People started to walk around it, admiring it and asking why the last brick had not been put in the space. The prophet said, "I am that brick and I am the seal of the Prophets (Khatam al-nabiyyin)" (Al-Bukhari, Sahih 18). Why did he close down all the doors of Prophethood for others ?

In the Quran Muhammad is referred to as a nabi (Prophet) 75 times during the Meccan period but was referred to as a rasul (messenger) 331 times all through the Medina period. Are both the words Interchangeable (Fazel, 1993 : 22) ?

Whether Prophets are Born or Made?

61. We say "there is no God but Allah and that Muhammad is His Prophet", but the Arabic title of Muhammad is rasul'u'llah or God's messenger. Muhammad views that apostle stands as founder and leader at the beginning of a series formed by his representatives, the Prophets (Wensinck 1924 : 168-169). If Prophets are not made, but are born then how could Muhammad become a Prophet at the age of forty ?

Muhammad was in the Beginning

62. On what basis did the Prophet claim : "I shall be pre-eminent amongst the descendants of Adam on the Day of Resurrection and I will be the first intercessor and the first whose intercession will be accepted by Allah" (Mus 4 : 5655) ?

Who were the 124000 Prophets?

63. If Allah being a Transcendent Being needs the help of intermediaries called Prophets for communication and sent one lakh twenty four thousand prophets to the world out of whom only 315 have brought messages or Books (according to Ibn Hanbal) why did the Quran mention only 25 prophets including 3 prophets from the New Testament who are as follows :

Sr. No.	Names of the Prophet mentioned in the Quran	Biblical Names
1.	Adam	Adam
2.	Idris	Enoch
3.	Nuh	Noah
4.	Hud	Hud

21

5.	Salih	Salih
6.	Ibrahim	Abraham
7.	Lut	Lot
8.	Ismail	Ishmael
9.	Ishaq	Isaac
10.	Yaqub	Jacob
11.	Yusuf	Joseph
12.	Shuaib	Jethru
13.	Ayyub	Job
14.	Dhul-kifl	Ezekiel
15.	Musa	Moses
16.	Harun	Aaron
17.	Dawud	David
18.	Sulaimen	Solomon
19.	Ilyas	Elijah, Ellias
20.	Al-Yasa	Elisha
21.	Yunus	Jonah
22.	Zakariya	Zachariah
23.	Yahya	John the Baptist
24.	Isa	Jesus
25.	Muhammad	

Why is a single prophet from other countries not mentioned in the Quran ? Is it deliberate or is it mere ignorance ?

Was Ishmael a Wild Man or a Prophet?
64. Can we accept Ishmael as a messenger and a Prophet (19 : 54), whereas the Old Testament describes him as a wild man, his hand shall be against every man, and every man's hand against him (*Gn* 16 : 12) ?

Can a Beast be a Prophet too?
65. The Quran confirmed that Allah brought a beast to speak (27 : 82) who preached like the prophet and had the authority of Moses and the wisdom of Solomon. (al-Baidawi; Abd Al-Fadi 1997 : 274-275). What is the difference between a prophet and a beast ?

Why to Confine Prophets between Nile and Euphrates?
66. All the Quranic prophets upto the Holy Prophet of Islam were born between the two rivers, the Nile and the Euphrates. Did the other parts of the world remain without any prophet (Muslim note 339, p. 105) ?

Paranoia or Prophetic Presentation?
67. Let us read carefully the claim of Muhammad as recorded by Bukhari :

> Narrated Ayesha : The truth descended upon him while he was in the cave of Hira. The angel came to him and asked him to read. The Prophet replied, "I do not know how to read. The Prophet added, "The angel caught me (forcefully) and pressed me so hard that I could not bear it any more. He then released me and again asked me to read and I replied, 'I do not know how to read.' Thereupon he caught me again and pressed me a second time till I could not bear it any more. He then released me and again asked

22

me to read but again I replied, 'I do not know how to read (or what shall I read) ?' Thereupon he caught me for the third time and pressed me, and then released me and said, 'Read in the name of your Lord, who has created (all that exists) has created man from a clot. Read ! And your Lord is the Most Generous," (96.1-3). Then Allah's Apostle returned with the Inspiration and with his heart beating severely (*Buk* 1.1.3).

In this recorded fact did the angel introduce anywhere that he himself was Gabriel ? How could Muhammad know that the angel was none other but Gabriel ? If Gabriel was an angel sent by God how could he not know that Muhammad was illiterate ?

The Hira cave experience of Muhammad indicates that he was much inquisitive *to study* that innets in his subconscious mind. Sujit Das believes that Muhammad had the impression of the story of Hassan and took the model of the semitic tradition of revelation of Moses (2010 : 50).

Who made Muhammad a Prophet?
68. Is not it a fact that both Khadija and Addas (not Addas who helped Muhammad in 619 when he sought refuge in Tayif) helped Muhammad to be a Prophet? Addas was a Christian monk from Nineveh who settled in Mecca and Khadija brought Muhammad to him and described his mental condition after returning from Hira mountain. It was Addas who linked his incident with angel Gabriel and gave confidence to Muhammad that it is nothing but divine revelation and placed him in the hierarchy of prophethood.

Seal of Prophethood
69. Do you also accept Muhammad as a prophet because he had a fatty tumor like *Zir-al-Hijla* or egg of a *partridge* on his neck between his shoulders (*Buk* 1 : 189; 4 : 741; *Mus* 30 : 5790; *Daw* 32 : 4071) ? How can one claim a physical deformity as a sign of prophethood ?

Did Jesus Prophesize on Muhammad
70. Jesus told his disciples that after him God would send a Comforter (Jn 14 : 16), *Parakletos* ("Renowned") in Greek and Ahmad (praised) in Arabic. Since "Ahamd" and "Muhammad" are derived from the same root, it is not wrong for Muhammad to claim to be the *Paraclete*. If this way the translation goes then one can read the gospel as follows : "Remember when Jesus said, "Verily I am an apostle of God, giving good tidings of a prophet that shall come after me whose name will be Ahmad" (61 : 6). Did Muhammad forget that the comforter is a Holy Spirit and he will descend on the Day of Pentecost ? After the ascension of Christ should the Holy spirit wait for over six centuries to come in the form of Muhammad ?

Arabia had a Prophet too ?
71. The two Meccan suras (10 :47; 16 : 36, 89) claim that God sent to every nation a prophet from among its own people. But the Bible says, however, that the prophets and messengers were exclusively from the children of Israel, being sent first to them and then to all the world. If the claim of the Quran is true, why did no prophet arise and preach in Africa, Europe, America, Australia and Asia ? Muhammad possibly strengthened his own weak situation to claim himself as a

messenger of God and gave strong reason that if these nations had their own prophets, then why not let the Arabs have their own. And that was Muhammad.

Prophets before Muhammad

72. When there were so many prophets sent to Arabia like Shu'aib to the tribe of Madyan (7 : 85) in the north-west Arabia, Hud sent to the tribe of Ad (7 : 65), Salih (7 : 73) to the tribe of western Arabia, why did Allah repeatedly tell us that no prophet had appeared in Arabia before Muhammad (32 : 3; 36 : 6) ?

Why was Muhammad Accepted ?

73. Is not it a fact that Muhammad was accepted as a prophet in Mecca because they had no previous revelation, and no books, and no male god like Allah ?

Why did Muhammad Please the Jews ?

74. Why did Muhammad try to please the Jews ? Is it with a motive : desire for a reconciliation and establishing his identity as a prophet with the general idea that each prophet was sent to a particular community, and that the community to which he was sent was the Arabs (3 : 64 : 57) ?

Unlike Moses did Muhammad have a Complete Book ?

75. When the Jews demanded Muhammad to bring a complete Book from heaven as Moses brought the Torah, Muhammad instead said " Would you question your messenger as Moses was questioned of old (2 : 108) ? Did not the Jews ask such question to Moses ?

Prophet against a Prophet

76. Is not it a fact that Muhammad belittled Moses ? Jabir Bin 'Abdullah narrated that when Umar came to Allah's Messenger, He said : "We hear the narration from the Jews, which sounds pleasing to us, so should we not write some of them ?" Whereupon he said : 'Do you want to be baffled as the Jews and the Christians were baffled ? I have brought to you (guidance) bright and pure and if Moses were alive now there would have been no alternative left for him but to follow me' (*Tir* 177).

"If (Moses) were alive (now), and he found my prophethood, he would have definitely followed me" (*Tir* 194, *Darimi* and *Mis* 1/20).

Prophet was Mortal like Others

77. Is not it a fact that the death of Muhammad could not be believed by Umar, who later became the second caliph, for which Abu Bakr had to recite the Quran which clearly stated that the Prophet cannot be immortal (39 : 30; *Buk* 5 : 711) ?

Prophet doubted his own Prophethood

78. Did not Muhammad doubt Allah's revelation and doubted his own prophethood (10 : 94) ? Why did Allah not give him the power of miracles like other prophets (11 : 17) ? Why was he in dilemma for which he had exchanged a verse in the place of another verse (16 : 101-103) ?

Can a Messenger be a Prophet ?

79. If Muhammad was not a Prophet but a messenger, how can he claim himself to be the Last Prophet ? Was he not merely a messenger, may be the last messenger ? After being a Prophet did he foretell the future ? Did he show any sign of divine sanction for his revelation ? Did he perform any miracle like Ibrahim walked on fire, Moses changed a stick into a serpent and Jesus cured the leper and raised the dead ? Instead Muhammad became apologetic and said :

I have no power to do any good or bad, even to myself.

Only God has the power and does as He pleases,

If I had the knowledge about the unseen

I would have enjoyed abundance of good.

And no evil would have befallen me.

Verily, I am just a warner

And a bringer of glad tidings

To those who believe in God (7 : 188).

Prophethood is Challenged

80. Is not it a fact that in the Battle of Ohad the Prophet faced the "Satanic wrath" of Abu Sufyan, his deadly enemy, in which he was spared his life ? Can you deny the fact that the superiority of Muhammad as the Prophet was challenged by Musailima who came to be known as the Prophet ? The two confronted each other in the battle of al-Yemama for establishing superiority in prophethood and unfortunately Musailima lost the battle. Does it mean his prophethood is lost ?

If God had no Son why a Messenger ?

81. If Muhammad could sarcastically say about Jesus : "If the most Gracious had a son, I would be the first of his worshippers (43 : 81). One can similarly say, "If the most Gracious had a messenger, that too the last messenger, I would be the first of his worshippers."

Extermination of Prophets by the Prophet

82. Is not it a fact that before, during and after Muhammad many including a woman proclaimed Prophethood ?

When Musailima bin Habib of Yamama wrote to Muhammad for sharing prophethood with him and divide the world fifty-fifty, does not the prophet reply him : "From Muhammad the Prophet of Allah to Musailima the Liar. Undoubtedly the whole of this earth belongs to Allah and He gives it from among his people to those whom He desires to give and for the pious is triumph, in the end" (Tareekh-e-Tabari, p. 1749; Nadvi 2007 : 52) ?

Did not Musailima gather a large following, entirely by peaceful means, and claimed that half of Arabia "belongs to him."'? During that period a woman named Sajah bint Hartha Tamimi declared herself as a Prophetess. To strengthen her position did she not marry Musailima the Prophet ?

What about Tulaha Asadi, who called Muhammad a pretender and Muhammad retaliated by calling him a false prophet. He was later defeated by Khalid ibn Walid and accepted Islam not with good grace (49 : 14) ?

This created a lot of confusion and problem for Prophet Muhammad to exterminate this epidemic of prophethood. Did not Prophet Muhammad and Hazrat Abu Bakr elect Khalid bin Walid to start an expedition with Thabit bin Qais Ansari and others to curb them ? Did not Walid kill the followers of Prophet Taliha Sherjeel bin Hasna and annihilate Musailma ? The Muslims suffered large casualties. Many Huffaz-e-Quran were killed. At last Hazrat Wahshi was killed. Still the Prophethood was not out of danger. The wife of Musailma who proclaimed Prophethood, escaped and ran away to Basra where she unfortunately died after a few days ? Aswad Ansi, who proclaimed himself a prophet during the life time of Muhammad was also killed (Tareekh-e- Yaqoobi, vol.2.p. 147; Nadvi 2007 : 53-

25

54). How could Prophet Muhammad tolerate any other Prophet when he declared himself to be the last prophet ?

A Prophet or a Mad Poet ?

83. What was Muhammad for the Meccans---- a Prophet or a mad man ? Here are some examples from the Quran : "The Hypocrites and those in whose hearts is a disease said : "Allah and His Messenger promised us nothing but delusion; they have promised only to deceive us" (33 : 12).

"Then they had turned away from him and said : "One taught by others, a madman !" (44 : 14).

"They said : "Are we going to abandon our gods for the sake of a mad poet " (37 : 36) ?

To save him from public embarrassment does Allah not console him with the Quranic revelation : "By the Favor of Allah, you are neither a soothsayer, nor mad" (52 : 29) ?

Allah could not Save his Prophet

84. Being a messenger of Allah how did he not reveal to Muhammad that the ewe had been poisoned ? The story goes like this :

A Jewish captive young woman named Zaynab enquired and learnt that the Prophet liked the leg portion of goat or sheep very much. So she took a goat slew it, and roasted it. Then she poisoned the goat with a fatal toxin, and added the poison to the legs and shoulder of the animal. At sunset, after Muhammad had led the people in the evening prayer, he moved to depart while she was still sitting at his post. He inquired about her, and she answered, "O, Abu Qasim, this is a gift I brought you." Muhammad ordered it to be taken from her. It was spread in front of him while his companions were still present; among them was Bishr. Muhammad said, " Come over." They sat around the food, and Muhammad picked up a leg of the ewe and took a bite. When Muhammad had swallowed the meat, Bishr also swallowed what he had in his own mouth. The people with them ate as well.

By eating the flesh Bishr became dark as a black mantle and Muhammad took a piece from the ewe and chewed and threw it away. But Bishr took a bite from the ewe and swallowed it.

Muhammad then sent for the Jewess and asked her, "Did you poison the ewe ?" She said, "Yes". He asked, "What made you do so ?" She answered : "You had done to my people that for which you are known. You killed my father, my uncle, and my husband, and caused my people grievous damage. So I said that if you are a king, we will rid ourselves of you, and that if you are a Prophet, it will be revealed to you." It was said that Muhammad spared her life. It is also related that he ordered her to be crucified (Ibn Saad's *Tabaqat Kubra*; section on "What Poisoned Muhammad").

When Muhammad was afflicted with the illness that caused his death, he said to Ayesha : "O Ayesha, I still feel the pain of the food with which I was poisoned at Khaibar. This is the time of the cutting off of my jugular vein (death), because of that poison." When the sister of Bishr visited Muhammad during the illness which caused his death, she was told, "This is the time of the cutting off of my jugular vein, because of the poisoned meal which I ate with your brother" (*True Guidance* I : 1991 : 108-111).

In another account it is said that the Prophet after eating a portion of poisoned roasted sheep asked the Jews of Khaibar : "Have you put the poison in this roasted sheep ? They replied : "Yes". He asked: "What made you do that ?" They replied : "We intended to learn if you were a liar in which case we would be relieved from you, and if you were a Prophet then it would not harm you" (*Buk* 7 : 669). Subsequently it caused the death of the Prophet.

Last Prophet to End all Prophets

85. Why did Allah tell Muhammad : *Khatam-al-Nabiyyin*, the last of the chain of the Prophets ? Did He close and seal the Prophethood after Muhammad (33 : 40) ?

Muhammad said : "There will be no Prophets after me." On another occasion he said : "My relation to the long chain of the Prophets can be understood by the parable of a palace. The palace was most beautifully built. Everything was complete therein except the place for one brick. I have filled in that place and now the castle has been completed" (Bukhari & Muslim; Maududi 1984 : 59).

How can we believe that Muhammad is the last Prophet when Manes (276), the Persian founder of an influential semi-Christian sect active in Arabia long before Muhammad, also declared that he was the last and the greatest of the Prophets and the Paraclete (Walker 1999 : 201) ?

Death of a Prophet

86. No Prophet died as helplessly as Prophet Muhammad. Was it a glorious death like Jesus or Socrates? He was worried about cursing the Jews and the Christians, much worried about the colourful artistic graves of their Prophets, which were taken as places of worship. He intended to warn the Muslims of not turning his grave as a place of worship thus his grave was not made conspicuous (*Buk* 5 : 725).

In such a fatal illness he asked : Where will I be tomorrow ? Where will I be tomorrow ? Means in which of his wives' house his stay will be tomorrow. His wives allowed him to stay wherever he wished. So he stayed at Ayesha's house till he breathed his last. Before leading a prayer meeting he asked Ayesha to pour on him the water of seven skinned barrel (*Buk* 5 : 727). He started covering his face with his woolen sheet, and when he felt short of breath, he removed it from his face. The prophet loved to have his teeth cleaned with a Siwaak tooth stick and Ayesha softened it and cleaned his teeth. When the last moments came his head was resting between Ayesha's chest and chin and through that Siwaak stick she cut it, chewed it and her saliva mixed with his saliva at his death (*Buk* 5 : 731).

Death be not Proud

87. Is not it a fact that the deadbody of Muhammad was laying but his relatives were much worried about the share of inheritance, as if they were eagerly waiting for his death ? There was no sign of sorrow. As at the time of his death, Muhammad did not declare a successor, there was strong disagreement about who should become the next ruler, Abu Bakr and Umar the most intimate friends of the Prophet abandoned the corpse of their dead master, and left it without a burial place, in a hurry to ensure his political succession (Warraq 2000 : 182).

Forecast is Falsified

88. Muhammad being a Prophet forecasted that the five things which nobody knows except Allah are :

    1. nobody knows what will happen tomorrow.
    2. nobody knows what is in the womb.

3. nobody knows what he will gain tomorrow.
4. nobody knows at what place he will die, and
5. nobody knows when it will rain.

Out of the five prophecies (*Buk* 2 : 149) at least two prophecies are falsified. Does not the physician determine the sex in the womb and can rain not be forecasted by the weather studies ?

Prophecy of the Prophet Falsified
89. Is not it a fact that before death Muhammad proclaimed that he would not be leaving inheritance to his family members (*Mus* 19 :4355), but the very next day of Muhammad's death, Fatima, Ali and Al-Abbas came to Abu Bakr to demand their share in the inheritance ? Did Abu Bakr give any thing to Fatimah (*Mus* 19 : 4349) ? This made her very angry and she left and did not talk to him till her death (*Tab* 9 : 196, 197). Abu Bakr died two years after assuming the caliphate and Umar became the next caliph. But, Ali and Ibn Abbas had never allowed the dispute to die out-- they still wanted the money, like the wives of the Prophet (*Mus* 19 : 4351).

The Prophet's three Answers :
90. Abdullah bin Salam asked three questions (*Buk* 5 : 275) to the Prophet and he answered them :

Q.	What is the first sign of the hour ?

A.	It will be a fire that will collect the people from the East to the West.

Q.	What is the first food which the people of Paradise will eat ?

A.	It will be the caudate (extra) lobe of the fish-liver, as the first meal which the people of Paradise will eat.

Q.	Why does a child attract the similarity of his father or his mother ?

A.	As for the child, if the man's discharge preceeds the woman's discharge, the child attracts the similarity to the man, and if the woman's discharge proceeds the man's, then the child attracts the similarity to the woman.

Are these answers convincing ? Decide.

Who said he is the Last among Prophets ?
91. An Islamic dogmatic argument often follows the following pattern : "He is the last prophet." Who says so? "The book says so." Why should the book be believed? "Because it is the word of God." Who says it is the word of God ? "He said so." Why should we believe him ? "He is the prophet of God." We have now come back, full circle, to the first proposition, with which we started and can go on in circles till kingdom came and get nowhere except by the final argument which alone can end such dogmatic arguments-- the sword or the gun (Sabab 2004 : 218).

Last Prophet with Last Mosque
92. Is it true that the prophet said, "I am the last prophet and the mosque I am constructing is the last mosque." If by the term "last mosque" it is understood that no other mosque will be built in the dispensation of Islam then it is not so. Similarly the term *khatam al-nabiyyin* (seal of the prophets) refers to the fact that the prophet confirmed the preceding prophets, and thus the peoples of Arabia, who had not accepted the prophethood of the prophets of the past, particularly those of

the Ibrahimic tradition, were summoned to recognize them [Rawshani, *khatamiyyat* (129 BE : 30-31]. Moreover, there are variant meanings of *seal* suggested in the Quran; one verse states that on the Day of God a "choice" wine will quench the thirst of the Righteous, "whose seal (*khitam*) is musk" (83 : 26).

Does not the word *khatam* (seal) mean "the last" in a temporal sense to early Muslims ? There are instances in classical Arabic poetry and Hadith literature to suggest that the word *khatam* (seal) was used to mean "the one who confirmed" (the prophets of the past) and was understood in a honorific way as "the best" (of the prophets) [Fazel. 1993 : 28].

Seal and Successorship of a Prophet

93. Is not it a fact that *khatam al-anbiya* (seal of the prophets) also found their way into hadith literature ? For instance, there is a saying of the Imam 'Ali that "Muhammad is the Seal of the Prophets (*khatam al-anbiya*) and I am the Seal of the Successors *khatam al-was iyyin* (*Majlisi, Bihar* 4-5). If *seal* solely meant termination, then how can one understand 'Ali as sealing the successorship, when there were to be eleven Imams after him according to Shi'i belief, and the Caliphate was to continue after him in the history of Sunni Islam ?

Ahmad a Prophet Next to the Last

94. If Mirza Ghulam Ahmad had the visions and hallucinations more accurately like Muhammad why to deny him as the promised Imam-i-Mehdi?

Who is the Last Prophet ?

95. What is wrong if Mirza Ghulam Ahmad declared himself a Prophet ? In a country like India where at least a hundred godmen declare themselves God, Ahmed too claimed : He is Adam, he is Nuh, he is Ibrahim, he is Isaac, he is Yaqoob, he is Israel, he is Moosa, he is Dawood, he is Isa-ibn-e- Maryam, he is Muhammad and at last in 1904 declared himself as Lord Krishna (*Radiance* 1988 : 2).

When Prophethood was Reincarnated ?

96. Is it not a fact that Mirza Ghulam Ahmad claimed to be an inspired Prophet to synthesize all religions under Islam and declared himself to be not only the manifestation of Prophet Muhammad but also the second advent of Jesus as well as Krishna and disregarded the finality of Prophethood with Muhammad ?

The Purpose of Prophet Muhammad

97. If all the previous Prophets of God were sent only to their people, their nations and their complete message was meant for a particular time then was not Prophet Muhammad sent to the world as the last and final messenger of God with the message :

We have sent you (21 : 107) with guidance and the Religion of Truth, to make it prevail over all religions (48 : 28), for that take not the Jews and the Christians for your friends (5 : 51), kill them wherever you catch them (2 : 191). Take not for friends unbelievers (4 : 144), fight the unbelievers who are near to you (9 : 123). Allah will punish them by your hands, execute, or crucify them or cut off their hands and feet from opposite sides, or exile them from the land (5 : 33) and fight the unbelievers until no other religion except Islam is left for them (2 : 193).

Prophecy on the 12th Imam

98. Is it possible to accept the leader of the Muslim community only from the family of Muhammad that too to the succession of Ali's descendants ? Among the number of divisions in Shi'ah, the "Twelvers" believed that the 12th Imam disappeared and went into seclusion somewhere in 870 AD but he would reappear to lead the Muslims as the Mahdi or Messiah, who will, at the end of time, establish justice on earth. Is not it the indication that Prophet Muhammad talked about these twelve Muslim rulers, who will rule all the Islamic world and all of them will be from Quraish (*Buk* 9 : 329) ?

7- Muhammad and his Magic Lamp

Miracle is a miracle if it is not understood. Explain it you will find there is no miracle but every event is too limited by the senses. If we say any event is a miracle, exceeding the known laws of nature, due to divine intervention, then there is nothing like a wonderful thing or a great and splendid or conspicuous deed. Therefore Prophet Muhammad instead of performing any miracle told the illiterate Arabs that the Quran is the miracle of miracles. If they doubt his statement then they should produce a *sura* of the Holy Quran.

To our surprise Muhammad performed many miracles among his supporters such as he had an over night journey to Jerusalem and ascended to the seven heavens where he talked with ancestors like Adam, Ibrahim, Moses and Jesus. Not only that Muhammad had performed many miracles such as multiplying bread (*Buk* 5.59.428), producing water for an army for ablution from a small pot (*Buk* 1.4.170, 1.4.194, 1.7.340, 4.56.779, *Mus* 30. 5656-9), multiplying dates (*Buk* 4.56.780), splitting the moon in two parts (*Buk* 4.56.831, 5.58.208, 5. 58.209, 6.60.388-91). Once he invoked Allah to bless the inhabitants of Medina with rain, and following this there was rain for seven days until the valleys flooded (*Buk* 8.73.115). He visited the towns of Jinns and some Jinns converted to Islam (*Mus* 26. 5559). Once he stuck a huge solid rock and the rock became like sand (*Buk* 5.59.427). He fought with a big demon and subdued him (*Buk* 1.9. 450). When companions of Muhammad departed from him on a dark night, they were led by two lights like lamps (Allah's magic light) lighting the way in front of them till they reached their houses (*Buk* 1.9. 454, 4.5.833) and the list goes on.

A few miracles can be cited here how Prophet Muhammad could perform miracles although he did not believe in the miracles of Moses and Jesus. We are very much doubtful about his miracles. Here are a few questions that strike our mind often.

Miracles help the Unbeliever to Believe
99. When the Jews and the Arabs asked Muhammad to perform a miracle to prove his Prophethood he declined to do so with the plea that if he performs a miracle like the ancient they won't believe it (17 : 59). Then why did Allah send Moses, Elijah, and Christ with Miracles ? Why will the people of unbelief believe the message of Allah to be true ?

Miracles before the Followers no Miracle
100. Is it not a fact that when the Arab dignitaries asked Muhammad to prove his prophethood and the divine revelation of Quran with some miracles or other signs, he failed to do so ? Was he not overcome by anxiety and distress when he could not

perform anything to testify his Prophethood and was thus silenced by the wise men of Arab ? Had he performed some miracles like the splitting of the moon or making water flow from between his hands which are ascribed to him by his followers before the wise men, he would not have had to feel offended and worried before his clans men and could have been easily accepted as a Prophet. (*Tabari's Commentary* on Sura 17 : 93-95; *Guidance* I p.79).

A Magical Ring

101. We read, "Certainly We tried Solomon, and we cast upon his throne a mere body; then he repented. He said, 'My Lord, forgive me, and give me a kingdom such as may not befall anyone after me' " (38 : 34, 35).

Muslim expositors claimed that Solomon killed the king of Sidon and took his daughter Jarada as captive, for she was beautiful, later she wept over her father in Solomon's house. Therefore, Solomon commanded the devils to make a statue of her father. When they made it, she set it before her and worshipped it for forty days. Now Solomon had a ring he always wore. He would give it to his wife Amina only when he went in for purification. It so happened that once Satan appeared to Amina in the shape of Solomon, took the ring from her, sat on the throne, and married Solomon's wives ! He continued reigning for forty days. Meanwhile Solomon was cast away and rejected by all who saw him. Satan flew away, and the ring fell into the sea. Several fishermen caught some fish and gave Solomon two of them as wages for his service in carrying the fish for them. When he ripped a fish open, he found the ring in its belly, so he put it on his finger, and his kingdom was restored to him (*Tab* 23 : 158).

What is this magical ring supposed to be ? How can whoever wears it become king ? Being a spirit, how can Satan marry flesh-and-blood women ? Where in the historical records is it said that King Solomon was a beggar and a carrier of fish for forty days (Abd Al - Fadi 1997 : 255 - 256) ?

Turn Safa into Gold

102. Is not it a fact that Prophet Muhammad advocated : "Every Prophet was given miracles because of which people believed, but what I have been given, is Divine Inspiration which Allah has revealed to me. So I hope that my followers will outnumber the followers of other Prophets on the Day of Resurrection" (*Buk* 6 : 504)?

Once the Quresh tribe, citing the examples of Moses and Jesus, told Muhammad to perform some miracles to strengthen their faith on him. Muhammad asked : "What kind of thing do you want ?" They answered : "Oh, that you would turn Mount Safa into gold ! Raise up some of our dead, and we will ask them if what you say is true or false, and show us angels bearing witness to you." Muhammad said : "If I do some of what you say, will you believe me ?" "Yes" ! they answered. "By Allah ! If you do that, all of us will follow you." Muhammad began praying and praying that Allah would turn Mount Safa into gold. When he saw Safa was not moving he consoled himself by saying : "Allah is compassionate. Had it come it would have caused an earthquake or fallen upon us to our destruction (Walker 1999 : 220). Finally Gabriel came and said to him, "If I want to, it will be gold. But if they do not believe you, we will torture them. Or you let go of them until they repent." Muhammad said : "Until they repent." Whenever Muhammad was asked to perform a miracle like those of Moses or Jesus, he would fail. All he could say was, "you do not believe" (*al Tabari's Commentary* on Sura 6 : 109; CQV 1994 : 106; Abd Al-Fadi, 1997 : 371).

Miracle of Miracles

103. When Prophet Muhammad quoted the Quran that if you are in doubt regarding the revelation then produce a *sura* like, (2 : 23) and consider the Quran, the miracle of miracles, what is the need to perform any miracle ? But Muhammad did perform miracle, was tempted to do so by feeding the multitudes by multiplying the bread (*Buk* 4 : 778, 781) just like Jesus and multiplying water in two barrels yet the skins were full to satisfy all the people (*Buk* 4 : 771), his meals used to glorify Allah while he was eating and this glorification was heard by his companions (*Buk* 4 : 779), and like Jesus he ascended to the heaven (*Buk* 1 : 345; 5 : 227).

Aren't these few acts of miracles indeed the handiwork of his followers who imposed a few supernatural acts on Muhammad which are not valid because they contradicted the saying of the Quran ? Followers are followers. They could have told boldly that miracle is a miracle if it is not understood. Explain it, it will be either a trick or science.

Splitting the Moon

104. When the people of Mecca demanded from Muhammad that he should show them some miracles, Muhammad split the moon into two parts between which the Meccans could see the Hira mountain (*Buk* 5 : 208-211;6 : 387-390), whereas others saw at Mina that moon was split up into two. One of its parts was behind the mountain and the other one was on this side of the mountain (*Mus* 4 : 6725) for a very short time. The Arabs thought the moon to be about the size of a basketball. Do they have any idea that it is a mass of 734,556,000,000 tonnes and it is 384, 403 km away from Arab or the world ?

Night Journey to Heaven

105. Before ascending to heaven on the night of *Miraj* the roof of his house was made open and Gabriel descended. He opened up his chest and washed it with the water of Zam-zam. Then he brought a golden tray full of Wisdom and Belief and poured it in his chest and then closed it. Then he took hold of his hand and ascended to the nearest heaven (*Buk* 1 : 345; 2 : 75, 700).

Is it believable that Muhammad had a night journey to Jerusalem and then to seven heavens where he talked with Adam, Idris, Moses, Jesus and Ibrahim (*Buk* 1 : 211, 345) ?

Where is the actual Jerusalem ?

106. Is it believable that the night journey of Muhammad from Kaaba to Jerusalem and from Jerusalem to his heavenward ascension a reality or is it a dream ? Is there any description of the real Jerusalem by Muhammad in Hadith or is it a mere claim of Ibn Abbas (*Buk* 5 : 228) ? Does not the heavenward ascension start at a time when no one could see him ?

Night Journey from Mosque to Mosque

107. Who arranged a night journey for Muhammad from the sacred mosque to the farthest mosque ? If the answer is Allah (17 : 1), then the next question comes : which one is the farthest mosque for Muhammad ? The Farthest Mosque is *al-Aqsa* in Jerusalem, say the Muslim scholars. From Jerusalem Muhammad started his heavenward ascension. Was *al-Aqsa* in existence at the time of Muhammad ? Was not the mosque built a hundred years after his death, during the reign of the Ummayad Caliph, Abdalmalik b. Marwan in 684 ? After visiting the city of Jerusalem he sent for his governors throughout the Islamic world, saying that Allah directed him to build the Dome of the Rock and *al-Aqsa* Mosque, and that he did not want to carry this out unless his subjects agreed. Letters came to him from all around the Islamic world commending the matter and saying that he should embark on what he planned to do. Marwan built the Dome and the Farthest Mosque to divert the people from making the pilgrimage in Mecca at the time when Abdallah b. al- Zubair had gained control over Hijaz (*Taba*; Qtd. CQV. 1994 : 183).

History tells us that when Muhammad visited Jerusalem there was no existence of any temple or Mosque. The Romans had already destroyed it by 70AD and as late as 691 AD the Jupiter temple was built by the Romans there.

Night Journey from al-Hijr
108. The heavenward ascension of Muhammad started from Kaaba or from al-Hijr ? Was he not asleep in the house of Umm Hani after the evening prayer ?

Umm, Abu Talib's daughter said : "He (Muhammad) slept in my home that night after he prayed the final night prayer. A little before dawn he woke us, saying, "O Umm, I went to Jerusalem." He got up to go out and I grabbed hold of his robe and laid bare his belly. I pleaded, "O Muhammad, don't tell the people about this for they will know you are lying and will mock you" (*Ish* 184).

Can it be denied that when Muhammad recounted his tale of ascending to the seventh heaven, did many Muslims not lose their faith on Muhammad and left him ? His closest friend Abu Bakr was at first taken aback. He was puzzled. He had two choices -- either to abandon Muhammad by accepting that he was a fraud, or remain with him by believing his absurd tales. Ibn Ishaq depicted :

"Many Muslims gave up their faith. Some went to Abu Bakr and said, 'What do you think of your friend now ? He alleges that he went to Jerusalem last night and prayed there and came back to Mecca.' Bakr said that they were lying about the Apostle. But they told him that he was in the mosque at this very moment telling the Quresh about it. Bakr said, "If he says so then it must be true. I believe him. And that is more extraordinary than his story at which you boggle" (*Ish* 183).

Allah revealed, "When We said to you 'Indeed, your Lord encompasses all people.' We did not make the vision which We showed to you... except to be a trial for people..." (17.60).

Allah was always with him to save him from such kind of embarrassment.

Water in the Wilderness
109. Is it believable that on one occasion when the Muslims needed water, Muhammad called for a pot, the pot was small enough for one to spread one's hand in. Then he made water flow out of his fingernails into the pot until everyone had all the water they needed. There numbers were more than eighty (*Buk* 1 : 170, 194; 4 : 773, 774, 775, 776, 779; *Mus* 4 : 5656).

Miracles are with Allah Only
110. If signs or miracles are with Allah, why didn't He allow Muhammad to perform it (29 : 50) ? Is it not a lame excuse to say, "I am indeed a clear warner" ?

8- The King has no Clothes

Nothing is secret about the wives of Prophet Muhammad. Historians like Ibn Ishak, Ibn Hisham, Ibn Saad, Ibn Hanbal, al-Tabari never hesitated to describe the married life of Muhammad in detail. But most of his historians are of the opinion that he was giving himself up to female company. Tor Andrae commented : "What kind of Prophet is this man, who only thinks of marrying" (1960 : 188) ?

By a special revelation Muslims were allowed to have upto four wives but the Prophet could have as many as he can. According to Thomas Pattick Hughes "Muhammad had eleven wives, but according to some traditions he had twenty two (1977 : 400). Everything is done in the name of Allah (33 : 52). Nabia Abbott was bound to comment : "The prayerful and perfumed Prophet of Islam, was avowedly a great lover of the ladies" (1985 : XV).

Khadija the Prophet Maker
111. Is not it a fact that Khadija first married to Abu Halal Ibn Zarara of Bani Tamim and had two sons by him, Halal and Hind. Hind later died in the Battle of the camel fighting on the side of Ali. Khadija married a second husband, Atiq Ibn Ayaz Makhzumi, to whom she bore a daughter named Hinda. It is after the death of her second husband that she, from her balcony, saw her future husband returning with the trade caravans from Syria (Narayan 1978 : 166). She elevated her trade supervisor to the state of her husband despite the difference in age. It was her charity from which Muhammad made his fortune. Did not she find him an orphan who was wandering ? Did she not give him shelter and guidance, removed all his burden and raised him to a respectable position ? A friend found in need became a friend indeed.

Who brought Hope for Muhammad ?
112. Is it not a fact that the marriage with Khadijah was a turning point in Muhammad's life ? Was not it a custom in Arab that minors did not inherit property from their parents ? Therefore Muhammad had no share from his father's and grandfather's side. Did not Muhammad's marriage to a widow obtain him enough capital after her death, though his only sorrow was none of his boys survived childhood ?

Why unlimited Wives ?
113. Is not it a fact that the Prophet was patiently waiting for the death of Khadija after which he could bring polygamy into practice ? After her death in 620 he got permission from Allah that men can have four wives at best (4 : 3) and Muhammad had special privilege divinely sanctioned to have more than four wives besides any number of servile women (33 : 49-51) ?

Sexual Appetite of a Prophet
114. Is it a fact that Muhammad used to have intercourse with his nine wives be it night or day (*Buk* 1 : 267, 270 ; 7 : 142) ? He was given the strength of 30/40 men of the men of Paradise. This strength was given by Gabriel who brought a kettle from which Muhammad ate. It was beyond comparison, surpassed all beings in the strength for sexual intercourse (Mualim's *Sahih*, section on Ayesha's Bounty; *Tabaqat* by Ibn Sa'd, section on Muhammad's wives and Ayesha's bounty Vol.1; *Ihya Ulum al-Din* by al-Ghazzali, section on marriage; CQV 1994 : 261).

Besides eleven wives he would often choose new sexual partners from the women captured during his conquests (*Buk* 1 : 367). It excludes beautiful women who offered themselves to Muhammad, and slave girls or the girls who were purchased (*Buk* 7 : 22-23).

Does not Anas quote Muhammad as having said : "I was given excellence in four things more than any other man : generosity, courage, intercourse and killing". Sahih informs us what Muhammad said, "My great love is prayer, but greater than this is my love for perfume and women" (Iyad, *al-shifa*; *True Guidance I.* 1991 : 101).

Such claims were made to impress the Arabs who at that time believed that ceaseless sexual activity could give the pleasure of Paradise (Morey 1992 : 190). Is the claim of Muhammad true ? Hadith reports a different opinion : "Muhammad was influenced by the magic that he used to think he had had sexual relations with his wives while he actually had not " (*Buk* 7 : 660; 6 : 60, 658; *Mus* 26 : 5428) ?

Rights of Man

115. Is not it a fact that when Ayesha asked Muhammad : "Should not a woman be ashamed to give herself to a man" (*Al-Bukhari* and others Nikah 29; *Tafsir* al-Sura al-Nur 24 : 11; *Muslim*, Nikah 65, Rada 50; *al-Tirmidsi*, Tafsir al-Sura al-Nur 24 : 4; Ibn Maja, Nikah 57; Ahmad b. Hanbal VI 60, 158; Qtd. *CQV* 1994 : 234-235). Muhammad uttered a verse from the Quran, "You may put off whom you will of them, and whom you will you may take to yourself; and if you seek any you have set aside, there is no fault in you" (33 : 51).

Then Ayesha said : "Indeed, Allah hastens to do what you desire." Muhammad took to himself Ayesha, Hafsa, Umm Salama, and Zainab; these he slept with on a regular basis. He put off five of his women : Umm Habiba, Maimuna, Sawda, Juwairiyya, and Safiyya; these he slept with whenever he wanted to. (al-Zamakhshari's Comment on Sura al- Ahzab 33 : 51; Qtd. CQV. 1994 : 234-235).

Special Rights of Muhammad

116. Is not it a fact that Allah gave Ten rights to his beloved messenger, which were not granted to any other believer ? According to Muhammad al-Ishmawi the rights are as follows :

I.   The right to cool shade.

II.   The right to bounties.

III.   The right to nine wives at once.

IV.   The right that his wives marry none other than him.

V.   The right to marry a woman who offers herself to him (33 : 49).

VI.   The right to put away any wife, take any wife, and seek again the wife he set aside (33 : 51).

VII.   The right to seize the best of any bounty, be it slave man, slave girl, or breastplate, and with or without his participation in the battle (*Sira Halabiyya,* Vol.2).

VIII.   The right to demand that his sons-in-law ask permission if they desire to marry other women. In one incident, Muhammad did not allow Ali (who had already married his daughter, Fatima) to marry a woman from the tribe of Hisham b. Mugaira (*Sira Halabiyya,* section on the conquest of Banu Selim).

IX.   The right to look at a woman who was not his wife and to be alone with her, to prevent him from lusting (*Sira Halabiyya,* on the conquest of Banu Mustaliq).

X.   The right to have sexual relations during Ihram, the pilgrimage (*Sira Halabiyya,* section on Imrat al-Qada) (*True Guidance* I 1991 : 101-102).

Adam had One : Prophet had Eleven

117. Is it not a fact that Abraham had two wives and one concubine (*Gn* 16 : 1; I *Chr* 1 : 32), Jacob had two wives and some concubines (*Gn* 35 : 32), David had seven wives (2 *Sam* 3 : 2-5) and Prophet Muhammad had eleven wives and a few concubines ? Was not Muhammad more progressive than earlier Prophets and generous enough to allow his fellow Muslims to marry women of their choice, two, or three, or four (4 : 3) ? How is something which is unlawful for others be lawful for him ?

Zaid offered his Wife to his Father

118. Muhammad had a foster son named Zaid who was very loyal to his foster-father. Zaid married Zainab bint Jahsh, who was a cousin of Muhammad. Zainab, Zaid's wife, whom Muhammad saw was dressed in a chemise and veil over her face, when he went to Zaid one day on a certain errand. She was light skinned, and her physical appearance was perfect among the women of the Quraish, so that he was bewitched by her beauty. Then he said : "Praise be to Him, who changes the hearts," and left. When Zaid arrived home, she told him, and he went about the matter with prudence. He came to Muhammad and said : "I want to leave my wife." Muhammad said to him : "What is the matter with her ? Did she do anything to make you suspicious of her ?" Zaid said : "No, by Allah. All I saw in her was good. But she treats me as inferior, on account of her nobility, and she hurts me with her tongue (i.e., with what she says)." So Muhammad said : "Keep your wife to yourself, and fear Allah concerning her." Yet, after this, Muhammad said that Allah rebuked him and said to him, "Why did you say : 'Keep your wife to yourself?' Were you afraid that the people would find fault with you and say : 'He ordered a man to divorce his wife and afterward he himself married her ?' Muhammad, do not fear the people."

Anas said : "Zainab used to boast to Muhammad's other wives and say : 'It was your fathers who gave you in marriage, but it was Allah himself who gave me in marriage, from above seven heavens.' She used to say to Muhammad : 'I pride myself with you on three things, which none of your wives can pride herself on : You and I have the same grandfather, Allah married me to you from heaven, and the mediator (of our marriage) was Gabriel' (*Al-Tabaqat al-Kubra* by Ibn Sa'd; section on Muhammad's wives; Qtd.CQV 1994 : 233-234).

This incident created a great embarrassment and a lot of controversy among the believers and this did not befit his position as a prophet but Allah was there to fulfil the salacious desires of Muhammad and He gave a clean chit saying : "Prophet, we have made lawful for you the wives to whom you have granted dowries and the slave girls whom Allah has given you as booty, the daughters of your paternal and maternal uncles and of your paternal and maternal aunts who fled with you, and any believing woman who gives herself to the prophet and whom the prophet wishes to take in marriage. This privilege is yours alone, being granted to no other believer" (33 : 50).

If the law maker is the law breaker then who will make the law ?

Fatima did not marry Abu Bakr

119. During Muhammad's time in Arab *Shighar* marriage was in practice, where two men can exchange their daughters as their wives. Prophet had his agreement with Abu Bakr to exchange their daughters with each other. According to the agreement the child Ayesha married the Prophet at the age of six at Abu Bakr's house in Medina. But Muhammad could not discharge his duty to give his daughter Fatima to Abu Bakr. Was he not waiting for a command from Allah which never reached the Prophet ? The Prophet could not convince Fatima and Abu Bakr gave up his hope to have Fatima as his wife. At last the Holy Prophet commanded : *(la shighara fi'l-Islam),* that is, the exchange of daughters or sisters is forbidden in Islam (*Hvoice* Sept., 2007 : 20).

Allah : the Marriage Broker

120. Is not it a fact that Allah the Great and Almighty could reduce Himself to a marriage broker for Muhammad ? Hadith writer recorded :

"Ayesha reported Allah's Messenger having said : I saw you in a dream for three nights when an angel brought you to me in a silk cloth and he said : Here is your wife, and when I removed (the cloth) from your face, lo, it was yourself, so I said : If this is from Allah, let Him carry it out" (*Mus* 31.5977).

Why did Muhammad remarry after Fifty ?

121. When Muhammad, being a young man of 25 married Khadija, a twice widowed lady, 15 years senior to him, he did not dare to look at any other woman, although he was living in a polygamous society. Just after the death of Khadija at the age of 50 why did he marry Ayesha whose age was only 6 ? Had not Ayesha's father Abu Bakr already given word to his friend Mutim for his son ? How was a father of a daughter forced to change his decision to give his girl child to a 50 year old man ?

Girl of 6 with Man of 50

122. The Muslims are very much worried when they are asked to remove Quranic study at the Madrasa. Will you feel comfortable when your children will be taught that Prophet Muhammad married a six year old bride Ayesha when he was 50 ? Can you justify that a girl is matured enough at the age of six or nine ?

In many Muslim countries this heinous criminal practice is protected by law. In fact there is no minimum age for marriage either for men or women in Islamic law. Ayatollah Khomeini said, "A man can have sexual pleasure from a child as young as a baby." According to Saudi Arabia's most senior cleric, Sheikh Abdul-Aziz Al Sheikh, the country's grand mufti : "Ten-year-old girls are ready for marriage. Those who say that ten or twelve year old girls are too young to marry, are 'unfair' to them" (Das 2010 : 233).

Why to marry during Hajj ?

123. Was not it a rule for pilgrims that they must not marry and give someone in marriage in the sacred state (while wearing ihram)... *(Daw* : 2.10.1837; 2 : 187; 2 : 197) ?

Did Muhammad observe this Quranic rule ? Once when he went to Mecca to perform the Hajj and a proposal of marriage was offered to him, he quickly accepted the offer and married the woman even though he was in sacred state wearing irham.

"Ibn 'Abbas said : The Prophet married Maimunah while he was in the sacred state (wearing ihram)" (*Daw* 2.10.1840).

Auto-erotic Sexual Mono-Games of the Prophet

124. Can we imagine a Prophet with an "auto-erotic sexual mono-game" with a girl of nine ? It can be quoted as it is from the Islamic sources :

"Narrated Ayesha : The Prophet and I used to take a bath from a single pot... During the menses, he used to order me to put on an Izar (dress worn below the waist) and used to fondle me" (*Buk* 1 : 298).

"Muhammad put his cheek and chest in between the naked thighs of a menstruating Ayesha" (*Daw*, 13 : 0270).

"Muhammad used to kiss and suck Aisha's tongue while they were fasting" (*Daw*, 13.2380).

"Ayesha said : 'During menstruation, I used to bite off meat from bone, the Prophet would take the bone from me and place his mouth at the same spot to eat of it where I had been biting : when I drank water, he would take the vessel from me and place his lips at the same spot where I had put mine'' (Vol 2; Qtd. Das 2010 : 120).

An Excellent Example of the Prophet

125. Can it be an "excellent example" (33 : 21) when Ayesha confessed:

"Al-Aawad and Hammam reported Ayesha as saying : I used to scrape off the (drop of) semen from the garment of the Messenger of Allah" (*Mus* 2 : 567).

"In case I (Ayesha) found that (semen) on the garment of the Messenger of Allah dried up, I scraped it off with my nails" (*Mus* 2 :572).

"Narrated Sulaiman bin Yasar : I asked Ayesha about the clothes soiled with semen. She replied, 'I used to wash it off the clothes of Allah's Apostle and he would go for the prayer while water spots were still visible' (*Buk* 1 : 231).

"Narrated Ayesha : 'I used to wash the semen off the clothes of the Prophet and even then I used to notice one or more spots on them'' (*Buk* 1.4.233).

Encouraged Child Marriage

126. Is it not a fact that in ancient Arab, i.e. in the age of *Jahiliyah* (ignorance), every evil took place except child-marriage. Even the Quran tells about the right age for the marriage (4 : 6) and in another verse it clearly says : "Marry women whom you like" (4 : 3). Here "woman" cannot be interpreted as "girl" or female child in relation to marriage. In such case the marriage of Salm, son of Umme Salma with the daughter of Hazrat Hamzah was allegedly arranged by the Prophet himself (Niazi p.4), and how did the prophet marry Ayesha, the six-year-old beautiful daughter of Abu Bakr which was consummated when she was nine. They remained together for nine years till the Prophet's death. When the Prophet came to her she was frightened (1 : p.526; Shaikh 1999 : 50). Does it not encourage child marriage using children for sexual pleasure or Pedophilia ?

The Jealous Husband

127. Is it not a fact that Muhammad married more than eleven times ? In his old age when he married a girl of six he suspected his friends and visitors and put his beautiful girl wife Ayesha behind the curtain, because he did not want his friends to look admiringly at her. Once Muhammad held a banquet on the night he married Zainab and he invited guests and served them a meal. He wished them to leave afterwards, because his mind was on his bride. He stood up to let them know he wanted to leave, so some left. He stood up once more, but some stayed. He stood up a third time, and then they all left. So he entered his house (where the bride was), and Anas followed him, but he prevented him (from coming in) by letting down the curtain : On behalf of Muhammad did Allah not say to his friends : "O you who believe, do not enter the prophets' homes unless you are given permission to eat, nor shall you force such an invitation in any manner. If you are invited, you may enter. When you finish eating, you shall leave, do not engage him in lengthy conversations. This used to hurt the prophet, and he was too shy to tell you. But Allah does not shy away from the truth. If you have to ask his wives for something, ask them from behind a curtain. This is purer for your hearts and their hearts. You are not to hurt the messenger of Allah. You shall not marry his wives after him, for this would be gross offence in the sight of Allah" (See *Asbab al-Nuzul* by al-Suyuti on Sura al-Ahzab, 33 : 53; CQV.1994 : 235).

Thereafter did Allah not send a message to the wives of the Prophet : "O Prophet, tell your wives and daughters and the women of other believers that they shall lengthen their clothes. Thus, they will be recognized (as righteous women) and not annoyed" (33 : 59).

Ayesha's Inspiration to receive Revelation

128. Is it not a fact that Muhammad received the inspiration for many of his *suras* while in Ayesha's presence ? When Umm Salama complained to him about the favouritism shown to Ayesha, did he not dismiss her, saying : "Trouble me not about Ayesha ? She is the only one in whose company I receive any revelations" (Walker 1999 : 226) ?

Ayesha's Dress brings Revelation

129. Is not it a fact that Ayesha relates that Muslims knew the day when she and Muhammad would spend time together. They would bring their gifts to Muhammad on that very day, in order to please him. As a result of which the wives of Muhammad were divided into two groups : Ayesha, Hafsa, Safia, and Sawda; and Um Salama and the others. Um Salama's group requested her to have Muhammad ask the Muslims to bring their gifts anytime, regardless of where he might be staying. Muhammad, while wearing women's clothing, said to Um Salama : "Do not hurt me concerning Ayesha. The revelation never came to me while dressed in a women's dress, except when wearing Ayesha's dress." Um Salama refrained from asking Muhammad about the matter again.

Did not the rest of the wives ask Fatima, Muhammad's daughter, to express their concern to him. Upon hearing the request from Fatima, Muhammad replied : "Do you not love the one I love ? Then love Ayesha !" (*True Guidance* I 1991 :

100-101). The Prophet is supposed to be equal to all his wives but his special concern for Ayesha brings hostility among his other wives.

Ayesha Jealous of Khadija
130. Is it not a fact that Ayesha was more jealous of Khadija, the dead wife of Muhammad as Muhammad spoke highly of her and used to mention her name very often (*Buk* 5 : 163-165) ?

Is it Wrong to be Beautiful ?
131. Is not it a fact that after attacking Khaybar, Muhammad took as a captive a very beautiful teenaged-girl named, Safiyyah and married her without paying any dowry (*mehr*) and thus violated Allah's instruction (*Buk* 5.59.523,524) ? Did not he claim that marrying Safiyyah was in itself a respect for her (*Mus* 8.3326) ? Before falling into the hands of Muhammad, Safiyyah was the legal wife of a Jewish man. Muhammad had killed Safiyyah's husband and her father after subjecting them to brutal torture, and finally beheaded them.

Muhammad was supposed to wait for four months and ten days before he could even touch her but he did not do that. Bukhari says Muhammad married Safiyyah and gave a grand feast at the wedding; then he had sex with her (*Buk* 4 : 143).

More Wives More Woes
132. Is it not a fact that Prophet Muhammad was in constant trouble with his wives ? Ayesha, the daughter of Abu Bakr, and Hafsa, the daughter of Umar were at times the problem makers. Were they influenced by the women dominated society of Medina (*Mus* 2 : 3507-3511) ?

Why did Muhammad suspect his Wives ?
133. Was not Muhammad sexually weak ? Therefore he could not perform any better sexual act than sucking little Ayesha's tongue and fondling other wives (Das 2010 : 235). In such a situation he is bound to suspect his wives and spy behind his back.

"Narrated Anas : The Prophet said, "Straighten your rows, for I see you from behind my back" (*Buk* 1: 686).

"Narrated Anas bin Malik : Once the Iqama was pronounced and Allah's Apostle faced us and said, "Straighten your rows and stand closer together, for I see you from behind my back" (*Buk* 1 : 687).

"Anas b. Malik reported : The messenger of Allah said : Complete the rows, for I can see you behind my back" (*Mus* 4 : 872).

Allah worried about the Wives of Muhammad
134. Is it not a fact that Allah was much worried about Muhammad's wives and constantly revealed him through the Quranic verses about how to handle their disputes and demands ?

Ayesha's Marriage to Jubayr broken off
135. Is it not a fact that in order to tie up with Muhammad, Abu Bakr and his wife Umm Ruman broke off their 6 year old daughter Ayesha's marriage with a young man named Jubayr ibn Mutam and gave her hand to Muhammad, a young man of 52 ? Did this not please the parents of Jubayr, because they were pagans and they anticipated that the marriage might lead to the boy's conversion to Islam ?

Allah Partial to the Prophet

136. Is Allah not partial when he gave dispensation to the prophet to defer or accept any number of wives at his own whim and discretion (33 : 51) but He grants a Muslim not to have more than four wives ? This gave a chance to his favourite wife Ayesha to comment : "I feel that your Lord hastened in fulfiling your wishes and desires" (*Buk* 6 : 311).

Fasting and Kissing

137. Do kissing and fasting go hand in hand ? In all religious rituals is not it an unpardonable sin ? Did not Muhammad kiss Ayesha while observing fast even during Ramadan (*Mus* 2 : 2438, 2446) ? Is it possible for a person to control his desires (*Buk* 3 : 149) when he is unable to control kissing his wife ?

Is Menstruation an Injury ?

138. When the Holy Quran says : "They ask you about menstruation. Say : 'It is an injury. Stay away from women during their menstrual periods and do not approach them until they are cleansed. When they have cleansed themselves, then come to them from where Allah has commanded you" (2 : 222). Why did Muhammad not spare his wives when they were in heavy menstruation ? He used to order Ayesha, his nine year old wife to put on Izar (dress worn below the waist) fondled her in bath, even when she was in her menses (*Buk* 1 : 298). Does he not use to put his cheek and chest in between the naked thighs of a menstruating Ayesha... (*Daw* 1 : 270) ?

Disobedient Servant of Allah

139. Is not it a fact that any sexual activity during daytime is forbidden by Allah (2 : 187) as well as during the fasting days ? How did Muhammad disobey Allah by sleeping with Umm Salama during her period, kissed her while fasting ? Did he not use to take bath from the same pot often having sex under a woolen sheet (*Buk* 1 : 319) and used to kiss and embrace (his wives) while he was fasting (*Buk* 3 : 149) and used to kiss and suck Ayesha's tongue while they were fasting (*Daw* 13 : 2380) ?

Ayesha Scandal

140. Is not it a fact that after defeating Banu Mustaliq, as Muhammad resumed the return journey, Ayesha, his youngest wife, lost the way while searching for her necklace ? A young soldier, Safwan b. Mu'Attal Sulami Zakwani, recognised her and gave her a lift back home. Though it was an innocent journey, the Prophet's enemies created a nasty scandal out of it subjecting him and Ayesha to a great deal of distress.

Though Ayesha was faultless, Allah found it necessary to devise an impossible law of evidence to protect the Prophet, and punish accusers. Does this incident, which is purely personal to Muhammad, not become the law for the whole Muslim world that one should produce four eye-witnesses to prove his innocence or he is liable to receive eighty lashes (24 : 1-4) ?

Forbidden means Forgiven

141. Is not it a fact that Muhammad used to divide time equally among his wives, spending night with each of them in turn in order to prevent jealousy ? Unfortunately the day when it was his wife Hafsah's turn, she had been to her father. Unexpectedly on her return she was surprised to see Muhammad in her bed with Mary the Coptic, his legal concubine, a present from the ruler of Egypt Al-Moqawqus. She was furious and she threatened to expose him to others in the harem. Muhammad had to please her by saying "Keep my secret, I will consider

41

Mary the Coptic unlawful to me." But Hafsa told Ayesha which prompted Muhammad to divorce Hafsa. He retired with Mary and stayed aloof from his wives for a month and returned again to Harem. How again did he bring back Hafsa and make Mary lawful thus breaking his oath ? Of course Allah sanctioned this through a revelation : "O Prophet ! Why holdest thou to be forbidden that which Allah has made lawful to you" (66 : 1)   ? (Al-Sira al- Halabiyya; vol. III; section on Muhammad's Wives and Concubines; CQV, 1994 : 260).

Killing the Husband and Marrying the Widow : No Crime

142. When Muhammad claimed one-fifth share of the booty in Allah's name or the best woman captured in a raid, he felt a strong sense of entitlement of having special privileges from his followers. He did not feel the need to follow any code of ethics because he was specially entitled to defy Allah's rules. His behaviour even stunned his followers. He justified all his actions by bringing Allah's revelations whenever he liked. Also, those who doubted Allah and his messenger were punished to death.

Narcissistic entitlement can be appropriately presented by two simple words, "I deserve". Is it not a fact that when Muhammad took Safiyyah to bed for sex on the very same night he had killed her husband and many male relatives after attacking Khaybar, and, when he took Rayhana to bed on the same night he had killed her male relatives of Quraiza tribe Muhammad justified his action by uttering the above two pet words of a Narcissist, "I deserve".

Following Hadith gives us a clue about Muhammad's one track thinking mind : "Narrated Abu Usaid : ...The Jauniyya (a lady from Bani Jaun) had been brought and lodged in a house in a date-palm garden ... When the Prophet entered upon her, he said to her, "Give me yourself (in sex) as a gift, "Can a princess give herself in marriage to an ordinary man ?" The Prophet raised his hand to slap her so that she might become tranquil. She said, "I seek refuge with Allah from you" (*Buk* 7: 182).

The Prophet died on Ayesha's Arms

143. Is not it a fact that the last days of the Prophet were miserable ? In the words of Ayesha the youngest wife of Muhammad :

The apostle came back to me from the mosque that day and lay in my bosom. A man of Abu Bakr's family came into me with a toothpick in his hand and the apostle looked at it in such a way that I knew he wanted it, and when I asked him if he wanted me to give it to him he said Yes; so I took it and chewed it for him to soften it and gave it to him. He rubbed his teeth with it more energetically than I had ever seen him rub before; then he laid it down. I found him heavy in my bosom and as I looked into his face, to his eyes were fixed and he was saying, "Nay, the most Exalted Companion is of paradise." I said, "You were given the choice and you have chosen, by Him Who sent you with the truth !" And so the apostle was taken. Ayesha said : The apostle died in my bosom during my turn : I had wronged none in regard to him. It was due to my ignorance and extreme youth that the apostle died in my arms. Then I laid his head on a pillow and got up beating my breast and slapping my face along with the other women (*Ish* 1955 : 682).

Ayesha became Widow at the Age of 18

144. Is it not a fact that Muhammad deprived his wives of remarrying after his death ? Did Ayesha not become a widow at the young age of 18 and remained a widow all through her life ?

42

How were the Wives of the Prophet Different from Others ?

145. In what respect were the wives of the Prophet different from other women for which Allah dictated in the Quran : "O wives of the Prophet, you are not the same as other women, if you keep your duty, you shall not speak too softly, lest he in whose heart is a disease aspire to you, but utter customary speech" (33 : 32) and "You shall settle down in your homes and not mingle with the people excessively, the way you used to do in the old days of ignorance. You shall observe prayers, and give the obligatory charity, and obey Allah and his messenger. Allah wishes to remove unholiness from you" (33 : 33) ?

Why the Prophet's Wives cannot Remarry ?

146. Is not it a fact that when Al-Suyuti said in *Asbab al-Nuzul :* "Talha came to one of the Prophet's wives and talked with her; he was her cousin. But Muhammad said to him : 'You will never do this again.' Talha said : 'But she is my cousin, and Allah knows that neither I nor she said anything abominable.' But Muhammad said : 'There is none more jealous than Allah, and there is none more jealous than me.' He left, and after that he said : 'On death of Muhammad I will surely marry Ayesha after him.' When Muhammad heard about it, he said : ...neither marry his wives after him."

Immediately the verse descended : "...It is not right for you, you should annoy Allah's messenger or that you should marry his widows after him at any time. Truly such a thing in Allah's sight is an enormity (33 : 53).

Does it not reflect that there was no objection for Muhammad to marry widows but he disallowed his wives to marry after his death ? Truly was he not a jealous husband ?

Is Father marrying his Daughter not Sinful ?

147. The widows of Muhammad were prevented from remarriage on the ground that as wives of Muhammad they were mothers of the faithful and as such marrying their sons was unpardonable sin. If his wives were mothers he was supposed to be father to the faithful. Does it not mean that being father Muhammad married his daughters ?

Why Ayesha was Against Ali ?

148. Is not it a fact that when Ayesha married Muhammad she was six and Muhammad was above 50 ? When Ayesha came of age Muhammad was in his late fifties or early sixties and probably impotent. In this case Ayesha was bound to be frustrated and this frustration turned to jealousy against Fatima and her children. Did not Ayesha stand in the way of Fatima's husband Ali in becoming the Caliph. Did she not revolt against him though she was defeated in the Battle of the Camel ? Was she not very angry and her hatred for Muhammad can be seen when she said before her death to be buried outside the building where Muhammad was buried, and not with him (*Sabab* 2004 : 214-215) ?

9- The Forbidden Questions

In the Pre-Islamic Arabia loot and raid were never common as it were considered hateful and shameful. The Arabic word for raid is "ghazzua" which means killing or enslaving the kafirs. If somebody kills many kafirs, in Islam, he is respected as "ghazi".

The loot from the kafir is legal for a Muslim. The distribution of the loot or booty, which includes the men, women and children, is done according to well-defined regulations described in the Quran and the Hadith. The first fifth of the loot goes to the Prophet or the Caliph and in their absence to the *mullah* who is in charge. The balance four- fifths are shared by the rest of the fighters who took part in the raid.

However, the Prophet had explained to his followers that since he was the Last Prophet for all times to come, such raids had now been sanctioned by Allah. Thus the property taken from the kafirs now was quite in order.

History shows that Muhammad murdered numerous people whose only crime was writing poems against him. Asma was murdered in her house for writing a poem against Muhammad, Kaab was murdered for writing poems against Islam, Muhammad gave orders to kill al- Hawayrith for insulting him, killed a woman named Sara who had once insulted him, and killed Abdullah's two singing girls for singing songs about Muhammad.

Sujit Das remarks that Muhammad created such an atmosphere of terror that no one could disagree with him. He was a man of the extremes and only of the extremes. It is recorded in Sunaan *Abu-Dawud* (38. 4348) that once a blind Muslim murdered his slave woman by pressing a dagger in her belly that killed her on the spot. In the morning, Muhammad called the man to explain why he committed such horrendous murder. The man stood up while trembling and said that the woman used to abuse and ridicule Muhammad and hence she was killed. Hearing this Muhammad said, "Oh be witness, no retaliation is payable for her blood." The message that Muhammad wanted to send was clear---If anyone insults me, he should be put to death and the killer will not be charged (Das 2010 : 117). Few more examples can be cited as evidence.

Does not the Prophet use Quran as Weapon ?
149. When did the revelations descend-- at the will of the prophet or at any time he wanted to curse his opponents (3 : 12) ? And is that why when one of his companions Abu Ruhm al-Ghifari accidentally hurt Muhammad's foot, he was terrified lest, the Prophet gets angry and curse him eternally through a Quranic revelation ?

Was Muhammad a Poor Man ?
150. Can you prove that Muhammad was a poor man with simple life ? Did he not gather a vast wealth during his Prophetic career and died as one of the richest men of Arabia ? Did he not admit :

'I have been made victorious with terror. The treasures of the world were brought to me and put in my hand" (*Buk* 4 : 220) ?

"The Prophet said, 'If you live long enough the treasures of Khosrau will be opened and taken as spoils. You will carry out handfuls of gold and silver" (*Buk* 4 : 793). Again "I have been given the keys of the treasures of the world by Allah" (*Buk* 4 : 795).

Was the Prophet Stone Hearted ?
151. Is it not a fact that the Prophet married one of his daughters to Abu Bakr. After she died while being punished for disobedience the Prophet married another daughter to the same man (*Darabi* 2007 : 48) ?

Trees also have Enemies
152. When Muhammad laid siege of the Jews of Banu al-Nadir in the vicinity of Yathrib, he had their palm trees cut down and burnt. When Muhammad was asked he legitimized his act by saying Allah sent him the message that the destruction of the enemies' tree during wartime is legitimate (59 : 5).

Three Signs of Hypocrisy
153. Is not it a fact that once the Prophet said, "The signs of a hypocrite are three : 1. Whenever he speaks, he tells a lie. 2. Whenever he promises, he always breaks it (his promise). 3. If you trust him, he proves to be dishonest" (*Buk* 1 : 32) ?

But whenever Muhammad disliked anyone, he often used to call them 'Hypocrite' means the worst form of unbelief, and it carries a terrible punishment under the Islamic law. Can we establish the fact that the Prophet was free from hypocrisy ?

Telling a lie to kill the enemies for the cause of Islam is divinely allowed in Islam as 'Taqiyya' or holy deception. Under Taqiyya, a Muslim is allowed to lie and say anything to deceive the non-Muslims.

In what way is Muhammad truthful in prescribing Taqiyya in Islam ?

Promises are made to Break
154. Did Muhammad ever keep his promise ? Did he not tell : "Allah willing, if ever I take an oath to do something, and later on I find that it is more beneficial to do something different, I will do the thing which is better, and give expiation for my oath" (*Buk* 4 : 361) ?

Did not Muhammad sign an agreement with the Meccans called "the treaty of Hudaybiya which demanded a cessation of hostility from both sides for a period of ten years . Did he not breach the treaty within just two and in January 630, he marched towards Mecca with an army of ten thousand fighting men ? The Quresh trusted Muhammad but Muhammad proved untrustworthy.

Forbidden Months are not Forbidden
155. Is not it a fact that in the pre-Islamic traditions fighting was prohibited during the holy months ? A proclamation from Allah and his messenger to the Muslims was : "When the forbidden months are past, then fight and slay the pagans wherever you find them" (9 : 5). But Muhammad broke this age-old agreement of the Arabs not to fight during the sacred months. In order to take revenge on his enemies he treacherously got the sanction from Allah to fight during the prohibiting months and considered it as the "Path of Allah" (2 : 217).

45

Then, after all this, the Quran defends the holy months and confuses the lunar and the solar year, claiming that the solar year is *Kufr* or "unbelief". But if the sacred months were of God, why then are they not observed throughout the whole Islamic world at present (*Al-Fadi*, 1997 : 219) ?

Making the Holy Month Unholy

156. How Muhammad misused the holy months in the name of Allah in order to take revenge on his enemies treacherously can be seen from the following incident. A month before the Battle of Badr Muhammad sent his cousin 'Abdallah Ibn Jahsh in the Jamuda al-Akhira giving him a letter asking him not to read the letter before having walked for two days. So 'Abdallah walked two days. Then he opened the letter and read it which said : "Go in the name of God, the Merciful, the Compassionate. With His blessings friends go till you reach Batn Nakhla where you will find camels that belong to the Quresh; and bring us some goods from them." 'Abdallah Ibn Jahsh and his eight men reached Bafn Nakhla which is between Mecca and al-Taif. After reaching there, they saw Amr Ibn al- Khudari, al-Hakim Ibn Kaysan, 'Uthman Ibn Abdallah Ibn al-Mughira and Hiraql Ibn Abdallah who were in charge of the camels. When they saw Muhammad's men, they were frightened. So Ibn Jahsh told one of his men to shave his head and go so that the people would think that these are native people and will do us no harm.

It was the last day of the second Jumada, and they thought it was in Rajab. They counselled among each other and thought that if they leave them tonight, they will enter into the holy place and will be safe. So they decided to fight the people. The Quresh and the inhabitants of Mecca ridiculed and criticized Muhammad for profaning the holy month, shedding blood and taking away their possessions. So Muhammad applied a Quranic verse and declared as what his men did as legal and divided the booty among themselves (*Abd Al-Fadi*, 1997 :354-355).

Are the idolaters not better than Muhammad to keep the holy months holy by not killing ? If the Quran prohibited fighting during the four sacred months that means killing the pagans in the other eight months was legal. Why then all Good Gods prohibit fighting and establish peace all through the year ?

Is Robbing Religious ?

157. Is not it a fact that Muhammad first started out saying that his followers could defend themselves if attacked, then he commanded them to go to war on his behalf, to gain wealth by robbing caravans. But as his army grew, his thirst for plunder also grew. So did he not order more and more wars to persecute other religions in order to gain more wealth ?

Badr's Booty : Source of Livelihood

158. Is not the battle of Badr one of the decisive battles of history where the booty distribution at the end of the battle encouraged the Muslims to earn their livelihood through wars ? In Muri's words :

In accordance with these commands, the booty was gathered together on the field, and placed under a special officer. The next day it was divided, near Safra, in equal allotments, among the whole army, after the royal fifth had been set apart. All shared alike, excepting that the horsemen received each two extra portions for their horses. To the lot of every man fell a camel, with its gear; or two unaccounted camels; or a leather couch, or some such equivalent. Muhammad obtained the famous camel of Abu Jahl, and a sword known by the name of Dzul Ficar. The

46

sword was selected by him beyond his share, according to a custom which allowed him, in virtue of the prophetic dignity, to choose from the booty, before division, whatever thing pleased him most (cf Sahih of Muslim, ed. Constantinople, 1329, Part IV, p. 146; Muir, *Life of Mahomet*, p. 113; Qtd. Zwemer 1939 : 27).

Booty in Allah's Name

159. Is not it a fact that Muhammad convinced the believers that use of booty from the spoils of war are lawful and good and he used to collect one fifth of the booty in Allah's name (*Buk* 1: 50) ?

The "greatest moral example in history" says Ibn Ishaq is that Prophet Muhammad chose robbery as his chief source of income. Indeed Muhammad deliberately used the spoils of war to lure people to Islam (1980 : 596).

Killing for Gold

160. Is not it a fact that Muhammad had killed people for the most trivial reasons ? When Kinana Ibn Ali al Huquiq, who was the leader of a Jewish tribe and whose fort was captured by the Muslims, tried to conceal the fact that he had gold Muhammad tortured him by having hot coals put on his chest till he was nearly dead, and then he was killed (*Maine* 1979 : 15-16).

A Prophet of War and Raids

161. Is not it a fact that Prophet Muhammad participated in 29 raids ? And was responsible for 47 raids and proxy wars where he sent his followers. It increased from 70 to hundred raids and proxy war which means an average of one raid per month. (*Abd Al-Fadi* 1997 : 394).

Because Allah said : O Prophet ! rouse the Believers to the fight. If there are twenty amongst you, patient and persevering, they will vanquish two hundred, if a hundred, they will vanquish a thousand of the unbelievers; for these are a people without understanding (8 : 65).

For every raid or war he got the inspiration from the above verse for which Muhammad never thought himself responsible.

Raids brought wealth, captive women, children, camels and other goods for the prophet and the followers. The men who want to live are bound to accept Islam or to suffer enslavement, exile or death (Walker, 1999 : 319-320).

If the last prophet of Allah who brought the last message to the world stoops down from the normal human standards of morality, then how does the morality of this self-asserted "Prophethood" rate ?

The Raid by Proxy on Ibn al-Khadhrami

162. In Sura al-Baqara 2 : 217 we read : "They will question thee concerning the holy month, and fighting in it." Is it not a fact that Muhammad made it lawful to raid in the holy months ?

Once Muhammad had sent out 'Abdallah Ibn Jahsh at the head of a raiding party consisting of 80 men. When they arrived at a place called Batn Nakhla they ambushed a caravan of the Quresh. 'Amr Ibn al-Khadhrami was in the caravan, and he was killed as the first of the unbelievers. Al- Hakim Ibn Kaysan and 'Uthman were taken captive as the first prisoners of war of Islam. The Muslims drove the caravan and the prisoners back to Muhammad, who grew angry because his friends

47

had raided and taken booty during the holy month. Afterwards, he made it lawful and allotted fixed portions of the booty to himself and his friends (*Abd Al-Fadi* 1997 : 394-395) .

Because Allah sent a message to his messenger : They ask thee concerning fighting in the Prohibited month. Say : Fighting therein is a grave (offence); but graver is it in the sight of Allah to prevent access to the path of Allah (2 : 217).

The Raid of Uhud

163. Once when Muhammad, with his 700 men was fighting the Arabs at Uhud, at first the Arabs ran away but later they turned around, fought back and won. They had already broken Muhammad's nose and his four front teeth and gashed his face. Muhammad was tired, defeated and friendless because his men had left him and were scattered while the Arabs were still after him. So he went to a rock and lifted it but could not. So he sat under an acacia tree. In the mean time one of the Arabs attacked Muhammad and tried to kill him. His standard-bearer defended Muhammad but instead was killed. The Arab thought that Muhammad was killed, so he rejoiced and declared that he has killed Muhammad after which the Arabian army withdrew. Later Muhammad started calling out his men, "Come and help me, God's servants", on which thirty men came and took him with great difficulty. On seeing how his men fled leaving him in distress, Muhammad started cursing them but on the other hand he also encouraged those who laid their lives for him by saying. "And that God may know who are the believers, and that He may take witnesses from among you" (3 : 140).

When the women who had waited long for him, his men said, "He is alive", upon which one of the women said, "I do not care; God has taken witnesses from among his servants."

Did Muhammad not quote this sentence as inspiration only because it was a huge consolation over their disastrous defeat at Uhud (*Abd Al-Fadi* 1997 : 395-396) ?

The Lesser Raid of Badr

164. Is it not a fact that in the raid of Badr the Muslims killed seventy men and captured seventy others ? Badr was a watering place between Mecca and Medina and belonged to a man called Badr.

There after Allah told to Muhammad : "And God most surely helped you at Badr, when you were utterly abject" (3 : 123).

The Raid of Hunain

165. Is it not a fact that inspite of having a huge army of twelve thousand men, the prophet had almost lost the battle of Hunain because most of his men fled in the middle of the battle leaving him alone ?

Muhammad had twelve thousand men with him during the raid of Hunain, a valley between Mecca and al-Ta'if. He already had ten thousand men and the other two thousand were war prisoners of the Mecca conquest who were later released and added up to the Muslim army. Seeing their vast number, Muhammad was confident of their significant win over this battle of Hunain. But after a fierce battle, the Muslims ran away leaving the Prophet alone with his uncle al-'Abbas and his cousin Abu Sufyan. When the servants of God called him, "O ye of the tree, O ye of the cow", they came and said, "At thy service," and fought for the Prophet and finally won over. The Prophet captured six thousand men and took huge number of camels and small cattles as war booty.

Allah reminded Muhammad : "God had already helped you on many fields, and on the day of Hunain" (9 : 25).

Poet Against a Poet

166. Is not it a fact that though Prophet Muhammad who like his grandfather Abd al-Muttalib and uncle Abu Talib was a reputed poet, yet he could not tolerate any other poets and said : "Those who go astray follow the poets" (26.224) ? Does he not say : "It is better for a man to fill the inside of his body with pus than to fill it with poetry" (*Buk* 8 :175) ?

Destruction of Pre-Islamic Poetry

167. Is not it a fact that the original works of pre-Islamic poets had not survived much after the advent of Islam ? Within hundred years of Muhammad's taking over Mecca, the Arab genius of poetry was totally erased (Warraq, 2000 : 151). The Egyptian scholar Taha Husayn, lamented that little of any genuine pre-Islamic literature had survived (Krizeck, 1964 : 60).

The Murder of Asma Bint Marwan

168. Why did Muhammad send Omayr the Blind to kill Asma Bint Marwan ? Her only mistake was that she wrote some satirical verses making fun of Muhammad and the citizens of Medina for being, "Like gluttonous people looking towards the cooking-pot"- that is, towards the advancement of Islam (Walker 1999 : 317).

Omayr went to her house at night when her children were sleeping and she was nursing her baby. He stabbed her in the chest and then went to the mosque to pray. Ibn Ishaq recorded the incident as follows :

"You obey a stranger who encourages you to murder for booty. You are greedy men. Is there no honor among you ?' Upon hearing this Muhammad said, 'Will no one rid me of this woman ?' Umayr decided to execute the Prophet's wishes. That very night he crept into her home while she lay sleeping surrounded by her young children. There was one at her breast. Umayr removed the sucking baby and then plunged his sword into the poet. The next morning in the mosque, Muhammad, who was aware of the assassination, said, 'You have helped Allah and His Apostle.' Umayr said, "She had five sons; should I feel guilty ?' 'No,' the Prophet answered. 'Killing her was as meaningless as two goats butting heads" (*Ish* : 676).

He told Muhammad what had happened, and Muhammad said, "Let no two goats but heads with one another for er sake !" He praised Omayr and said, "If someone desires to look at a man who helped God and His Messenger, let him look at Omayr. He gave him the title of "Omayr the Seeing" and told him : "You have done a service to Allah and his Messenger" (Abd Al- Fadi 1997 : 356-357; Rodinson, 1976 : 171; Walker 1999 : 317; Main 1985 : 8).

Now the question arises why wouldn't Muhammad murder her himself ? Why is it that every time Muhammad wanted someone to be killed, he always got someone else to do his killing ?

The Murder of Abu Affq the Jew

169. Why did Muhammad send Salim Ibn Umair to kill a 120 year old Jew ? Is it because he used to ridicule Muhammad in his verses and told the people of Medina to doubt Muhammad for his strange and dictatorial behaviour ? When Muhammad heard of this he felt it not as a threat to his life but a threat to his career as a prophet. He employed Salim Ibn Umayr to kill him. Salim knew that Affq is going to sleep in the courtyard of his house on the hot night. He went near him and drove his sword into his liver and killed him. Does this not force Ali Dashti to comment : "Thus Islam was gradually transformed from a purely spiritual mission into a militant and punitive organisation whose progress depended on booty from raids and revenue from the zakat tax" (1885 : 97).

In the same year, i.e., in June 624 after Muhammad had gained power in Medina, a man and his wife were murdered, again at Muhammad's instruction because they had written insulting verses about him and the new religion he was preaching (Frieling, 1978 : 33; Walker 1999 : 317).

Why was Abu Azza Killed ?

170. Is not it a fact that Abu Azza, a critic of Muhammad was beheaded because he used to write poetry urging the desert tribes not to join Muhammad's gang (Walker 1999 : 318)?

The Murder of Kaab Ibn al- Ashraf

171. Why did Muhammad employ his foster brother Abu Naila and four others to kill Kaab Ibn al-Ashraf ? His only mistake was that he had composed a lament on the Korayshis slain at Badr. In July 624 Kaab was with his newly married bride when Naila with his company went to him and called him with friendly words. He recognised the voice and came out confidently. One of the companions of Naila, Muslama said to Naila, as Kaab comes down, I will extend my hands towards his head and tell you to do your job. When he came down they said to him : "We sense from you a very fine smell. He said : Yes, I have with me a mistress who is the most scented of the women of Arabia. He said : Allow me to smell (the scent on your head). He said : "Yes, you may smell." So he caught it and smelt. Then he said : Allow me to do so (once again). He then held his head fast and said to his companions : Do your job (*Mus* 3 : 4436, 687) and they cut off his head and brought before the prophet while the prophet was praying and he asked : "How successful was the mission ?" They answered : "What you wanted was accomplished, O Messenger of God, "and threw Kaab's head in front of him (Abd Al- Fadi 1997: 557-558).

The same story is repeated by Bukhari in a different way : "Narrated Jabir bin Abdullah : The Prophet said, "Who is ready to kill Ka'b bin Al-Ashraf who had really hurt Allah and His Apostle ?" Muhammad bin Maslama said, "O Allah's Apostle ! Do you like me to kill him ?" He replied in the affirmative. So, Muhammad bin Maslama went to him (i.e. Ka'b) and said, "This person (i.e. the Prophet) has put us to task and asked us for charity." Ka'b replied, "By Allah, you will get tired of him." Muhammad said to him, "We have followed him, so we dislike leaving him till we see the end of his affair." Muhammad bin Maslama went on talking to him in this way till he got the chance to kill him" (*Buk* 4 : 270).

If a Prophet could murder people who disagree or criticise him what can we expect from the founder of a religion ?

The Murder of Abu Rafi 'Ibn' Abdallah

172. Why did Muhammad send Abdallah Ibn Atik with four persons to kill Abu Rafi-i, the merchant of Hijaz, and a pagan ? They secretly entered his fort in the night and called his name Abu Rafi-i. When he replied, Abdallah Ibn Atik proceeded towards the voice and killed him with his sword. Is this the way to eliminate the enemies of a prophet (*Buk* 4 : 264; 5 : 371) ?

Is not this incident repeated time and again by Tabari and Bukhari to ascertain in an Islamic way that it is not that Rafi was killed but Allah killed him ?

Here is the citation :

"In this year, it is said, the killing of Abu Rafi the Jew took place. The reason for his being killed was, it is said, that he used to take the side of Ka'b bin Ashraf against Muhammad" (*Tab* : VII.99).

"Narrated Al-Bara bin Azib : Allah's Apostle sent a group of persons to Abu Rafi. Abdullah bin Atik entered his house at night, while he was sleeping, and killed him" (*Buk* 5 : 370).

"I (the murderer of Abu Rafi) came to my companions and said, 'By Allah, I will not leave till I hear the wailing of their women.' So, I did not move till I heard them crying for the Jewish merchant. I said, 'Deliverance ! Allah has killed Abu Rafi" (*Tab* VII: 100).

Strange ! Did not the Muslims make their Allah a murderer !

The Murder of Salam Ibn Abi al-Haqiq

173. Is it not a fact that to please the Prophet, his disciples competed with each other to kill his enemies and be in his good books ? When the Al-Aws tribe killed Ka'b Ibn Abi al-Ashraf, Al-Khazraj tribe did not want to be left behind. Since Muhammad had ordered to kill Ibn Abi al-Haqiq, they asked the Prophet for five men from Banu Salma to help them kill al-Haqiq. The Prophet asked 'Abdallah Ibn 'Atik, Mas'ud Ibn Sinan, 'Abdallah Ibn Anis, Abu Qatada, Ibn Rab'i and Khuza'a Ibn Aswad to accomplish the mission and made 'Abdallah Ibn' Atik their leader but prohibited them to kill a child or a woman. When these men reached Khaybar at night they went to the house of Ibn al-Haqiq and closed all doors of his house. He was in his upper room. So they went there and called him. His wife asked them who they were and they told her that they were nomads looking for a place to stay. So she asked them to come in.

The moment they entered inside the room, they closed the door on her. And before Abi al-Haqiq could do something they stabbed him. His presence in the darkness could be indicated with his white body which looked like cotton lying on the bed. 'Abdallah Ibn Anis moved in closer and stabbed him once again with his own sword in the belly. When his wife shouted all of them pointed their sword to her but did not strike her. They would have struck her had the Prophet not forbidden them. After completing their work they left. While leaving, 'Abdallah Ibn' Atik, who had poor vision, fell off the ladder and possibly sprained his foot or hand. So his friends carried him and came back to Muhammad. They gave him the good news but each of them claimed to have killed Salam Ibn Abi Haqiq. So the Prophet examined their swords and concluded that Abdallah Ibn Anis had killed him because he could find traces of food on his sword (*Tab* : VII. 101; *Ish* 482; Abd Al-Fadi, 1997 : 358-360).

The Murder of Umm Qirfa

174. How could the Messenger of God be so sadist and cruel as to congratulate a man for his bestial cruelty ? Is it not a fact that Muhammad congratulated Zaid for having killed Umm Qirfa, and whose method of killing was beyond the limits of inhumanity ? Shortly before the murder of Ibn Abi-al-Haqiq, Umm Qirfa was killed by tying her two legs to two camels who were forced to walk in opposite directions until her body was ripped apart (Abd Al-Fadi : 1997 : 360).

The Murder of Ibn Sunayna

175. Is it not a fact that Muhammad once said, "Kill any Jewish you meet" ? Upon this Mahisa Ibn Masud killed Ibn Sunayana, a Jewish cloth merchant. But Huwaisila, another non-Muslim was annoyed by this incident and reprimanded Mahisa. Mahisa instead said : "The one who commanded me to kill, if he commands me to kill you then I will not hesitate to strike your neck off." Huwaisila was so scared hearing this that he thought it wiser to embrace Islam than to be killed.

Cruelty to kill Beni Quraizah Tribe

176. Is it not the height of cruelty to kill the entire male population of the Beni Quraizah, a Jewish tribe, on a single day and their women and children sold to slavery (33 : 26) ? It happened when the Prophet decided to massacre the entire clan and for that a ditch, big enough for burying 800 Jews, was dug the previous night in the market-place of Medina. The holy prophet commanded to bring forth the male captives in batches of five or six at a time. He ordered them to lie down, with the face down in a row on the brink of the ditch. Those who were busy chopping their heads off and kicking the corpses into the ditch were Prophet's uncle Jubair, Hamja, Talha and cousin Ali.

The noted historian W. Muir recorded : "The booty was divided into four classes---lands, chattels, cattle and slaves and Muhammad took a fifth of each. There were a thousand captives; from his share of these, Muhammad made certain presents to his friends of slave girls and female servants. The rest of the women and children he sent to be sold among the Bedawi tribes of Nejd, in exchange for horses and arms in the service of the state... The remaining property was divided amongst the 3,000 soldiers of Medina, to the highest bidder among whom the women were also sold" (1992 : Qtd. Brahmachari 2007 : 20-21).

Is not it a fact that Muhammad returned from the horried spectacle to solace himself with the charms of Reihana whose husband and all her male relatives had just perished in the massacre and in such a tragic event she refused Muhammad to be his wife rather preferred to remain as a slave or a concubine ?

What was the mistake of the Jewish tribe of Banu Quraiza ? Only that they were Jews and people of capacities.

Muhammad kills us for his Sport

177. Is it not a fact that while Muhammad told others not to kill people when in Mecca and, not to kill people at the Kaaba, when Muhammad heard that Ibn Khatal was taking refuge in the Kaaba, he said, "Kill him." He was dragged out and killed (*Buk* 3 : 72). Robert Payne rightly remarked : It is worthwhile to pause for a moment before the quite astonishing polarity of Muhammad's mind. Violence and gentleness were at war within him. Sometimes he gives the appearance of living simultaneously in two worlds, at one and the same moment seeing the world about to be destroyed by the flames of God and in a state of divine peace; and he seems to hold these opposing visions only at the cost of an overwhelming sense of strain. Sometimes the string snaps, and we see him gazing with a look of bafflement at the world around him, which is neither the world in flames nor the world in a state of blessedness, but the ordinary day-to-day world in which he was rarely at home (1962 : 84).

Can Islam tolerate Mockery

178. Is not it a fact that both Allah and Muhammad refused to answer questions and could never tolerate criticism ? It may be the reason that there is no convincing argument to defend their Faith. In the Quran Allah frankly confessed that mockery and criticism has no place in their religion : "When you hear His verses being disbelieved or mocked, do not sit with them until they engage in other talk, or else you will surely be like them. Allah will surely gather the hypocrites and unbelievers altogether in Hell" (4 : 140).

Why did Muhammad massacre the Jews of Nadir ?

179. When the Muslim army was defeated at the Battle of Uhud in 625 Muhammad desperately needed a victory and decided to attack the Jewish tribe of Nadir. The revelation helped him to spread a rumour saying that the Nadir were planning to kill him. But Nadir were a peace loving people and they surrendered on the condition that they be allowed to leave with their goods except their arms and to join their Jewish people at Khaybar (Warraq 1993 : 50). Among them there was a man called Nadir Ibn Haritha who was a story teller. His only mistake was that when Allah challenged to the unbelievers to produce *Suras* like those found in the Quran Nadir Ibn Haritha accepted the challenge, and wrote stories of the Persian kings and recited them like *Suras* (Sell 1928 : 208). Not only this he once told to the audience of Muhammad : "Are not my stories as good as Muhammad (Main 1985 : 15) ? When Muhammad heard this in 628 he attacked the Khaybar and massacred the Jews of Nadir. Did he not drive out all the Jews and Christians from the Arabian Peninsula with the words : "There was no room for two religions in Arabia" (Warraq 1993 : 150) ?

Muhammad also mercilessly burnt and cut down the date-palm trees of Bani Al-Nadir because Allah revealed to him : "What you cut down of the date-palm trees of the enemy, or you left them standing on their stems. It was by Allah's permission" (59 : 5; *Buk* 5 : 365).

Scribe who contributed for Quran

180. Can you think of an author who made the words of his scribe his own ? People should not know that the scribe is the real author of some portions of the Quran. For that Muhammad assured the scribe that he would not be killed but instigated other people to kill him.

'Abdallah Ibn Sa'd Ibn Abi Sarh, was the scribe of the Prophet. In the verse (Sura al-Mu' minun 23 : 12) that says, "We created man of an extraction of clay" when Muhammad reached the part that says, "...thereafter we produced him as another creature" (23 : 14), 'Abdallah suggested to add, "So blessed be God the fairest of creators !" in amazement at the details of man's creation. The Prophet immediately said, "Write it down; for thus it has been revealed." 'Abdallah doubted and said, "If Muhammad is truthful then I receive the revelation as much as he does, and if he is a liar, what I said was as good as what he said."

In *Al-Sira*, by al-' Iraqi, we read : There were 42 scribes of Muhammad; 'Abdallah Ibn Sarh al-'Amiri being one of them, and he was the first Qureishite among those who wrote in Mecca before he turned away from Islam. He started saying, "I used to direct Muhammad wherever I willed. He would dictate to me

'Most High, All-wise', and I would write down 'All-wise' only. Then he would say, 'Yes, it is all the same.' On a certain occasion he said, 'Write such-and-such,' but I wrote 'Write' only, and he said, 'Write whatever you like." So when this scribe exposed Muhammad, he wrote in the Qur'an, "And who does greater evil than he who forges against God a lie, or says, 'To me it has been revealed", when naught has been revealed to him" (6 : 93). So when Muhammad conquered Mecca, he commanded his scribe to be killed. But the scribe fled to 'Uthman Ibn 'Affan, because 'Uthman was his foster brother (his mother suckled 'Uthman). 'Uthman, therefore, kept him away from Muhammad. After the people calmed down, 'Uthman brought the scribe to Muhammad and sought protection for him. Muhammad kept silent for a long time, after which he said yes. When 'Uthman had left, Muhammad said, "I only kept silent so that you (the people) should kill him" (Abd Al-Fadi. 1997 : 366-367).

Eye for an Eye : Revenge for Hamza

181. Is it not a fact that when his uncle Hamza was killed in the Battle of Uhud, Muhammad was so angry that he swore to take revenge on the Qureish and killed seventy people in place of his uncle (Abd Al-Fadi 1997 : 361) ?

Khalid : the Sword of God

182. If Muhammad was a peace loving prophet why did he give the title "The Sword Of God" to Khalid who won his victory over the recalcitrant tribe of Bani Jazma, dwelt a day's march south of Mecca, and butchered most of his prisoners (Muir 1992 : 135, 193) ?

No Victory of Sword

183. How can Islam be called the religion of peace when it was spreaded by the sword ? Is not it a fact that the Prophet first used the sword to shed the blood of unbelievers in the battlefield of Badr for his mission (Zwemer 1939 : 25) ?

Can we ignore the famous verses attributed to Ali Ibn Abi Talib which are quoted everywhere in Arabia :

> *As-Saif wa'l Khanjar rihanuna,*
> *'Uffun ala'l narjis wa'l as*
> *Sharabuna dam a 'adauna,*
> *Wa jumjumat ras al kas.*

> **Our flowers are the sword and dagger,**
> **Narcissus and myrtle are nought;**
> **Our drink is the blood of our foemen,**
> **Our goblet his skull when we've fought.**

(*Arabian Peak and Desert*, p. 109 Qtd. Zwemer 1939 : 26; Al-Fadi 1997 : 361).

In the concluding chapter of Sir William Muir's *Life of Mahomet* he speaks of "The sword as the inevitable penalty for the denial of Islam" and continues : "The sword of Mahomet and the Coran are the most fatal enemies of civilization, liberty, and truth, which the world has yet known" (1992 : p. 322; Qtd. Zwemer 1939 : 25).

54

The Challenge accepted and Surpassed

184. Is it not a fact that in response to Muhammad's challenge to produce even one sura (10 : 39) like those in the Quran, many poets composed which equalled and even surpassed the suras in both style and content and when one of the poets was told that his verse failed to evoke the same ecstatic rapture as that of Quran, he replied, "Let mine be recited in the mosques for a hundred years, and then see" (Rodinson, 1976 : 92).

Had Hamzah ben-Ahed not written a book against the Quran with at least equal elegance, and Muslema another, which surpassed it (McClintock 1981 : 126) ?

Unpleasant Personality of Prophet Muhammad

185. Did Muhammad have a sense of humour and tolerate any one who joked about him or his prayer ?

Once one elderly man watched Muhammad and his disciples bowing and touching their foreheads to the dirt while reciting Surat-an-Najm at Mecca.

When the old man saw their foreheads becoming dirty, as a joke, he picked up some dirt and put it to his own forehead and said, "This is sufficient for me."

The old man was saying that if the important thing was to get dirt on your forehead when you pray, then it would be a lot easier to pick up some dirt and smear it on your forehead. Ha ! Ha !

Obviously, the old man's joke was directed against the Muslim pride over their dirty foreheads.

But Muhammad was not amused by the old man or his joke. The Muslims murdered the old man as a non-believer (*Buk* 2 : 173).

Did not Muhammad give orders to kill al-Hawayrith, a woman named Sara who had once insulted him and Abdullah's two singing girls for singing songs about Muhammad (Ibn Ishaq, p. 550-551) ?

Writing as Crime : Death as Penalty

186. When the Prophet challenged to produce ten suras (11 : 13) or even one sura (10 : 39) of Quran did not several poets like Abu Musa al Mozdar (d. 840), the Karmathian satirist Mutanabbi (d. 965), the blind poet Abu Ala Maari (d. 1057) and philosopher Muhadabuddin al-Hilli (d. 1205) produce their works which equalled the Quran in diction, style, beauty of language and content ?

What about Asma and Kaaba whose only crime was writing poems against Muhammad for which they were killed (Ish p. 675-676; 364-368) ?

Is it not a fact that Prophet Muhammad killed each and every writer and poet whose only crime was writing poems against him, in the same manner Muslims are now killing people like Van Ghog and threatening writers like Sulman Rushdie, Tasleema Nasreen and Wafe Sultan ?

Mukaffa killed for Imitating Quran

187. Was not Ibn Mukaffa, (d. 758) the first great prose writer, poet and translator in Arabic and a converted Zoroastrian tortured to death because he tried to imitate the Quran ? His limbs were hacked off one by one and thrown into the flames, then his trunk followed (Walker 1999 : 332).

Poet who claims his Poems Better than Quran

188. Did the Persian-born Arab blind poet Bashar ibn Burd not claim that his poems were better than the Quranic *suras* especially Sura 59 ? Was he not accused of introducing Zoroastarian dualism into Islam and thus was thrown into a swamp in Batiha in 784 AD (Walker 1999 : 332) ?

Prophet's Enemy is Allah's Enemy
189. Is the Almighty and the All-Merciful worthy of such petty vindictiveness as cursing Muhammad's opponents or throwing his enemies to the flames of hell for no major reason (111 : 1) ?

Can you prove the Prophet as a peace-loving person knowing well that he was massacaring the Jews of Kuraiza and Nazir clan and indiscriminately killed the Arab infidels organizing 82 raids and military campaigns during his ten years' stay at Medina ?

The Great Iconoclast
190. Did Muhammad not order the destruction of the Kaaba idols in 630 and the erasure of all the paintings from the walls and pillars ? The effigies of Ibrahim and Ishmael were destroyed, as they were shown holding the divine arrows of the pagan soothsayers. Does he not place a protective hand over the picture of Mary and the infant Jesus (Esin 1963, p. 109) ? The picture was said to have been painted by the artist Bakum (Pachomias) when the Kaaba was rebuilt after the accidental fire of 594. What happened to the picture is not stated, but no doubt it was disposed of in a suitable manner (Walker 1999 : 192).

Did Muhammad spare the Pagan Shrine ?
191. Is it not a fact that during the time of Muhammad, there were 360 idols in the Kaaba; every tribal community in Arabia had its own idol there, including notable goddesses Allat, Ozza and Manat ? The feet of these idols were fastened down with lead. Muhammad came to the Kaaba one day, struck each idol with a rod of iron, and the idols fell to the ground, while he said, "The truth has come, and falsehood has vanished away; surely falsehood is ever certain to vanish" ?

Pagans have every Right to Perform Hajj
192. Was Kaaba the Mosque for the Muslims ? It was originally a pagan's pagoda and after the invasion of Muhammad he destroyed 360 icons and made it a mosque. So the pagans equally have the right to perform Hajj and Muhammad has no right to stop them (*Buk* 6 : 178).

Muslims made Kaaba their Mosque
193. Is it not a fact that all the religions built their temples for their gods by their devotees with love, devotion and dedication as was Kaaba which was built by the pagans ? Did not the Prophet occupy Kaaba forcibly for his God Allah ?

Muhammad's Message for the Peace Loving World
194. Is not it a fact that when Muhammad was powerless and helpless in Mecca he preached : "There is no compulsion in Religion", but after he immigrated to Medina he became violent with his power and strength and started preaching in the name of Allah :

O Prophet ! rouse the Believers to fight (8 : 65).

If they ask you concerning fighting in the prohibited month. Say : Fighting therein is a grave offence. But graver is it in the sight of Allah to prevent access to the path of Allah (2 : 217).

Fighting is prescribed upon you, and you dislike it. But it is possible that you dislike a thing which is good for you, and that you love a thing which is bad for you (2 : 216).

Strive hard against the unbelievers and the Hypocrites, and be firm against them (9 : 73).

But when the forbidden months are past, then fight and slay the pagans wherever you find them (9 : 5).

I will instil terror into the hearts of the unbelievers, smite you above their necks and smite all their finger-tips off them (8 : 12).

Therefore, when you meet the unbelievers, smite at their necks, at length, when you have thoroughly subdued them, bind firmly (47 : 4). (For doing all this) Be not weary and faint-hearted, crying for peace (47 : 35).

Are these verses of Quran confined only to the Muslim warriors while they invaded Al-sham (Syria, Lebanon and old Phoencia), Faris (Iran), Jerusalem or is it for all times to come ?

Killing the Kafirs

195. If a religion under the threat of the sword, permits killing for the sake of Allah it cannot be a religion. How can a prophet tempt people to fight, desecrate the holy month, equip the tribes with war material and swords ? Does not Islam declare all non-Muslims to be Kafirs and are not Kafirs to be eliminated ?

Mistakes of Muhammad

196. Is it not a fact that more often than not, Muhammad acted wrongly ? When the Holy scriptures forbade any prophet to have prisoners of war why did Muhammad, on the Day of Badr, take seventy prisoners captive at the behest of Abu Bakr and spared their lives for a ransom ? Sura *The Spoils* attests to this : "It is not for any Prophet to have prisoners until he make wide slaughter in the land. You desire the chance goods of the present world, and God desires the world to come; and God is All-mighty, All-wise" (8 : 69).

It is related to the incident on the Day of Badr where seventy prisoners were taken captive, among whom were al-Abbas and Aqil b. Abi Talib. Muhammad consulted his friends concerning them. Abu Bakr said : "They are your people and relatives ! Spare their lives, and God may forgive you. Take a ransom from them to strengthen your friends." Umar said : "Behead them, for they are the chiefs of the infidelity. God has spared you the need for ransom money." But Muhammad refused to do so, saying : "God may soften some men's hearts, so that they become softer than milk. God may harden other men's hearts, so that they become harder than stone. Abu Bakr, you are like Ibrahim who said, 'He who follows me becomes one of mine; and he who disobeys me, you are Forgiver and Merciful.' But you Umar, you are like Noah who said, 'O Lord, leave not of the unbelievers a single one on earth." Then he gave his friends the choice, and they took the ransom. But he regretted this decision later. Because they pestered him, he claimed that the above verse came to him.

One day, Umar entered Muhammad's house and saw him and Abu Bakr weeping. He inquired about the reason, saying, "Tell me, so that I may weep if I can, or at least pretend to do so." Muhammad said : "I weep for your friends who took the ransom. Their punishment was displayed in front of me, and it is as close as this tree (he pointed to a nearby tree)." Thus, the verse, "It is not for any prophet to have prisoners," is a clear prohibition for taking prisoners of war. This happened on the Day of Badr. Muhammad also claimed that God commanded him and his people to kill the polytheists at the Battle of Badr; so by capturing them and not killing them, they had violated the commandment of God. Muhammad decreed a ransom, and he accepted it. That was wrong of him. Thus, Muhammad and Abu Bakr sat weeping for taking the ransom and for fear of imminent divine retribution (Razi's commentary on Sura *The Spoils* 8 : 71).

It is recorded in Sura *Repentance* 9 : 43 : "God pardon thee ! Why gavest thou them leave, till it was clear to thee which of them spoke the truth, and thou knewest the liars ?" This means : "God give you grace, O Muhammad : 'Why did you grant permission to those hypocrites who asked to be exempted from joining you in the expedition of Tabuk ?'"

Umar b. Maymun al-Awadi said : "Two things Muhammad undertook by himself without being commanded to do : the exemption he granted to the hypocrites and the taking of ransom money from the prisoners of the Battle of Badr" (Qurtubi's commentry on Sura 9 : 43). It is said that God reproved him for this. But if he were a true God, He would have punished Muhammad more severely. According to the Bible, when Achan stole some of the prohibited things, God punished the entire nation of Israel and delivered them to a foe who defeated them. When a king of Israel spared the life of one whom God had commanded to be killed, God punished that king severely, unlike what happened to Muhammad. If Muhammad had committed a detestable crime he deserved the severest punishment and the worst chastisement, but God had only reproved him, was kind to him and mindful of his feelings, then where is His holiness and justice (*The True Guidance*, I 1991 : 99-100) ?

Muhammad the Racist

197. Is not it a fact that being of a fairer complexion Muhammad (*Buk* I : 63, 167; 2 : 122, 141) referred the black people as "raisin heads" (*Buk* I : 662 ; 9 : 256) and prefered to keep slaves from the Black community (*Buk* 6 : 435) and at times insulted them by saying that if someone dreamt of a black woman, it was an evil omen for an approaching epidemic disease (*Buk* 9 : 162-163) ? This shocked the Black Muslims so much that racists like Elijah Muhammad and Louis Farakhan reacted with the words : "all white men are devils." They never spared Muhammad and Jesus (*Buk* 9 : 242; Morey 1992 : 182).

No Community so bad as to call them Apes and Swine

198. Can a community like the Jews be so bad as to transform them into apes and swines so that it may help Muhammad grow his own community (2 : 65; 5 : 60; 7 : 166) ?

Was Muhammad Sinless ?

199. When Muhammad was a child two angels appeared and took him and "expanded his breast (94 : 1-3) and cut his chest, they took out his heart and removed an impure clot (wizr) from it, then put back his heart and closed his chest again. Did they not purify him from the childhood ? If that is the truth why did Muhammad ask Allah several times for forgiveness of his sins ? Was he repentant when he married the wife of his adopted son Zaid (33 : 38; 40 : 56; 47 : 21) and waited for Allah's mercy ?

Or like several of the prophets Muhammad too committed grave sins by offering sacrifices to a heathen deity in Mecca ? (Guillaume 1954 : 119)

Repentance for Sin

200. Was Muhammad sinless, when he candidly confessed "O Allah, set me apart from my sins as the East and West are set apart from each other and clean me from sins as a white garment is cleaned of dirt. O Allah ! Wash off my sins with water, snow and hail (*Buk* I : 711) ? Did he not pray O my Lord ! Forgive my sins and my ignorance. Forgive my sins of the past and of the future which I did openly or secretly (*Buk* 8 : 407)? Did these sins mean torturing people by cutting off their hands and feet and burning out their eyes with hot irons (*Buk* 1 : 234), leaving them to bleed to death after cutting off their limbs (*Buk* 8 : 794-795) and making people die of thirst (*Buk* 8 : 796)?

Need for Forgiveness

201. Is it not a fact that the sins of Muhammad were many and that they weighed heavily upon him ? It is recorded in Sura *The Expanding* : "Did we not expand thy breast for thee and lift from thee thy burden, the burden that weighed down thy back" (94 : 1-3)? This indicates that God had to remove Muhammad's burden (sins) from his back, regardless of whether they were committed during the pre-Islamic period or any other time. Since all have sinned, everyone is under judgement, whether old or young, prophet or saint. So he was just as human as anyone else.

Sura *Victory* (48 : 2) says, "...God may forgive thee thy former and thy latter sins..." The sins mentioned in this verse are those which Muhammad committed before and after he claimed his prophethood. What proves that he was a sinner is verse 67 in Sura *The Believers* 40 : "And ask forgiveness for thy sin..." Sura *Muhammad* says : "Know thou therefore that there is no god but God, and ask forgiveness for thy sin, and for the believers, men and women. God knows your going to and fro, and your lodging" (47 : 21).

According to Abu Huraira, the Messenger says, "I ask forgiveness and repent to Him seventy times a day" (Buk : 8 : 319). The Prophet is repenting because he has sinned.

Muhammad in Hell

202. Inspite of his sins how can the prophet enter the paradise ? Dante, the greatest Latin poet, in his famous *Inferno* saw Muhammad in the Hell. Edward Said describes this episode how Dante saw him in hell : "Maometto"- Muhammad-turns up in canto 28 of the *Inferno*. He is located in the eighth of the nine circles of Hell, in the ninth of the ten Bolgias of Malebolge, a circle of gloomy ditches surrounding Satan's stronghold in Hell. Thus before Dante reaches Muhammad, he passes through circles containing people whose sins are of a lesser order : the lustful, the avaricious, the gluttonous, the heretic, the wrathful, the suicidal, the blasphemous. After Muhammad there are only the falsifiers and the treacherous (who include Judas, Brutus and Cassius) before one arrives at the very bottom of Hell which is where Satan himself is to be found (*Year Book of Muslim World* 1996 : 44).

Muhammad as a Mosaic Personality

203. Is it not a fact that the character of Muhammad was quite a mosaic, as Sir Norman Anderson summarizes :

For the rest, his character seems, like that of many other, to have been a strange mixture. That he was in the main simple in his tastes and kindly in his disposition there can be no doubt; he was generous, resolute, genial and astute : a shrewd judge and a born leader of men. He could, however, be cruel and vindictive to his enemies; he could stoop to assassination; and he was undeniably sensual (1976 : 60).

Muhammad as a Sahir

204. Is it not a fact that some of the neighbours feared Muhammad as a *sahir* or magician and an evident sorcerer (10 : 2; 15 : 15) who told lies (38 : 4) !

Has Wine some Profit ?

205. In Quran Allah said, wine and gambling are great sin and some profit for men... (2 : 219). Therefore Muhammad forbade drinking wine. But on the Farewell pilgrimage he drank it, as the books of *Sira* his biography recorded :

He got off from his camel and prayed two *rak'ahs*. Then he went to Sakis, (cup bearers) to drink some wine of dried grapes. When Al-Abbas said to him, "Shall I get something that we make in the house ?" Muhammad denied saying he would drink what the people drink and kept on drinking once, twice and even thrice.

Ibn Abbas said : once, the Prophet felt thirsty so they brought him some wine from the *sakis* (frowned cup bearers). He smelt it and asked for a bucket of water from Zamzam well. They added the water, and he kept on drinking until a man asked him : "Is this unlawful, O Prophet of Allah ?" He answered : "No".

(This *hadith* (tradition) is narrated by Yahya b. al-Yaman, as he heard it from al-Thawri, who heard it from Mansur b. Khalid, who heard it from Said, who heard it from Ibn Mas'ud al-Ansari; see Ibn Abdirabbih's Al-Iqd al-Farid; CQV 1994 : 47). Umm Ayman said : 'The Messenger of Allah said to me : "Bring me the wine from the mosque." I said to him : "I am menstruating !" He answered : "Your menstruation is not on your hand."

Here the Prophet saw no problem with his wife bringing the wine with her own hands, even though he himself banned a menstruating woman from entering a mosque. It goes without saying that Muhammad drank wine !

(*Al-Isaba fi Tamyiz al-Sahaba* (chapter on Umm Ayman), by the great Sheikh of Islam, Ibn Hajar al- Asqalani).

10- Jesus Versus Muhammad

In the Holy Quran Jesus is referred to as *Eesa* in Arabic and *Esan* in Hebrew. In the Quran Jesus is mentioned as a righteous Prophet (6.85), apostle to

Israel (3 : 49-51; 4 : 171; 5 : 78), who taught no false worship (5 : 119-120) but he was neither seen as God (5 : 19, 75) nor was mentioned as the son of God (9 : 30).

One thing we have to admit that the Holy Quran claims to be a special dispensation of the will of God and monotheism of Islam is purer and better than Zoroastrian dualism, Jewish Jehovahism and trinitarian Christinity. But would not you accept a fact that the Christian concept of God is far better than the Jews and the Muslims so far as mercy, kindness and holiness is concerned ?

Christ Born by the Spirit

206. Is not it a fact that unlike Christ, Muhammad was born of a father and mother like you and me and his birth was not announced by an angel, nor was he born by the spirit of God ?

Son of Mary was the Most Pure

207. Is not the Quranic verse, "Did we not open your breast" (94 : 1-3) supported by the Muslim scholars that when Muhammad was a child, two angels came for his heart surgery to purify him to become *al-Mustafa* or the chosen one", whereas Quran says the son of Mary was "most pure" from the birth (19 : 19) ?

Mary referred 34 Times in Quran

208. Is not the name of Mary, the mother of Jesus, repeated 34 times in the Quran and in contrast, the name of Muhammad's mother is never mentioned in the Quran, not even once ?

Muhammad's Middleman

209. Is not it a fact that Allah directly taught Jesus the Book, Wisdom, the Torah and the Gospel (3 : 48) whereas Allah remained far away from Muhammad and did not speak to him directly but dealt through a middle-man the Angel Gabriel ?

Prophecy for Muhammad why not for Jesus ?

210. If Bible is corrupted why do you quote Deuteronomy (18 : 18), Isaiah (42), and John (16 : 13) as the prophecy for Muhammad but do not accept Isaiah (53) as the prophecy for the crucifixion of Christ ?

Can Christ's Crucifixion be Challenged ?

211. If a look alike of Jesus died on the cross instead of Jesus (4 : 157) where is the documentary evidence to prove this except the Gospel of Barnabas---a 15th century forgery book by a Muslim ?

One Man One Wife

212. Is not it funny for a man to divorce his wife, marry her again, dismiss her again, re-marry her and dismiss her a third time. (*Buk* 34). He cannot marry her again until she has been married to another man at least for one night and when he dismisses her then her first husband can re-marry her ? Does it prove the equality between man and woman or it gives women a little higher status than a maid servant whereas Christ confirmed monogamy and prohibited any irresponsible divorces (*Mk* 10 : 6-12) ?

Can a Temple be used as a Trade Centre ?

213. Is it not a fact that Jesus did not like to make the temple of Jerusalem a temple for traders or businessmen (*Mt* 21 : 13-13; Lk 19 : 46) whereas Allah through Muhammad declared : "There is no harm for you if you seek of the bounty of your Lord during Hajj by trading etc "(2 : 198) ?

61

Fight and Slay the Pagans

214. Jesus was persecuted by the Jews but he commanded Peter : "Put your sword into its place, for all who take the sword shall perish by sword" (*Mt* 26 : 52). Even he preferred to shed his blood to save his enemies and prayed God : "Father forgive them, for they do not know what they do" (*Lk* 2:34). Like Jesus, Muhammad was equally persecuted in Mecca but when he became politically powerful he launched severe attacks and bloody wars against his enemies and got command from Allah :

> Slay them wherever you catch them, and turn them out from where they have turned you out...Such is the reward of those who reject Islam (2 : 191).

> Take not to yourselves friends of them, until they emigrate in the way of Allah; then if they turn away seize them and kill them wherever you find them (4 : 89).

> When the forbidden months are past, then fight and slay the

Difference between the Quran and the Bible

215. The major difference between Islam and Christianity is their inspiring scriptures---- the Quran and the Bible. In the whole of Quran we find "do unto them before they do unto you," kind of verses and consider the opponents as "Shatim-E-Rasool" or insulter of the prophet, whereas the New Testament tells about love and live. Now see the difference :

In the Holy Quran

Allah's curse is on the unbelievers (2: 89).

Allah is the enemy of the unbelievers (2 : 98).

Do not take Jews and Christians as friends (5 : 51).

Fighting is enjoined on you (2 : 216)

Those who believe fight in the way of Allah (4 : 76).

Fight those who do not believe in Allah (9 : 29).

Slay the unbelievers wherever you find them (2 : 191; 9 : 5).

In the Holy Bible

Love your enemies (Matthew 5 : 44).

Forgive those who trespass against you (Matthew 6 : 14).

Do good to those who hate you (Luke 6 : 27).

Bless those who curse you, pray for those who mistreat you (Luke 6 : 28).

The U.S. Attorney General John Ashcroft rightly remarked : "Islam is a religion in which God requires you to send your son to die for Him.

Christianity is a faith in which God sent His son to die for you" (Pollock 2002 : 8).

My Peace I give unto You

216. Is not it a fact that all Muslims for all time pray to Allah to grant peace to Muhammad ? Does not their prayer indicate that the peace of Allah has not yet come to Muhammad (33 : 56), whereas peace was with Jesus since the day he was born, the day he died and the day he was raised from death. Jesus said, "My peace I give unto you" (Jn 14 : 27).

Miracles through Love and Mercy

217. Is not it a fact that the miracles of Allah granted to Muhammad were the verses of the Quran or the words, whereas the signs of miracles of Jesus were miracles manifested in his work of love and deeds of mercy ?

Jesus Versus Muhammad

218. If the mission of Christ was to appear on this earth to express his love for mankind, and He sacrificed himself for their sake, can you cite a similar example from Islam that Muhammad too came with such glorious mission ? When a Quraish Pagan Uqba bin Abi Muait came and threw the intestines of a camel on the back of the Prophet, the Prophet did not raise his head from Prostration till Fatima (his daughter) came and removed those intestines from his back, and invoked evil on whoever had done this. But the Prophet instead of excusing them started scolding them : "O Allah ! Destroy the chiefs of Quresh, O Allah ! Destroy Abu Jahl bin Hisham, Utba bin Rabia, Shaiba bin Rabia, Uqba bin Abi Muait, Ubai bin Khalaf. At last all of them were killed in the battle of Badr (*Buk* 4 : 409).

Christ and Muhammad a Mismatch

219. When Christ said : Come to me, all who are tired and weary, I will give ye comfort" (*Mt* 11 : 28) has the founder of Islam spoken of himself anywhere in these or similar terms ? Instead of that Muhammad said : "O Allah ! Help me against them by sending seven years of drought upon the infidels, like the seven years of drought of the Prophet Joseph. "He also said : "O Allah ! Destroy Abu Jahl" (*Buk* 7 : 400).

Between a Sinner and a Sage

220. Does not Muhammad accept Jesus as the gift of a pure son whereas he himself was only a messenger (19 : 19) ? Was not Jesus sinless whereas Muhammad confessed thrice in the Quran for forgiveness of his sins (40 : 55; 47 : 19; 48 : 1-2)?

Jesus died to fulfil the Plan of God

221. Did not Muhammad die after suffering from high fever ? Did he not say that prior to his death he was poisoned by a Jewish slave-woman, whereas Jesus' death, according to the Quran, was fulfilling the plan of God (3 : 55) ?

Who is Great : Jesus or Muhammad ?

222. If life is greater than death then Jesus is greater than Muhammad because Muhammad died and was buried in Medina whereas Jesus died but Allah raised him from death (3 : 55; 4 : 158) therefore the grave of Christ prepared at Medina is yet empty ?

Did Muhammad copy Jesus ?

223. Is not it a fact that Muhammad tried to copy the events and words of Jesus ? It was said that, like Jesus, Muhammad chose twelve disciples to carry the message of Islam. Like Jesus, Muhammad gave a Sermon on the Mount, which ended, 'This day have I perfected your religion.' Jesus announced in the synagogue in Nazareth, 'This day is this scripture fulfilled in your ears' (*Lk* 4 : 21). Jesus's last words on the cross, 'It is finished' (*Jn* 19 : 30), find an echo in the words with which Muhammad ended his last sermon : 'I have finished my work ?"

Section II

The Miracle of Miracles

11 - Queries on Quran

Once the Meccans challenged Muhammad to perform a miracle as proof of his divine mission. He boldly referred to the book called the Quran, which was the last miracle taking shape under his supervision.

While I was at Cairo an Egyptian Maulabi enchanted me with the recitation of a few verses from Quran. Thougsh I could not understand anything from his recitation, I found an internal flow of music in his voice. That speaks of the power of music in the Quran.

Not only the Quran but the Pre-Islamic poetry too is melodious, rhythmic of balanced phrases. According to Benjamin Walker : "The music and harmony emerged from the interplay of vowels and consonants, and the beauty of expression. They discovered new metres and new rhythms, developed to the full opportunities their language offered for poetic eloquence, and set standards for excellence that later poets were long to emulate" (2002 : 79).

There is hardly any difference between the language of the Quran and the poetry of other poets of Arabia. No doubt it is a wonderful work of religious truth. Its language is superb, the depth of its meaning is profound. Therefore every word of the Quran is called infallible and it is the miracle of miracles. Such a book cannot be written by an unlettered man like Muhammad.

Allah made the first revelation through Angel Gabriel to Muhammad in 610, that too in a cave on mount Hira, known as Jahal al-Nur or the mountain of light. The revelation began during the holy month of Ramadhan when the Angel Gabriel called Muhammad "Recite" or read in the name of the Lord. That is the beginning of real education for Muhammad.

This Holy Book of Muslims, the Quran, means "recitation". Its shape and size is approximately the same length as the New Testament. The whole book is divided into 30 parts according to the holy month of Ramadan for recitation.

Every *surah* except one begins with the words *'bismillah-al-rahman al-rahim'* in the Name of God the Compassionate, the Merciful.

Allah speaks in the first person plural (We). It was sent down to Muhammad over some 20 years. The revelations were brought to him by the angel Gabriel when Muhammad was in a kind of trance or ecstasy. On his return to senses he recited the words of revelation to his scribes who had then written down on pieces of paper, stones, palm-leaves, shoulder blades, ribs and bits of leather.

The Quran is divided into 114 chapters or sura, that include Meccan 90 and Madinan suras 24 loosely arranged in their order and length. It begins with a short prayer called *fatihah* (opening) and ends with two or three shortest chapters. The larger chapters are sub-divided into sections, each section being called *ruku*. The chapters are of unequal length. The longest chapter contains about one - twelfth of the entire Book while the smallest contains only three verses.

In the 114 chapters or surahs there are 6, 239 verses or *ayahs* and there are 77, 934 words or *harf* and 323, 621 letters in the Holy Quran.

The *suras* revealed during Muhammad's flight to Mecca, where he spent 13 years of his life, are called *Mecca suras* and the *suras* revealed after the flight called *Madina suras*, where he spent the last 10 years of his life. The following period is arranged from the early Mecca period to the last Medina period.

Early Mecca Period	:	*60 Chapters* : 1, 17-21, 50-56, 67-109,
		III-114.
Middle Mecca Period	:	*17 Chapters* : 29-32, 34-39, 40-46.
Last Mecca Period	:	*15 Chapters* : 6,7,10-16, 22, 23, 25-28
Early Madina Period	:	*6 Chapters* : 2,8,47, 61,62,64.
Middle Madina Period	:	*12 Chapters* : 3-5, 24, 33, 48, 57-60, 63, 65
Last-Madina Period	:	*4 Chapters* : 9, 49, 66, 110.

We do not know the authority of the Holy Quran because Muslim scholars give a circular definition of it. If someone asks, the Muslims promptly answer "Quran is from Allah because Muhammad said so and how could you know that Muhammad was the messenger of Allah they reply because Quran says so. But neither Allah nor Muhammad could collect the revelation to preserve it for the benefit of mankind.

What is the need of one more Quran ?
224. What was the need of the Holy Quran when the doctrine of Unity had already been revealed to the world in the Torah, the book of Moses and the New Testament of Jesus ?

Is Quran for the Illiterate Arabs ?
225. In what way the Arabs were distinguished from others to receive such a book in their language ? Did they become wiser and more intelligent ?

Why did Allah choose an Illiterate to deliver the Quran ?
226. Why did Allah choose a Prophet who is said to be illiterate and giving the task to prepare the text of the Quran to an illiterate person casts aspersions on the choice of Allah Himself ?

Was the Quran sent from heaven, written in gold on a rich tablet to Muhammad or it was jotted down on bits of skin and palm-leaves "in a wild and semi-barbarous environment ?

For whom was the Quran written ?
227. Is it not a fact that the Quran itself claims that God has provided for each people a law given in the language of the people, so that they can read, study and understand it (41 : 44) ? And the Quran was in Arabic so it can be assumed that the Quran was for the Arabs only ?

Is not it a fact that the Holy Quran was revealed in Arabia and in Arabic language to warn the mother of cities and those around her (6 : 92) ? And the Quran clearly says :

"And thus We have inspired in thee a Lecture in Arabic, that thou mayst warn the mother-town and those around it, and smayst warn of a day of assembling whereof there is no doubt. A host will be in the Garden, and a host of them in the Flame" (42 : 7).

"Lo ! We have appointed it a Lecture, in Arabic that haply ye may understand" (43 : 3).

Or say they " He hath invented it ? Nay, but it is the Truth from thy Lord, that thou mayst warn a folk to whom no warner came before thee, that haply they may walk aright" (32 : 3).

"And thou was not beside the Mount when We did call; but (the knowledge of it is) a mercy from thy Lord that thou mayst warn a folk unto whom no warner came before thee, that haply they may give heed" (28 : 46).

"And We have made (this Scripture) easy in thy language only that they may heed" (44 : 58).

It is not for the townsfolk of Al-Madinah and for those around them of the wandering Arabs so stay behind the messenger of Allah and prefer their lives to his life" (9 : 120).

Is the Quran a Heavenly Book ?
228. Is it not a fact that the Quran was not a full transcript of the heavenly book as it was claimed to be and this is also confirmed by the Quran itself (18 : 109) ?

Can a Puppy stop Revelation ?
229. Is it not a fact that the revelation to Muhammad was delayed for 15 to 40 days because a puppy entered Muhammad's house hid under the bed and died ? Therefore Gabriel delayed coming to the Prophet. My question is :

What kind of a revelation is it that ceases because of a puppy ? And what kind of an angel is he who avoids a prophet because of a puppy ? What has a dog to do with the revelation of God ? Weren't most prophets, such as Ibrahim, Isaac, Jacob, Moses and David, shepherds of sheep who kept sheepdogs ? Why then haven't we heard of any of them being forsaken by heaven because of their dogs ?

Is the Quran Infallible ?
230. If Quran is the eternal and infallible word of Allah and contains the whole of Allah's final revelation to man why does it contain ambiguous verses and verses whose interpretation is only known to Allah (3 : 7) ?

Can Allah's Word be Changed ?
231. If God's word cannot be changed (6 : 34; 18 : 26) why did God replace a verse in place of another verse (16 : 101) and abrogate verse to oblivion to bring a better verse (2 : 106) ? Does it not imply that the unchangeable *archetypal Quran* in heaven also has a temporary relevance and can be subjected to alteration ?

Is the Quran a Complete Book ?
232. How can it be claimed that the Quran is a complete book when the book itself makes it clear that not all that was known about other apostles had been revealed to Muhammad (4 : 162), nor is it a compendium of morals or a legal code because Muslim law code is not purely based on it ?

Is there any way that memories would not falter over a period of fifty years while compiling the Quran and all those men who had died before the compilation of the Quran, must have taken some bits of the Quran with them for good ?

Why is the Quran recited in various ways ?
233. Is it not a fact that Muhammad had permitted people to recite the Quran in their own native dialect, so many vernacular texts were current in many parts of the Islamic world which were later banned by Muslim theologians (Grunebaum 1961, 152) ?

Missing Verse from Quran

234. Is it not a fact that after these copies of the Quran were prepared by Zaid a verse from Surat Ahzab (33 : 23) was missing and at last was found with Khuzaima-bin-Thabit al Ansari (*Buk* 6 : 509) ?

Records of many variant readings in the codices of both Salim and Ubai bin Ka'b exist but, as Ibn Mas'ud was especially singled out before the others by Muhammad himself, it is astonishing to discover that his text varied from the others (including Hafsah's) so often that the different readings involved are set out in no less than *ninety pages* of Arthur Jeffery's collection of variants in the various codices. The author has taken his evidence from numerous Islamic sources which are documented in his book. There are no less than 149 cases in Sura 2 *alone* where his text differed from the others in circulation, in particular the text of Hafsah.

Furthermore one of the reasons he gave for refusing to abandon his codex in favour of Hafsah's was that the latter text was compiled by Zaid-b-Thabit who was still only in the loins of an unbeliever when he had already become one of the closest companions of Muhammad (Gilchrist 1988 : 19).

Omission of *Bismilah*

235. Is it not a fact that Sura al-Tawba 9 begins without the invocation, "In the name of Allah, the Merciful, and Compassionate" (the Bismilah) ? Are we not bound to think that Suras al-Anfal 8 and al-Tabwa 9 are one Sura, and that no *Bismilah* was written between them ?

☐Is it wrong to think that this introductory phrase was not original part of the Fatiha, nor was it from the other Suras, that it was added later to the beginning of the Quran in the process of its compilation (Al-Mashih 1993 : 16) ?

Why Sura 12 not Acceptable ?

236. Is Sura 12 not rejected by the Ajarida and Maymuniya sects as unworthy to form part of a Holy Book because it contains the story of eroticism of Joseph and Zulaykha ?

Shiite Muslims worried about Missing Verses

237. It is said that once one Sura originally had 200 verses in the days of Ayesha. But by the time Uthman standardized the text of the Quran, it had only 73 verses ! A total of 127 verses had been lost, and they have never been recovered. Do the Shiite Muslims not claim that Uthman left out 25 per cent of the original verses in the Quran for political reasons (McClintock 1981 : 152) ?

Is the Text of Quran Authentic ?

238. After the death of Muhammad and the battle of Yamaamah (633) when a great number of soldiers who knew the Quran by heart had been killed, can there be an accurate and authoritative text of the Quran ? While editing and compiling the Quran in the book form does Uthman not say to the three Qureshi persons : "If you differ with Zaid bin Thabit on any point of the Quran, then write it in the language of Quresh, as the Quran was revealed in their language" ? So they acted accordingly (*Buk* 4 : 709; 6 : 507).

No Trustworthy Quran

239. Is it worthy to believe that Zayd ibn Thaabit's copies on sheets available to Caliph Umar was enough for the text of Quran ? The copies that was handed over to

Caliph Umar by Zayd ibn Thaabit who was with Umar till his death came to his daughter Hafsah and she again handed over the copies to Caliph Uthman, who consulting those who knew the Quran by heart, compiled the text. Can it be trustworthy ?

Topkapi Quran of Istanbul
240. Why the Muslim authorities refused to release the photocopy of the ancient Topkapi manuscript of Istanbul, one of the three oldest Qurans in existence ? Out of fear or was there any other reason ?

Why was Quran communicated in Piecemeal ?
241. Why was the Quran communicated to Muhammad in piecemeal although they have existed (17 : 106) on a preserved tablet or Lawh al-mahfur in Allah's presence since eternity ?

It creates doubt in our mind as to why the Quran came to Muhammad in pieces, parts of it having been given at a certain time, and others having been delayed ? To avoid such questions from the non-Muslims, Muhammad sometimes even replied that Gabriel delayed in coming to him, owing to some dogs (Abd Al-Fadi-1997 : 328).

Ayesha brings Revelations to Muhammad
242. Why did Muhammad usually get revelations only when he slept with Ayesha (*Buk* 3 : 755) and not when he slept with other wives ? Is it because except Ayesha, all his wives were grown up and matured. It was not that easy to convince them about his revelation from Allah via Gabriel. Whereas Ayesha was ready to believe in whatever Muhammad told her about Gabriel, and revelations and he once said :

"O 'Aisha' This is Gabriel and he sends his (greetings) salutations to you." 'Ayesha said, "Salutations (Greetings) to him, and Allah's Mercy and Blessings be on him," and addressing the Prophet she said, 'You see what I don't see" (*Buk* 4 : 440).

Quran descended at Odd Times
243. Is it not a fact that the Quranic revelations descended upon Muhammad unexpectedly at odd times while he was eating, riding or having his hair washed ?

Why Earlier Copies of the Quran were Burnt ?
244. Was the Quran first collected by Caliph Uthman ? There were numerous texts of the Quran available in Syria, Armenia and Iraq. Uthman collected (*Buk* 4 : 709) the manuscript of the Quran which was in possession of Hafsah, one of the wives of Muhammad and the daughter of Umar, and ordered Zaid-b-Thabit and three others to make copies of the text and to correct it wherever necessary. Bukhari has recorded :

Uthman sent to every Muslim province one copy of what they had copied, and ordered that all the other Quranic materials, whether written in fragment manuscripts or whole copies, be burnt (*Buk* 6 : 510).

Weren't the copies of the Quran that differed from the copy of Uthman nonetheless from God ? Why then did Uthman burn them if a standard text was already in existence ? And if they were the oracles of God, why didn't He keep them from being burned and lost for ever ? Why did Uthman replace the copies of the Quran with another one; burning the others, and keeping his own and was much worried to send his copy of Quran to Damascus, Basra and Kufa, the capital cities of the great Muslim empire ?

Revision of the Quran by Allah

245. Is the holy Quran in chronological order or at times some verses are cancelled and some verses are replaced by other verses ? If it is not so then why does Allah say in the Quran :

Allah does not abrogate any verse but substitutes something similar or better... (2 : 106).

Allah doth blot out or confirm what He pleaseth : with Him is the mother of the Book (13 : 39).

Allah substitutes one revelation for another (16 : 101).

If Quran is free from contradictions why Allah himself admits : "Whatever verse we abrogate, or cause you to forget, we will bring a better one than it or one like it" (11 : 100).

Can Quran be easily corrected ?

246. Is it not a fact that once Ibn Umm Maktum, a blind man from Mecca requested Muhammad to correct a verse to exempt him to join in a Jihad because of his blindness ?

"Narrated Al-Bara : There was revealed : 'Not equal are those believers who sit (at home) and those who strive and fight in the Cause of Allah' (4.95). The Prophet said, 'call Zaid for me and let him bring the board, the inkpot and the scapula bone (or the scapula bone and the ink pot).' Then he said, 'Write : 'Not equal are those Believers who sit', and at that time 'Amr bin Um Maktum, the blind man was sitting behind the Prophet. He said, 'O Allah's Apostle ! What is your order for me (as regards the above Verse) as I am a blind man ?' So, instead of the above Verse, the following Verse was revealed : 'Not equal are those believers who sit (at home) except those who are disabled (by injury or are blind or lame etc.) and those who strive and fight in the cause of Allah" (4.95; *Buk* 6 : 512).

Can you deny the fact that Muhammad very clearly had corrected, deleted, modified the contents of a verse to suit his purpose ?

Meaning of the Quran known to Allah Alone

247. Is it not a fact that there are many interpretations, many readings and meanings of the Quranic verses and the Arabs claim that the true meaning is known only to God ?

Is the Quran Manifesto of Muhammad ?

248. Is it not a fact that Muhammad's constant recourse to Quranic revelation to control his wives, silent his opponents, or forestall objections to his conduct and solve local political problems which he couldn't deal on his own reduced the significance of Quranic verses as revealed through the divine inspiration of Allah ?

Prophet's Personal Opinion on Quran

249. Is not it a fact that the Quran does not merely contain the words of God but also personal reflections of the Prophet. The opening Sura Fatihah of Quran is recited :

In the name of the Merciful and Compassionate God, Praise belongs to God, The Lord of the worlds, the merciful, the compassionate, the ruler of the day of the day of judgement ! Thee we serve and Thee we ask for aid. Guide us in the right path, the path of those Thou art gracious to; not to those Thou art wroth with, nor of those who err" (1 : 1-7).

Is it addressed to God in the form of a prayer or *Appah*, who is praying himself, or, it is Muhammad's words of prayer to God ? By adding the imperative "say" in the English translation of the Quran at the beginning of the Sura this difficulty is removed. Does the word "say" occur in the original Arabic version of the Quran (Das 2010 : 149) ?

Quran : the Personal Notebook of Muhammad

250. Is it not a fact that Muhammad's contemporaries scorned his revelations as a series of his own self-induced inventions (11 : 16), by which he falsely provided sanction for his deeds and misdeeds ? Did they not reject the holy text as a lie which he had forged (25 : 5) and denounced him as a fabricator of the Quran (16 : 103) ?

Quran : the Autobiography of the Prophet

251. Is it not a fact that the Quran is the autobiography of Prophet Muhammad ? According to Ayesha the youngest and dearest wife of the Prophet, the Quran faithfully mirrors the life of the Prophet and it also establishes the fact that the *seerat* of the Prophet and the Quran are essentially synonymous" (Yusuf. 22 Sept., 1991 : 3) .Are not many of the verses a solution to many of the problems Muhammad faced and answers to everyday social and political situations like orders for his troops, making peace treatise with tribal chiefs or distribution of booty after a raiding expedition (8 : 41); incidents that occurred with his wives Ayesha, Zainab, Khadija, Maryam al-Qibtiyya (Mary the Copt), Hafsa, Umm Hani and the rest. The Quran even records his vulnerability to magic as well as the incantations he used to ward it off. It also records some of the Companions' words, presuming they, too, were the "sending down of the All-wise, the All- knowing ?"

Quran as the Newspaper of that Time

252. Is Muhammad not the author of the Quran which he used as a kind of newspaper, publishing orders of the day, bulletins, judgements on domestic affairs and other local topics and responses to questions at public meetings ? Benjamin Walker rightly remarked : Western scholars too have concluded that the Quran is a very human document, reflecting many sides of Muhammad's own personality. Muhammad's authorship, they believe, is confirmed by internal evidence provided by the borrowings, the abrogations, the amendments, the contradictions, the stylistic flaws, the adhoc nature of many passages, and other indications of Muhammad's personal opinions, his desires and demands, his preferences and prejudices. They have tended to dismiss the idea of divine authorship through the angel Gabriel or a similar agency. The Italian Arabist Leone Caetani spoke of the Quran as a kind of newspaper, publishing orders of the day, bulletins, judgements on domestic affairs, and similar matters of current topical interest. It has been variously spoken of as Muhammad's 'Day Book', 'Utterances', 'Diary', 'Table talk', 'Sermons', 'Autobiographical Notes' or 'Discourses'. And quite definitely all his own work (1999 : 168-169).

Quran gives Importance to Alexander the Pagan King

253. It is said in the Quran (18 : 83-88) that Zulqarnain was Alexander the Great, a courageous person like ram having two horns, i.e., his crown had two horns.

How could the Quran make of the pagan king, Alexander, a prophet who spoke to God and received an oracle from Him ? How could the Quran say that he visited a spring in which the sun set ? How could he be a prophet or even a believer when in fact he was an idol-worshipper and, moreover, claimed he was the son of Amon, the sun-god ?

Quran a Product of 23 Years

254. Is it possible to believe that without any physical existence of Allah Muhammad could receive His revelations intermittently through the agency of an angel Gabriel from the age of 39 (609 AD) till his last breath (632 AD) that was nearly for 23 years ?

Two Speakers in Quran

255. When Allah is the only speaker of the Quran, should it not be written in the first person ? But it contains many instances that confuse the reader regarding the identities of the two speakers. One is Allah and the other Muhammad ?

Why the Quran is written in Third Person ?

256. Is not the Quran written in third person which proves that it is neither the word of Allah nor that of Muhammad ? For example Then will Allah say : "O Jesus the son of Mary ! recount My favour to thee and to thy mother" (5 : 110).

Epileptic Author of the Quran

257. Some of the people agree that the Prophet was sincere and truthful but allege that he was suffering from epilepsy and during the epileptic seizures he recited what later became the Quran (*Islamic Voice* Jan 2004 : 23). If it is not so, why did Muhammad answer to followers repeatedly that when Angel Gabriel approached him : " I hear the sound of a ringing bell or banging metal. Then, I step quickly down from my horse or camel and cover my head. He then presses so hard on me that I think I will die. When he speaks, I can never forget his words which I reveal to you" (Al-Masih : nd 17).

Is it not a fact that "Muhammad was subject to epilepsy and found curious confirmations in the notices that recorded his experiences during the process of revelation" (Margoliouth 1905 : 89; al-Masih 1993 : 15-16) ?

Muhammad failed to bring a written Quran

258. Did not the Jews ask Muhammad to bring down a written message, like the two tablets God gave to Moses (4 : 153) ? Why did Muhammad fail to do so ? Does not the Quran consist of answers to questions people asked ? Did Muhammad ask Allah to give him a written Book, and was his petition denied ? Or did Muhammad fail to make such a petition ? If he asked and his petition was refused, why did Allah refuse Muhammad's prayer ?

Muhammad praising Allah in the beginning of the Quran

259. Who is the author of the Quran ? Allah or Muhammad ? If it is the revealed word of Allah then does Allah begin by saying "In the name of Allah" and praise Himself as the "Most Gracious, Most Merciful." Again who says "Praise be to Allah" Muhammad or Allah Himself ?

Could Allah say "You do we worship" and "You we ask for aid or help".

It would have been more proper to say, "*bika nastain*," for this means "by you we are aided"; but as it is written in Arabic, "*Wa iyyaka nastain*" means "with you we are aided."

Would Allah need to ask for guidance to the straight path ? Does it mean that Allah is praising Himself or Muhammad is praising Allah ?

Did Muhammad prepare the Quran ?

260. Is not it a fact that Muhammad did not prepare the manuscript of the Quran before his death and the portions of the Quran were scattered on palm leaves, rocks and bones (*Buk* 6 : 509) ?

Is Quran a Hoax ?

261. Did Abdulla ibn Saad, the foster-brother of Uthman, later the third caliph--- not scandalize Muhammad saying that his revelations were a hoax (Glubb 1979 : 308) and he dictated simply what came into his head (Thaalibi 1968, 69) ? More over he had helped the Prophet to alter the wording of his revelations and on one occasion he added a concluding phrase to complete a verse that Muhammad was composing (23 : 14) ?

Quran is Hidjaz

262. How many non-Arab Muslims know that the language in which Muhammad delivered his revelations was in his own Meccan dialect Hidjaaz which was very much in use during the time of Muhammad and he liked the rhythmic prose by the Arabs, in which their sooth sayers and poets used to speak ?

Why Quran in Seven Dialects only ?

263. Why did Allah send Gabriel four times to convey His message to Muhammad to recite the Quran in Koraysh, Hawazin, Thakif (the dialect of Tayif) and Hodayl as well as three dialects of the Kahtan Arabs namely Tayi, Tamim and Yemeni, i.e. in these seven dialects only besides his own mother tongue ? Why did Allah confine the Quran into seven dialects when there are about 6, 912 living languages in the world ?

What is the Language of the Quran Like ?

264. Is the Quran written in clear language (16 : 103) or in ambiguous language (3 : 7) ?

Quran a Miracle of Miracles ?

265. Is it not a fact that all the Prophets in the past were miracle mongers, like Moses' contemporaries were excellent in magic ? So, his major miracle was to defeat the best magicians of Egypt of his days. Jesus' contemporaries were skillful physicians. Therefore, his miracles revolved round raising the dead and curing the blind and the lepers. The Arabs, the contemporaries of Muhammad, were known for their eloquence and magnificent poetry. So, Muhammad's miracle was different from his predecessors, because his miracle of miracles was his Quran what he received from Allah through angel Gabriel (17 : 88).

It may be a miracle for Muhammad but not for the Arabs. Comparing the seven pre-Islamic poems (Muallaqat) and the pieces of rhythmic prose of al-Hariri in what way is the Quran more eloquent ?

74

Isn't Imru'al-Qais more expressive than Muhammad ? Aren't the poems of al-Mutanabbi, al-Farid, and the speeches of Quss Ibn Sa'ida just as eloquent as the Quran ?

After reading them can any one call the Quran a work of miracle ? This poetry competition between God and man is ridiculous and Muhammad the representative poet of God seems less gifted. If you accept Muhammad as illiterate, he had no idea of other poets of the world those who were his contemporaries mainly Hebrew, Greek and Roman. This challenge of Allah through Muhammad is nothing compared to the other poets of the world.

What is the need to produce a Book like Quran ?
266. It has been said that Quran is the word of Allah because no one has ever been able to produce a book like it. Is it necessary to produce a book like Quran, so contradictory, full of errors and violence ?

Produce a Sura like it
267. When Allah challenged the poets through Muhammad by saying "If you are in doubt as to what We have revealed from time to time to Our servant, then produce a Sura like it" (2 : 23). Has not Quran adopted the same style of poetry as Quss b. Saida used to write who lived in Mecca before the advent of Quran ? Does not Ibn Kathir relate that Muhammad often asked Abu Bakr to read something of Quss' poetry to him ?

Let us examine a translation of a passage, bearing in mind that this English translation cannot reflect the Arabic rhyme :

"Where is he who oppressed and tyrannized ? He collected and knew it, and said : 'I am your most high Lord.' Were they not richer than you ? Did they not live longer than you ? Lo ! they were callously crushed under the moist earth. Indeed, it tore them down mercilessly. Behold, their bones are worn out, their houses vacant, inhabited by the howling wolves (see the biography of Quss b. Saida in *Shuara al-Nasraniyya qabl al Islam* by Louis Sheicko; see also *Al-Bidaya wa al-Nihaya* by Ibn Kathir; *Tarih al-Umam wa al-Muluk* by al-Tabari; and *Al Kamil by Ibn al-Athir* see also "The True Guidance, part 5; 1994 : 10)".

Muhammad not only was acquainted with Quss' poetry but also with his contemporary poets such as : Umaiyya b. Abi-al-Salt, Waraqa b. Nawfal and Zaid b. Amr b. Nufail. After reading their poetry nobody can dare to claim that Quran is the best poetry anthology.

Is the Quran a Clear Book ?
268. Is it not a fact that although the Quran describes itself as a "Clear book" (2 : 2, 12 : 2), some of its passages are difficult and in need of interpretation for which the work of commentry, *tafsir and ta'wil* has been increasing day by day ?

Is Quran a Special Poetry ?
269. Is not it a fact that Persian and Arabic are poetic languages and therefore shahnameh or the Robeyat Khayam or the Poetry of Nader Naderpour are more poetic than the Quran ? All poetry are revelations from innate ideas.

Other excelled the Quran in Style and Beauty
270. Is it not a fact that the Mutazilis circulated the works of other earlier Arab poets in competition with the Quran to show that they far excelled the Quran in stylistic beauty and moral excellence ?

Can God reject His own Verses ?

271. The Quran existed long before the creation of the world as the "mother of the book" (13 : 39). If Quran was written in heaven (*Buk* 9 : 643) how do the earthly pre-Islamic sources exist in Quran and are found in great abundance ?

Large Part of Quran Missing or Lost

272. If Quran is written in heaven how was one verse cancelled (*Buk* 4 : 57), one of the verses of Surat Al-Ahzab missing (*Buk* 4 : 62), how the revelation about those who were killed at Bir-Maura, and the Quranic verse they used to recite, was cancelled later on (*Buk* 4 : 69), how another verse of Quran concerning those martyrs was cancelled (*Buk* 4 : 299) ? At the Battle of Yamama the casualties were heavy among the Qurraa of the Quran (those who knew Quran by heart) so a large part of Quran might have been lost and perished with them (*Buk* 6 : 509).

Disagreement between Makki and Madani Suras

273. Can you deny the fact that the early Meccan Suras and the later Medinan Suras are very distinct in their style, theme and purpose ? The Meccan Suras which comprised one-third of the Quran could be recited, orally transmitted, full of visionary power, poetic fervours, more tolerant towards other faiths, with high idealism and deep religious conviction, whereas the Medinan suras are the result of the Prophet's conscious mind, consisting of exhortations, appeals, regulations and proclamations, having a more didactic and legalistic tone engrossed with intolerance towards punishing the disbelievers, that is the reason why they are not suitable and are never used in public worship or other religious occasions.

1. Should major concepts of the Makki verses be the negation of polytheism and idolatry and inviting people towards monotheism and monotheistic beliefs, then which of the following verses is Makki ?

 a. Surat-ul-Fateha (Chapter "Opening")

 b. Surat-ul-Jom'a (Chapter "Friday")

 c. Surat-ul-Saff (Chapter "The Ranks")

 d. Surat-ul-Kauthar (Chapter "The Heavenly Fountain")

2. If one of the signs of Madani verses is the issue of Jihad against the polytheists, hypocrites and paganists then which of the following verses is Madani ?

 a. Surat-ul-Dhariyat (Chapter "The Scatters")

 b. Surat-ul-Waghe'a (Chapter "The Great Event")

 c. Surat-ul-Tahrim (Chapter "The Prohibition")

 d. Surat-ul-Rahman (Chapter "The Beneficent")

A Portion of Quran in the Stomach of a Goat

274. Can we think of Quran as a complete book ? As per *Sunaan ibn Majah* (3 : 1944); during preparation of Muhammad's funeral some verses were lost when a domestic goat entered the house and ate them. Since several Muslim scholars had recorded this Hadith, it must be true. How can Divine words be eaten by a goat and thus lost forever, when the Quran claims to have been revealed word by word and letter by letter (Das 2010 : 140) ?

 If nobody could change a word of Allah (10 : 64) and or alter a word of the Quran (6 : 34) then it is better to bring from the original copy of Quran, the mother of the book (43 : 3), the concealed book (55 : 77) and a well guarded tablet (85 : 22) from the heaven by any devoted Muslim.

12- Grammatical Errors in the Quran

If Allah wrote the Quran in heaven on a stone table it should be perfect and none can write any verse like that (10 : 37-38). To our surprise the Holy Quran is neither in perfect Arabic nor it is free from grammatical errors. Arabic, one of the Semitic languages, comprises 28 characters, all consonants, vowels being expressed either by positioned points or, in some cases, by insertion of the letters *alif, waw* and *ya* in positions where they would not otherwise occur, thereby representing the long *a, u* and *i* respectively. Its alphabet is not original rather it is developed from a script used in Nabatacan Aramaic. As Arabic had different consonants than Aramaic, jdiacritical dots came to be used to eliminate ambiguous readings of some letters, and these remain a feature of the script and it is written from right to left.

The Arabic grammar is entirely different from the languages of Europe as all words are based on verbs, and in turn, all verbs are based on a root of three consonants. For example, the consonants "k," "t," and "b" give the general meaning of writing. Thus we get : "ma*k*ta*b*a" (library), "ma*k*ta*b*" (office), "ki*i*ta*b*" (book, and "ku*t*oo*b*" (books). Unlike English, French and Spanish, Arabic does not make plurals by adding "s" or "es." From these three consonants, hundreds of related words and verb forms are derived. While very logical to the Arab linguistic mind, it is an extremely difficult barrier for the Westerner to hurdle. Granted, they have many words from similar roots in English, French and Spanish, but the roots *per se,* are not the "meat and potatoes" of the grammatical system.

Classical Arabic, the language of the Quran, is used today occasionally in writing and rarely in speech (Wordsworth 1999 : 99). Some of the *'Ulama* of Islam have even counted the total number of the alphabetic letters which are contained in the Holy Quran and have said :

> The letter "Alif" (the first Arabic alphabetic letter) has occured 48940 times; the letter "Ba'a" (the second Arabic alphabetic letter) has occurred 11420 times; and the letter "Ta'a" (the third alphabetic letter) has occurred 1404 times; and so on. They have reckoned the total number of dots used in the Holy Quran and recorded them as 1520030 in number (*Tehran Times* 10 : Feb : 88 : 6).

Inspite of great sincerity and seriousness to compile the Quran Michael Cook and Patricia Crone find the Quran , strikingly lacking in overall structure, frequently obscure and inconsequential in both language and content perfunctory in its liking of disparate materials and given to the repetition of whole passages in variant versions. On this basis, it can be argued that the book is the product of a belated and imperfect editing of materials from a plurality of traditions (1977 : 18).

Ibn Warraq, too was confused with the structure of the Quran and was sorry to say : "My idea is that the Quran is a kind of cocktail of texts that were not all understood even at the time of Muhammad. Many of them may even be a hundred years older than Islam itself. The Quran claims for itself that it is 'mubeen', or clear. But (contrary to popular belief) if you look at it, you will notice that every fifth sentence or so simply does not make sense... the fact is that a fifth of the Quranic text is just incomprehensible. If the Quran is not comprehensible, if it can't even be understood in Arabic, then it's not translatable into any language. That is why Muslims are afraid. Since the Quran claims repeatedly to be clear but is not--

there is an obvious and serious contradiction. Something else must be going on" (1995 : 739-744).

Abdallah Abd al-Fadi explains the inner structure of the language of the Quran to show how it is a highly inflected language that assigns the role or function of a word according to its case ending, not according to its position in a sentence. The case endings of words are, therefore, very important in understanding a given text or phrase, and if these case endings are confused or jumbled, the reader will not be able to grasp the meaning. The cases in Arabic are : the nominative, the accusative, the genitive and the apocopate. The nominative case is the case of the subject or predicate. The accusative case is the case of the object or of any noun that directly follows an accusative particle, like inna or its "sister particles", or any noun that comes after *kana* or its "sister verbs". What we may call with a bit of license the genitive case, or more descriptively, the construct case, is the case of the second term of an *idafa* (addition) construction. Verbs can be put in the apocopate form in Arabic, which results in the loss of a vowel, when they are preceded by certain particles or when they are in a subjunctive or conditional clause. The first part in such a clause is called the *protasis*, and the second is called the *apodosis*.

Another aspect of Arabic is the consistent agreement of gender and number between the nominal and verbal subject and the predicate, between the noun and the adjective that qualifies it, and between the verb and the noun that carries out the action (the agent) [n.d. 173].

Out of modesty or expressing his innocence Muhammad himself admits that he was *Ummi* or illiterate. If we accept his statement true we have to admit that because he was illiterate he was supposed to make mistakes while re-speaking the Quran. But how could Allah dictate such grammatically erroneous verses to Muhammad ? Sometimes Allah refers to himself in third person singular (He), then shifts to first person plural (We), and sometimes to first person singular (I and Me). We will find these kinds of errors in the entire Quran. Quoting a prominent Islamic scholar, M.A.S Abdel Haleem; Sujit Das affirms the most common type of shifting is from 3rd to 1st person over 140 instances, then 1st to 3rd person is the second largest nearly 100 instances, 3rd to 2nd person nearly 60 instances and 2nd to 3rd person about 30 instances (2010 : 153). Here are a few grammatical errors in the Quran quoted from Abd al-Fadi, a great scholar of Arabi as well as the Holy Quran :

A Nominative Noun that should be Accusative
275. We read in Sura al-Ma'ida 5 : 69 : "Surely they that believe, and those of Jewry, and the Sabaeans..."

إِنَّ الَّذِينَ آمَنُوا وَالَّذِينَ هَادُوا وَالصَّابِئُونَ

This verse in the original Arabic has the word for Sabaeans *(Sabi'un)* in the nominative, but it ought to be in the accusative because it is added to all the previous nouns that are accusative themselves as a result of following *inna*. Thus the word for Sabaeans should have been *Sabi'ina*, which appears in Suras al-Baqara 2 : 62 and al-Hajj 22 : 17.

The Subject is Incorrectly Accusative
276. We read in Sura al-Baqara 2: 124 : "My covenant shall not reach the evildoers."

قَالَ لَا يَنَالُ عَهْدِي الظَّالِمِينَ

This wrong and awkward translation is in fact a result of an unbelievable grammatical mistake in the Arabic Qur'an. The Qur'an meant to say, "The evildoers shall not attain to my covenant, "but since the word *al-Zalimin* ("the evildoers") appears in the accusative rather than the correct nominative, the translator ended up saying that the covenant does not reach the evildoers, an image that is very foreign to the Arabic mind. In fact, the Quran should have simply said-*Al-zalimun*, and the problem would have been solved !

A Feminine Subject with a Masculine Predicate
277. We read in Sura al- A 'raf 7 : 56: "Surely the mercy of God is nigh..."

اِنَّ رَحْمَتَ ۖ اللّٰهِ قَرِيبٌ مِنَ الْمُحْسِنِينَ

In this verse, the Arabic for "nigh" is *qaribun*. This predicate is masculine while the subject *rahmah* ("mercy") is feminine. Had the Quran preserved the agreement between the subject and the predicate, it would say *qaribatun*.

A Wrong Gender and Incorrect use of Plural
278. We read in Sura al-A'raf 7 : 160 : "And We cut them up into twelve tribes, nations."

اِنَّ رَحْمَتَ ۖ اللّٰهِ قَرِيبٌ مِنَ الْمُحْسِنِينَ

The Arabic rendering of this verse reads : *"Wa qatta'nahum ithnatay 'ashrata asbatan."* There are two grammatical errors in this sentence; the first is the feminine number *ithnatay 'ashrata*, and the second is the plural noun *asbatan*. The word "tribe" is masculine and requires a masquline number; also, a noun used in conjunction with a number above ten should be singular. Therefore the Quran should have said : *"Ithnay 'ashra sibtan."*

An Incorrect Plural Verb and Pronoun
279. We read in Sura al-Hajj 22 : 19 : "These are two disputants who have disputed concerning their Lord."

اِنَّ رَحْمَتَ ۖ اللّٰهِ قَرِيبٌ مِنَ الْمُحْسِنِينَ

This sentence reads thus in Arabic : *"Hadsan khasman ikhtasamu fi rabbihim."* The verb *ikhtasamu* ("disputed") is plural, and the possessive pronoun in the word *rabbihim* refers also to a plural antecedent. The Quran ought to have attached a dual ending to the verb and a dual possessive pronoun to the word *rabb*. The sentence should be : *"Hadsan Khasman ikhtasama fi rabbihima."*

A Relative Pronoun in a Wrong Singular Form
280. We read in Sura al-Tawba 9 : 69 : "You have plunged as they plunged."

وَخُضْتُمْ كَالَّذِي خَاضُوا

The Arabic relative pronoun *alladhi*, unlike our English "who" or "that", is subject to declension. That means it does not remain the same with every noun it refers to. It can receive a plural or a dual ending. The word "as" in this verse is actually the translation of the relative pronoun *alladhi* in the singular form. It should have been in the plural form since it refers to a plural pronoun. Thus the Arabic should read : *"Khudhtum kalladhina (instead of al-ladhi) khadhu."*

A Verb is Apocopate instead of Accusative
281.We read in Sura al-Munafiqun 63 : 10 : "Expend of what We have provided you before that death comes upon one of you and he says, 'O my Lord, If Thou wouldst defer me unto a near term,
so that I may make freewill offering, and so I may become one of the righteous."

وَأَنْفِقُوا مِنْ مَا رَزَقْنَاكُمْ مِنْ قَبْلِ أَنْ يَأْتِيَ أَحَدَكُمُ الْمَوْتُ فَيَقُولَ رَبِّ لَوْلَا أَخَّرْتَنِي إِلَى أَجَلٍ قَرِيبٍ فَأَصَّدَّقَ وَأَكُنْ مِنَ الصَّالِحِينَ

The Arabic for "I may become" in this verse is *akun*, with the medial vowel struck off as though it is apocopated. Actually, it should be in the accusative because it is added to the accusative verb *al- sadaqa* ("make freewill offering"). The correct sentence should be : *"Fa' assadaqa wa akuna* (With a long *u*)..."

A Plural Pronoun refers to a Singular Antecedent

282. We read in Sura al- Baqara 2 : 17 : "The likeness of them is as the likeness a man who has kindled a fire, and when it lit all about him God took away their light."

مَثَلُهُمْ كَمَثَلِ الَّذِي اسْتَوْقَدَ نَارًا فَلَمَّا اضَاءَتْ مَا حَوْلَهُ ذَهَبَ اللَّهُ بِنُورِهِمْ

The Quran ought to have attached a singular possessive pronoun to the singular antecedent "man". Thus the verse should read : "...a man who has kindled a fire... God took away his light."

Accusative Instead of Nominative !

283. We read in Sura al-Nisa' 4 : 162 : "But those of them that are firmly rooted in knowledge, and the believers believing in what has been sent down to thee, and what was sent down *before* thee, that perform the prayer and pay the alms, and those who believe in God and the Last Day-- them We shall surely give a mighty wage."

لَكِنِ الرَّاسِخُونَ فِي الْعِلْمِ مِنْهُمْ وَالْمُؤْمِنُونَ يُؤْمِنُونَ بِمَا أُنْزِلَ إِلَيْكَ وَمَا أُنْزِلَ مِنْ قَبْلِكَ وَالْمُقِيمِينَ الصَّلَاةَ وَالْمُؤْتُونَ الزَّكَاةَ وَالْمُؤْمِنُونَ بِاللَّهِ وَالْيَوْمِ الْآخِرِ أُولَئِكَ سَنُؤْتِيهِمْ أَجْرًا عَظِيمًا

The Arabic word for "perform the prayer" is *al-muqimina*. The word is put in the accusative for no legitimate reason. It should have been *al-muqimuna*, for it is added to the nominative words that preceded it, namely *al-rasikhuna* and *al-mu'minuna*, and should agree also with the nominative ones coming after it, namely *al-mu'tuna* and *al-mu'minuna*.

A Governed Genetive Noun is Accusative !

284. We read in Sura Hud 11: 10 : "But if We let him taste prosperity after hardship that has visited him, he will say, 'The evils have gone from me'; behold, he is joyous, boastful."

وَلَئِنْ اذَقْنَاهُ نَعْمَاء بَعْدَ ضَرَّاء مَسَّتْهُ لَيَقُولَنَّ ذَهَبَ السَّيِّءَاتُ عَنِّي انَّهُ لَفَرِحٌ فَخُورٌ

In Arabic, nouns coming after *ba'da* (meaning "after") are supposed to be in an *idafa* construct (addition construct), and should have a *kasra* (an *i* vowel) at the end as a case indicator if they are singular or feminine. But in this verse the word *dharra'a* that comes after *ba'da* has a *fatha* (an *a* vowel) instead, as though the word is accusative ! The word should have been spelled *darra'* !

An Incorrect Plural of Multitude

285. We read in Sura al-Baqara 2: 80 : "The fire shall not touch us save a number of days."

لَنْ تَمَسَّنَا النَّارُ إِلَّا ايَّامًا مَعْدُودَةً

The Arabic reads : "...*illa ayyaman ma'duda*." In the Arabic language there is a feature that is unique, namely the plural of multitude (which refers to a great number of things or people) and the plural of paucity (which refers to a small number of things or people). The words in this verse were uttered by common folk who wanted to say that the days of their chastisement were numbered and few. Therefore the Quran should have used *ma 'dudat*, which is the plural of paucity, rather than *ma 'duda*, which is a plural of multitude.

An Incorrect Plural of Paucity

286. We read in Sura al-Baqara 2 : 183, 184 : "O believers, prescribed for you is the Fast, even as it was prescribed for those that were before you-- haply you will be godfearing-- for days numbered."

كُتِبَ عَلَى الَّذِينَ مِنْ قَبْلِكُمْ لَعَلَّكُمْ تَتَّقُونَ
ايَّامًا مَعْدُودَت

The Arabic for "days numbered" is *ayyaman ma'dudat*, which is a plural of paucity. The number of days the Muslims fast in Ramadan, however, is thirty days, which requires a plural of multitude. These words should have been *ayyaman ma'duda*.

A Wrong Plural Ending

287. We read in Sura al-Saffat 37: 123-130-132 : "Elias too was one of the Envoys...Peace be upon Elias."

وَإِنَّ إِلْيَاسَ لَمِنْ الْمُرْسَلِينَ
سَلَّمٌ عَلَى إِلْ يَاسِينَ
إِنَّهُ مِنْ عِبَادِنَا الْمُؤْمِنِينَ

The Arabic Quran has two spellings for Elias in this passage. The one in the beginning of the quotation is *Ilyas*, while the other is *Ilyasin*, as if it were plural ! In fact, the author of the Quran was so fond of rhyme that he often sacrificed the rules of grammar for the sake of it. He said in Sura al-Tin 95 : 1-3 : "By the fig and the olive and the Mount Sinai and this land secure." In Arabic, he changed the word for Sinai (sina') to its plural form (sinin) for the same reason !

A Noun in Place of an Adjective

288. We read in Sura al-Baqara 2 : 177 : "It is not piety that you turn your faces to the East and to the West. True piety is this : to believe in God and the Last Day."

لَيْسَ الْبِرَّ انْ تُوَلُّوا وُجُوهَكُمْ قِبَلَ الْمَشْرِقِ وَالْمَغْرِبِ وَلَكِنَّ الْبِرَّ مَنْ ءامَنَ بِاللَّهِ وَالْيَوْمِ الْاخِرِ
وَالْمَلَئِكَةِ وَالْكِتَبِ وَالنَّبِيِّنَ

A more precise translation of the last part of this verse is : "But piety is he who believes in God and the Last Day." In Arabic there are two similar words, namely *birr* and *barr*. The first means "Piety", while the second means "pious". So in order to correct the verse, we think it more accurate to say, "...But pious is he who believes in God and the Last Day."

Accusative Instead of Nominative

289. We read in Sura al-Baqara 2 : 177 : "And they who fulfil their covenant when they have engaged in a covenant, and endure with fortitude misfortune, hardship and peril."

وَالْمُوفُونَ بِعَهْدِهِمْ إِذَا عَهَدُوا وَالصَّبِرِينَ فِي الْبَأْسَاءِ وَالضَّرَّاءِ وَحِينَ الْبَأْسِ

The Arabic for "and endure" is *wa al-sabirin*, which is a plural noun added to "and they who fulfil" *(wa al-mufuna)*. But it is in the accusative, c ontrary to the rules of grammar. It should have been *al-sabirun*-just as nominative as *al-mufuna*.

An Incorrect Tense

290. We read in Sura Al Imran 3 : 59 : "Truly, the likeness of Jesus, in God's sight is as Adam's likeness; He created him of dust, then said He unto him, 'Be', and he was."

إِنَّ مَثَلَ عِيسَى عِنْدَ اللَّهِ كَمَثَلِ ءادَمَ خَلَقَهُ مِنْ تُرَابٍ ثُمَّ قَالَ لَهُ كُنْ فَيَكُونُ

The Arabic of this verse reads : "...then said he unto him, 'Be', and he is." Of course the context requires the past tense-- not the present tense-- as indeed the translator understood it.

A Conditional Clause with no Apodosis

291. We read in Sura Yusuf 12 : 15 : "So when they went with him, and agreed to put him in the bottom of the well, and We revealed to him, 'Thou shalt tell of this their doing when they were unaware."

فَلَمَّا ذَهَبُوا بِهِ وَاجْمَعُوا انْ يَجْعَلُوهُ فِي غَيَبَتِ الْجُبِّ وَاوْحَيْنَا اِلَيْهِ لَتُنَبِّئَنَّهُمْ بِامْرِهِمْ هَذَا وَهُمْ لَا يَشْعُرُونَ

Where is the apodosis (the consequence clause of a conditional sentence) of the sentence ? Actually, if we omit the "and" that comes before "We revealed", the sentence would be straightened out !

The Meaning is Obscured by Odd Structure

292. We read in Sura al-Fath 48 : 8,9: "Surely We have sent thee as a witness, good tidings to bear, and warning, that you may believe in God and His Messenger and succour Him, and reverence Him, and that you may give Him glory at the dawn and in the evening."

إِنَّا أَرْسَلْنَاكَ شَهِدًا وَمُبَشِّرًا وَنَذِيرًا
لِتُؤْمِنُوا بِاللَّهِ وَرَسُولِهِ وَتُعَزِّرُوهُ وَتُوَقِّرُوهُ وَتُسَبِّحُوهُ بُكْرَةً وَأَصِيلًا

This sentence is disrupted because of a sudden shift from addressing Muhammad to addressing other people. Apart from this, the accusative pronoun in "succour Him, and reverence Him" refers, beyond doubt, to Muhammad, who was mentioned earlier, not to God as the English translator understood it. But "give Him glory" refers to God. The entire verse is chaotic. The reader cannot be expected to understand its true meaning from the arrangement of words. It is *Kufr* ("unbelief") to say "and succour Him, and reverence Him, and that you may give Him glory at the dawn and in the evening" about Muhammad, since glory should be given to God alone. It is also *kufr* to make such a statement with reference to God, since God almighty is not in need for succour or help !

A Diptote Receives the Nunnation

293. We read in Sura al-Insan 76 : 15 : "And there shall be passed around vessels of silver, and goblets of crystal."

وَيُطَافُ عَلَيْهِمْ بِءانِيَةٍ مِنْ فِضَّةٍ وَأَكْوَابٍ كَانَتْ قَوَارِيرَا

The Arabic word *qawariran* which was translated as "crystal" is in fact a diptote; that is, it has two cases only and cannot receive the final *n* that distinguishes the triptotes. But the Qur'an seems to have been unaware of this grammatical rule, or rather to have done violence to it, to maintain the rhyme !

The same error occurs in verse 4 of the same sura (al-Insan), where we read : "Surely We have prepared for the unbelievers chains, fetters, and a Blaze." Here the Arabic word for chains *(salasilan)* is given a final *n* in violation of the same rule.

A Predicate with an Incorrect Gender

294. We read in Sura al-Shura 42 : 17 : "God it is He who sent down the Book with the truth, and also the Balance. And what shall make thee know ? Haply the hour is nigh."

اللّٰهُ الَّذِي أَنْزَلَ الْكِتٰبَ بِالْحَقِّ وَالْمِيزَانَ وَمَا يُدْرِيكَ لَعَلَّ السَّاعَةَ قَرِيبٌ

The last part of this verse in Arabic is : *la 'alla al-sa' ata qaribun*. There is no gender agreement between *al-sa'ata* ("hour") which is a feminine subject, and *qaribun* ("nigh") which is a masculine predicate !

Pointing out the Obvious

295. We read in Sura al-Baqara 2 : 196 : "Or if he finds none, then a fast of three days in the Pilgrimage, and of seven when you return, that is ten completely."

مِنَ الْهَدْيِ فَمَنْ لَمْ يَجِدْ فَصِيَامُ ثَلٰثَةِ أَيَّامٍ فِي الْحَجِّ وَسَبْعَةٍ إِذَا رَجَعْتُمْ تِلْكَ عَشَرَةٌ كَامِلَةٌ

There was no need to add "completely" in this verse, for who would think that three and seven make nine ?

A Sudden Transition in Person

296. We read in Sura Yunis 10: 22 : "And when you are in the ship-and the ships run with them with a fair breeze, and they rejoice in it, there comes upon them a strong wind."

حَتّٰى اِذَا كُنْتُمْ فِي الْفُلْكِ وَجَرَيْنَ بِهِمْ بِرِيحٍ طَيِّبَةٍ وَفَرِحُوا بِهَا جَاءَتْهَا رِيحٌ عَاصِفٌ

This sudden transition from the second person to the third person is not good grammar; it would have been preferable to maintain the second person throughout the entire text.

A Singular Pronoun instead of a Dual One

297. We read in Sura al-Tawba 9: 62 : "But God and His Messenger-- more right is it they should please Him."

وَاللّٰهُ وَرَسُولُهُ أَحَقُّ أَنْ يُرْضُوهُ

Why wasn't the pronoun referring to God put in the dual form, since in this verse both God and the Messenger are to be pleased ?

A Plural Noun used in Place of a Dual One

298. We read in Sura al-Tahrim 66: 4 : "If you two repent to God, yet your hearts are inclined."

إِنْ تَتُوبَا إِلَى اللّٰهِ فَقَدْ صَغَتْ قُلُوبُكُمَا

Al-Baidawi says that Hafsa and 'Aisha were being addressed with this verse. But in spite of this, the Arabic for "your hearts" *(qulubukuma)* is in the plural form ! Can two people have more than two hearts ? (These above 24 Grammatical errors are Quoted exactly from al-Fadi 1997 : 174-185).

Is the Holy Quran Badly edited Scripture ?

299. Is it not a fact that Quran, the last text of Allah, is not arranged chronologically, or subjectwise or themewise ? Therefore it is toilsome and wearisome, and a mass of confusions, contradictions and inconsistencies.

Historian Edward Gibbon has described the Quran as "an incoherent rhapsody of fable, and precept, and declamation, which sometimes crawls in the dust, and sometimes is lost in the clouds" (1941, Vol .1 : 365).

The German scholar Salomon Reinach rightly stated : From the literary point of view, the Quran has little merit. Declamation, repetition, puerility, a lack of logic and coherence strike the unprepared reader at every turn. It is humiliating to the human intellect to think that this mediocre literature has been the subject of innumerable commentaries, and that millions of men are still wasting time in absorbing it (1932 : 176).

Even the Muslim scholar Ali Dashti laments the literary defects of the Quran : "Unfortunately the Quran was badly edited and its contents are very obtusely arranged. All students of the Quran wonder why the editors did not use the natural and logical method of ordering by date of revelation, as in' Ali b. Abi Taleb's lost copy of the text" (1985 : 28).

Mc Clintock and Strong's *Encyclopaedia* concludes : "The matter of the Koran is exceedingly incoherent and sententious, the book evidently being without any logical order of thought either as a whole or in its parts. This agrees with the desultory and incidental

Displacement in Order in the Quran

300. When in the Quran Allah is described : "Say : 'He is Allah, One, Allah, the Everlasting Refuge, who has not begotten, and has not been begotten, and equal to Him is not any one" (112 : 1-3).

Don't you find a displacement of order to say "Who has not begotten, and has not been begotten."; for it is impossible to beget before one has been begotten first ?

If we think Allah is One and Everlasting how can He be confined to a specific time ? "Who has not begotten", can be paraphrased as "does not beget." This phrase suggests the Universal nature of God and it includes all possible tenses.

In the *Comments on Quranic Verses* (1994 : 266) it is suggested that : the most important principles of eloquence in Arabic to avoid any vague expressions or confused ideas that would render the text difficult for the reader to understand. On this basis, our simple paraphrase proves to be more eloquent and accurate !... this sura in its corrected form, for God, literally speaking, was not born and does not give birth ! To rephrase the *sura* in the following order :

"Say : 'He is God, One, God, the Everlasting Refuge, who has not been begotten, and does not beget, and equal to Him is not anyone."

Repetitive Sentences in the Quran

301. Is it not a fact that in the Quran there are many repetitions which create irritation instead of being eloquent ? Take for example the Sura 55 : 16. The question : "Then which of the favours of your Lord will ye deny ?" is repeated 29 times. These verses were : 16, 18, 21, 23, 28, 30, 32, 34, 36, 38, 40, 42, 45, 47, 49, 51, 53, 55, 57, 59, 61, 63, 65, 67, 69, 71, 73, 75 and 77. Why do these verses ask the same questions and what for it is repeated is known to Allah only.

Prefixed Letter and Meaning

302. Why does God confuse when He mentions some hidden meaning of the signifying letters that prefix some suras ? For instance, the letter *N* that prefixes Sura 68 stands for nun means, 'fish', signifing the sea-monster Behemoth, the letter *Q* prefixed to Sura 50 stands for Qaf, the ring of mountains that encircles the earth. Thirteen of the twenty-nine suras mentioned begin with the letters *AL*, out of these, six begin with *ALM*, five with *ALR*, and one each with *ALMS* and *ALMR* ? Ok, we understand the letters *AL* may signify *Al*, 'God', with the name of a pagan deity concealed in the remaining letters. The Mesopotamian sun-god Sin, worshipped in Arabia as far as the Hadramaut, may be hidden in the letters that head Sura 36, consisting of the letters *YS*, which in Arabic read *Ya Sin*. Has it not been interpreted as *'Ya insan'*, meaning 'O man !', but it might simply be read as an invocation to the sun-god, 'O sin !' (Walker 1999 : 155-156).

Problems in Spellings in the Quran

303. Is it not a fact that the earliest form of Arabic writing was deficient in many ways and the earliest copies of the Quran had many problems of spellings, vowelization and their meaning which led to discrepant readings and conflicting interpretations ?

Are Quran, Sura and Aya Foreign Words ?

304. Is not the "Quran" *Sura* (the portion of scripture), *aya* (sign) borrowed from the Syrian Christians (Walker 1999 : 195) ?

Foreign Words in Quran

305. Is it a fact that the Quran was not written in pure and clear Arabic (26 : 193-195), though its purpose was to make it easy, in Arabic in order that they may give heed (44 : 58) ? Mutazili writer and master of Arabic prose Amr ibn Bahr, known as al-Jahiz, the "goggle eyed" has said that the Quran represents good-writing but not the perfection of Arabic (Walker 1999 : 162) ? If it is in pure Arabic why are there many foreign words in the Quran ? This is a brief list :

Persian words with Quranic Reference

Abariq (ewers)	56 : 18
Ara'ik (couches)	18 : 31
Ghassaqan (pus)	78 : 25
Istahraq (brocade)	18 : 31 (Istabar)
Jinn (spirit)	51 : 56
Sijjil (baked clay)	105 : 4
Suradiq (Pavilion)	18 : 29

Assyrian Word

Abraham	4 : 4

Akkadian Word

Adam	2 : 34

Hebrew Word

Allah	1 : 1 (Hebrew *Eloah* and Syriac *Ilaha*
Aaman (believe)	also in Aramaic
Harb (rabbi)	9 : 31 (Haver)
Jahannam (Gehenna)	8 : 36 (Gey Hinnom)
Ma'un (charity)	107 : 7
Sabt (sabbath)	27 : 124
Tawrat (Torah)	3 : 50

Syric Words

'Adn	9 : 72
Fir'awn (pharaoh)	73 : 15
Salaat (Prayer)	
Sura	9 : 124
Taghut (idols)	2 : 257 (Teghutha)

Zakat (freewill offering)	2 : 110 (zkhutha)

Pahlavi Words

Firdaws (paradise)	18 : 107
Huri	55 : 72
Maqalid (keys)	39 : 63
Zanjabil (ginger)	76 : 17 (also in Sanskrit)

Aramaic Words

Harut	2 : 102
Marut	2 : 102
Sakina (shekinah)	2 : 248

Greek Words

Al-Kauther (Katharis)-Abundance (Sura 8)
Iblis (Devil)
Injil (Gospel) means evangelion 3 : 48
Zelqarnain (Alexander the Great) (18 : 83 ff; 5 : 86)

Ethiopian Word

Mishkat (niche)	24 : 35

Latin Word

Sirat (path)	1 : 4

Egyptian Word

Tabut (ark)	2 : 247

Sanskrit Words

Zanjabil (ginger)	76 : 17
Qalam (Kalam, Pen)	
Kafur (Kapur, comphor)	
Feel (peel, elephant)	
Fund (Vrind, troop)	

Disorder in the Quran's Arrangement

306. When Muhammad himself could not arrange 114 suras of the Quran, why to blame the editors that they have kept some Meccan suras in Medina and vice versa; why is it that the subject changes at times abruptly and except for the first sura, why the suras are arranged with the longest at the beginning and the shortest at the end ?

As a reader of the Quran don't you feel it is a jumble of disjointed material, without order, continuity or unity of any kind and absolute absence of chronology?

13 - Authenticity of Hadiths

After the death of Prophet Muhammad the Muslims soon turned to the facts of his life. To imitate his life style as a model they wanted to know every detail of his life. The holy Quran was not enough therefore, a few scholars started collecting information about his acts and words which was later called *Hadith* or the traditions about Muhammad.

The authors collected materials on Muhammad from different sources. These sources are called *Sira* (biography).

The early sources of Islam and the biography of Prophet Muhammad rest on Ibn Ishaq's *Sira* (biography) written within 200 years of the Prophet's death. The Sira's chronological presentation is similar in style to Christian Gospels. His work contains too much information that is devastatingly unfavorable to the Prophet (Das 1010: 7).

Next to *Sira, al-Tabari* is a store house of information. Al-Tabari a Persian historian, a commentator of Quran, collected oral tradition and huge materials on Muhammad like the works of Abu Miknaf, al-wiquid, Ibn sa'd and Ibn Ishaq.

No more we get the book of Ibn Ishaq in original except an abridged work which survives in Ibn Hisham and al-Tabari (Das 1010 : 9).

The collection of Hadith involved travelling and meeting the people who were contemporary and closely related to the Prophet.

Both the Quran and the Hadith (Sunna) are regarded as works of revelation, though their mode of expression differs. If the Quran is the recited revelation by the angel Gabriel to Muhammad, the Hadith are unrecited revelations of the life and deeds of the Prophet. The Hadith is the Quran in action, the Quran provides the text the Hadiths the context.

In the Hadiths every word is dropped from the lips of the Prophet, "every nod or shake" of his head was important and no selection of actions was done. Therefore everything irrespective of good or bad incidents of Prophet's life is reflected in the Hadiths.

The word Hadith is derived from the Arabic root "Hdth" which means "to happen", or "to tell the happenings." It includes the Prophet's style of dressing, his appearance, manner of standing, sitting, walking and speaking and the way he washed his hands, ate his food, tied his turban etc.

These are known as the six *sahih* (sound) Books. These six books are well documented. It speaks in the first person such as : It was related to me by A, on the authority of B, on the Authority of C, on the authority of D, from E. A companion of Muhammad must say the events. These chain of names must come to prove the event for its authenticity.

Out of quite a large number of Hadiths, most Muslim theologians accept only six Hadiths of which two collections are most important and most often cited as authentic. They are al-Bukhari and Sahih Muslim.

Matters Disgraceful to Discuss

307. Why did Ibn Hisham while abridging Ibn Ishaq's work omit things which Ishaq recorded in his book ? In the earliest biography of Prophet Muhammad Hisham was apologetic while writing "I have omitted things which are disgraceful to discuss and matters which would distress certain people" (Guillaum 1955 : 691). Does it not mean that many unpleasant events of the Prophet are not worth mentioning?

What is in Bukhari ?

308. Is it not a fact that Bukhari (870) examined 600, 000 traditions out of which he chose some 7, 275 as genuine ? Recent critics cut this number down still further. In fact Bukhari's interest was in law so he made the framework of his collection and fitted the legal code into it. Does he not repeat one matter into different headings while for some sections he could find no tradition at all ? And were those matter not, in addition to some of the incidents of Muhammad's life and his sayings, bits of folklore, quotations and adaptation from the Bible and later history (Tritton 1951 : 32) ?

Are Sa'd and Tabari Historical ?
309. Did not Bukhari and Muslim reject 90% of the materials collected by the historians such as Sa'd and Tabari, because they collected whatever they heard about the prophet, without any verification (Zakaria 1991 : 27) ?

Unbelievable Portions in Hadith
310. Did not the Umayyad dynasty, who were not approved by the pious, invent traditions which inculcated unquestioning obedience to the government to counteract the teaching of the pious because the pious insisted that it is God alone who should be obeyed ?

Muhammad said, 'Who obeys me, obeys God; who obeys the *imam*, obeys me; who does not obey me, does not obey God; who does not obey the *imam*, does not obey me.'

Do not curse rulers; if they do justice, reward is theirs and it is yours to be grateful; if they do wrong, guilt is theirs and it is yours to be patient.

If a crop-eared Abyssinian slave is made ruler over you, obey him.

Pray behind any *imam* (Tritton 1951 : 33).

The last sentence, besides being political, condemns the censoriousness to which zealots inside and outside Islam are prone.

Two Dots change the History
311. Is it not a fact that Muhammad had an estate at Fadak, which, on his death, both his family and the state claimed ? Does not one tradition say, "A prophet has no heirs; what he leaves is made into a charitable trust ?" The political meaning is that the descendants of 'Ali have no right to the throne for this right is determined by the community. Did not the Shi'a alter the text, two dots below one letter instead of one dot above, so that it read, "What we have left as a charitable trust cannot be inherited (but everything else can)"; thus getting support for their legitimate claims (Tritton 1951 : 32-33) ?

Only 1% Hadith is True
312. Is not it a fact that there are about 500,000 Hadiths which are, beside the Quran, the second source of the Sharia ? And only 4, 800 of these are considered to be genuine ? Does this not mean that only 1% of all Hadiths is true and the rest are fabricated lies (al-Masih 1996 : 31) ?

14- Contradictions Within

If God is one and his scriptures are one there should not be any contradiction in his words and work, His scriptures should agree with each other. But it is not so. The Universal God Allah in one place says there is no change in his words (10 :64;

18 : 27) but he changes his words and substitutes one revelation for another (18 : 101). There are as many as thousands of contradictions in the Holy Quran.

How can something be both being and nonbeing at the same time. Aristotle remarked : It is impossible for some quality to exist and not to exist at the same time and in the same manner. These contradictions in the Holy Quran can be solved if we interpret his words as man's words to God. Let us try to interpret them sincerely.

Can there be any change in the Words of Allah

313. What do we believe there is no change in the words of Allah (10 : 64 ; 18 : 27) or He will substitute one revelation for another (18 : 101). This kind of unbelievable number of gross contradictions and absurdities are there in the Holy Quran.

Is Indecency Permitted ?

314. Allah does not command indecency (7 : 28) or He allows indecency (17 : 16) ?

Who will be Saved ?

315. Muslims and others will be saved (5 : 69) or Muslims only will be saved (3 : 85) ?

Creation through Six or Eight Days ?

316. Is not the Quran contradicting with the Bible on creation-- one says six days (*Gn* 1 : 31) the other says eight days (4 days + 2 days + 2 days = 8 days) (41 : 9-12) ?

Earth created on the Third or the Fifth Day ?

317. Whether earth was created on the third day (*Gn* 1) or it took two days to be created and to spread out it took two more days (41 : 9-11) ?

How Long is One Day ?

318. One day for Allah is thousand years (32 : 5) or fifty thousand years (70 : 4) ?

Allah confused Biblical Chronology

319. Is it not a fact that Allah confused God's chronological order, and jumbled together the names by keeping David and Solomon before Job, Joseph, Moses and Aaron ? Why are Zechariah, John and Jesus mentioned before Elias ? Why is Ishmael mentioned after Isaac, Jacob, David, Solomon, Job, Joseph, Moses, Aaron, Zechariah, John, Jesus and Elias ? Why are Elisha and Jonah mentioned before Lot (6 : 84 : 86) ?

The chronological order is confused and topsy turvied in the Quran. Ibrahim, his nephew Lot, his two grandsons Ishmael and Isaac, his great grandson Jacob and his great great grandson Joseph lived around 2000 BC, Moses and Aaron lived around 1300 BC David and his son Solomon came after them. Elias (or Elijah) and his disciple Elisha lived during the era of the Kingdom of Israel (between 1004-926 BC). Jonah is the last Old Testament prophet mentioned in the Quranic verse, when, in fact, Zechariah, John the Baptist and Jesus followed him as prophets in the New Testament era (Abd al-Fadi n.d. 50-51).

Historical Chronology and the Quran

320. Is it not a very serious charge against the integrity of the Quran that the historical chronology is not maintained in this book ? As if Nimrod and Ibrahim, Haman and Moses, Mary and Aaron were living in the same place and same time, even the events like flood and Moses, the tower of Babel and Pharoah happened at the same time ?

God could change the History

321. Once Pharaoh said to Haman : 'Council, I know not that you have any god but me. Kindle me, Haman, a fire upon the clay, and make me a tower, that I may mount up to Moses' god; for I think that he is one of the liars (28 : 38).

Again Pharaoh said, "Haman, build for me a tower, that haply so I may reach the cords" (40 : 36).

Does the Quran not say that Haman was Pharaoh's minister, while history tells that Haman was the minister of King Ahasuerus (486-465 BC), and that there is a thousand years' difference between them ! Besides, Pharaoh was king of Egypt (1991-1778 BC) while Haman served in the Persian Empire ! Being so separated from one another by distance and time, how could Haman have been a minister to Pharaoh ?

In the book of Esther, Haman was the villain, who plots to massacre the Jews and was eventually hanged on the gallows that he had prepared for Mordecai ?

Historical Mistake on Golden Calf

322. Is it not a historical mistake to tell that the Jews made the golden calf in the wilderness at the suggestion of the Samaritan (20 : 88, 96) because Torah says that the Samaritan did not come into existence for many centuries, until after the captivity of Israel first by the Assyrians and then by the Babylonians ?

Muhammad Mis-Quotes Moses

323. Is it not a fact that like Quran, the Hadith puts speeches into the mouths of Noah, Moses and Jesus, which they could not have spoken because it is different from the vocabulary and the doctrines they preached (*Buk* 1 : 74, 78, 124) ?

The 70 people whom Moses chose are those who are being spoken of here when they said : "O Moses ! We shall never believe in you until we see Allah plainly (2 : 55). In another place when Rafia b. Khuzaima asked Muhammad : "If you are, as you claim, an apostle of Allah, then ask Allah to speak that we might hear his words, or perform a sign that we might believe in you." Muhammad replied : "The Jews asked Moses to show them Allah plainly, they were seized for their presumption, by thunder and lightning (4 : 153). Was Muhammad not avoiding the question by misquoting the Torah ? According to Torah they asked Moses to speak to God and to allow them to stand at a distance, lest they die (Ex 20 : 18-21).

Ibrahim's Father Azar or Terah ?

324. Was Ibrahim's father Azar (6 : 74) or Terah (*Gn* 11 : 27) ?

Did Ibrahim ever live in Mecca ?

325. Is not it a fact that in order to bring Ibrahim into the mainstream of Islam Quran claimed that he lived in Mecca and found the sanctuary of the Black Stone with his son Ishmael (3 : 95-97) ?

If it is not a legend why did the Egyptian scholar Taha Husayn question whether Ibrahim had ever been in Mecca (Guillaume 1983 : 156; Walker 1998 : 16) ? Is there any evidence that Ibrahim and Ishmael had any connection with the region of the Hejaz in general or with Mecca and the Kaaba in particular (Walker 1998 : 16) ?

Is there any archaeological, epigraphic or documentary evidence, that Ibrahim ever set foot in Arabia and let alone built the Kaaba ? The archaeological evidence proved that Ibrahim never lived in Mecca but it is clearly evident that Ibrahim came from the city of Ur, which has been found in Iraq and then moved west to Palestine.

Putting Ibrahim in Mecca is a Mistake

326. Allah says that the first House of worship appointed for men was at Bakka (a variant of Mecca), full of blessing and of guidance for all the worlds. Therein are clear signs the station of Ibrahim... It is the duty of all men towards God to come to the House as pilgrim (3 : 96-97).

If it is so we should know that the heathen built Kaaba for the worship of Saturn and other gods. The Arabs used it as a destination of pilgrimage to venerate their gods. It is a gross mistake to say that the Kaaba was the house of God or the station of Ibrahim. How could the house of idols be identified as the house of God ? As we all know Ibrahim lived in the land of Canaan and never set foot on the Arabian Peninsula. What relationship is there between a Hebrew and the Arabs ? How could a Hebrew who lived in Canaan be a resident of the Hijaz ?

Where is Ibrahim and where is Arab ?

327. Was it not a strategy for Muhammad to bring the Jews to his fold for which he adopted Ibrahim, as the common ancestor of the Jews and the Arabs (4 : 125; 22 : 78) ?

How the Arabs were the Descendants of Ibrahim ?

328. If all the Arabs of the Middle East are the descendants of Ibrahim, what happened to all the Akkadians, Sumerians, Assyrians, Babylonians, Persians, Egyptians, Hittites, etc. who lived before, during, and after Ibrahim ? What happened to all those millions of people who were not Ibrahim's descendants ? Where did they go ?

Ishmael or Isaac ?

329. Is it not historically wrong to state that the son to be sacrificed was Ishmael whereas the commentators like Ibn Omer, Ibn Abbas and Abdulla ibn Ahmad agree with the Biblical version that the son was Isaac (Walker 1998 : 16) ?

Legitimate Son of Ibrahim

330. Is it a fact : "God chose as the best the children of Ishmael, the son of Ibrahim. From Ishmael's descendants, God chose the Quresh (the tribe of Muhammad) as the best of people; from the Quresh, God chose the Banu Hashim (Muhammad's clan) as the best of people, and from the Banu Hashim, God chose Muhammad as the best of all men"... (*Tir* Vol : 2) or are the Jews the descendants of Isaac who was the legitimate son of Ibrahim borne by his wife, Sarah, whereas Ishmael was the son of Hagar, an Egyptian maid-servant of Sarah who was made pregnant by Ibrahim ?

How is Ibrahim the first Muslim ?

331. If Ibrahim was not a Jew, not yet a Christian; but he was an upright Muslim because he joined no gods with Allah (3 : 67), so can you accept the Vedantins as the first Muslims as Vyasha and Sankara never tried to join any god with the God ? Historically how can you connect Ibrahim with the Islam of Muhammad ?

Who is First ?

332. Who was the first to believe ? Ibrahim or Moses (6 : 14 versus 7 : 143) ? Both cannot be First.

Quranic and Biblical Joseph

333. Is not it a fact that sura 12 of Quran tells the story of Joseph which is quite different from the biblical account ?

Was Enoch Idris ?

334. In Quran why did Allah replace the name of Enoch the Prophet (*Gn* 5 : 21-24, *Heb* 11 : 5) as Idris (19 : 56-57) ?

Mistakes about Moses

335. Did Pharoah's wife adopt Moses (28 : 8-9) or Pharoah's daughter (*Ex* 2 : 5) ?
Did Noah's flood take place during Moses' time (7 : 136) ?
Did Haman live in Egypt during the time of Moses and worked for Pharoah's tower of Babel (40 : 37) or he lived in Persia and was in the service of King Ahasuerus (*Esther* 3 : 1-2)?
Was crucifixion in practice at the time of Pharoah (7 : 124) ?

Are Job and Isaac Contemporary ?

336. What has Job got to do with Isaac, the father of Jacob (6 : 84) ? Are they contemporary ?

Was Job a Cruel Husband ?

337. Regarding Job it is said in the Quran (38 : 44) that he takes in his hand a bundle of rushes, and strikes his wife.
How could the pious and patient Job, who endured the loss of children, servants and cattle, get angry with his wife ? The Bible bears witness to his kindness and forbearance, especially with his wife. Wasn't it he who said to her, "You speak as one of the foolish women speaks. Shall we indeed accept good from God, and shall we not accept adversity" (*Job* 2 : 10) ? How could it possibly befit Job to vow to beat his wife a hundred lashes for merely delaying ? Would God really solve the dilemma of Job's failure to fulfil his oath by advising him to take a bundle of rushes with a hundred stalks and strike her once ? How could Job marry Joseph's granddaughter ? Job was a predecessor of both Joseph and Jacob. This story is one of the many Jewish fables told in the Quran as truth.

Change in Quranic Name

338. Is it not a fact that during Muhammad's time Arabic translation of the Bible was not there for which in Quran the man who bought Joseph, Jacob's son, was named Aziz (12 : 21) though he was Potiphar (*Gn.* 37 : 36) ? Can proper noun be changed like Goliath as Jalut, Korah as Karun, Soul as Talut, Enoch as Idris, Ezekiel as Dhu'l-Khifl, John the Baptist as Yahya and Jonah as Yunus ?

Truth about Abrah Stoning Birds
339. Is it a fact that the elephant army of Abrah was defeated by birds dropping stones of baked clay upon them (105) or Abrah's army withdrew their attack on Mecca after smallpox broke out among the troops (Guillaume 1954 : 21) ?

What happened to Pharaoh ?
340. Was Pharaoh saved (10 : 89-92), or did he drown (17 : 102-103; 28 : 40) ?

Samaritan or Aaron who made the Golden Calf ?
341. Did the city of Samaria exist when Israelites came out of Egypt and travelled through Sinai ? Did the Samaritan make a golden calf for Israelites (20 : 85-88) or it was Aaron who made the calf for them ?

Who was Joseph's Father ?
342. If the children of Jacob admitted that their father was a Prophet (4 : 163) how could they contradict him and accuse him of being in error (12 : 8) ?

Not Towa but Hereb is the Holy Land
343. Is it the holy valley of Towa (20 : 12) or Hereb in Sinai (*Ex* 3 : 1-5) where God asked Moses to take his sandals off his feet, because that was a holy ground ?

Contradictory Revelation
344. If Allah reveals the Injit or New Testament to Prophet Jesus (57 : 27), Torah to Prophet Moses (11 : 110; 87 : 19), Zabbur or Psalm to Prophet David (4 : 163) and there is no difference between one another (2 : 136;4 : 163) why did Allah contradict and revised his revelation from time to time ?

Noah led the People into Error
345. How could it be possible for Noah, being a prophet, to ask God to increase the people in error (71 : 24) ? Neither did Noah love error, nor is God the source of error. Bible says that "Noah was a just man, perfect in his generations" (*Gn* 6 : 9), and that he was simply "a preacher of righteousness" (2 *Pet* 2 : 5).

Was Cannan Noah's Son ?
346. Was Canaan Noah's son who refused to embark with him onto the ark and thus drowned (11: 42-43) ? Is it not contradictory to what the Bible says that, Noah had only three sons : Shem, Ham and Japheth, each of whom had a wife. This makes those who embarked in the ark eight in number : Noah and his wife, and his three sons and their wives. Was Canaan even born when the Flood took place ?

Is it not a fact that Canaan was not Noah's but Ham's son who was born after the flood (*Gn* 10 : 1, 6, 15) ?

What Quran says about Mary and her Father ?
347. Did Mary give birth to Jesus under a palm tree (19 : 23) or in a stable (*Lk* 2 : 1-20) ?

Was Mary the mother of Jesus as well as the sister of Moses and Aaron (19 : 28) ?

Was Mary's father Imran (66 : 12) ?

Does not the Quran confuse Moses' father with Mary's father ?

Imran is Moses' and Aaron's father but the Quran by mistake called Jesus' mother the sister of Aaron (19 : 28;3 : 35-36).

Was not Mary, the mother of Jesus, born almost 1, 500 years after Miriam the sister of Aaron ?

Was Zechariah the Guardian of Mary ?

348. Was Zechariah the guardian of Virgin Mary (3 : 37) or the husband of Elizabeth, the cousin of Virgin Mary (*Lk* 1 : 5) ?

Was Mary with her Husband ?

349. Why does the Quran not give us any clue as to why Virgin Mary had withdrawn from her people to an eastern place and taken a veil apart from them, before she received the good news of Christ (19 : 16-21) ? Why would a virgin live by herself, away from her people, bearing in mind that the Quran claims she lived in the Sanctuary under the care of Zechariah contrary to what the Bible claims that Mary lived in Nazareth and was betrothed to Joseph the carpenter (*Lk* 1 : 26-36) ?

Mary was the Daughter of Heli or Amran ?

350. If Virgin Mary was the daughter of Heli (Lk 3 : 23) how come the Quran claims she was the daughter of Amran (Imran) (66 : 12), the father of Prophet Moses, and that she was the sister of Aaron (19 : 27-28) Moses' brother ? Does Mary and Amran, Moses and Aaron belong to the same age or was there not a gap of 1,400 years between Mary and others (Ex 6 : 20) ?

Was Hagar's Situation like Mary's Situation ?

351. Is not it a fact that the Quran (19 : 22-26) confuses between Hagar and Virgin Mary ? Both had different situation . It was Hagar who escaped to the wilderness with Ishmael but not Mary. Allah provided her and her son a spring of water to drink whereas Mary was not in need of water to drink.

Did Moses not know about Crucifixion ?

352. Can you prove that crucifixion by death as a punishment started during the time of Moses in 1500 BC (2 : 124) ?

Was Muhammad in the Beginning ?

353. When asked Muhammad replied that he was made prophet when the body and soul of Adam were still in the making (*Tir* vol. 2) or was the dignity of the messenger thrust on him when he was forty years of age ?

How many Drank that Water ?

354. How many people drank that water which flew out of Muhammad's fingernails into the bowl ?

70 persons (*Buk* 4 : 774) or
80 persons (*Buk* 4 : 775) or
around 300 persons (*Buk* 4 : 772) or
1500 persons (*Buk* 4 : 776; 5 : 473) ?

Is Wine Allowed or Forbidden ?

355. Is wine forbidden (5 : 90) or is it allowed (47 : 15; 83 : 25-26) ?

15- Quran on Trial

To put the Quran on trial, let us see how the Quran begins trial on Zindiq. Their only mistake is that they secretly opposed the dogma of Islam. Special Magistrates were appointed to arrest, imprison, behead or crucify them. Ibn Warraq (2003 : 43-54) and Sujit Das (2010 : 259-263) cited a number of cases here how these Zindiqs faced the trial :

The first person who was executed on the charge of a Zandaqa was Djad Ibn Dirham by the order of Ummayyad caliph in 742 or 743 CE. He denied the Divine attributes of Quran. He also accused Muhammad of lying and denied resurrection. Around 760 CE, another famous Zindiq named Ibn al-Muqaffa was executed for attacking Islam, its Prophet, and its concept of God. He was killed in the most horrible manner--- his limbs were cut off one by one and fed into a blazing fire.

From 786 CE, special magistrates were appointed to pursue the zindiqs. Abu Nuwas, one of the greatest of classical Arabic and Persian poets, was accused of Zandaqa. He was fond of wine. Once he entered a Mosque drunk as ever and when the Imam recited the verse 1 from Sura 109, "*Say ! O you unbelievers...*", Abu Nuwas is said to have cried out "*Here I am*". He was handed over to religious police. He was imprisoned on other occasions as well for insulting Islam.

Zindaqa even penetrated the Hashemite family (The Hashemites trace their ancestry from the great-grandfather of Muhammad, although the definition today mainly refers to the descendants of Muhammad's daughter, Fatimah). Several members of this family were executed or died in prison. Ibn Abi-I-Awja (executed 772 CE) casted doubt on the justice of some of the punishments described in the Quran. He also disbelieved that Islamic pilgrimage was ordered by god.

Bashshar Ibn Burd came from a noble Persian family. He was tortured for glorifying the ancient memories of Iran. He was also disrespectful towards the institution of pilgrimage. On one occasion, he left for the pilgrimage but stopped on the way and spent his time drinking. As the pilgrims were returning, he joined them and pretended on arrival to have completed the entire pilgrimage. He also ridiculed the Quran many times with his satires and denied resurrection.

Hammad Ajrad who was executed in 777 CE wrote some verses, which were parody of Quran and preferred those verses over Quranic verses during the prayer.

One of the greatest poets in Arabic language was Al-Mutanabi (in Arabic, one who pretends to be a Prophet). He rejected Muslim religious dogmas regarding it as spiritual instruments of oppression. He also began revolutionary propaganda and claimed to be a Prophet with a new Quran. He was imprisoned.

Ibn al-Rawandi (827-911) was an early skeptic of Islam and a critic of religion in general. In his early days he was a Mutazilite scholar but after rejecting the Mutazilite doctrine he remained in Shi'a Islam for a brief period of time and later rejected Islam completely. According to him, the Quran, far from being a miracle and inimitable, is an inferior work from literary point of view, since it is neither clear or comprehensible, nor of any practical value and certainly not a revealed book.

Perhaps the greatest freethinker in the whole of Islam was Muhammad Ibn Zakariya al-Razi (865-925). His general philosophy was that no authority was beyond criticism. He was a true humanist and had boundless faith in human reason. Al-Razi argued :

On what ground do you deem it necessary that God should single out certain individuals (by giving them prophecy), that he should set them up above other people, that he should appoint them to be the people's guides, and make people dependent upon them ?

If the people of this religion are asked about the proof for the soundness of their religion, they flare up, get angry and spill the blood of whoever confronts them with this question. They forbid rational speculation, and strive to kill their adversaries. This is why truth became thoroughly silenced and concealed.

Al-Razi maintained the view that reason is superior to revelation and salvation is only possible through philosophy. The Prophets, the billy goats with long beards, as Al-Razi disdainfully described them cannot claim any intellectual and spiritual superiority. These billy goats pretend to come with a message from God, all the while exhausting themselves spouting their lies and imposing on the masses blind obedience to the '*words of the master*'. As for the Quran, it is but an associated mixture of '*absurd and inconsistent fables*'. Al-Razi continued, "you claim that the evidentiary miracle is present and available, namely, the Koran. You say : 'Whoever denies it, let him produce a similar one'. Indeed, we shall produce a thousand similar, from the works of rhetoricians, eloquent speakers and valiant poets, which are more appropriately phrased and state the issues more succinctly. They convey the meaning better and their rhymed prose is in better meter. ... By God what you say astonishes us ! You are talking about a work which recounts ancient myths, and which at the same time is full of contradictions and does not contain any useful information or explanation. Then you say : 'Produce something like it' ?"

The Holy Quran is above the human laws. So in the Quran there is but one reference to Shariah : "*We put you on a path; follow it*" (45 : 18). Which path ? That path, which are floridly lacking the morality. Like the Holy Quran there are many holy scriptures in the world but why did the Holy Quran become the subject matter of adjudication in a court of law.

The Quran may be beyond human laws but it cannot be free from human critics. Ibn Warraq reveals how the early rulers of Islam had mercilessly criticized Muhammad, Islam and Allah ? He cited an example of a Muslim leader who said : "If there were a God, I would swear by his name that I did not believe in him" (2003 : 42).

Caliph al-Walid II who ruled during 783 is said to have stuck the Quran onto a lance and shot it to pieces with arrows. He wrote poem, a similar type of Quranic verse and mocked the Quran as follows :

You hurl threats against the stubborn opponents,
well then I am a stubborn opponent myself.
When you appear before God at the day of resurrection,
Just say, 'My Lord, al-Walid tore me up.'

Explaining Walid II , Warraq said, "An intensively cultivated man, he surrounded himself with poets, dancing girls and musicians and lived the merry life of a libertine, with no interest in Allah, Muhammad and Islam altogether"(2003,42).

Let us see how the heavenly book is judged by our earthly judges :

Calcutta High Court dare not touch the Quran

356. Is not it a fact that on 29th March 1985 one Chandmal Chopra filed a writ petition in the Calcutta High Court demanding a ban on the Holy Quran because it promotes hatred and communal enemity ? Under Section 95, Criminal Procedural Code and Sections 153 A and 295 A, of the Indian Penal Code, any publication can be immediately banned which vitiates communal harmony by hurting the religious feelings of any community. But the Court was undone and did not dare to touch the holy book Quran and gave the following verdict :

> I state that according to the Islamic belief the Holy Quran is a Divine Book.It contains the words of God Almighty revealed to His last Prophet Muhammad. The verses of the Holy Quran were revealed on the happenings of particular events and its each and every verse has a connotation of its own on different and separate background.

> I further state that as the Holy Quran is a Divine Book no earthly power can sit upon judgement on it and no court of law has jurisdiction to adjudicate it. The Holy Books like the Quran, the Bible, the Geeta, the Granth Sahib, etc., or their translations cannot be the subject-matter of adj`udication in a court of law. All Holy Scriptures are immune from judicial scrutiny.

> I submit that this Honourable Court has no jurisdiction to pronounce a judgement on the Quran, the Holy Scriptures of the Muslims all over the world, each and every word of which, according to Islamic belief, is unalterable (Bhatty 1985 June : 31-32).

The Honourable court did not consider the case seriously. The verses quoted from the Holy Quran practically indicate no difference between Allah and the Prophet. Allah utters at the wish of the Prophet. Once the favourite wife of Muhammad, Ayesha, told the Prophet : "I find that Allah is prompt to proclaim commandments in accordance with your desire." May be true.

Quran on Trial by the Delhi Metropolitan Court

357. Does not the Holy Quran, a guide for the Muslims, teach that Kafirs must be eliminated, if they cannot be converted (5 : 10) ? Like the aforesaid Ayat there are 23 more verses of Quran which teaches that a Muslim may stay in the company of non-Muslims and may form a common *Ummat* as friends to fight a common enemy but once he gains strength, he should vanquish them.

It is clear from the aforesaid Ayats that in them there are commands for ill-will, enemity, hatred, duplicity, fraud, dispute-tusssle, looting and killing. Due to these reasons in this country and in this World there occur riots between Muslims and Non-Muslims. As long as the above command giving Ayats are not eliminated from the Quran Majeed, riots cannot be stopped.

In 1985 Delhi Administration filed a case against Serva Shri Inder Sen Sharma and Raj Kumar Arya in the court of a Metropolitan Magistrate, Delhi for publishing the aforesaid hand bill. On 30.7.86 the court while acquitting both the accused gave the judgement as under : "With due regard to the Holy Book of "Quran Majid", a close perusal of the Ayates shows that the same are harmful and teach hatred and are likely to create differences between Mohammadans on one hand and the remaining communities on the other."

Section

III

Searching the Sources of the Quran

16- The Source of Monotheism

The Holy Quran cannot be considered a new book in the history of mankind. It existed long before Prophet Muhammad brought it down. It is said that Prophet could hardly read or write but he was quite influenced by other religions like Pagan, Sabeans, Jewish, Christians and the Persian thoughts that were already in existence a thousand years before. Muhammad easily borrowed and incorporated these ideas in his new found scripture.

Monotheism in Pre-Islamic Period

358. Is monotheism a new concept that Islam contributed to the world philosophy ? No. It was there in Arab and in the Jewish religion. The following is a summary of what we found in *Bulugh al'Arab fi Ahwal al-'Arab* concerning the monotheists who lived before Islamic times :

The Arabs used to worship according to the law of Ibrahim, the friend of the All-Merciful, which had been passed on to them through his son Ishmael. They believed that God is one with no associate or helper, and that He is the All-hearing, the All-seeing. They used to pray, fast, make the pilgrimage, and pay the *zakat*. But with the passing of the years they went astray, differed in opinion and were divided into factions over worship. Only a remnant did not change or alter the law of Ishmael the son of Ibrahim; they abided by the practices of the past, such as venerating the Kaaba, circumambulation around the Kaaba *(tawaf)*, the minor and the major pilgrimage, etc... Thus they became divided : some remained steadfast in monotheism, while others adhered to other cults. The Arabs before Islam were not used to approaching women during their monthly period. They also determined that divorce was official if it was repeated three times, provided that the first and the second time could be abrogated. They used to run around the Kaaba seven times (vol. 2, chapter on the religions of the Arabs before Islam. al-Fadi.n.d : 122-123).

Some Suras begin with Pagan Gods

359. Is it not a fact that the word *Allah* was derived from *al* or *Allat* meaning god and as a pagan temple Kaaba was known as the House of Allah or *Baitullah* ?

Is it not a fact that the titles of most of the chapters or suras of the Quran resemble the names of the pagan gods, like Tarik, a stellar god which is the title of sura 86, similarly the titles of sura 110 and sura 91 preserve the names of Nasr, the god of Himyar and Shams, a solar deity respectively ?

Are the titles of Allah not reflected in many pagan names which survives in Islam such as : *Wadd,* a moon-god, was assimilated into and survived in al-Wadud, 'the Loving'; *Munim,* worshipped in north Arabia survives in al-Mani, the Withholder'; *Salm,* a deity of Tayma, in al-Salaam, 'the peace'; *Kaus* or Kayis, regarded as the consort of Manat, is retained in al-Kawi, 'the Strong'; *Aziz* of north Arabia is preserved unchanged in al-*Aziz*, 'the Mighty'. The pre-Islamic designations of God, al-Rahman, 'the Merciful', and al-Rahim, 'the Compassionate', remain conspicious in Islam (Walker 1999 : 43) ?

Pre-Islamic Practices in Islam

360. Is not it a fact that Muhammad adopted most of the pre-Islamic pagan practices in Islam ? He could remove 360 idols from Kaaba but not their customs and systems.

Muhammed borrowed the pagan system of bowing and praying towards Mecca. The following is quoted from an Arabic book titled *Al- Milal wa-al Nihal* by al-Shahrastani :

The Arabs during the pre-Islamic period used to practice certain things that were included in the Islamic Sharia. They, for example, did not marry both a mother and her daughter. They considered marrying two sisters simultaneously to be a most heinous crime. They also censured anyone who married his stepmother, and called him *dhaizan*. They made the major *(hajj)* and the minor *('umra)* pilgrimage to the Kaaba, performed the circumambulation around the Kaaba *(tawaf)*, ran seven times between Mounts Safa and Marwa *(sa'y)*, threw rocks and washed themselves after intercourse. They also gargled, sniffed water up into their noses, clipped their fingernails, plucked the hair from their armpits, shaved their pubic hair and performed the rite of circumcision. Likewise, they cut off the right hand of a thief. (vol.2, chapter on the opinions of the pre-Islamic Arabs; al-Fadi. n.d. 122).

Why pre-Islamic Friday for Muslims ?

361. When Muhammad emigrated to Medina, the Muslims suggested him that the Jews worshipped God on the Sabbath day, the day on which God rested after creating the Universe in six days, the Christians had their day on Sunday, the day of resurrection of Christ. But the Muslims have no special day for worship. Muhammad made the wrong choice, and made Friday as the day of prayer. Did he not accept the Friday from Ka'b Ibn Lu'ay who was preaching the people on that day and not because it was the day approved by Allah through his revelation (*Bulugh-al-'Arab fi Ahwal al- 'Arab* vol.1. p. 250 Qtd. al-Fadi. n.d. 126) ?

Pre-Islamic Sacred Months

362. Were not the sacred months (9 : 5; 47 : 4) of Rajab, Dhu al-Qa'da, Dhu-al-Hijja and Muhrram adopted by Muhammad from the pre-Islamic Arabs ? During these months raids, taking revenge, war, fighting and disputes were forbidden. These months were the months of reconciliation and peaceful co-existence. Does not Muhammad betray the Arabs when he contradicted himself with the verse : "They ask you concerning fighting in the prohibited months" say : "Fighting therein is a grave offence : but graver is it in the sight of Allah to prevent access to the path of Allah, to deny Him..." (2 : 217) ?

17 - Sabaean Influence

Long before Muhammad, Sabaeans, an ancient Aramaic speaking people, dominated the religion of Arab. They believed in an astral religion in which they worshipped moon as the male and sun as the female deity. Alongwith moon and sun (41 : 37) they followed Seth, Enoch, Noah and angels and worshipped other deities such as the stars. Muhammad borrowed the Lunar calendar from Sabaeans and instituted the fasting stands with the appearance of a crescent moon and did not cease until the crescent moon reappeared. Later this practice was adopted as one of the five pillars of Islam (Morey 1992 : 42). Therefore the Ramadan fast was not a part of the revealed religion nor was a part of the Christian religion but a borrowed tradition of the Sabaeans.

Sabaean taught how to perform Hajj and Umra

363. Is it not a fact that the Sabaeans, who worshipped stars, prayed seven daily prayers five of which resemble the Islamic prayers, fasted one month out of a year and went on pilgrimages to Safa and Marwa, (2 : 158) were the pre-Islamic ancestors of the Muslims ? Have the Muslims not borrowed many of their customs from the Sabaeans ?

Sabaeans' Fasting influenced Islam

364. Is not it a fact that among the Sabeans, fasting was insisted as an essential act of religion and during the month of Tammuz, they were in the habit of fasting from sunrise to sunset, without allowing a morsel of food or drop of liquid to pass their lips (Doane 1948 : 179) ?

Sabaean influence on Namaz ?

365. Is not it a fact that Muhammad regarded the Sabaeans as the people of God given religion because they believed in Allah and the Last Day and worked righteously (2 : 62; 5 : 69; 22 : 17) ? Muhammad Shukri al- Alusi said, "The Sabaeans have five prayers similar to the five prayers of the Muslims. Others say they have seven prayers, five of which are comparable to the prayers of the Muslims with regard to time, that is, morning, noon, afternoon, evening and night; the sixth is at midnight and the seventh is at forenoon. It is their practice to pray over the dead without kneeling down or even bending the knee. They also fast for one lunar month of thirty days; they start their fast at the last watch of the night and continue till the setting of the sun. Some of their sects fast during the month of Ramadan, face the Kaaba when they pray, venerate Mecca, and believe in making the pilgrimage to it. They consider dead bodies, blood and the flesh of pigs as unlawful. They also forbid marriage for the same reasons as do Muslims"(Bulugh al-'Arab Fi Ahwal al-'Arab vol. 2. chapter on the Sabaeans; Al-Fadi n.d. 121-122).

Is there any originality in Muslim Namaz ? Does not Muhammad copy the prayer system from the Sabaeans ?

18- Impact of Hanif

Hanif is a Syrian-Christian loan word, which means those who have moved away from idolatry. The Zorostrians, Jews, Christians and Sabaens were the Pre-Islamic religious communities who were monotheists and did not worship idols of God. Muhammad in his early days knew them (22:17).

Influence of Hanifa on Quran

366. Is not it a fact that Muhammad learnt many things from the Hanifa, as taught by Zaid Ibn Amr ? Even he referred *hanif* with praise (4 : 125), for its pure faith and no idolator (6 : 161) and for its confession of the unity of God who they believed is Compassionate and Forgiving. All these Quranic references indicate indirectly Hanif only. Muhammad was influenced by Zaid Ibn Amr's poems especially the one against idolatry. We quote this poem from Abd Al-Fadi :

> *Is it One Lord or a thousand lords*
>> *That I should pay homage when matters are divided ?*
> *I abstained from both al-Lat and al-'Uzza,*
>> *I pay no homage to either 'Uzza or her two daughters,*
> *Nor do I visit the two idols of Banu Amr.*
> *I do not pay homage to Hubal, either;*
>> *It being a lord in age past when my dream was easy.*
> *I wondered, and nights have things to wonder at,*
>> *As the days, too; which only the discerning knows.*
> *It is that God destroyed many a man,*
>> *Who lived a dissipated life-style.*
> *And saved others by the righteousness of some,*
>> *So that the little child among them grew chubby.*
> *As the person felt unsatisfied, he repented*
>> *Just as the winded-driven twig fluctuates.*
> *But I worship my Lord the Compassionate One,*
>> *So that the forgiving Lord may forgive my guilt.*
> *So keep the godliness of God your Lord,*
>> *Which, when you keep, you shall not perish.*
> *The righteous have paradise for a dwelling-place,*
>> *But the unbelievers have the heated Fire,*
> *Shame in this life, and when they meet their death,*
>> *They find things that bosoms cannot bear.*

Has not Islam shaped its major tenants from Hanafa (1997 : 323-324) ?

Muhammad too a Hanif

367. Is not it a fact that before the rise of Islam a group called the Hanifs, who claimed themselves as the spiritual descendants of Ibrahim, influenced Muhammad so much that he too claimed that his religion started with Ibrahim and that he too is a Hanif (Parrinder 1971 : 465) ?

Influence of Hanif on Muhammad

368. Is not it a fact that Hanifs were already in Arab long before Muhammad and many of his disciples were Hanifs ? Did not Muhammad hear the sermons of Hanif *Koss ibn Sayda*, of the Lyad tribe in about 610 ? Did he not consider Ibrahim as Hanif who was also an exponent of monotheism (21 : 52) as he was neither a Jew nor a Christian (3 : 67) but a Hanif (16 : 120-121) ? Did he not borrow the titles of Allah as al-Rahman (the merciful) al-Rabb(the Lord) and al-Ghafur (the Forgiving) from the Hanif ?

19 - Jewish Sources

The message that was being revealed to Muhammad in Medina appears to model Islam on the older religions like Judaism and Christianity. Muhammad followed the Jewish practices in Mecca like facing towards Jerusalem while worshipping and declaring Jerusalem as his *quibla* and commanded his followers to fast on the Jewish Day of Atonement, the Fast of Ashura on the 10th of the Jewish month of Tishri. When the Fast of Ramadan was instituted, that of the 'Ashura was not forbidden and he had a tendency to make Islamic practices similar to that of the Jews and encouraged his Medinan followers to continue Jewish practices which they had adopted (Watt 1956 : 199).

Jewish Monotheism

369. If Islam stands for monotheism and Jewish faith rests on monotheism, why in their early days did the Muslims fight against the Jews and compel the Jews to accept Islam as their religion ?

From the Books of unlearned Jews

370. Following is a list of the themes Muhammad inserted into the Quran. The corresponding Quranic verses and references in the original Jewish writings are also provided :

(1) Cain learns how to bury his brother from a raven (Sura al-Ma'ida 5 : 30-35).(See Perqui Rabbi Eliezer,Chapter 21).

(2) Nimrod casts Ibrahim into the fire, but the fire could not burn him (Suras al-Baqara 2 : 260, al- An'am 6 : 74-84, al-Anbiya' 21 : 52-72, Maryam 19 : 42-50, al-Shu 'ara' 26 : 69-79, al-'Ankabut 29 : 15-16, al-Saffat 37 : 81-95, al-Zukhruf 43 : 25-27, and al-Mumtahina 60 : 40); found also in *Midrash Rabba*, chapter 14, section on Genesis 15 : 17).

(3) King Solomon consults with *jinn*, birds and an '*ifrit*. Also, a hoopoe delivers news about the queen of Sheba and how her throne was brought to Solomon (Sura al-Naml 27 : 17-45); found also in the Second Targum on the book of Esther.

(4) Implanting lust in the two angels Harut and Marut, and their drinking wine, fornicating, killing and teaching sorcery to the people (Sura al-Baqara 2 : 96); found also in Midrash Yalkot, chapter 44.

(5) A mountain is raised above the Jew's heads (Sura al-A'raf 7 : 170); found also in Avodah Zarah, Chapter 2.

(6) A golden calf that lows (Suras al-A'raf 7 : 157 and Ta Ha 20 : 91); found also in *Pirqei Rabbi Eliezer,* chapter 45.

(7) The seven heavens and the seven gates of Gehenna (Suras al-Isra' 17 : 46, 48 and al-Hijr 15 : 44); found also in the *Hagiga* (section 9, Chapter 2) and *Sefir Ha-Zohar,* chapter 2.

(8) A throne on the water (Sura Hud 11 : 9); found also in the exegesis of Rashi on Genesis 1: 2.

(9) The battlements, which are meant to be the fine partition between paradise and hell (Sura al-A'raf 7 : 44); found also in the *Midrash* on the exposition of Ecclesiastes 7 : 14.

(10) A flood consisting of boiling water (Sura Hud 11 : 42); found also in the books *Rosh Hashana* (16 : 2) and *Sanhedrin* (108).

(11) A guarded tablet (Sura al-Buruj 85 : 21, 22); found also in *Pirqei Avot*, section 5, chapter 6.

Heavy borrowings from Old Testament

371. Was Muhammad illiterate ? Was his journey confined to Syria and that too for business undertaken by Arab trade caravans ? Was he not well informed about the Prophets of the past ? Did Muhammad not absorb many of the teachings from the Talmudic sources because the Jews had a strong presence in al-Madina and Yemen ? And can we deny that most of the stories and legends in the Quran were borrowed from the Old Testament ?

The Quran includes accounts of the **story of Adam**, which is for example, repeated in Suras 2, 38, 20, 7. **The story of Noah** is repeated in Suras 7, 10, 11, 21, 25, 26, 29, 37, 71, 54, and 23.

The **story of Ibrahim** is repeated in Suras 3, 21, 19, 14, 11, 15, 51, 6 and 37.

The **story of Lot** is repeated in Suras 37, 7, 16, 29, 26, 21, 54 and 11.

The s**tory of Moses** is repeated in Suras 28, 20, 26, 7, 2, 10, and 4.

The **story of Solomon** is repeated in Suras 38, 2 and 16.

The **story of Jonah** is repeated in Suras 21, 37, 68, and 10.

Besides, Muhammad could remember David and Solomon no less than 33 times, the tale of Noah recollected some 30 times as well as heading a chapter and the sura of Joseph in the longest narrative given in the Quran.

A selected subjectwise list is given below of how many references are there from Old Testament.

Creation of the world in six days : 7 : 54; 10 : 3; 11 : 7; 25 : 59; 32   : 4; 57 : 4.

Creation of heaven : 2 : 29; 23 : 17; 23 : 86; 41 : 11; 65 : 12.

Day and night : 6 : 96; 17 : 12; 25 : 47; 28 : 73.

Adam was created from : Dust 3 : 59, Earth 11 : 61; 18 : 37; 2 : 5; 30 : 19; 35 : 11, Nothing 19 : 67; Water 22 : 5; 23 : 13-14; 40 : 67; 27 : 14; 75 : 37-38; 96 : 2.

Creation of Eve : 4 : 1; 7 : 189; 39 : 6; 42 : 11.

Adam names everything : 2 : 30-33.

The constitution of the **prohibited tree** : 23: 20;24 : 35; 95 : 1-2.

Allah's covenant with Adam : 20 : 115.

Tempted by Satan : 7 : 20-21, 27; 20 : 120-121.

The fall of man : 7 : 22-23; 20 : 121.

Explusion from paradise : 2 : 36; 7 : 24; 20 : 123.

The curse : 2 : 36; 7 : 24-25; 20 : 55; 22 : 66.

Eve's pregnancy. The fall of the first human beings : 7 : 189 f.

Two sons of Adam 5 : 27-31.

Cains repentance : 5 : 31.

Allah commands Noah to build the ark : 11 : 36-37; 23, 27-28.

The flood : 6 : 6; 11 : 40, 23 : 27; 54 : 11-12.

The ark : 54 : 13-14; 69 : 11-12.

The call to enter the ark : 11 : 41.

Destruction of sinful mankind : 7 : 64; 10 : 73; 21 : 77; 26 : 120.

Allah puts an end to the water : 11 : 44.

Allusion to the **tower of Babel** : 40 : 36-37.

Ibrahim's dispute with his father : 6 : 74; 19 : 42-48; 21 : 52-   57; 43 : 26-27.

Ibrahim destroys the idols of his father : 21 : 58.

Ibrahim's **dispute with Nimrod** : 2 : 268; 14 : 15, 50 : 24.

Lot believes Abraham : 29 : 26.

Ibrahim's Intercession for the sinful cities : 11 : 74-75; 29 : 31-32.

The **wickedness** of the people of Sodom : 11 : 77-79; 15 : 67-72; 27 : 54-56.

Destruction of the city of the sinners : 11 : 82; 15 : 66; 73-74; 21 : 70; 26 : 172-173; 27 : 58; 29 : 35; 37 : 136; 51 : 37; 54 : 34; 37-38.

Ibrahim sacrifices his son : 37 : 102-113.

Ibrahim's descendants : 2 : 133; 6 : 84, 11 : 71; 12 : 6, 38; 19 : 49-50,58; 21 :71-72; 29 :27;37:112-113; 38 : 45-48.

Ishmael : 2 : 125, 133, 136; 3 : 84, 4 : 163; 6 : 86; 14 : 39; 19   : 54; 21 : 85; 38 : 48.

Joseph hears the dream of the king and Interprets it : 12 : 46-49; 7 : 130.

Joseph before Pharaoh : 12 : 54-56.

The Egyptians believe that there will be no mesenger from God after Joseph : 40 : 34.

Pharaoh kills the Jewish boys : 2 : 49; 7 : 141; 14 : 6; 28 : 4; 40 : 25.

The fear of Moses' mother : 28 : 10.

Moses' mother puts him into the box : 28 : 7; 20: 38-39.

Moses' sister is to look after the little box : 28 : 11.

Moses' sister offers the mother of Moses as a nurse : 20 : 40; 28 : 12.

Pharaoh's wife supports Moses : 28 : 9.

Pharaoh, the enemy of Moses, has to bring him up : 28 : 8; 20 : 39; 26 : 18.

Moses grows up : 28 : 14.

Moses kills one of his enemies and the consequences of this act : 20 : 40; 26 : 21; 28 : 33; 15-19.

The burning bush : 20 : 9-10; 27 : 7-8; 28 : 29-30.

Allah gives Moses the signs that he is to perform before Pharaoh : Ta Ha 20 : 17-24, al-Naml 27 : 10-12, al-Qasas 28 : 31-32, al-Nazi' at 79 : 20.

Aaron as the substitute of Moses : 7 : 142; 19 : 53; 20 : 29- 36; 25 : 35; 26 : 12-14; 28 : 34-35.

Moses and Aaron are afraid to go to Pharaoh : Ta Ha 20 : 45-46, al-Shu'ara' 26 : 12-15, al-Qasas 28 : 33-35.

Pharaoh holds a **secret council against Moses** : 20 : 60- 65; 26 : 34-40.

The plagues : 7 : 133-134; 17 : 101.

Pharaoh, the man of the poles, wants his minister **Haman to build him al tower** : 28 : 6, 8, 38; 29 : 39; 38 : 12; 40 : 24; 36-37; 89 : 10.

The people of Moses are to **go out of Egypt** : 2 : 50; 17 : 103; 20 : 77-78; 26 : 52; 44 : 22-24.

The **passage through the sea** 2 : 50; 7 : 138; 10 : 90; 20 : 77; 26 : 63-66; 44 : 30-31.

The **destruction of the Egyptians** in the sea : 2 : 50; 7 : 136; 8 : 54; 17 : 103; 20 : 78; 26 : 66; 28 : 40; 29 : 39; 43 : 55-56; 51 : 40; 85 : 17-18.

Pharaoh alone is saved : 10 : 90-92.

Moses strikes water out of a rock : 2 : 60; 7 : 160.

The people receive shadow from clouds as well as **Manna and Quail to eat** : 2 : 57; 7 : 160, 20 : 80-81.

Allah's covenant with the children of Israel : 2 : 40; 83- 84; 4 : 154; 5 : 70; 7 : 169.

The Ten Commandments : 2 : 40-46; 83, 177; 6 : 151-152; 17 : 22-37; 23 : 1-11; 25 : 63-74; 46 : 10-12.

Moses and the **40 days of the conclusion** of the covenant : 2 : 51; 7 : 142, 145; 19 : 52; 28 : 44.

The golden calf : 2 : 53-54 and 92; 4 : 153; 7 : 148-150; 20 : 83-85; 87.

Moses rebukes the people regarding the sin of the calf : 2 : 54; 7 : 151; 20 : 86.

Moses receives the tablets anew : 7 : 154.

Israel imitates an idolatrous people : 7 : 138-140.

The sacrifice of the yellow cow : 2 : 67-70.

How to expiate with **the yellow cow** : 2 : 71-72.

David and Solomon pass judgements : 21 : 78.

Solomon, David's successor : 27 : 16; 38 : 30.

Solomon's insight and wisdom : 27 : 15, cf 21 : 79.

Solomon commands the wind : 21 : 81; 34 : 12; 38 : 36.

Solomon and the ant : 27 : 18-19.

Jonah judges the might of Allah to be small : 21 : 87.

The fish devours him : 37 : 142.

Job's character : 6 : 84; 38 : 44.

The Characters of Old Testaments in Quran

372. Can you deny the fact that there are atleast 30 characters borrowed from the Old Testament with or without context ? They were :

	Bible	*Quran*
1.	Adam	*Adam*
2.	Aaran	*Harun*
3.	Abel	*Abil*
4.	Abraham	*Ibrahim*
5.	Cain	*Qabil*
6.	David	*Daud*

7.	Elios	*Ilyas*
8.	Elijah	*Alyasa*
9.	Enock	*Idris*
10.	Ezra	*Uzair*
11.	Gabriel	*Jibril*
12.	Gog	*Yajuj*
13.	Goliath	*Jalut*
14.	Issac	*Ishaq*
15.	Ismail	*Ishmael*
16.	Jacob	*Yacub*
17.	Job	*Aiyus*
18.	Jonah	*Yunus*
19.	Joshua	*Yusha*
20.	Joseph	*Yusuf*
21.	Korah	*Qurum*
22.	Lot	*Lut*
23.	Magog	*Majuj*
24.	Michael	*Mikail*
25.	Moses	*Musa*
26.	Noah	*Nuh*
27.	Pharoah	*Firaun*
28.	Saul	*Talut*
29.	Solomon	*Sulaiman*
30.	Terah	*Azar*

Stories from Jewish Sources

373. Is it not a fact that many of the stories in Quran came from the Jewish sources, the Talmud, the Midrash, and many apocryphal works such as :

1. The source of Sura 3 : 35-37 is the fanciful book called *The Protevangelion's James the Lesser.*
2. The source of Sura 87 : 19 is the Testament of Abraham.
3. The source of Sura 27 : 17-44 is the Second Targum of Esther.
4. The fantastic tale that God made a man "die for a hundred years" with no ill effects on his food, drink, or donkey was a Jewish fable (Sura 2 : 259 ff.).
5. The idea that Moses was resurrected and other material came from the Jewish Talmud (Sura 2 : 55, 56, 67).
6. The story in Sura 5 : 30, 31 can also be found in pre-Islamic works from Pirke Rabbi Eleazer, the Targum of Jonathan ben Uzziah and the Targum of Jerusalem.
7. The tale of Abraham being delivered from Nimrod's fire came from the Midrash Rabbah (see Suras 21 : 51-71; 29 : 16, 17; 37 : 97, 98).
   It must be also pointed out that Nimrod and Abraham did not live at the same time. Muhammad was always mixing people together in the Quran who did not live at the same time.
8. The non-biblical details of the visit of the Queen of Sheba (Saba) in Sura 27 : 20-44 came from the Second Targum of the Book of Esther.
9. The source of Sura 2 : 102 is no doubt the Midrash Yalkut (chapter 44).

10. The story found in Sura 7 : 171 of God lifting up Mount Sinai and holding it over the heads of the Jews as a threat to squash them if they rejected the law came from the Jewish book Abodah Sarah.
11. The story of the making of the golden calf in the wilderness, in which the image jumped out of the fire fully formed and actually mooed (Suras 7 : 148; 20 : 88), came from Pirke Rabbi Eleazer.
12. The seven heavens and hells described in the Quran came from the Zohar and the Hagigah.
13. Muhammad utilized the Testament of Abraham to teach that a scale or balance will be used on the day of judgement to weigh good and bad deeds in order to determine whether one goes to heaven or hell (Suras 42 : 17; 101 : 6-9). (Morey 1992 : 149-150).

Jewish influence on Muhammad

374. Is it not a fact that in South Arabia, more than a century before the rise of Islam, there had been a Jewish kingdom which had been destroyed by Ethiopian Christian invaders, who came to avenge the persecution of Christians in the area ? There were also widely scattered Arabic-speaking Jewish tribes, particularly in the Oasis of Yathrib, who offered many opportunities to the Arabs to become acquainted with Judaism because of their trading connections to the regions up the north. Is this not the place where Muhammad was to settle when his position in Mecca became untenable, and where Muhammad learnt monotheism (Parrinder1971 : 465) ?

Muhammad learned Judaism from Abdias

375. Can you deny the fact that while living in Mecca, Muhammad had been friendly with a learned rabbi named Abdias ben Salom who, it is said, recited the Jewish scriptures to Muhammad, described Jewish traditions and gave him other information that was of use to him in the composition of the Quran ? Did not the learned rabbi Abdias ben Salom, himself later become a Muslim as Abdulla Ibn Salam and is believed to be the "witness" mentioned in the Quran (46 : 9) (Walker 1999 : 181) ?

Divorce Rule of Jews is a Carbon Copy in Islam

376. Can we deny the fact that the divorce rule is followed from Jews. When a woman is divorced, she must wait for three months before she can re-marry. This period, is called *iddat*. At the end of this period, if she is found with child, she must be delivered of it before she can marry again. Are these rules also not copied from the Jews, according to whom a divorced woman or widow cannot marry another man till ninety days be passed after the divorce or death of the husband ?

Corrupt Judaism in Quran

377. Can we prove that Judaism at the time of the revelation of the Quran was corrupt both in practice and doctrine and therefore Islam was the need of the day ? If Muhammad did not like Torah how could he record the ancient scrolls of Ibrahim and Moses (87 : 18-19), and also find some excerpts from the sayings of Isaiah, David, Ezekiel, Jonah and others, whose words were the revealed Books of the former people (26 : 196) ?

Quran is distorted Old Testament

378. If Muhammad is not the author of the Holy Quran but Allah inspired him and revealed his words through him why 75% of the Quran is composed of distorted laws and stories from the Old Testament ?

Why Muslims accept Bible as being inspired by Allah though there are many gaps between the Quran and the Bible ?

Can you deny the fact that Quran was influenced by the Old Testament, at times word by word ? Such as "An eye for an eye, a nose for a nose, an ear for an ear, a tooth for a tooth" (Sura 5 : 49 ; Ex 21 : 23-24).

Does not the Bible say, "On the day of the Lord, the heavens shall be rolled together as a scroll" (*Isa* 34 : 4). "On that day will we roll up the heavens as one rolleth up written scrolls", says the Quran (21 : 104).

Some biblical texts quoted in the Quran are acknowledged as quotations. Thus 'the righteous shall inherit the earth' (21 : 105) is taken direct from the Old Testament (*Ps* 37 : 29).

20 - The Bible Speaks Through Quran

The Christian influence on Muhammad was immense since his childhood . His nurse Umm Ayman was an Abyssinian Christian. In his boyhood he met the monk Bahira in Syria (Walker 1999 : 189).

During the days of Muhammad Christian Evangelists from south Yemen used to come to Mecca in the month of the pilgrimage and hold discourses in the inner court of the Kaaba. Muhammad might have listened to such sermons. (Al Masih. *Islam Under* p. 43). Not only that, Christianity was widespread in Arab and there were renowned Churches like the "Kaaba of Najran."

There were also learned bishops like Quss Ibn Sa'ida, famous for his eloquent speeches. Muhammad heard him at Suq 'Ukaz. Among the Christians there were innocent martyrs like the yemenite Christians against whom some Jewish people revolted, killing them by throwing them into a trench which they set on fire (Abd Al-Fadi, 1997 : 392). Muhammad referred to that in the Quran (85 : 4-7) and praised the priests of Christianity for their piety (5 : 82)

Christianity was widely spread in the Ara kingdom of Ghassan, Byzantine Church and Nestorians were there at al-Hira and Persia and there was another well-known Christian Community at Najran to the South and East of Mecca (Parrinder 1971 : 465).

Muhammad as a boy also came in contact with a Nestorian monastery in Busra, and grew deeply interested in the religious and philosophical views of the monks and upon reaching manhood, some say, he came more and more under Nestorian influence (Head 1969 : 141).

From the Books of unlearned Christians

379. (1) Is not it a fact that the story of the men of the cave, or the seven sleepers (Sura al Kahf 18 : 8-26) is found also in Gregorious' *The Book of the Glory of the Martyrs,* vol. one, chapter 95.

(2) The story of Mary : how she vowed herself to God, how Zechariah took charge of her, and how the angels provided her with food (Sura Al Imran 3 : 31, 32, 38-42); is found also in the books *Yerut Euangelion* (chapters 3, 4,5,7,8,9,11,15) and *The Death of Our Father, the Old Carpenter* (chapter 3, on the Life of Mary).

(3) Mary's withdrawal from her family to a distant place, and the falling down of ripe dates by the command of her Baby (Sura Maryam 19 : 23, 24); is found also in *The Book of the Story of Mary's Birth and the Childhood of the Saviour*, chapter 20.

(4) Christ creates birds out of clay (Sura al-Ma'ida 5 : 110); is found also in the Greek book, *The Book of Hooma the Israelite*, chapter 2.

(5) The denial of Christ's crucifixion and His likeness being cast upon another (Sura al-Nisa' 4 : 157); this is in line with Basilides' heresy, which maintains that Christ cast His likeness upon Simon of Cyrene, so that he was crucified in His place; followers of this heresy assumed this is what happened, for they held that Christ had no real body, but took upon Himself only the likeness of a body.

Christians who influenced Muhammad

380. The Muslim scholars who try to prove that Muhammad was illiterate and therefore borrowed nothing from *Torah* or *Injil* cannot refute the facts that when Muhammad had visions Khadijah took him to her Christian cousin Waraqa ibn-Naufal, probably the leader of a house church in Mecca and a distant relative of Muhammad, who initiated Muhammad (Al-Masih. *Islam Umen.* 23). Did he not listen to Abu Takbiha, a Greek Christian preacher, and was influenced by Tamim al-Dari on the eschatological ideas ?

The Arabs of Mecca said that Muhammad was taught these stories by another man, who was a mortal like himself (16 : 103) and not by Allah as he claimed. They disagreed as to who that man was. Al-Qurtubi reported that Muhammad knew a blacksmith in Mecca called Baalam, who was a Christian. The idolators saw Muhammad going in and out to him, therefore they said : "It is only Baalam that teaches him." Ikrima said : "Muhammad used to entertain a slave of the Mughirites called Yaish, who could read the Scriptures. Therefore the Quresh said : "He is teaching him." It was also said that Muhammad often sat at the Marwa with a Roman Christian slave owned by the Hadramites, whose name was Jabr, and he could read the Scriptures. Ubaidallah b. Muslima said : "We had two slaves from the people of Ain al-Tamr, one was called Yasar whose surname was Abu Fakiha, and the other's name was Jabr. They worked in Mecca as sword markers and used to read the *Torah* and the *Injil*. They were reading one day when Muhammad sat with them, and he found rest in their words whenever the unbelievers hurt him. The idolators said therefore that Muhammad was learning from them. Al-Farra said : "The Arabs said that Muhammad was learning from Aish, a slave owned by Huwaitib b. Abd al Uzza, who was a non-Arab Christian converted to Islam." Others said : "It was Addas, the slave of Utba b. Rabia" (see al-Suyuti's *Asbab al-Nuzul* on this verse; CQV. 1994 : 180).

One God Concept of Muhammad

381. Is not it a fact that Michael Hart, the author of the book *100 : A Ranking of the Most Influential Persons in History,* argued and proved that Muhammad got the concept of one God from the Jews and Christians who were small in number and were living in Mecca (*Year Book of Muslim World* 1996 : 79) ? When Muhammad was 40 years old, he became convinced that this one and true God (Allah) was speaking to him, and had chosen him to spread the true faith.

Borrowed Phrases from the Bible

382. Is it not a fact that Muhammad easily picked up information, and phrases probably through conversation with the Jews and Christians. These phrases are quoted by Margoliouth as follows :

"tasting death," "to bring from darkness to light," "to pervert the straightway of God," "the trumpet shall be blown," "to roll up the heavens as a scroll is rolled up," "they have weights in their ears," "the new heavens and the new earth," "the first and second death," "that which eye hath not seen nor ear heard nor hath entered into the heart of man," "a camel entering a needle's eye," "as far as the East is from the West, so far hath he removed our sins from us" (1905 : 60-61).

Judgement Day and Resurrection Islam borrowed from Christians

383. Are the concepts like the Judgement day and resurrection in the Quran not directly borrowed from the New Testament (Ju 1 : 6; Rom 2 : 2, 2 : 16; Mt 17 : 7, 23; Cor 15 : 21) ?

Quran borrowed from the Bible of Jesus

384. How wonderfully Muhammad followed the footsteps of Jesus. If we sincerely search we will find how both Jesus and Muhammad chose twelve disciples to propagate their message among mankind. Like Jesus Muhammad too gave a Sermon on the Mount, which ended : "This day have I perfected your religion", which long before Jesus announced in the synagogue in Nazareth : "This day is this scripture fulfilled in your ears" (*Lk* 4 : 21). Jesus pronounced his last words on the cross : "It is finished" (*Jn* 19 : 30), similarly Muhammad ended his last sermon with the words : "I have finished my work." A few examples can be cited from the sayings of Jesus and Muhammad :

New Testament

1. It is easier for a camel, to go through the eye of a needle than for a rich man to enter into the kingdom of God (*Mt* 19 : 24; *Mk* 10 : 25; Lk 18 : 25).

2. The foolish said to the wise, "Give us of your oil; for our lamps are gone out." But the wise answered saying, "Not so, lest there be not enough for us and you. Go rather and buy for yourselves" (*Mt* 25 : 8-9).

3. Jesus said, 'It is easier for a camel to pass through the eye of a needle, than for a rich man to enter the kingdom of heaven' (*Mt* 19 : 24).

4. 'For the earth bringeth forth fruit of herself; first the blade, then the ear, and after that the full corn in the ear' (*Mk* 4 : 28).

5. 'There are many other things which Jesus did, which if they were to be written down, I suppose that even the world itself could not contain the books that should be written' (*Jn* 21: 25).

6. 'Now we see through a glass darkly; but then face to face' (1 *Cor* 13: 12).
7. 'Where two or three are gathered together in my name, there am I in the midst of them' (*Mt* 18 : 20).
8. Jesus said, "He that loveth father or mother, son or daughter more than me is not worthy of me' (*Mt* 10: 37).
9. St. Paul writes. 'Eye hath not seen nor ear heard, neither have entered into the heart of man, the things which God hath prepared for them that love him' (1 *Cor* : 2

The Quran

1. To those who reject our signs and treat them with arrogance, no opening will there be of the gates of heaven, nor will they enter the Garden, until the camel, can pass through the eye of the needle (7: 40).
2. On that day the hypocrites, both men and women, shall say to those who believe, "Tarry with us that we may kindle our light at yours." It shall be said, "Return ye back and seek light for yourselves" (57: 13).
3. 'Heaven's gates shall not be opened to those who charge us with falsehood nor shall they enter paradise until a camel passeth through the eye of a needle' (7: 38).
4. This is their picture in the Gospel: "They are as the seed which putteth forth its stalk, then strengtheneth it, and it groweth in the ear, and riseth upon its stem" (48: 29).
5. If the seas were ink it would be insufficient for the words of the Lord' (18 : 109).
6. In the Quran, 'Faces on that day shall be bright, gazing at their Lord' (75: 22).
7. Three persons cannot meet secretly but God is the fourth' (58: 8).
8. None of you is a believer till I am dearer to you than your child, your father and the whole of mankind. (Mu. 1: 71).
9. 'No soul knoweth what joy of the eyes is reserved as a reward for good works' (32: 17).

Muhammad rectified Moses and Jesus

385. What had gone wrong in the system of Moses which Jesus was commissioned to rectify and similarly what subsequently went wrong with the New Testament which brought Muhammad to set right in the Quran ?

Does he not admit that he contributed nothing but the "tales of the ancient" which he repeated in the Quran four times (6 : 25; 8 : 31; 25 : 5; 68 : 15), and which Muhammad has caused to be written and they are dictated before him morning and evening (25 :5). The parable of the sower and that of the labourers in the vineyard have been imitated in tradition too.

113

386. Is it not a fact that whenever Muhammad was in doubt about his Quran, he admittedly fell back to the Bible as a reference for his saying ? Does he not admit that the Torah was the plain command of Allah (5 : 43) ? Does he not affirm that the Gospel judge by what Allah hath revealed therein (5 : 47) ? At times he agreed and disagreed with the ideas of Jesus. Does he not mention Jesus in the Quran in his own words like :

> Jesus, a righteous Prophet : 6 : 85.
> Angels...Gabriel and Michael : 2 : 97-98.
> Birth of Jesus : 3 : 45-47, 19 : 22-23.
> Jesus the messenger to Israel : 3 : 49-51.
> Crucifixion of Jesus not true : 4 : 157.
> Jesus sent with Gospel : 5 : 46, 47.
> Jesus not the son of God : 9 : 30.
> Message and Miracles : 5 : 110, 19 : 30-33.

21 - Quran Quotes the Ancient Poets of Arab

The Holy Quran cannot be accepted as an original text rather the Prophet has plagiarized the pagan poets of Arab. It was a practice of the then poets of Arab to hang up the poems upon the Kaaba and Muhammad unhesitatingly recited those poems and added them to his revelation. Quoting Warraq, Das writes : One day, Fatima, the daughter of Muhammad, was reciting two passages from Sabaa Mu'allaqot (2010 : 14). Suddenly she met the daughter of Imra'ul Qays, who cried out : "O that's what your father had taken from one of my father's poems and calls it something that has come down to him out of heaven" (1998 : 235-236). Let us see how far it is true.

Quran : an Interpolation of Ancient Wisdom of Arab
387. Is not it a fact that the sonorous verse and rhythmic prose in the early style of the Quran had been composed long before Muhammad's time, both by poets and by religious and social reformers like Zayid ibn Amr, Koss ibn Sayda, Omayya of Tayif and others ? Did not the Prophet's Meccan opponents, contrast Muhammad's inspirations with the ancient Arab wisdom and the verses in which they were enshrined, often came out in favour of the older works (Walker 1998 : 161) ?

Quran quotes Imru'al-Qais
388. Is it not a fact that Prophet Muhammad was very fond of ancient poetry and listened to the poetry of Umayya b. Abu as Salt as time and again and loved a great pre-Islamic poet Labid (*Mus* 4 : 5602-5606) ? Therefore in the Quran it is said it is nothing but the "tales of the ancients." Muhammad quoted the fairy tales of the ancient in the Quran without reference. Here is a glaring example of Imrual-Qais, a Pre-Islamic poet who died in 540, thirty years before the birth of Muhammad. Abd Al-Fadi quotes the famous poem of al-Qais, from which the Quran quotes several lines. These are indicated in italics below :

> *The hour has drawn nigh : the moon is split,*
> Revealing a doe that hunted my heart and bolted away.

She has white and black eyes;
   Her features never cease to amaze me;
She has sleepy eyes
   With stark contrast between black and white.
She passed by me on the feast-day in her adornment;
   Shot me, took in hand, and hamstrung (me),
With arrows of deadly glances,
   And left me as the wattles of a pen-builder.
If she stays away from me for an hour,
   This hour would be the most distressing and afflictive.
Beauty has been engrossed upon her cheeks
   With musk-powder as a brief line.
It is the routine of the moons to travel by night,
   But I saw the night travelling by the moon.
By the white forenoon and the brooding night.
   Distinguished by light, what a blooming thing !
When I saw her embarrassment, I said,
   "The hour has drawn nigh, the moon is split."

The first part of the first sentence and the last line occur in Sura al-Qamar 54: 1, where it says, "The hour has drawn nigh: the moon is split." The second line of the third sentence is found in Sura- al-Qamar 54 : 29, where it says, "Then they called their comrade, and he took in hand, and hamstrung her." The fourth line of the third sentence is found in Sura al-Qamar 54 : 31, where it says, "And they were as the wattles of a pen-builder." The first line of the seventh sentence is found in Sura al-Duha 93 : 1,2 where we read : "By the white forenoon and the brooding night." Imru' al-Qais also wrote :

   She came forward; and the lovers from behind,
      As though they slide down out of every slope.
   And she came on the feast-day in her adornment;

      So for the like of this let the workers work.

The second line of this poem is found in Sura al- Anbiya' 21 : 96, where it says, "When Gog and Magog are unloosed, and they slide down out of every slope." The last line of this poem is found in Sura al-Saffat 37 : 61, where it says, "For the like of this let the workers work" (1979 : 311-312).

22 - Borrowing from Zoroastrian

Though Christianity is a Jewish heresy, and Islam a Christian heresy their source is the same, i.e., the semitic religions. Their God is one though their temples are different. They differ with Zoroastrianism and Hinduism because Zoroastrianism has a missing link with the ancient Hinduism. And Hinduism itself stands like a mighty banyan tree under which no religion can grow.

There lies a fundamental difference between the Semitic religions and Hinduism. Semitic religions believe in a single prophethood, a single text book of the prophet and a specific way of life. For the Christians Christ is the only son of God, New Testament is the only text book about Christ and they follow a single pattern of life approved by the Church. For the Muslims Muhammad is the last prophet of the prophethood, Quran is the only textbook of Muhammad and they follow a single pattern of life guided by their Quran and Hadith. Whereas Hinduism does not claim Prophethood by any single prophet or avatara, no single text book is prescribed for the Hindus and a Hindu chooses his own way of life suitable for his situation.

A Hindu may visit or may not visit a temple, may believe a single god or a host of gods and goddesses or may not believe any god or goddesses, a Hindu may even declare himself not a Hindu, yet Hinduism won't deprive him from any of his rights until and unless he is accepted by any of the semetic religions. Let us see how Islam is influenced by Zoroastrianism ?

The Opening of the Quran with Zoroastrian Words

389. Is not it a fact that every chapter of the Quran, excepting only the ninth, opens with the words *"Bismillah uar Rahman er Rahim"* which exactly correspond to the formula with which the Zoroastrians begin their books, viz., *"Banam Yazdan bakhshish gar dadar"* which means in the name of the most merciful God (Prasad 1966 : 10) ?

Zoroastrian Formula in Islam

390. Is not it a fact that the celebrated formula of the *"La-Elah-illillah"* which means there is no God but God is a mere paraphrase of the Zoroastrian formula, *"Nest ezad magar Yazdan"* (Prasad 1966 : 10).

From the Books of unlearned Persians

391. The Quran testifies that al-Nadr Ibn al-Harith used to rebuke Muhammad for merely copying the sayings of the Persians and receiving nothing by revelation. It is a matter of common knowledge that the Persians ruled over a large number of Arabian tribes before and during Muhammad's lifetime. Therefore, the stories of their kings, beliefs and legends circulated among the Arabs and left their stamp on Muhammad, who recorded many of them in his Quran. Al-Nadr Ibn al-Harith, too, used to relate the accounts of the Persian kings to the people, and would often say, "By God, Muhammad has nothing better to relate than I do; and his narration is nothing but the fairy-tales of the ancients that he has had written down, just as I have." To which Muhammad answered, "When our signs are recited to him, he says, 'Fairy-tales of the ancients". (Sura al-Qalam 68 : 15). Muhammad even went so far as to curse al-Nadr in the Quran, saying, "Woe to every guilty impostor who hears the signs of God being recited to him, then perseveres in waxing proud, as if he has not heard them; so give him the good tidings of a painful chastisement" (Sura al-Jathiya 45 : 7,8).

How could Muhammad curse al-Nadr, when he knew that he had quoted a great deal of the Persian legends in his Quran, such as the ascension of Artioraf Namak and the description of paradise with its wide-eyed *huris* and lads ? Moreover, Muhammad made his instructor, Salman the Persian, one of the Companions ! Consider the following subjects, which Muhammad copied from Persian sources :

116

(1) The ascension of Artioraf Namak. The original story (written roughly 400 years before the Hijra) says that the Magi sent Artioraf's spirit to heaven while he was in a trance. The purpose of this ascension to heaven was to acquire knowledge of what was there and to bring news of it back. So Artioraf ascended to heaven by the guidance of an archangel and wandered about from one level to another, gradually ascending higher and higher. Having acquired knowledge of everything, the good god Ahura Mazda ordered him to return to earth and tell the Zoroastrians about what he saw. Muhammad apparently took the story of the ascension of Artioraf Namak and turned himself into the main character, saying, "Glory be Him, who carried His servant by night from the Holy Mosque to the Further Mosque the precincts of which we have blessed, that We might show him some of Our signs. He is the All-hearing, the All-seeing" (Sura al-Isra' 17 :1).

In his account of the Night Journey, Muhammad said, "I was brought a white beast smaller than a mule and larger than a donkey, called al-Buraq; it would place its hoof at a distance equal to the horizon. I sat upon it and Gabriel took off with me till he reached the lower heaven. He called upon God for help and I saw Adam. Then he brought me up to the second heaven and I saw Jesus and John (the Baptist); then he brought me up to the third heaven and I saw Joseph; then he brought me up to the fourth heaven and I saw Idris. After that he brought me to the fifth heaven and I saw Aaron. Then he brought me up to the sixth heaven and I saw Abraham. After that I returned to the lotus tree in the seventh heaven *(Sidrat al-Muntaha)* and saw four rivers, among them were the Nile and the Euphrates. Afterwards, I was brought a vessel of wine, a vessel of milk, and a vessel of honey, and I took the milk. He said, 'This is the instinct which you and your people have'" (*Mishkat*, p. 518-520).

(2) Paradise : its *huris* and youths. Muhammad took the belief in the existence of the *huris* in paradise from the Zoroastrians, who said that in heaven will be found the spirits of luminous, young, and pretty girls, and that the reward of war heroes will be an eternity with the youths and *huris*. The Indians likewise believed in the *huris*. As for the word *huri*, its meaning can be traced to the Avestan and old Persian languages, in which it refers to the sun and its light. It is the same as the Pahlavic word *hour*, which developed in modern Persian into *hur* (See also The Book of the Laws of Manwa; chapter 5, verse 89). So in keeping with this Persian belief and expression, the Quran refers to *"huris*, cloistered in cool pavilions" (Sura al-Rahman 55 : 72), and "wide-eyed *huris* as the likeness of hidden pearls" (Sura al-Waqi 'a 56 : 22, 23).

(3) Muhammad's instructor : Salman the Persian. The Quran testifies that it was Salman the Persian who dictated the Persian stories to Muhammad. We read in the Quran : "And We know very well that they say, 'Only a mortal is teaching him.' The speech of him at whom they hint is barbarous; and this is speech Arabic, manifest" (Sura al-Nahl 16 : 103).

Salman was a Persian who was converted to Islam. He also became one of the companions. It was he who advised Muhammad to dig a trench at the time when Medina was under siege, which advice Muhammad readily took. It was also he who advised Muhammad to use catapults in the invasion of Banu Thaqif in al-Ta'if. The Arabs accused Muhammad of receiving assistance from him when compiling the Quran, and of falling back on him as a source for many stories and phrases. Although Muhammad said that Salman was barbarous (a non-Arab) and that the Quran was Arabic, this does not rule out the fact that the contents and intention may have come from Salman, whereas the Arabic style of phraseology may have come from Muhammad (Abd al-Fadi 1997 : 320).

The Night Journey borrowed from Persians
392. Is not this story of the heavenward ascension of Muhammad borrowed from the books of the Persians and their ancient legends which were written 400 years before the Migration in a Persian book entitled : Artioraf Namak (*CVQ* 1994 : 184) ?

Zoroastrian influence on Islam
393. Is it not a fact that one of the ancient religious communities the Zoroastrians had established their fire-temples in Muzdolite, a station near Kaaba and the sacred well Zamzam, the Black Stone within the Kaaba were nothing but the relics left by them ? According to Benjamin Walker; "Zoroastrian angelology and demonology have influenced Judaism, Christianity and Islam" (1999 : 27).

Prophet Muhammad knew the Zoroastrians as magi or the Majcus (22 : 17) and kept them in high esteem like Hanifs who were against idol worship.

Zamzam for the Zoroastrians
394. Is there anything to be proud about the well of Zamzam, the story related to Hagar ? Did this well Zamzam not exist long before Islam, because it was sacred to the early Zoroastrians who muttered their prayers there with a low buzzing sound, after which the well was named (Walker 1999 : 46) ?

Is Blackstone a Relic left by Zoroastrians ?
395. Is not it a fact that there is a reference of *Magians* (22 : 17) or Zoroastrian in the Quran, who were classified among the hanifs-- those who had abandoned idolatry ? They seem to have been established in Arabia from very ancient times. Their fire-temples are mentioned in some early Arabic texts, and one of them was situated in Muzdalifa, a 'station' of the Kaaba pilgrimage. The sacred well of Zamzam near the Kaaba was also sacred to the early Zoroastrians. How can you deny that the Black Stone within the Kaaba might not have been a relic left by them ?

23 - The Story of Cave Men from the Greeks

We cannot eliminate the Greek influence on the Holy Quran. Even Allah could quote the character of Alexander the Great (Zulqarnain) means the two-horned man who was changed with a mission by him in the text of Quran (18 : 83 ff; 5 : 86). The Meccan sura al-Kahf may be called a lesson on the brevity and mystery of life that include the story of the companions of the cave who slept therein for a long period and yet thought they had been there only a day or so.

Gilbert Grandguillaume remarks how the existence of Greek terms in the Quran is attested, even if it is not always acknowledged by the exegetes. Citing Greek terms in the Quran he quoted suraAl-Kauthar which means "abundance" is a word from Greek Katharis. The spoils of war (Sura 8) from Greek "libation", the term that for Berque means "flighty birds." Recalling Badal comes from the Greek, meaning "hurl" : "pelting birds" (Sura 105) (2010 : 57-58). Let us see how the Greek story of cave men reflects in the Quran :

The Story of Cave Men from the Greek

396. The Christians became sinner and the king and the Roman Emperor Diocletian killed the people who refused to worship idols. Fearing the persecution 309 youths entered to a cave with a dog named Qitmir. They were faithful to the true God. After many years the shepherd opened the door of the cave, and the angel woke the youths up. One of them went out to buy food for them with the money that was with them. When he presented the money, the people found it exotic and thought he had chanced on a treasure. (al-Razi's, Ibn Kathir's and al-Tabari's commentaries on Sura al-Kahf. 18 : 9-22) Is this story not a carbon copy of the ancient Greek legend entitled, "The Story of the Seven Sleepers" which was widespread at the time of Muhamamd ?

If the revelation ceased to come to Muhammad, Gabriel said to him that he would not enter a house wherein there is a dog, how then did the angels turn to the Men of the Cave while their dog was stretching its paws out on the threshold (Sura al-Maida 5 : 4) ?

Behind this story there is another story, so Allah reveals these verses in Sura al- Kahf (18 : 9-25) to Prophet Muhammad. "Quraish sent a group of people to the Jews in Medina to get them some information concerning Muhammad, whether he was really a prophet or only a pretender. When the delegates of the Quraish arrived at Medina and met its Jewry, they said : 'Ask him about these three, about certain youths who disappeared in the former age. What has become of them ? Their story is surely a marvel. And ask him about a wandering man who reached the two extremities of the earth. What was his story ? And ask him about the spirit. What is it ? If he tells you, he is a prophet, but if he does not, he is a liar. When they asked Muhammad these questions, he answered from the uncertain and indefinite information which he knew.' The Quran's answers, therefore, do not go beyond saying : 'Your Lord knows very well how long you have tarried,' and 'Say : "My Lord knows very well their number" (Al-Nisaburi narration Qtd. *CQV*. 1994 : 195-196).

24 - Alif Lam Mim and the Concept of Aum

I first suspect when I find the similarity between the Aryan and Arabian Hajj rituals. It cannot be disbelieved that once Kaaba was a Shrine of the Pagans where 360 idols were worshipped during the Pre-Islamic period. Only to please these gods and goddess the Pagans bowing and postrating shaving the hair, wearing a white robe, circumambulating around a square and revered the black stone with kiss and drink the sacred water of Zamzam. It is so similar to a Hindu pilgrim that the Muslim historian Firishta writes : "Before the advent of Islam, the Brahmans of India were always going on Pilgrimage to the Kaaba, for the worship of the idols there" (Qtd. Robert Spencer 2011 : 30).

To establish this connection Robert Spencer quotes Klaus K. Klostermaier who writes the records of Arabo-Indian trade with Egypt as far as 2743 BC. There were, for instance land routes through Basra or along the sea that appear to have gone through Arabia. Klostermaier continues to says :

"For several centuries a lively commerce developed between the ancient Mediterranean world and India, particularly the ports on the Western coast. The most famous of these ports was Sopara, not far from modern Bombay, which was recently, renamed Mumbai. Present day Cranganore in Kerala, identified with the ancient Muziris, claims to have had trade contacts with ancient Egypt under Queen Hatsheput, who sent five ships to obtain spices, as well as with ancient Israel during King Solomon's reign. Apparently, the contact did not break off after Egypt was conquered by Greece and later by Rome" (Qtd. Spencer 2011 : 30).

The historians have traced the connection of India with Mesopaotamia and Sumeria during Mahenjodaro period. During the Babylonian period India had trade of luxury goods at the Shatt al-Arab and Dilmun that is Bahrain.

India exported gems, ivory, cinnamon, pepper, ginger, rice, sandal wood, camphor, dyes, honey made from reeds and raw cane sugar. Indian cotton fabrics and richly hued textiles and silk were in great demand in Arab. Swords, bows and arrows were sold in high price and spears made of bamboo were bought from India. To our surprise the third Caliph Othman, in building the prophet's mosque in Madina, made the roof out of Indian teak (Walker 1999 : 17). During that time Buddhist missionaries were spreadout and preached Buddhism. Wasil ibn Ata (d. 749) was influenced by Buddhism (Walker 1999 : 308).

Imagination of Seven Heavens

397. Can we believe that there are seven heavens, and the earth is (65 : 12) for mankind and Allah lifted himself to heaven and travelled seven heavens (2 : 29) to set it up as a roof well protected (21 : 32) ? Are all the seven heavens created in two days and the lower heaven is decorated with lamps (41 : 12) and holds back heavens lest it fall upon the earth, save by his leave (22 : 65) ? If Allah created seven heavens smooth and closely fitted, one on top of the other with six other heavens as roofs he must have created our earth together with six other earths like it. How could it be that the millions of s-   tars floating in limitless space are lamps fixed in an imaginary roof ?

Concepts of Fourteen Worlds

398. Is there any novelty in mentioning of seven heavens (17 : 46; 23 : 88; 41 : 11; 65 : 12) and seven hells (15 : 44) in Quran ? Much earlier than the advent of Islam, the Hindus and Zoroastrians had this concept of Seven Upper world (*Sapta Urdhvalokas*) and seven Under world (*Sapta Adholokas*) mentioned into as fourteen worlds or *Chathurdasa Bhubanas* such as :

Sapta Urdhvalokas (Seven Upper Worlds)	**Saptha Adholokas** (Seven Under Worlds)
(1) *Bhuloka*	(1) *Athala*
(2) *Bhuvarloka*	(2) *Vithala*
(3) *Swarloka*	(3) *Suthala*
(4) *Mahahloka*	(4) *Talathala*
(5) *Janalok*	(5) *Rasathala*
(6) *Tapah*	(6) *Mahathala*
(7) *Satyalok or Brahmalok.*	

(7) *Pathala.*

Hindu Thought through Zoroastrian Influence

399. Is not it a fact that the Quran records
1. The story of a flying trip through seven heavens
2. The Huries of Paradise
3. Paradise with its wine, women, and song
4. Azazil and other spirits coming up from Hades
5. The bridge of Sirat
6. The king of death
7. The peacock story
8. The concept of seven heavens and fourteen worlds.

which were borrowed either from Zoroastrianism or Hinduism ?

Which Adam of which Age ?

400. Like so many Yugs (Ages) and so many Indras in Indian scriptures did Muhammad not echo hundred thousand Adams of whom we are the children of the last Adam ? Does not Muhammad affirm that there have been 1, 24,000 prophets since Adam and he himself is the last of them ? By saying so does not Muhammad tell a story quoted by Ibn al- Arabi in *Futuhat Makkiya :*

Once Moses asked God, show me some of Thy marvels. God asked him to go to a certain place. There was a pit, yet a desert, and none to talk with. Moses threw a pebble in the pit, and from within came a voice : "Who are you ?" Moses introduced himself by giving his geneology upto Adam -- and he was proud of knowing so much-- but continued the invisible talker : "Which Adam ? For every ten thousand years somebody comes and throws a pebble in this pit, and on question gives exactly the same name and geneology as yours, and the pit is fast filling with these pebbles !" (Hamidullah 1979 : 14-15).

Is Kapila Dhu'l-Kifl ?

401. Does not Muhammad Hamidullah suspect that the fig tree mentioned in the Quran (95 : 1) may refer to the Bodhi tree and Buddha's birth place Kapila-Vastu which is supposed to have given the name of the Prophet *Dhu'l-Kifl* from Kapila (1979 : 19) ?

Allah is Everywhere not only at Kaaba

402. Is it not a widespread tradition that Guru Nanak the founder of the Sikh religion once visited Mecca ? One day he was lying on the floor of the mosque, with his legs stretched out towards the Kaaba. A steward who happened to be near invited him to adopt a more respectful attitude towards the House of Allah. The subtle-minded Nanak replied : "Take my legs, and turn them in the direction where God is not." The Steward did not insist further, and went away.

Meaning of Alif Lam Mim

403. Why do you boast that "Alif Lam Mim" (ALM), a shorter prayer in the first chapter, devoted to the praise of God only the subject matter of the book commencing with the second chapter, the first verse of which begins as : "A.L.M. This is the Book; in it is guidance sure, without doubt, to those who fear Allah", of the Quran, cannot be understood because of the profound mysteries of the letters.

But there is no mystery in it. If we read from right to left, this figure of OM represents the numbers 786. That is, Islamic symbol of 786 is made from Hindu symbol of OM. If we split Om into three strokes 7, 8, 6 as above separately in Sanskrit and rewrite each number 7, 8 and 6 from right to left, we get the Islamic 786.

When God has revealed the entire *Quran* for the benefit of mankind, how can God keep its symbol *A*lif *L*am *M*im (7l) a secret ? The letters

Alif (A) |
Lam (L) J
Mim (M) P

are nothing but Alif (A), Wao (O) and Mim (M), i.e. A,O,M or 'Om'.

Lam (L) can be pronounced as Wao (O), according to Arabic grammar, under certain circumstances. In Arabic we write Shamsaldin, but you read it as Shamsuddin. When we write Nizamaldin, but we read it as Nizamuddin. Does not Lam (L) become silent here and give the sound of Wao (O or U) ? According to Arabic grammar, when Lam (L) comes between a vowel and a consonant, it becomes silent and gives the sound of Arabic Pesh (O or U). Similar is the case here with Alif (A), Lam (L), and Mim (M). Here Lam (L) is in between the vowel Alif (A) and the consonant Mim (M) and therefore, it becomes silent and gives the sound of O or U. Accordingly, Alif, Lam and Mim give the sound of Alif (A) Wao (O or U) and Mim (M), i.e. AOM or AUM. This is nothing but 'Om'. It is clearly and unambiguously 'Om' and nothing but 'Om'. Hence the word OUM and Allah refer to the same God. Let us see the similarities between Oum and Allah :

25 - The Words of Umar Reflect in the Quran

'Umar Ibn al- Khattab had a piece of land in the upper section of Medina, and the only way he could get to it was through a *beit midrash* (house of prayer) that belonged to the Jews. So it was that whenever he was there, he would sit down and listen to what they had to say. Once they said to him, "There is none among Muhammad's friends that is dearer to us than you, and we have ambitions for you. Umar said, "By God, I have not come to you out of love for you, or because I am doubtful of my religion; rather I come to you to gain more insight about Muhammad." They said, "Who of the angels is Muhammad's friend that comes to him ?" He answered, "Gabriel," they said, "That is our enemy." 'Umar said, "Whosoever is enemy to God and His angels and His Messengers, and Gabriel, and Michael--surely God is an enemy to him." When Muhammad heard of it, he said that it was so revealed to him, and recorded it in his Quran in Sura al-Baqara 2 : 98. Later Muhammad said to Umar, "Your Lord was in agreement with you, 'Umar" (Al-Fadi 1997 : 312).

Umar's Contribution to Quran

404. Wouldn't it have been more correct for Muhammad to say that Umar was in agreement with his Lord, and not the other way round ? What strikes us as even more strange is the fact that Muhammad plagiarised the sayings of Umar and claimed that they were revealed ! In that case, is Umar to be considered an inspired prophet, or did Muhammad plagiarise the sayings of another and claim them as revelation ?

Al-Bukhari and others reported that Umar said, "I was in agreement with my Lord on three things : : When I said, 'O Messenger of God, I would that you take Abraham's station for a place of prayer' (Muhammad took the words from his mouth and had them recorded in his Quran in Sura-al-Baqara 2 : 125 : "Take to yourselves Abraham's station for a place of prayer"). And when I said, 'O Messenger of God, both the righteous and the unrighteous come in to your wives; why not order them to use a curtain' (Muhammad took the words from Umar's mouth and had them recorded in Sura-al-Ahzab 33 : 53). And in the incident of jealousy (over Ayesha), where his wives were gathered against him. Therefore Umar said to them, 'It is possible that if he divorces you, his Lord will give him in exchange wives better than you." (Muhammad also took these words verbatim and had them recorded in Sura al-Tahrim 66 : 5). Are God's words taken from the mouths of mere men (Abd Al- Fadi. 1997 : 312-315) ?

Section
IV
Believe it or Not

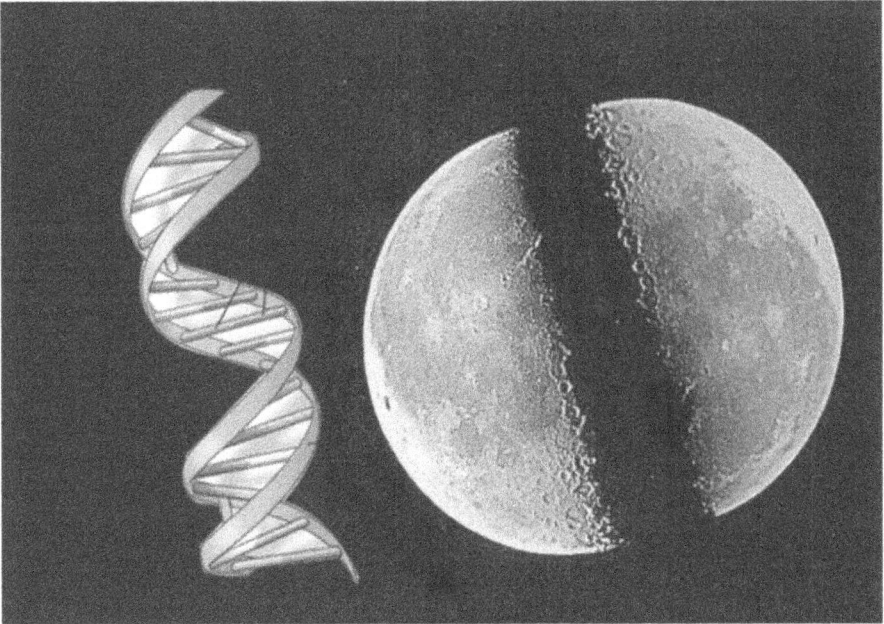

26 - Quaranic Science

Once Prophet Muhammad said : "He who leaves home in search of knowledge is walking in the way of God." The search for knowledge started in Arabia when Aristotle and Plato were translated in 800 AD. John Bowker remarks : it created tension between thinkers who favored reason and those who preferred the guidance of revelation. And he admits : "Arab medicine was based on Greek and Indian learning, and the works of Galen, of 2nd century CE were fundamental to it (1997 : 74). The 16th century Algebra, Logarithms, and Algorithms which are named after the great al-Khwarizmi of Khiva (d 846 CE), are all inventions of Arab mathematicians. Their use of the Indian number system made great advances possible (Bowker 1997 : 174).

Here we cannot ignore Al-Razi, who was born in 850 AD at Rayy near modern Teheran and who was an encyclopedia of medicine with many extracts from Greek and Hindu authors as well as his own personal observations (Khan, *Radiance* 9-15 Feb, 1992 : 7). Al-Razi left his mark in the field of surgery too.

In the field of astronomy the Bowayh sultan built an observatory in his palace at Baghdad in 982 AD where Abdal-Rahman Al-Sufi, Ahmad-al-Saghni and the celebrated Abu-Al- Wafe were engaged in exploring the space.

In the field of optics and particularly in the problems of vision al-Kandi (786-866), the first Muslim scientist discovered the most fundamental principles of optics that rays issue in all directions from every point of the surfaces of the eye, with behavior analogous to that of external light.

But one has to admit that Islamic theory of science is not based on reason and sound logic about the creation. But it is more romantic than scientific. In the Quran it is said : "We have adorned the lowest heaven with lamps" (67 : 5). And it is also said : "The creations of these stars are for three purposes. i.e., as decoration on the sky, as missiles to hit the devils, and as signs to9 guide travellers" (*Buk* 4 : 420). Let us see some more instances of Quranic scientific theory.

Sun Runs and Rests
405. Does the sun run to a fixed resting place (36 : 38) or it is a stationary star that does not move ?

No Clash between Sun and Moon
406. Is it Allah's arrangement that both sun and moon are swimming in the sky and the sun is not permitted to catch the moon, nor can the night outstrip the day (36 : 40) ?

Sun sets in Mud Pond
407. Is it possible to reach the place where the sun sets in the spring filled with water and mud (18 : 83-86) ?

Allah postpones the Date to Astray Unbelievers
408. Is not it confusing to determine the difference between solar and lunar calender when Allah postpones the date to astray the unbelievers to fight (9 : 36-37) ?

Moon has its Station
409. Is the moon determined by its station, till it runs like the old lower part of a date-stalk (36 : 39) ?

Hide and Seek Game between Crescent and Eid
410. Is it always possible to see the new crescent to determine the beginning of a month ? Though the month shall have 30 days but it will be 29 days if the new moon is seen on the evening of the 29th day. If the Lunar month begins on the day immediately following the day of conjunction (eclipse) whether it is visible at a particular location or not then the incoming month will be counted from 2nd day only and Ramadhan fasting would be one day less. If Shawwal in moon is correctly sighted on the 29th, Ramadhan would have only 28 days and therefore Muslims are forced to extend Ramadhan onto the Eid day, which is a day, prohibited for fasting, as the days and dates must coincide. Is it necessary to fix the month based on the visible crescent which may fall on 2nd or 3rd ?

Eclipse caused Fear
411. Is it not a fact that the Prophet had no idea of Solar or Lunar eclipse ? Was he not afraid of Solar and Lunar eclipse as if the Day of Judgement has arrived (*Buk* 2 : 167) ? Out of fear did he not offer prayer and invoke Allah till the eclipse was over because his son Ibrahim had died on that day and it was there in his mind (*Buk* 2 : 161, 170) ?

Magic Number in the Quran
412. Does the Islamic calender accept 365 days in a year ? If not then how can we interpret the word *Shahr* meaning month which is repeated twelve times in the Quran as equal to the number of months in a year and the word *Yum* meaning day which is repeated 365 times in the Quran as equal to the number of days in a year. Moreover, how does one interpret both the words *Satan* and *maleeke* (angels) which are repeated 88 times and *hayat* (life) and *mut* (death) which are repeated 145 times ?

Thunder is an Angel
413. Is thunder an angel (13 : 13) who is entrusted with the clouds and drives them away at the will of Allah or is it electricity generated by the collision of positively and negatively charged ions in the clouds which create sound ? Can we say that thunder rebukes the clouds ? Is it poetry or science ?

Stars are Ammunition for Angel
414. Is an angel, the size of a man, holding the stars like pieces of ammunition for stoning Satan (67 : 5; 37 : 6-10; 15 : 66-18) ? Can the angel use star as war materials which are nothing but an enormous galaxy floating at huge distances in limitless space ?

Note for the Astronomers
415. Are stars created by Allah as missiles to hit the devils, as Muhammad says (*Buk* 4 : 420) ?

Is Earth Flat ?
416. If the earth is egg shaped (79 : 30) why did Allah repeatedly say that He has made the earth as a carpet spread out (71 : 19), so that one can go about therein, in spacious roads (71 : 20) ?

Mountains keep the Earth from Moving

417. If Allah created the heavens without any visible pillars (31 : 10) stretched out the earth and set therein firm mountains (13 : 3), as paperweight to support the earth so that it would not fall down somewhere, (15 : 19; 16 : 15; 21 : 31) how was it possible to stretch out the earth, flatten and motionless, when we know that it rotates on its axis once in every 24 hours and revolves around the sun once a year ?

Mount Qaf encompasses the Earth

418. Allah swore by the mountain Qaf when He says : "Qaf by the glorious Quran" (50 : 1). Mt Qaf holds a prominent place in Quran.

When 'Abdallah Ibn Salam inquired of Muhammad, saying, 'What is the highest peak in the world ?' Muhammad said, "It is Mount Qaf" He asked, 'And what is it ?' Muhammad said,' It is of green chrysolite, to which the sky owes its greenness.' What is the height of Mount Qaf ?' Muhammad answered, 'It is a journey of five hundred years !' He asked him further, 'How long does it take a man to cover its circumference ?' He answered, 'It is a journey of two thousand years.'

Is it not a fact that the story of Mt.Qaf actually originated from the Hebrew word *qav* which can be translated as "line" and *tohu* which means emptiness or formlessness ? The word *tohu* (*Gn* 1 : 2) refers to green line encompassing the entire world from which darkness issues. Is it not ridiculous to interpret the horizon or *tohu* which is an imaginary line as a majestic mountain chain ?

Mountain can be like Canopy

419. When Allah said He will uproot the mountain and leave it above like a canopy (7 : 171; 4 : 154) does he intend to intimidate the Jews and force them to receive the law of Moses ? Doesn't this do away with the scientific law of gravitation and the moral law of divine love (*CQV* 1994 : 128-129) ?

Islamic Genetics

420. Is it not a fact that the statement "genetics is the key to the physical characteristics of one's children" is defied by Muhammad who believed : If a man has sexual intercourse with his wife and gets a discharge first, the child will resemble the father, and if the woman gets her discharge first, the child will resemble her (*Buk* 4 : 546) ?

Man created from ejected Liquid

421. Is it a fact that man was created from ejected liquid (a drop emitted) proceeding from between the backbone and the ribs (86 : 6-7) or from the sperm originated from the mid--gut section of a man's body ?

Is Abortion before 120 Days no Killing ?

422. Is it a fact that the fetus' "moment of humanity" is calculated at 120 days in the Quran after conception when "ensoulment" takes place ? According to Hadith the Quran alludes to four stages before ensoulment. According to Islam, the embryo takes human shape 40 to 42 days after conception. Some Islamic jurists would allow abortion upto 40 days "for social reasons". Others would permit it up to 120 days "for medical reasons". After that, it would be considered the same as killing according to Ibn-Hazim, a prophet of the tenth century. However, abortion thereafter to save the woman's life would be considered the "lesser of two evils."

Fever comes from the Heat of Hell

423. Does fever come from the heat of Hell, so put it out (cool it) with water (*Buk* 7 : 619) ?

Spitting is Medicating

424. Is it not a dirty practice of Muhammad to spit into the hands of his followers so that they could rub the saliva on their faces (*Buk* 3 : 891) ?

Healing through Spit

425. Is it possible to cure a man with eye trouble by spitting in his eyes as Muhammad was doing (*Buk* 4 : 192; 5 : 51) ?

How far was Muhammad justified while claiming that all manner of diseases could be cured with his spit (*Buk* 7 : 641) ?

Is it believable that Muhammad, by waiving his hand over the wound, reciting the Quran, and by applying his spit to the wound, snake bites, scorpion stings, and all kinds of illness, could heal them (*Buk* 7 : 637-642) ?

Remedy for Plague

426. If you hear of an outbreak of plague in a land, the prophet said do not enter it, but if the plague breaks out in a place while you are in it, do not leave that place (*Buk* 7 : 624). Is it the remedy for Plague ?

Kill Snakes having Stripes

427. Why should we kill the snakes having stripes over them and having short tail ? Do they really cause miscarriage of a pregnant woman and affect the eyesight adversely (*Mus* 4 : 5544) ?

27 - The End of Reason

Doubt is knowledge and faith is ignorance. Doubt is the mother of all inventions and discoveries. Human society gains more in doubt than in belief. Newton doubted the falling of an apple and gravitation was discovered , Marcony threw a pebble to the pond and discovered the wave lines in the air. People are cheated not because they doubt but because they believe. Can one hear a crying palm tree, a talking wolf, Jinn eating dung and bones, angel having 600 wings etc. If you believe these unbelievable things add a few more impossibilities.

Results of changing Sabbath Day

428. How is it that Allah commanded the Jews to hallow friday but they disobeyed God and chose Saturday ? The additional command of Allah relating to the Sabbath was that they should not do any work including fishing on the Sabbath day. It would have been really amusing had the fish known the Sabbath day and appealed to the Jews on that day and swim away and would not be seen again till the next sabbath hence be saved. Satan now tempted them to go fishing as a result Allah transformed them into apes howling at one another (7 : 163; al-Tabari's commentary on Sura al-Araf; *CQV.* 1994 : 127-128). Does it not mean Allah misguides and confuses His people ?

Can Birds Fight with Stone ?

429. We read in the Sura al-Fil 105 : 1-5 : "Hast thou not seen how thy Lord did with the Men of the Elephant ? Did He not make their guile to go astray ? And He loosed upon them birds in fights, hurling against them stones of baked clay and He made them like green blades devoured."

Al-Baidwai explained : It has been reported that the Battle of the Elephant took place in the year of the Prophet's birth. Abraha al-Ashram, the king of Yemen, who reigned before Ashama the Negus, built a church in San'a and called it *Qalis* most likely from the Greek ecclesia. He hoped to turn the Pilgrims' attention to it. It happened that a man from Kinana went forth and stayed in it overnight, which angered Abraha. He, therefore, swore to tear down the Kaaba. He went forth with his army having with him a strong elephant named Mahmud and another she-elephant. When he prepared to enter, and mobilised his army, the elephant arrived, and whenever they pointed it toward Mecca, it knelt down and remained there. But whenever they pointed it toward Yemen, or any other direction, it would trot away. So God Almighty sent birds.

But we do not understand why did the elephant prefer to help the heathen and refrain from helping the Christians, refusing to walk whenever they pointed it toward the Kaaba of the heathen, and trotting away whenever they pointed it toward Yemen ? How did the birds comprehend this and join the heathen in war against the Christians ? How did the flocks of birds understand one another, know the exact spot of the battle, bring along pebbles, carry them with their beaks and feet, and stone the army of the Christians without hitting the heathen ? How could it be that God would side with the elephant, the birds and the pagan worshippers of the Kaaba against the Christians ? And finally, how could a pebble "smaller than a chick-pea" fall down from the beak of a bird onto a man's head, penetrate his skull, chest and abdomen, and exit from his rectum (Abd Al-Fadi, 1997 : 285-286) ?

Is Thunder an Angel ?

430. Is thunder an angel who proclaims the praise of Allah (13 : 13) ? Answering to the question of Ibn Abbas the Prophet said : Thunder is an angel entrusted with the clouds and entwined shreds of fire with which he drives the cloud (*Al-Baidawi*). Muhammad did not know that thunder and lightening are natural phenomena resulting from the collision of positive and negative charges in cold and hot air, not from any angels ?

Cave Life of 309 Years

431. How was it feasible for seven young men, together with their dog, to live for 309 years without eating, drinking, walking, urinating or defecating; seemingly awake, but yet asleep, turning right and left in their sleep, while their dog was stretching its paws on the threshold (18 : 9-26) ?

Is not this myth a second century myth of Christian youths who went to sleep in a cave for 300 years because they were persecuted for their faith ? The hero of this was a Christian not a Muslim as the Muslim claim.

Tortured in the Grave

432. Muhammad heard the voices of the dead persons in their grave. Once Muhammad went through the graveyards of Medina and heard the voices of two humans who were being tortured in their graves. By hearing the conversation between two dead people Muhammad said, "They are being punished, but they are not being punished because of a major sin, yet their sins are great. One of them never used to save himself from (being soiled with) the urine, and the other used to go about with calumnies (Namima)." Then Muhammad asked for a green palm tree leaf and split it into two pieces and placed one piece on each grave, saying, "I hope that their punishment may be abated as long as these pieces of the leaf are not dried" (*Buk* 8.73.81).

Dream or Reality ?

433. How are we going to interpret the following facts from the life of Prophet Muhammad :   Once during the childhood two men in white clothes came to Muhammad with a golden basin full of snow. They took him and split open his body, took his heart and split it open and took out from it a black clot which they flung away. Then they washed his heart and his body with that snow until they made them pure (*Ish* : 72).

Chest Operation of Muhammad

434. Can one believe when Muhammad was in Mecca, the roof of his house was opened and Gabriel descended, opened his chest, and washed it with Zamzam water. Then he brought a golden tray full of wisdom and faith and having poured its contents into his chest, he closed it (*Buk* 1.8.345).

Eating and Talking Bread

435. Muhammad's eating and talking bread shout out loud to glorify Allah (*Buk* 4 : 56, 779).

A Talking Wolf

436. Unis bin Amar became Muslim when he was amongst his sheep and suddenly a wolf caught a sheep. He shouted. The wolf set on its tail and addressed him : "Do you forbid me the provision which Allah has provided me ?" When I clapped my hands the wolf said : There is something more curious and wonderful than this : that is, Allah's messenger in those palm trees inviting people to Allah (Islam). This changed his life (*Buk* 5 : 40).

Cry of a Palm Tree

437. When the prophet used a pulpit while delivering a sermon, the trunk of a palm tree started crying like a pregnent she-camel because he did not stand beneath the tree to preach so the prophet went to it, caressing the tree to stop its crying (*Buk* 2 : 13-14, 41; 4 : 783).

Food of the Spirit

438. The *Jinn* or spirits eat dung and bones (*Buk* 5 : 200) ?

Tying Satan in a Pillar

439. Is not it a fact that when Muhammad was offering prayer Satan came in front of him and tried to interrupt his prayer, but Allah gave Muhammad an upper hand and Muhammad choked him ? Muhammad thought of tying Satan to one of the pillars of the mosque till Muslims got up in the morning and saw Satan. But Allah made Satan return with his head down (humiliated) (*Buk* 2.22.301). Is it a hallucination or reality ?

Satan can Stay in your Nose

440. Muhammad would suck in water up his nose and then blow it out because Satan stays in the upper part of the nose all night (*Buk* 4 : 516).

Satan urinates in the ears of those who fall asleep during *namaz* (*Buk* 2 : 245).

Gabriel's Six Hundred Wings

441. The angel Gabriel has 600 wings (*Buk* 6 : 60, 380). He can also take the form of a human being (*Buk* 4 : 56, 827).

Foretell the Number of Dates in a Garden

442. Muhammad could estimate the number of dates, a garden would contain before it was harvested (*Buk* 2 : 559).

Iron becomes Soft

443. Iron changes its property in David's hand (34 : 10-11) and becomes as flexible and soft as wax without being heated or hammered.

Muhammad spit on a Dry Well and filled it with Water

444. Is it not a fact that when Muhammad spat into a dry well, it was filled with enough water to satisfyed 1400 men and their camels (*Buk* 4 : 777; 5 : 471, 472)?

Can you Believe

445. a. Mountains and Birds can praise Allah in Human Tongue (34 : 10).

b. That Solomon flew on the wind and moved (34 : 12).

c. That Jinn built temple (34 : 12) and once a tree informed Muhammad that the Jinns hear the Quran (*Buk* 5 : 58, 199).

d. That Prayer brings rain (*Buk* 2 : 55) ?

Section

V

Aslim Taslam
(Accept Islam and Submit to Allah)

28 - Be : It Becomes

The creation story of semitic religions is a myth. In the Quran it is said : Who is it that sustains you from the sky and from the earth ? Or who is it who has power over hearing and sight ? And who is it who brings out the living from the dead and the dead from the living ? And who is it who rules and regulates all affairs ? They will soon answer, "Allah" (Sura 10 : 31; Trans. Esposito 1995 : 1 : 77).It begins with the Babylonian story of creation through water and Egyptian story of mud of the Nile river and Greek chaos surrendered by water and darkness. Throughout the Bible and the Quran God or Allah is identified as the creator.If Allah commanded "*Kun Fayakoon*" or "Be ! And it becomes", who was there to obey his command ? We are not supposed to ask such questions to God who is not answerable.

Allah's command on Creation
446. Before the creation when Allah commanded or *Kun Fayakoon* "Be ! It becomes" who was there to obey His command ?

Earth or Heaven : Which was created First ?
447. The earth was created first (41 : 9-12) or the heaven (79 : 27-32) ?

Why Woman is Uglier than Man ?
448. Is it a fact that man becomes more beautiful with increasing years but woman more ugly because Adam was created out of dust but Hawwa out of a bone (Gibb 1974: 138?

Height of Adam
449. Was Adam really 60 cubits tall means as tall as a three-storey building (*Buk* 4 : 543) ? How tall were Eve and her Children ?

Hawwa offered her Husband the first Wine
450. Is it not a fact that Hawwa, though her name does not occur in the Quran (7 : 19) offered her husband the first wine, before the forbidden fruit and caused mankind eternal grief (Gibb 1974 : 138) ?

29- Unity of Godhead

Bedouins were animists. They associated spirits with rocks and springs and trees. They were also influenced by the Semitic religion existing in that land. Besides such beliefs they had their goddesses of importance like al-lat, al-Uzzah, and al-Manat, alongwith a superior male deity whom they called Allah. The annual festival was held at the shrine of al-manat at Ukaz, not far from Mecca. In Mecca itself there was a temple of their principal God called Hubal near the well of Zamzam. The temple was built in rectangular stone. Each clan erected their own deity. A certain month of the lunar calendar was considered sacred. During that time fighting was forbidden, people of different tribes came to Kaaba not only for piligrimage or trade but for poetry competition (Parrinder 1971 : 465).

Besides the Bedouins, Arabia was home to a large Jewish and Christian community. Though the population of the Christians was less than the Jews the Christians had their community at Najran to the south and east of Mecca. To help them, the Ethiopian Christian invaders destroyed the Jewish kingdom in South of Arabia. Inspite of the Jewish and the Christian background Arabia still reminded us of the gods and goddesses till the period of Muhammad. Let us see how the goddesses of Arabia took a prominent place in their culture. How Allah was accepted as a special identity can be seen in these following questions.

L stands for Divine

451. Is it not a fact that the phoneme *L* was divine in all Semitic languages ? So the Babylonians and Assyrians called their god as *Ilu*, the Hebrew *Elohim*, the Aramaean *Alaha*, the Arabians *Ilah* or *Allah*, the Nabataean *Elh* or *Alh* and the Canaanite *El*. ?

The Word "Allah" derives from Elohim

452. Is it not a fact that in Arabic language, the name *Allah* is derived from *al-el-hu* and "El" or Allat, which is an old Semitic name for God meaning "The strong and the almighty ?"

The Jewish name for God is Elohim and the plural is *hum* whereas Allah *hu* is used as singular.

When the Muslims do not believe that Jesus was ever hung on the cross why do they claim that Jesus said on the cross "Eloi Eloi Lama Sabachthani" means "Allah, Allah Lama Sabachthani" ? Can you prove "Eloi" is not a Hebrew word (*Ps* 21:)?

Definition of Allah

453. Is Allah a spiritual Being or some sort of mental illusion or a hegemonistic idea of Muhammad ? Does He represent man's quest for knowledge or is He a projection of a less edifying source in man's psyche ? Allah seems to be helpless and tries to communicate through a favourite intermediary like his only son Jesus or the last messenger Muhammad. Once Allah and his messenger have decided a thing, where is a choice for the believers ?

Abdullah means Servant of God

454. If Allah is the Islamic connotation of God, how is it that the word 'Allah' was in use as proper noun among the pre-Islamic Arabs, for example, Muhammad's pagan father's name was Abdullah where *abd* means servant and *Allah* means God, so it means "servant of Allah" ?

Allah the Pagan and Jewish God

455. Is it not a fact that to please the Jews and the pagans Muhammad adopted their deity *El* (*Gn* 16 : 23; 17 : 1, 21 : 33; 31 : 13; 35 : 7) for whom Jacob once erected the alter called : "El-Elohe-Israel" which means "El the God of the Israel." ?

Why 99 Names of Allah ?

456. Is not it a fact that Allah has 99 most beautiful names; 72 of which are used in the Quran 1286 times ? Sometimes they contradict, even cancel each other out. As a result, the Islamic theologian Al-Ghazali wrote that Allah is everything and nothing. He cannot be grasped by the human mind and is greater than we can comprehend; he rules and governs all and is the sole controller of the universe (Al-Masih. *Islam Under* 13).

Pagan Titles of Allah

457. Is it not a fact that out of the 99 titles given to Allah many of them are borrowed and modified upon the names of the pagan gods ? Are the names *al-Wadud*, "the loving" not derived from Wadd, a moon-god; *al-Mani*, "the Withholder" from the North Arabian god Munim, *al-Salaam*, "the Peace" from the Tayman deity Salm; *al-Kawi*, "The strong" from Kayis who is regarded as the consort of Manat and has not Aziz, the Arabian god been retained as *al-Aziz*, "the mighty" ? Are the names *al-Rahman*, "the Merciful" and *al-Rahim*," the Compassionate" not derived and preserved from pre-Islamic times which were the designations used for pagan gods (Walker : 1998 : 43) ?

Allah is a Noun not a Verb

458. Are not the 99 names of Allah merely nouns and not verbs because as nouns they were simply signifying something but as verbs they did not necessarily produce any action ?

Allah or Huwa which one is Correct ?

459. Which manuscript of the Holy Quran is correct--- the Tashkent MSS or the modern Egyptian Quran ? In 5 passages : 2 : 284; 2 : 283; 3 : 37; 3 : 109 and 5 : 119 the Tashkent MSS uses the word 'Allah' while the modern Egyptian Quran, uses the word 'Huwa' (the pronoun 'he'). Which word do you believe is in the "preserved master tablet" and "mother of all books" in heaven ?

Is Allah All Powerful and the Most Merciful ?

460. Compared to Allah are you sure that other gods are powerless either to harm or benefit you (5 : 76) ?

Is it not a fact that though the Quran says Allah is the "most merciful" and the "most compassionate" but He always considers the unbelievers as his enemies (2 : 90) and He wants to send these unbelievers to hell where they will be given to drink boiling fetid water (14 : 16) ?

Allah does not need change in Pagan's Prayer

461. The idolaters will say : If Allah had wished, we should not have been idolaters, neither our fathers, nor would we have forbidden ought (6 : 148); means the all powerful Allah did not guide the idolaters. Does it not prove that Allah had prescribed mercy for Himself (6 : 54) ?

I'm insignificant because Allah Wished It

462. If Allah is the defender and the destroyer and if He is the guide and the tempter, He saves whom He wills and condemns whom He wishes (76 : 31) how can He be called compassionate and merciful ?

Creatures belong to the Creator

463. Can you deny the fact that in Islam everybody is a slave of Allah ? None can claim to be free and independent or live for himself because mankind belongs to the creator as He has created us.

Nobody has seen Allah the Invisible

464. Is it a fact that Muhammad saw Allah in clear horizon (81 : 23), and he saw him descending (53 : 13), from heaven and filling the space with the greatness of his bodily structure ? Is it not the greatest lie against Allah (*Mus* 337) ?

Has Allah a Face ?

465. Does Allah have a face (28 : 88; *Buk* 9 : 502) ?

Is Allah Deaf ?

466. Why do the Muslims shout while uttering *"Allah-O-Akbar"* ? Does it mean Allah is deaf or absent ? Prophet Muhammad said One who is All-Hearing and Near to you why do you call Him in louder voice (*Mus* 4 : 6526-6528) ?

How a Spirit gives Speeches

467. If Allah is an Essence for the Sunnies why do they go on repeating the Quran, the speech of Allah ?

Is Allah High and Great ?

468. In the Holy Quran time and again Allah says : "He is oft-forgiving, most merciful, All-knowing, All-wise, High and Great." How many times should Allah repeat these adjectives after noun ? In a Persian Proverb it is said : "you said it once I believed you. You said it again I doubted you, if you mention it for the third time I know that you were telling a lie."

Identity of Allah

469. Are the Gods of the Jews and Christians and the Allah of the Muslims identical or is their association accidental ? It is like St. Paul's endeavour to make the unknown God paramount at Athens to the exclusion of all other deities ? Did not Margoliouth rightly remark that the Jewish and Christian records narrated how their Allah had despatched messengers, and such a messenger he might be. The message was in many cases subordinate to the dignity of the office, just as we think of a King's ambassador as a high official, rather than as the bearer of a definite message. For the contents of the message he had to go back to Jewish and Christian Scriptures, until the course of events provided him with plenty to say (1905 : 79-80).

Allah an Idolatry Identity

470. Does not the Prophet give an international identity to a tribal idol called Allah, and prove God's covenant with Abraham and Ishmael and not with Abraham and Isaac ?

Can Allah be replaced with Rahman ?

471. Can one deny that since the word "Allah" had pre-Islamic origin, Muhammad wanted to replace it with the word "Rahman" ?

Father does not mean Mother's Husband

472. When Muhammad says Allah has no daughters and no son, in a physical sense, He means Lat, Uzza and Manat cannot be the daughters and Christ cannot be the only son of Allah ? In a spiritual sense God, the Father, evokes thoughts of love, tenderness, compassion and protectiveness, does it mean "your mother and Allah had sexual intercourse to produce you !"

Needs of Allah

473. If Allah is self-sufficient, why does He need more Muslims ? If He is all powerful why does He ask humans : "If ye will help the cause of Allah, He will help you" (47 : 7-9) ? Why should Allah create such people whom He hates ? Either He is not a creator or He is not the All-knowing.

137

Is Allah a Jealous God ?

474. Is not it a fact that ten deities of the pre-Islamic Arabs mentioned by name in the Quran : Allat, Uzza and Manat (53 : 19); Jibt and Taguth (4 : 54); Nasr; shaped like an eagle; Yaguth, like a lion; Yahuk, like a horse; Sowa, like a woman; and Wadd, like a man (71 : 23) were believed to have formed a circle of 360 monolithic figures around the sacred shrine ? Some were tall standing stones; some were crudely fashioned in human or animal shape. Some reputedly were prehistoric, dating back to the antediluvians of Noah's time (Walker 1998 : 44).

Why did Muhammad discard them all to establish the importance of Allah who proved to be a jealous, cruel, angry, and proud God of the Muslims ?

No Alternative to Allah

475. The Quran exhorts "there is no God but Allah and Muhammad is his Prophet". If that is so, where is the place of Buddhists, Jains, atheists and agnostics and people who do not know Allah ?

Islam starts with Negation

476. Don't you think the foundation of Islam rests on Negativity, or Negation which means disowning of all existing creeds, beliefs, culture and history, because they repeat in their prayer "There is *no* god, but God" ? Here "No" means denial of anything that is non-Islamic.

Negative Concept of God

477. Is it not confusing to say : There is no god except God. That means we can say there is no dog, except a dog; there is no horse except a horse (*Year Book of Muslim World* 1996 : 46) ?

Why God swears on Himself ?

478. Is it necessary for an Almighty God to take oaths like any ordinary man, as when He swears by the fig and olive, and by Mount Sinai (95 : 1); by the declining day (103 : 1); and by the stars, the night and the dawn (81 : 15-18) ? We ask : Why does the Almighty have to swear on Himself (91 : 5) ?

Is it not a fact that many criticized the Quran on the fact that God swears or takes oaths like any mortal (95 : 1; 103 : 1; 81 : 15-18) ?

Why does the author of the Quran swear by the sun, the moon, the day, the night, heaven, the earth, the soul, the forenoon, the fig, the olive, Mount Sinai, Mecca, and the stars (89 : 1-5; 91 : 1-9; 93 : 1-3; 95 : 1-4; 86 : 1-4) ? Does a truthful person who tells the truth need to swear by an oath to confirm his saying ?

Why do we add Muhammad's Name with Allah ?

479. Why do the Muslims recite *the Kalima* "There is no God but Allah (47 : 21) Muhammad is the messenger of God," (48 : 29) though nowhere in the Quran this creed is clubbed together ? Is not the second part of this creed opposed by Abu Sofyan the longtime opponent of Muhammad ? Why did Muslims add Muhammad's name alongwith Allah which Muhammad did not like (Walker 1999 : 224)?

Is it necessary for the All Merciful Allah to curse the opponents of Muhammad, or those in which he consigns 'Muhammad's enemies like Abu Lahab and his wife to the flames of hell (111 : 1) ? Does it not mean Muhammad created his own concept of Allah to satisfy his unbound lust for women, power and money ?

138

Islam means Allah with Muhammad

480. Is not it a fact that though Allah admits He has no partner, how is it that Muhammad became His senior partner, almost equal to Allah by integrating his name with that of Allah in the *Kalmah* ? If Islam is a religion of monotheism why is it said : "Obey Allah and His Messenger" ? Does it not mean that Allah is nothing without Muhammad or more properly, Allah and Muhammad are one and the same person ?

According to James Tirmze (vol.2) if on the day of judgement Muhammad would occupy the right hand side of Allah's throne, and will be the first person who would be appointed as the intercessor and would unlock the gates of paradise and would be the first to enter the paradise followed by his followers then what is the need of an Allah for the Muslim world ? Did not the Prophet say :

"Whoever obeys me, obeys Allah, and whoever disobeys me, disobeys Allah, and whoever obeys the ruler I appoint, obeys me, and whoever disobeys him, disobeys me'" (*Buk* 9.89.251; 4 : 52.203 : *Mis* 1 : 144).

"Allah addressed the believers and said, 'In Allah's Apostle you have a fine example for anyone who hopes to be in the place where Allah is" (*Ish* : 467).

"Those who speak negatively of Allah and His Apostle shall be cursed" (33.57).

"For he who insults you (Muhammad) will be cut off" (108.3).

Is not it a fact that when Muhammad speaks as the representative of Allah who is unseen and unheard where is the scope to distinguish between Allah and Muhammad ? Are not they synonymous to each other and their voice is one ? Does not Allah become a mere decorative figure to serve the purpose of Muhammad only ? Can one believe Muhammad to be a slave of Allah ? Do slaves control their masters ? Does not this statement make Muhammad identical with Allah ?

Is not Allah a Puppet in the Hands of Muhammad ?

481. It is said that Muhammad was a humble servant of Allah. But does he not use and misuse Allah so much that Allah becomes a puppet in the hands of Muhammad and he does so to command an unquestionable obedience from his followers ? Does the Prophet not ascertain : "Whoever obeys me will enter Paradise, and whoever disobeys me will not enter it" (*Buk* 9.92.384).

30 - The Abode of Allah

The origin of the word "God" can be traced back to the ancient European tribal religion and accepted by all religionists as the only God for the whole of the universe. The Hebrew God was called "elah", "EL" and "Elohim". Elah became "Allah" in Arabic language. The entire semitic religions share one God. The Jews, Christians, Muslims and Baha'is accept the God of the Hebrew as their God. Muhammad in the Quran says about the same God or Allah as follows :

We believe in the revelation which had been sent down unto us, and also in that which had been sent down into you; our God and your God is one, and unto Him are we resigned (29 : 45-46).

In another verse Allah said of Himself as :

God ! There is no god but He, the living, the self-subsistent. Slumber seizes him not, no, nor sleep. To Him belong all that is in the heavens and upon the earth. Who is there who intercedes with Him except with His permission ? He knows what has appeared as part and as yet to come, and there is no share in his knowledge except by His will. His throne extends over the heavens and the earth, and their preservation wearies him not. He is the All-sublime, the All-glorious (Surah 2 : 255, Trans. Esposito 1 : 76).

The Jews should feel proud of Ibrahim, the first man who brought them back from pagan deities to one God who is Indivisible, Omnipotent and Eternal. Through Ibrahim the Jews got a God who could take care of a small group of semitic tribes and established an eternal contractual relationship.

The desert God of Israel became the Lord of the Universe when a Jew named Jesus came out of a narrow domestic wall and declared himself a Masiha for mankind. The same God comes to the hand of a semitic idolatrous race called Muslims at a very difficult time of history when Christianity was rising and Zorastrianism was slowly wining away. Richard Carlyon rightly remarked :

> Islam arose at a period of history when the two other main religious trends of the area, Christianity and Zorastrianism, were experiencing difficulties; difficulties over which the former was to triumph and under which the latter to collapse (1981 : 303).

Keith W. Stump remarked : "God may be dead in the West, one observer has commented, but he is very much alive in the Middle East" (1981 : 15) whose name is Allah. Allah is the supreme deity of certain ancient Arab tribes, such as those living in the Hejaz (29 : 61), a name said to be derived from the root *al*, "god", which itself is based on the phoneme *L*, the nucleus of the divine name in many semitic languages. The sound is pronounced with the tip of the tongue turned up and back against the roof of the mouth, so that it is full-throated and heavy.

To distinguish Allah from other gods, He was given the title "Allah Taala" (God the most High). In another reference from the Old Testament it is said that Jacob erected the alter called "El-Elohe-Israel" means "El the God of Israel." El was the God head of the Syro-Palestinian pantheon and *yahwe* was a part of that great God El (Dt 32 : 8-9).

For Islam Allah is One and Unique, has no partner and no equal. But the one God concept brought an innumerable misery to mankind. He is bound to be a dictator under the nondual concept and bound to be a jealous God. Schopenhauer in one place says :

> Indeed, intolerance is essential only to monotheism; an only God is by nature a jealous God who will not allow another to live. On the other hand, polytheistic gods are naturally tolerant they live and let live. In the first place, they gladly tolerate their colleagues, the gods of the same religion and this tolerance is afterwards extended even to foreign gods who are, accordingly, hospitably received and later admitted, in some cases, even to an equality of rights...thus it is only the monotheistic religions that furnish us with the spectacle of religious wars, religious persecutions, courts for trying heretics, and also with that of iconoclasm, the destruction of the images of foreign gods, the demolition of Indian temples and Egyptian colossi that had looked at the sun for three

140

thousand years; all just because their jealous God had said "Thou shalt make no graven image." And so on, (Qtd. Warraq 1993 : 49).

Now let us examine how far Schopenhauer is true in his saying through various questions concerning the Quranic God :

Kaaba before Creation

482. Can you believe that Kaaba floated like foam on the water forty years before the creation of the heaven and the earth, and it was after this time that the earth was spread out and the angels used to make ritual circumambulations *(tawaf)* around a house built below the celestial Throne *('arsh)*. Later on, God sent angels to build another house on the earth, so that the earthly creatures might do the same thing as the heavenly creatures (Hamidullah p. 74) ?

The First Centre for Human Race

483. Though Muslims call the Kaaba "Albayt alharaam" (5 : 97) and it is considered the inviolable institution of obedience to Allah's Sharia, the pue mosque: :Al-mashjid al-haraam" (see Quran 2 : 196; 5 : 97; 9 : 19; 48 : 25), but what is the proof that the Kaaba was the first centre established for the cultural advancement of the human race except for a verse in the Quran (3 : 96) ?

Builder of Kaaba

484. If Kaaba was built by Adam, destroyed in the flood of Noah and rebuilt by Ibrahim and his son Ishmael where is the chance to call it a pagan shrine ? And if it is not a Pagan shrine then how were 360 idols worshipped there ? Was Ibrahim not an idolator ? Is there any scriptural indication that Kaaba was ever destroyed in the flood of Noah ?

Is there any historical evidence that the foundation of the Kaaba was laid by Adam and completed centuries later by Prophet Ibrahim and his son Prophet Ishmael ?

How Ibrahim built the Kaaba ?

Myth

485. Muslims claim that Ibrahim built the House. They claim that Allah sent al-Sakina to locate its site. Al-Sakina, they say, was a fast-blowing wind that had two snake-like heads. Others say it was inverted while blowing. Ibrahim was commanded to set up the House at the place where the wind resides. So Ibrahim traced it until it reached the specific location where he was to build the House. Ibn Abbas said : "Allah sent the wind as big as the Kaaba. Ibrahim followed its shadow until it stopped at the location of the House. Ibrahim was called : 'O Ibrahim ! You shall build the House as big as its shadow, no more, no less !' The wind is said to have cleaned the area surrounding the Kaaba until the foundation appeared. This explains what Sura al-Hajj (22 : 26) says : 'And (remember) when We prepared for Ibrahim the place of the (holy) House.' While Ibrahim was building, Ishmael handed him the stones. This is the meaning of 'Ibrahim was raising the foundations of the House"(See Ibn Kathir's commentary on Sura al-Baqara 2 : 125-127).

Reality

The Torah teaches that Ibrahim moved neither to the Kaaba nor to Arabia. He left Ur of the

141

Chaldeans with his father, and they both lived in Haran and then moved on to Canaan. Ibrahim passed through the land to the locality of Shechem, to the oak of Moreh. From there he departed to the mountain on the east of Bethel and there he built an altar to the Lord. He journeyed on, going southward. Then he lived in the land of Egypt. He ended up at the place where he built the first altar. When he parted with Lot, he lived in the land of Canaan. Scriptures never state that he went into the Arabian Peninsula and built the Kaaba. (See Old Testament; Qtd. *Light of Life* 1994 : 38).

History of Idolatry since Noah

486. Is it not a fact that Amr Ibn Luhai is the person accountable for the idolatry of all the Arabs since he was the first one to introduce idols to the Arabian Peninsula and to place them around Kaaba and some of those idols had already been there since Noah's time ? Does not Noah indicate in Sura 71 : "Abandon not your gods : abandon neither Wadd nor Suwa; neither Yoguth nor Yauq nor Nasr' (7 : 23; *CQV* 1994 : 108-109) ?

Was Kaaba a House for Idolaters encroached by Allah ?

487. How could Kaaba, the House of Allah be a place of visitation and a sanctuary be a house for idol worship (2 : 125-127) ? Can we deny the fact that each tribe of Arab found or introduced in the Kaaba their domestic idols ? That is how 360 idols of men, eagles, lions and antelopes alongwith the Syrian chief statue of Hubal, of red agate, holding in his hand seven arrows without heads or feathers speak of pre-cosmic antiquity.

Is not it a fact that being built originally for the worship of the planet Saturn, every subsequent conqueror used the Kaaba as a place for practising the rites of his own religion, and allowed the people to worship their gods ?

The Kaaba, which was a temple of polytheists, was closed after Muhammad conquered Mecca with a fear that it might be influenced by the polytheists so he left no trace of polytheism there. Muslims thought that if non-Muslims were disallowed to enter Mecca, their trade would be affected. Muhammad got a command from Allah : "Truly the Pagans are unclean, so let them not, after this year of theirs, approach the sacred Mosque and if you fear poverty, soon will Allah enrich you" (9 : 28). When paganism is unacceptable how could their temple be acceptable ? Allah could not think of a new temple. So by destroying the old temple He wanted to live there. Is this not unjustified for a justified Allah ?

Allah's Statue at Kaaba

488. Can you deny the fact that Allah was an Arabian God whose idol was worshipped in the Kaaba and was under the hereditary management of the Quresh, the Prophet's tribe who were known as the people of Allah (Shaikh, 1995 : 16).

Is Allah worshipped in Kaaba ?

489. Is it not a fact that the Kaaba was known as the House of Allah, "Baitullah" and Pre-Islamic poetry speaks of Allah as the "Lord of the Kaaba ?" And that the pagan custom of offering prayer to Allah and other secondary gods surrounding him known as the companions of Allah are mentioned in the Quran (6 : 137) of whom, the Meccans believe, Allah approves of and never forbids this kind of a worship to them (6 : 149) ?

Hu (He is) *al* (Allah or God) = He is God

490. Can one deny the fact that the pagan God Hubal, whose idol was much adored and worshipped in the Kaaba and who is considered to be a personification of Allah, is derived from the Semitic *Hu* meaning "He is" and *al* meaning god, *i.e.*, *He is God*? And that the Meccans invoked his name as a war-cry?

Pagan Practices in Kaaba

491. Is it not a fact that the Muslim writers have given the Kaaba a history of their own in order to remove its many pagan associations? Are they successful? Like the pagans, do the pilgrims not go round the Kaaba seven times, in a counter-clockwise direction and with each round they kiss the Black Stone, or bow or wave their hands towards it?

Do the pilgrims, as a pagan rite, not run seven times between Safa and Marwa?

Do the pilgrims not spend a night at the valley of Mina and the next day proceed to Arafat where once the shrine of the deity named *Jial* was worshipped and stand there from midday to sunset?

After visiting Arafat the pilgrims come to Mount Muzdalifa where once the thunder-god Kuza was worshipped (Wensinck 1974 : 124) and raise a great shout following Muhammad's farewell pilgrimage.

In the valley of Mina seven stones are thrown to Satan to remember Ibrahim encountering Satan which also was a pagan practice but is still retained by the Muslims.

Pre-Islamic Practice in Kaaba

492. Was not it a better *Ibadat* to Allah during pre-Islamic time when all the pilgrims, both male and female, went round and round stark naked and said : "We shall go before God in the same condition in which our mothers gave birth to us"?

Did not the Arabs worship natural objects like the heavenly bodies, stones, trees and wells? The Sabians were star-worshippers, the people of Himyar worshipped the sun, the tribes of Asad and Kinana the moon . The Kaaba is thought to have been dedicated to the Great Goddess, or to a lunar deity.

Did not the circumambulation of the Kaaba originally symbolize the motion of the planets (Rodwell 1915, p. 455)? Did not the three goddesses Allat, Ozza and Manat preside over the Moon, the planet Venus and Sirius (the Dog Star) besides other celestial bodies? The Quran refers to Allah as 'Lord of Sirius' (53 : 50; Walker 1999 : 46)?

Shrine for Seven Heavenly Bodies

493. Was not the Kaaba dedicated to seven heavenly bodies, therefore it was to be circumambulated seven times and the pilgrims had to run between the hills of Safa and Marwa seven times and seven stones were thrown by each pilgrim at Mina (Walker 1999 : 47)?

How is the Idol Bad but his Sword Good?

494. Why did Ali bring back a magnificent Sword from the hand of the pagan idol Tayi and keep this celebrated weapon, known as Dhulfikar as his personal sword? How can the sword be good if the idol is bad (Walker 1998 : 45)?

143

Idols will Return to Kaaba at the End Time

495. Another famous idol, Dhul Khalasa, carved out of white quartz, was situated at Tabala between Mecca and Sanaa. Arrows of divination would be used at his shrine. Does not Muhammad say that one of the signs of the end of the world would be the revival of Dhul Khalasa's worship (Walker 1998 : 44) ?

According to a prophecy attributed to Muhammad himself (Sale, 1886 : 90) , the Kaaba will be destroyed by the Ethiopians and will never again be rebuilt. The Arabs will once again pay homage to Allat, Ozza and their other deities and revert to their old pagan ways. In one hadith Muhammad says, 'The world will not pass away until the buttocks of the women of Daus wriggle again around the image of Dhul Khalasa and they worship as they were wont to do before Islam' (Faris 1952 : 32; Walker 1998 : 340).

31 - Daughters of Allah

Like any other temples in India Kaaba was a temple for the Arabs. In the Kaaba temple every tribe had its own deity. The deities were male, female, half-male, half-female. Their names were Hubal, Safaa, Naila, Al-Lat, al-Uzza, and Manat etc. Kaaba as a commercial and religious centre was a focal point through out the Arab world.

After the conquest of Mecca Muhammad entered the pagan temple where there were 360 idols around Kaaba. Muhammad then started hitting them with a stick in his hand and said : "Truth (Islam) has come and falsehood (disbelief) vanished. Truly falsehood was ever bound to vanish" (17 : 81; 34 : 49). That way he destroyed 360 icons in the temple.

It was a wonderful step the Prophet took to establish monotheism. But he was confused and to please the Meccians he brought back al-Lat, al-Uzza and Mannat- the three local idols worshipped in Mecca (353 : 19-20). But he soon realized his mistake and blamed Satan for misguiding him for setting up female partners with his Allah (4 : 116). Muslims are very uncomfortable with the satanic verses episode and this had been the subject of endless and bitter controversy (Walker 1998 : 111).

For this Satanic verses Muhammad had to run away from Mecca in shame. The shame of defeat was so much that Muhammad and Abu Bakr had to flee through the window in the back of Abu's house and went to a cave in Thawr, a mountain below Mecca (*Ish* 223 Qtd. Das 2010 : 6).

Goddesses were Prominent than God

496. Is it not a fact that the female deities like Allat, Uzza, Manat, the sun and the moon were more prominent than the male god Allah in Arabia ? Even *Kaaba* was derived from a word for *cube* or *Kaab* meaning *virgin* (Walker 1999 : 47).

Are Uzza and Manat Adam's Children ?

497. According to al-Tabari (9 : 145) the names of the children of Adam and Eve were Abd al-Uzza and 'Abd Manat. If it is so how could Adam take the idols of the Arabs as gods and named his sons after them ?

Safa and Marwa remind Manat ?

498. Was it not a question before the Ansars that they used to assume *Ihram* for worshipping an idol called *Manaat* which they worshipped at a place called Al-Mushallal before they embraced Islam (*Buk* 6 : 384) ? To tell the Ansars to perform Tawaf between Safa and Marwa did it not remind them of the pre-Islamic period of ignorance (*Mus* 2 : 2924) as they did not like to return to the old pagan rituals ? If *Tawaf* between Safa and Marwa is that important why is it not mentioned in the Quran, although in the Quran *Tawaf* of the Kaaba is mentioned ? Is it not the restoration of idolatry if the T*awaf* (Sai) between Safa and Marwa remains compulsory and is one of the symbols of Allah (*Buk* 2 : 706; 6 : 384) ?

Muhammad the Worshipper of Al-Uzza

499. Is it not a fact that Muhammad confessed to have at one time sacrificed a grey sheep to Al-Uzza and probably did so more than once, since after his mission he used to slaughter sheep for sacrifice with his own hands (Margoliouth 1985 : 70) ?

The Daughters of Allah

500. Is it not a fact that the three female deities mentioned in the Quran, Allat (the Goddess of war), Uzza (the Arabian Aphrodite) and Manat (the Goddess of destiny) (53 : 19) had Pre-Islamic pagan significance ? They were even referred to as "the daughters of Allah" (16 : 57) and were worshipped in the form of a cubical black stone. Can one deny the great regard they commanded on the Meccans and Qureshis who chanted invocations to them while circumambulating the Kaaba ?

Three Goddesses of Muhammad

501. Is it not a fact that Muhammad received a revelation from Allah that goddess Al-Lat worshipped at Taaif, the goddess al- 'Uzza worshiped at Nakhlah near Mecca by the Quresh tribe and goddess Manat whose shrine lay between Mecca and Medina were belovedly called the "Banat Allah," which means "daughters of God" ? Muhammad thought these goddesses might be regarded as divine beings whose intercession was effectual with Allah.

To get the support of the Meccans and to bring them to his fold Allah helped Muhammad to reveal *Surat an - Najm.* This delighted the Meccans and the exiled Muslims in Abyssinia returned to their homeland Mecca. After returning they could learn that the agreement had been of short duration. At this juncture Muhammad realised that *Banat-Allah* principle is going against his theory of Monotheism. The Prophet had very soon recognised these words as interpolations of Satan and had substituted for them the words which we now have in the Quran. He was forbidden to worship those other than Allah (6 : 56) and he considered these goddesses nothing but names (53 : 19-23) (Watt 1960 : 100-109; Encyclopaedia of Islam 1936 : 727).

Allah : the Moon God

502. Can we deny the fact that the phrase, : "no god but Allah" proves "Allah" is not just another word for "God" for the Muslims ? The transliterated phrase from Arabic reads, *"Lailaha illAllah."* A word by word translation into English would read : *La* (no) *ilaha* (god) *ill* (except or but) *Allah* (Allah). If "Allah" were the word for God, then the phrase would read, "there is no Allah but Allah. The Quran itself claims that Allah is the personal name of the Islamic God (17 : 110). If "Allah" were the word for God, then Islam's God is nameless. There is also no evidence that the word "Allah" is a contraction of the words "al ilah", which means, "the God". If it were, then again, the phrase would read, "there is no allah but allah".

Does it not prove that Muhammad completely hijacked Allah, which was prayed as moon god in Arabian Peninsula ? (See Google)

Allah in the eyes of Muhammad

503. Is not Allah different from Jehovah ? Are they one and the same God for all the Semitic religions ? If so why is Allah angry with the Jews, the chosen people of Jehovah and continues to rebuke the Jews for disbelieving His signs and slew His Prophets unjustly (2 : 61) ? Are not among the Jews, idolaters (5 : 82) and Christians good people for guidance (5 : 51) ? How Torah, once recognised as a Divine book for guidance (5 : 44) for the righteous (6 : 154) by Allah was perverted by the Jews (2 : 75) ?

Did not Muhammad declare : "Abu Huraira reported Allah's Messenger as saying : The last hour would not come unless the Muslims will fight against the Jews and the Muslims would kill them until the Jews would hide themselves behind a stone or a tree and a stone or a tree would say : Muslim, or the servant of Allah, there is a Jew behind me; come and kill him; but the tree Gharqad would not say, for it is the tree of the Jews" (*Mus* : 41: 6985) ?

Muhammad's Concept of Allah

504. When Muhammad looked at Allah, does not he see Allah as a light (*Mus* 1.341; 342) ?

Muhammad saw the signs of Allah in a green screen covering the horizon (*Buk* 6 . 60. 381).

Who is the Lord of the Dawn ?

505. Can you differenciate between the voice of Allah and the voice of Muhammad ? Who says : "I take refuge with the Lord of the Dawn" (113 : 1).

If Allah is the only God, then who is the Lord of the Dawn ? Does it not indicate 'Lord of the Dawn' must be more powerful than Allah ?

Who is the Second Person in the Quran ?

506. In the Holy Quran it is said : "Nothing of our revelation (even a single verse) do **We** abrogate or cause be forgotten, but **we** bring (in place) one better or the like thereof. Knowest thou not that Allah is Able to do all things" (2 : 106) ?

"Lo ! *We* inspire thee as *We* inspired Noah and the prophets after him, as We inspired Abraham and Ishmael and Isaac and Jacob and the tribes, and Jesus and Job and Jonah and Aaron and Solomon, and as We imparted unto David the Psalms" (4 :163).

"And We have not taught him (Muhammad) poetry, nor is it meet for him. This is naught else than a Reminder and a Lecture making plain" (36 : 69).

"*Our Lord* ! Lo ! it is Thou Who gatherest mankind together to a Day of which there is no doubt. Lo ! Allah faileth not to keep the tryst" (3 : 9).

"*Allah has said* : "Take not (for worship) two gods : for He is just One Allah : then fear Me (and Me alone)" [16 : 51].

In the first three verses who is that *We* ? Are they Muhammad and Allah ? Does not it mean Muhammad is more powerful than Allah ? In the second two verses who is addressing "Our Lord" ? Is it Allah Himself addressing to himself as "Our Lord" and "Allah has said" ? Who heard it, Muhammad or Allah ?

Satanic Verses became Divine Verses

507. Is it not a fact that in 616 Muhammad, to please his Meccan opponents, spoke of the three Goddesses as "the exalted damsels mounting upward to heaven, whose intercession may be sought," and in 630 he ordered their shrines to be destroyed and substituted the above verse as, "what, shall men have male progeny, and God female ? This a most unfair distinction" (53 : 21-2). Didn't he go on to say, "Would God choose daughters rather than sons" (37 : 153) ?

Muhammad confused of Voices Within

508. Is not it a fact that Muhammad was in constant fear of evil spirits, from the mischief of things Allah created, afraid of the night and afraid of sorcerers and women who cried to have influence on others by making knots and blowing on them ? This fear is often found in the Quran and climaxes into a deep fear of Allah (113 : 1-5). Does his fear not come from within, from Satan who whispered into his inner most being and he heard voices and was not sure which was from Allah and which was from Satan (114 : 1-5; 53 : 20-23) ?

Is Allah a Deceiver ?

509. Is not it a fact that Allah claims thirty times in the Quran that He misleads or sends astray people and that he is the greatest deceiver (*Allaahu Khayrul-maakiriin*) (3.54;8.30) ? Allah says that he leads people astray (4.88, 143;6.39, 126;7.178, 186; 9.51; 13.27, 31; 14.4; 16.93; 17.13, 97; 30.29; 35.8; 36.8-10; 39.23; 40.33, 34, 74; 42.44, 46; 74.31). Even the first rightly guided Caliph (al-Khulafa'u r-Rashidun) Abu Bakr (632-634 A.D.) said :   "I swear to Allah that I do not feel safe from Allah's cunning even if one of my feet is already inside Paradise..." (cited Khalid, 2005 : 99).

If this is the case then how are Muslims to differentiate between Allah and Satan?

Merciless Mercy of Allah

510. Can Allah be merciful when He frightens through the eclipse of the sun to scare Muhammad and his followers ? For example :

"Narrated Abu Musa : The sun eclipsed and the Prophet got up, being afraid that it might be the Hour (i.e. Day of Judgement). He went to the Mosque and offered the prayer with the longest Qiyam, bowing and prostration that I had ever seen him doing. Then he said, 'These signs which Allah sends do not occur because of the life or death of somebody, but Allah makes His worshipers afraid by them. So when you see anything thereof, proceed to remember Allah, invoke Him and ask for His forgiveness" (*Buk* 2.18.167).

Satan tempted Muhammad

511. Is it not a fact that Muhammad justified his mistake saying that all Prophets, at times are tempted by Satan who inspires them with his verses as if they were revealed by Allah which are later on rejected by Allah with new revelations (22: 52-53)?

Did it not happen with Muhammad once on account of the three goddessess when he was unable to distinguish the voice of Satan from that of Allah (53 : 20-28) ? Is it not possible then that there could be more verses in the Quran which could be of Satanic origin but which Muhammad assumed might be Allah's revelation ? Perhaps this prompted novelist Salman Rushdie to explore more on the

"Satanic Verses" which were already present in the Quran and were not invented by Rushdie for which Ayatollah Khomeni issued a fatwa of death against him ?

Quran behind the Satanic Version

512. Does not in Sura the Pilgrimage (22 : 52-53) Muhammad confess his temptation concerning the Satanic whispering ? What is the true, vital issue about the Satanic verses in the Quran ?

Was Muhammad infallibly inspired as he himself was bewitched so that he began to imagine that he had done a thing which infact, he had not done ? Does it happen because he was under Satanic inspiration (*Buk* 4 : 400, 490) ?

When praising their Idols did not Work

513. Is it not a fact that when Muhammad came to know that his method of establishing leadership over his people by praising their idols did not work, rather the people used it as a weapon against him, he immediately repented and sought forgiveness by saying : "My heart is overwhelmed by Satan; thus, I ask God for forgiveness one hundred times a day" (Albani : *Mishkat*, Tradition 2324).

Satanic Verses to Please the Meccan

514. If Allah is one and the only one why did Muhammad compromise by acknowledging the existence of three goddesses alongwith Allah-- Lat, Uzza and Manat (53 : 20-23) ? Did he not visit Kaaba and in the presence of the elders of Mecca, recited the verses still found in the Quran ? Is it due to severe persecution of his followers who emigrated to Ethiopia, a Christian state or to please the Meccan (Al-Masih 1990 : 19) ? This brought an endless and hot controversy among the Meccans and commentators like al-Wakidi, Ibn Hisham, Ibn Saad, al-Tabari, al-Zamakshari, al-Baydawi and Jalaluddin were perplexed with this subject.

Why to Please the Idolators ?

515. Is it not a fact that Muhammad, under increasing pressure, acknowledged the existence of the three goddesses alongside Allah : Lat, Uzza and Manat (53 : 20-23) ? When the people of Mecca heard this confession did they not delightfully revoke their ban on him thus allowing his 83 followers, who had taken refuge in Ethiopia, a Christian state following severe persecution to return home again ? But to their utter surprise Muhammad regretted his words about the three goddesses. Did he not later confess that his verse about the three goddesses was the whispering of Satan thus rejecting the whole verse as the Satanic Verse ?

We do not know why after the death of Muhammad, the "Satanic verses" were not included in the text of Quran (Thompson 1965 : 13-36).

Why to disclose the Satanic Verses ?

516. Why did Imam Malik, one of the founders of the four principal schools of Muslim theology and a contemporary of Ibn Ishaq (d. 768) call discloser of Satanic Verses "a devil" (Zakaria 1991 : 13) and blame his contemporary historians like Waqidi (757-822), Ibn Sa'd (764-845) and Tabari (839 -923) and made them responsible for "digging the only intelligible clue" (Muir 1894 : 88-89; Zakaria 1991:13)?

Is not this *Satanic Verses* a discredit to Muhammad and his worshipping Allah of a doubtful nature which strikes at the very root of monotheism ?

Is it not a fact that, at one point of time, Muhammad praised the Qureshite idols El-Lat, El-Uzza and Manat to appease the polytheistic tribe ? Allah revealed the Sura to him, "Have you considered El-Lat and El-Uzza and Manat the third, the other ?" (53 : 20) and goes on to say : "Those are the lofty cranes whose intercession is desired." Though he recited it in his prayer, it was later deleted from the Quranic text. When Gabriel said, "I have not brought you these words," Muhammad claimed that someone in Gabriel's form came and threw them in his mouth, (Razi's Commentary on Sura The *Pilgrimage* 22 : 51). Some of his supporters defend Muhammad saying that Satan came in the garb of Gabriel and placed it in Muhammad's tongue. How, then, can we deny that Satan would not have recited the rest of the Quran on Muhammad's tongue ?

Prophet's Sin of Idolatry

517. Is it not a fact that idolatry is considered as one of the most heinous crimes in Islam (4 : 5 ; 116) ? Allah can forgive the sin of adultery but not idolatry. (Albani; *Mishkat,* Tradition 26; True Guidance I, 68). Inspite of knowing this did Muhammad not commit the sin of idolatry though he claimed to have falsely extolled the idols to please and convert the people of his tribe ?

Prophet should be with his Parents in Hell

518. Is it not a fact that Muhammad's mother and father are languishing in hell because they were idolators ? When Muhammad prayed for their forgiveness, he was reprimanded and was revealed the following verse : "It is not for the Prophet and the believers to ask pardon for the idolators, even though they be near kinsmen" (9 : 113) ? How then did Allah pardon Muhammad when he praised the idols Al-Lat, Al-Uzza, Manat ?

32 - Kiss Allah Through the Black Stone

Stones are stones. Islam being a religion of the iconoclasts the black stone kept at the corner of the House of Allah is of more concern for us than the 360 idols worshipped there long before the advent of Islam. What may be the importance of this black stone can be seen through the tradition of Islam.

It is said : As it had fallen down from the sky it is linked with Adam. When God expelled Adam from Paradise and sent down to earth, He caused him to fall on the site of the Sacred House, which trembled like a boat. God then sent down the Black Stone--the 'Angular Stone' *(rukn)*-which at that time glittered because of its intense whiteness. Adam took the Stone and retained it. And he was commanded : 'Walk, O Adam !' So he set out and went as far as the region of Hind (India) and Sind, and here he stayed for as long as God pleased. Then Adam felt the nostalgia with a longing to see the Angular Stone, so he was commanded : 'Make the pilgrimage'. This he did, and he was welcomed by the angels, who expressed the good wishes : 'May this pilgrimage be accepted as a pious action on your part ! Two thousand years ago we also made pilgrimage to this House (*Hamidullah* p. 74).

Black Stone : from Heaven to Earth

519. Is it not a fact that the Black Stone was a meteorite that fell from the skies in prehistoric times, and that the Kaaba was built to house it ? It lies embedded in the eastern corner of the Kaaba, about five feet from the ground, and it was worshipped by the ancient Arabs and continues to be revered by the Muslims till this day.

Paganism restored in Kaaba Shrine

520. Was not it embarrassing for the new convert to Islam to accept the Black Stone at Kaaba to love and kiss, when the Prophet destroyed 360 idols, scraped the paintings of Ibrahim and the angels from the walls and sanctioned the use of the well Zamzam and restored the boundary pillars defining the sacred territory around Mecca (Noss 1974 : 517; McDowell 1982 : 154) ?

Black Stone has a History

521. Is it not a fact that long before the advent of Islam the Kaaba was known as the House of Allah in order to house a sacred black stone ?

According to the commentator Ibn Abbas (d. 687), Muhammad said that the Black Stone came down from paradise, and at the time of its descent it was whiter than milk; but the sins of men who touched and kissed it caused it to become black. According to an old tradition of the Persians, the stone was allegedly the emblem of Saturn and one of the relics left in the Kaaba by their hero Mahabad (Hughes 1977, p. 155; Walker 1999:39).

Is not it a fact that some time in the third century AD the Jurham guardians are said to have removed the black stone and thrown it into the well of Zamzam. In 603 it was broken into three pieces by the catapults of the Omayyad army, and it was later stolen by the Karmathians and allegedly pulverized.

We very much doubt whether the same stone is there in Kaaba or not ?

Is the present stone not an irregular oval some seven inches in diameter, with an undulating surface ? It is made up of a dozen smaller stones of different shapes and sizes, apparently not of the same composition, held together in a cement mixture and now well smoothed, the whole being set in a silver mounting (Walker 1999: 39)?

Why to Kiss the Black Stone ?

522. Whenever the question of idol worship arises Muslims argue that they do not worship the Black Stone but they love to kiss it as Allah made the Kaaba, the Sacred House (5 : 97). Is it not the Pre-Islamic rite of the Pagans to kiss the Black Stone which Muhammad had preserved ?

Umar b. Khattab while kissing the Black Stone said : "By Allah, I am kissing with full consciousness of the fact that you are a stone and that you can neither do any harm nor good; and if I had not seen the Prophet kissing you, I would not have kissed you" (*Mus* 2 : 2914; *Buk* 2 : 667).

Why Umar blindly kissed the Black Stone for the sake of Muhammad as a mark of respect we do not know. Accept it or not, it is a pre-Islamic idol very much revered by the pagans. Why did the Prophet leave that stone in the Kaaba though he removed 360 idols is yet to be answered.

If Islam is against idolatry why did Muhammad incorporate kissing the black stone as one of the rites of the pilgrimage, like the idolators ? Why did he seek the favour of idolatrous Arabs by honouring the stone together with Allah ? If kissing is showing reverence and veneration (*Tabbarah, The Spirit of Islam.* p. 173) to the Black Stone what is the difference between the Muslim practice of Kissing and the Catholic practice of Kissing the statute of virgin Mary ?

Importance of Black Stone for the Prophet

523. When Muhammad said : "I recognised the stone in Mecca (means *Hajr-E-Aswad*) which used to pay me salutations before, my advent as a Prophet and I recognise that even now, (*Mus* 4 : 5654); it confirms that prior to his advent as a Prophet he was before Adam, which contradicts his claims that he received his first revelation when he was forty; the stone used to pay him salutations "means he was a regular visitor to the temple, before he became the founder of Islam; this statue used to salute him is a form of worship. Does not the above sentence indicate that Muhammad was inspired by idolatry ?

Why the Black Stone was returned from Bahrein ?
524. Is not it a fact that the Holy Black Stone called Sang-e-Aswad was once taken by the followers of the Kiramata sect of Ismailis to their capital Bahrein ? How was it returned to Kaaba again ?

Why Black Stone in Silver Band ?
525. If the Black Stone is not an idol why is it said that when Allah expelled Adam from the paradise, He gave Adam the Black Stone which is now built into the eastern wall of the Kaaba and consists of three large pieces and some fragments, surrounded by a stone ring and held together by a silver band ? A stone which is an object of worship is bound to be an idol.

Why the Muslims Love the Three Stones at Kaaba ?
526. Though Muhammad condemned all forms of idolatry, but stroking or kissing the Black-Stone was never regarded as a form of worship. The caliph Umar (d. 644) said of the Black Stone, 'I know you are nothing but a stone that neither harms nor helps.., If I had not seen the messenger of Allah kiss you, I would never kiss you myself.' If it is true why are the two stones besides the Black Stone one *asaad* (lucky) and the other *makami Ibrahim* (the place of Abraham) there for the pilgrims to touch with devotion ? Why is the *makami Ibrahim* covered in a gilded cage and kept in a little building just outside ? Is it believable that Ibrahim while constructing the original shrine was said to have stood on the stone ?

Islam encourages Idolatry
527. How can one deny that the Prophet has categorically prohibited Muslims from drawing pictures or sculpting statues of animals or human beings but while performing ritualistic worship before an object does it not lead us towards *shirk* or idolatry?

Muhammad in Description
528. How did Prophet Muhammad look like ? There is no photo or potrait available because of the restriction imposed by Muhammad. What little we know about his physical appearance is from the descriptions available in the Hadith which says :

He was of medium height, having broad shoulders, with his hair hanging down on the lobes of his ears (*Mus* 4 : 5770) and was neither very curly nor very straight (*Mus* 4 : 5773). But he was a hairy man (*Buk* 4 : 272). Some of his hairs was red because he used scent (*Buk* 4 : 747). He had the most handsome face amongst men and he had the best disposition (*Mus* 4 : 5772). He had a broad face with reddish wide eyes, and lean heels (*Mus* 4 : 5776), and had an elegant white colour (*Mus* 4 : 5778). He had a rosy colour, neither absolutely white nor deep brown (*Buk* 4 : 747). He had a few white hair in his beard (*Mus* 4 : 5786) the seal near the shoulder of the size of a pigeon's egg (*Mus* 4 : 5789).

What is the difference between a verbal description and a painting ? If an artist converts this description to the form of a painting why is there a hue and cry among the Muslim world ? Does not the description create a mental image ?

Inspite of that, painting and illustrated manuscripts of Muhammad available in Persia, Turkey, Syria, Egypt and North Africa show the Prophet's face, usually bearded, with piercing eyes and a halo around his turbanned head (Walker 1999 : 232-233). I have seen the portrait of the Prophet in many libraries like British Library, London and Harvard College Library, USA where he is shown with his face blanked out in different anthologies of religions.

Is Calligraphy an Art Icon ?
529. Don't you think that the exquisite calligraphy which adorns the text of the Quran, inscribed in the great mosques like that of Ibn Tulun in Cairo, the mosque of Cordoba and of Istanbul are not art or painting which is forbidden in Islam ?

Quran becomes an Icon
530. Can you differentiate between an idol and an icon ? The Hindu has the temple with idols in a corner of his house and the Muslim has the Quran kept reverentially in the corner of his house. Hindus have their idols and Muslims have their icon. None can touch unless he or she is pure. None can sleep with their feet towards it. Not only pictures or sculptures but a literary work can be an icon. It takes the *form* of a mental image. The *Quran* can be compared with *Guru Granth Saheb*. Both the Sikhs and the Muslims worship icon which are their respective Holy Books but their aesthetics is one. Does it not prove that the Muslims who break the idols of others keep their icons safe ? Attack is the best defence.

No Painting, Music and Poetry
531. Is it not a fact that Muhammad disliked painting, music and poetry ? Did not once Muhammad say that those who decorate their tombs and churches with painting "were the worst part of all creations" (Main 1985 : 14) ? Do the Muslim architects not decorate their Mosques and Minarets with intricate arabesque ornamentation ? It may be a fact that music, painting and poetry engender immorality, lust and licentiousness but most importantly they soften one's heart and a man with a soft heart is unfit for Jihad.

Why to keep Photographs at House ?
532. Is it not a fact that one should not keep a photograph in his/her house as no angel will enter by seeing a photo (*Mus* 3 : 5246; *Buk* 7 : 843) ? Whoever makes a picture in this world will be asked to put life into it on the Day of Resurrection, but he will not be able to do so (*Buk* 7 : 846). Once Ayesha had hung on the door a thin curtain having pictures on it. Muhammad took hold of that curtain and tore it and said : The most grievous torment for the people on the Day of Resurrection would be for those who try to imitate Allah in the act of creation (*Mus* 3 : 5258; *Buk* 7 : 844).

Concession for the Pictures of Tree
533. No Muslims should keep any kind of photographs in their house. To a question Prophet Muhammad replied : Whoever makes a picture will be punished by Allah till he puts life in it and he will never be able to put life in it" (*Buk* 3 : 428). Inspite of such clear cut principle of the Prophet in the same passage why did Abbas make correction by saying : "If you insist on making pictures I advise you to make pictures of trees and any other unanimated objects ?" Abbas perhaps thought trees have no life.

Section
VI

The Peace to End All Peace

33 - What is in the Name

What Islam means to us ? Is it a religion of peace ? If it is the religion of peace why does it preach against the Jews, Christians and other non-Muslims as infidels and kafirs ? Since iconoclasm is an article of faith of Islam, is it a matter of religious rite for the Muslims to destroy places of worship belonging to others and building mosques there on ? If you do agree please try to answer these questions :

Is Islam a borrowed Word ?

534. Is it not a fact that the word "Muslim" itself is a loan word borrowed from the Syrian Christians to signify "devotion to God" (Jeffery 1938 : 63) ? Did not Muhammad borrow this word from the same semitic root and make Ibrahim (3 : 60), the household of Lot (51 : 36) and the Jews, Christians and Muslims before the advent of Islam (28 : 53; 3 : 45) ?

Is Islam a New Religion ?

535. If we accept Muhammad as an *Ummi* or unlettered (7 : 157) we have to admit that he had a good memory because of which he collected religious information from the Jews, Christians and Zorostrians to formulate his new religion, Islam. Even he did not dare to change any pagan practices, rather he included the ceremonies of the pilgrimage to Mecca. Did he dare to claim any originality in founding a new religion ? Didn't he tell that he had started and continued the religion of Ibrahim ?

Islam started after the Prophet's Migration to Medina

536. Can you accept the fact that Islam does not begin with the birth of Muhammad, nor with his revelations nor with the formation of the original Islamic community at Mecca, nor even with the martyrdom of the Muslims during the twelve years of persecution at Mecca rather it started with the Hijra, the migration to Medina, on 16th July 622 AD as the beginning of the Islamic calender ? Did the date not mark the turning point in Islam as a date not of spiritual but of political prophesy ?

Islam Versus Muhammedanism

537. If no Buddhism without Buddha, no Judaism without Judah, no Christianity without Christ what is wrong to name Islam after Muhammad, *i.e.,* Muhammadanism as he was the founder of his religion ? Can we think of Islam (5 : 3) or Muslim (22 : 78) without Muhammad ? Muhammad is Islam and Islam is Muhammad. But why Muhammad did not dare to call his religion after his name when the Muslims declare : "Muhammadur rasul Allah" or Muhammad is the messenger of God". What is wrong to name Muslims as Muhammadans ?

Is the World for Muslims ?

538. Does not Islam advocate that the world belongs to Allah and Muslims are his chosen people ? Does not Islam classify humans as Muslims, Jews, Christians and Kafirs or Infidels ? Does not it show Islamic contempt and hatred towards nonbelievers ? Does not Islam exhort believers to kill, convert or enslave the Kafirs through a technique called Jihad, a very pious activity prescribed for the Muslims ?

Why to be Proud of Ishmael ?
539. Is not it a disgrace to say that the Muslims were the descendants of Ishmael, the first-born son of Abraham ? Was not Ishmael the illegitimate son of Ibrahim by an Egyptian concubine, a bonded woman who is not of the Semitic race ? Was he not outside God's covenant with Ibrahim ? As told by Moses he was "a wild man, his hand will be against every man" (*Gn* 16 : 12). Therefore God made an everlasting covenent with Issac (*Gn* 17 : 18) not with Ibrahim or Ishmael.

Free Entry but no Exit
540. Did not the Prophet say : "If somebody (a Muslim) discards his religion (of Islam), kill him." (*Buk* 4 : 260) and record the murder of those who left Islam for another religion (*Buk* 5 : 630; 1 : 6, 48) ?

Islam : the Product of Topography
541. Do you accept the environmental factors, the barren and harsh land, the poverty of the conflicting tribes, the presence of Jewish and Christian settlements among the Arabs, and the religious conflicts of the age that awakened a chord in the mind of Muhammad and fired his soul to establish Islam ?

Kinds of Priests in Islam
542. It is said that Islam is a religion without a priest or a clergy. What you think of Foqaha, Motakallamin, and Mohaddasin (the FMM), the experts on Islamic jurisprudence ? Who are these Imams, Ulamas, Faqih and Qadis ? Do they not constitute a kind of Priesthood or Clergy ? One thing cannot be denied that priests are not born but priesthood is thrusted upon.

Who represents Islam ?
543. Who represents true Islam ? Wahabite ? In 1900 Abd al- Aziz al- Sa'ud tried to restore the former Wahabite Kingdom with its strong puritanical ideas. Al-Sa'ud's son King Fahd an alcoholic cannot represent Islam. The Sunnites, who constitute 90 per cent of the Islamic population in the world or the Shiaes ? Neither of them as they were divided into sects. Can Muatazilites influenced by Greco-Byzantine philosophy represent Islam ? Can the Sufis and Dervishes do so ? Can collective trances and mysticism signify Islam (Al-Masih. Islam Under...6-7) ?

Has Apostasy any Right to Live ?
544. Does not Islam speak of two types of apostasy----one, a person born of Muslim parents who later rejects Islam is called a *Murtadd Fitri* and the other who first converts to Islam and later leaves it is called a *Murtadd Milli* ? Did not the Prophet order to kill those whoever changed their Islamic religion (*Buk* 9 : 57) ?

Does not the first twenty years , immediately after the death of Prophet Muhammad on 8th June 632, record the killing of about fifty to sixty thousand apostates in Arabia itself in these wars of apostasy (Ibn Warraq 1995 : 32) ?

Fighting Spirit of the Bedouins
545. Is it not a fact that Muhammad studied the mental attitude of the Arabs that too the fighting spirit of Bedouins and diverted them to jihad ? In this context Gabriel, formerly a student, teacher and scholar of Azhar University writes :

> One of the stronger characteristics of Arabs in Muhammad's time was that they were known for being extremist in everything----extreme love, extreme hate and no tolerance of others who were different from them...

This extremist mentality did not change at all after Islam. As a matter of fact Islam embraced many of the core characteristics of this Arabic culture. There was no moderation, no reconciliation with others... Many non-Arab Muslims such as Iranians, Afghans, Pakistanis, Indians and others have adapted and adopted these behaviours as the way of their new religion.
(Hitti 2001 : 66-67; Paliwal. *Jihad in the Way of Allah*, p. 61).

This suggests Muhammad was bound to be with the fighting spirit of the Arabs and to fulfil the fierce monotheism he became intolerant towards other religions.

Is Islam a Religion of Iconoclasts ?

546. Since iconoclasm is an article of faith of Islam, is it a matter of religious right for the Muslims to destroy places of worship belonging to other religions and building mosques there on ?

Didn't Muhammad begin his religion by destroying Kaaba, shrines for idolators in Mecca and thereafter Muslims destroyed thousands of temples in India, and many synagogues and churches in Middle East, Europe and North-Africa ?

Prophecy about Islam

547. Does not Prophet Muhammad forecast the future of Islam 1400 years ago : "Islam initiated as something strange and it would revert to its old position of being strange. Just as it started, it would recede between the two mosques (that is between the old mosques of Mecca and Medina) and would recede to Medina just as the serpent crawls back into its hole (*Mus* 1 : 270-272) ?

Uris Prophecy on Arab and Islam

548. Does not Leon Uris in his best seller "The Haj" foretell the future of Arabs in the following words :

Islam is unable to live at peace with anyone. We Arabs are the worst. We can't live with the world, and even more terrible, we can't live with each other. In the end it will not be Arab against Jew, but Arab against Arab. One day our oil will be gone alongwith our ability to blackmail. We have contributed nothing to human betterment in centuries, unless you consider the assassin and the terrorist as human gifts. The world will tell us to go to hell. We, who tried to humiliate the Jews, will find ourselves humiliated as the acum of the earth.

And he continues :

Hate is our overpowering legacy and we have regenerated ourselves by hatred from decade to decade, generation to generation, century to century. In ten, twenty, thirty years the world of Islam will begin to consume itself in madness (*Teheran Times,* Nov.28, 1984 : 3,2).

Should not the Muslim states learn from Mustafa Kemal Ataturk (1881-1938) how to abolish the sultanate, the Ottoman empire, and establish a secular republic ? Did he not replace shariah law to secular justice system, banned polygamy, allowed Muslim women to marry non-Muslims ? The thrice said Talak system was replaced by civil divorce system, women were given legal equality, including the right to vote, hold government office, and work in business, right to education for women, Arabic script replaced by Roman alphabet, Gregorian calender replaced the Islamic calender and the Quran being translated into Turkish so that ordinary people could read it, instead of relying on the Mullahs and

Maulabis for interpretations (Cherry 2002 : 21-22) ? Is not it the best way to protect all Muslim Nations and bring them to the mainstream of mankind ?

Trade and Marriage Forgo Swords

549. Is it true that Islam spreaded in Indonesia and Malaysia without swords through peaceful means ? Was it not through the Arab businessmen who converted them to Islam ? Is it not a fact that business knows no religion. Through business the Arabs entered Indonesia and Malaysia and established marriage relations with the natives and multiplied ? Inspite of that Indonesians till today are proud of Ramayan and earn by performing Ramayana dance drama throughout the world and do not like to change their Hindu names and culture. If asked by the foreigners they reply that they have changed their religion but not their forefathers. In the words of Geoffrey Parrinder :

> From a very early time, the Islands of Indonesia were visited by Arab traders who established colonies along the coasts, and brought their religion with them. The influence of the traders was reinforced by the presence of numerous Sufi saints and preachers, and by the tendency of the Arabs everywhere to intermarry with the local population. By the fifteenth century, there were already Muslim sultanates and kingdoms in the islands which were moving gradually towards the condition of a majority Muslim population which they have today (1971 : 481).

Interest-free Banking is no Banking

550. Is not it a fact that the Koreans hate the concept of interest to such an extent that both receiving and paying interest have been forbidden in Korea ? Do all the Muslim governments throughout the world have their banking systems run exactly the same way as in the European countries except the hypocrisy that they refer to *interest* as *profit* ?

Have not all Arab countries lent their Petro-dollars to the West on highest possible rates of interest, and also pay interest on the borrowings made on the international money markets ? Is it possible to run a national economy or exercise monetary control without the interest-mechanism ?

Islam leads to Lethargic Contentment

551. If Islam means resignation to the will of God, should not such a religion kill Man's initiative, damp all his efforts to meet the challenges of the dynamic environment and thus lead him to a lethargic contentment ?

34 - Quran and Kafirs

When the Prophet was once asked by a man : "Should I join Jihad ? The prophet asked the man : "Do you have parents ?" The man said : "Yes." The Prophet replied : "Then strive by serving them" (Salfuddin, I, Nov. 2001 : 8).

But to our surprise, when the prophet appointed any one leader of an army, he ordered them : "Fight in the name of Allah and in the way of Allah...When you meet your enemies who are polytheists... invite them to (accept) Islam. If they refuse to accept Islam, demand from them Jezia (tax), if it refuge to pay tax, seek Allah's help and fight them" (*Mus* 3 : 4294).

157

In the Quran the term *Jihad-fi-sabillah* (Jihad for the cause of Allah) has been used 26 times, *Qutal* (kill) has been used 79 times. Out of 24 suras revealed in Medina (622-632) 19 are concerned with Jihad (2-5, 8-9, 22, 24, 33, 47-49, 57-61, 63 and 66), seventeen suras explain the rules and virtues of Jihad (Paliwal 2007 : 2).

When Allah's messenger was asked : "What is the best deed ?" He replied : "I have been ordered (by Allah) to fight against the people until they testify that none has the right to be worshipped but Allah, and that Muhammad is Allah's Messenger" (*Buk*1 : 24). "Know that Paradise is under the shades of spears" (*Buk* 4 : 73).

In Islam; love, brotherhood and forgiveness are insignificant. More important issues are ill-will, hatred, animosity, death and destruction of the infidels, who because of their nonbelieving status do not consider Muhammad as a messenger of God.

After 23 years of preaching, the core message of Muhammad remained the same. Islam's main message is that Muhammad is a messenger and that people must obey him. Beyond that, there is no other message. Failure to recognize him as such entails punishment, both in this world and the next. Monotheism, which is now the main argument of Islam, was not originally part of the message of Muhammad" (2008: 16).

So Duglas MacArthur remarks : "Everything is permissible in war in order to gain an advantage for ends justify the means."

Are Pagans Unclean ?
552. Is it true that the pagans are unclean (9 : 28) therefore let them not approach the sacred mosque says Allah to Muhammad ?

Unbelievers have no Right to Survive
553. How are you going to explain these following verses-- as the metaphorical battles or as moral crusades : "O believers ! When you meet the unbelievers in hostile array, never turn your backs to them (8 : 15). Kill those who join other Gods wherever you find them" (9 : 5) ?

The Fate of the Unbelievers
554. Why do the non-Muslims believe another scripture as true ? If they do not accept Islam they will be treated as hypocrites and unbelievers and they will be sent to hell (4 : 140) ?

The Kafir - Hating Community
555. How should a Muslim treat a non-Muslim or a kafir or a non-believer ? In the Holy Quran Allah says to the Muslims not to strive against the unbelievers such as : Heed not the hurt (33 : 48), no compulsion in religion (2 : 256), extend money to them (2 : 272), leave them alone (3 : 19; 6 : 107; 10 : 99-100), calling them with goodwill (16 : 125). But in various verses in the Quran Allah seems to be more cruel to the unbelievers and has passed order to the Muslims to kill them (8 : 65), fight with them(2 : 193), extract money from them (9 : 29), persecute them (4 : 89; 47 : 4; 9 : 71), call them with the sword (4 : 84) ? No Muslim should be killed in Qisaas (equality in punishment) for killing a kafir (disbeliever) (*Buk* 9 : 50).

Infidels and Atheists are to be killed not Burnt
556. Is it not a fact that the Quranic verses descended to justify his killings of the infidels (47 : 4) and release him from his oaths (66 : 2) ?

Is it not a fact that some atheists were brought to Ali and he burnt them. The news of this event, reached Ibn Abbas who said, "If I had been in his place, I would not have burnt them", as Allah's messenger forbade it, saying, "Do not punish anybody with Allah's punishment (fire)." I would have killed them according to the statement of Allah's Messenger, "Whoever changed his Islamic religion, kill him" (*Buk* 9 : 57).

35 - Jihad in Allah's Cause

'Jihad' is an Arabic word derived from 'Jahada' which means to strive or to struggle. Does it have anything to do with the strive against one's own evil inclination, or to fight in self-defence or to fight in the battle field against oppression and against aggression ? If so why Muhammad said : "I have been commanded to fight against people, till they testify to the fact that there is no God but Allah, and believe in me (that) I am the messenger (from the Lord) and in all that I have brought." And when they do it, their blood and riches are guaranteed protection on my behalf except where it is justified by law, and their affairs rest with Allah" (*Mus* 1 : 29-33, 2; 2634; 4, 196).

Why Muslims are translating Jihad as Holy war ? The translation of 'Holywar' in Arabi would be *al-harbu-al muqaddasah* but Jihad comes from the Arabic word *al-Jahd* which means 'tireless or to serve Allah tirelessly.' Is this translation satisfactory ? Can there be a spiritual meaning of Jihad as inner struggle, directed against one's worst impulses and the outer struggle, directed against a society that refuses to allow Muslims to worship (Schafer, May 2002 : 16) ? Has Jihad not become an institution for killing the infidels rather than indicating an event ?

The Prophet has said : "Acting as Allah's soldier for one night in a battlefield is superior to saying prayers at home for two thousand years" (*Maj* 2 : 166; *Buk* 4 : 50-52) and encouraged the Jihadis by saying : "He who travels to participate in a Jihad, the dust he encounters in the process, shall become fragrance for him on the Day of Judgement" (*Maj* 4 : 2775).

Khawarij's Concept of Jihad
557. Did not the Khawarij change the concept of Jihad from aggressive idealism to "enjoying good and forbidding evil" ?

Jihad for the Cause of Allah
558. Is it not a fact that Jihad was so important to Muhammad that he made it the second most important deed in Islam ? When Allah's apostle was asked, "What is the best deed ?" He replied, "To believe in Allah and his Apostle." The questioner then asked, "What is the next (in goodness) ?" He replied, "To participate in Jihad (religious fighting) in Allah's cause" (*Buk* 1 : 25-26; *Mus* 1 : 148, 149, 152).

Is Jihad among the Five Pillars ?
559. If Jihad is an inescapable duty in Islam why did Allah not include it in the five basic cannons--- Kalama, Rosa, Zukat, Imam and Haj ? If Jihad is not included in the five pillars of Islam why did Muhammad say : "Leaving for Jihad is the way of

Allah in the morning or in the evening will merit a reward better than the world and all that is in it" (*Mus* 3 : 4639) and again he says : Jihad is a part of faith. Through this a Muslim will be recompensed by Allah either with a reward of paradise or booty (*Buk* 1 : 35), and it is next to Allah (*Mus* 1 : 148-149). Is it for any spiritual reasons or to fulfill a political need ?

Many Faces of Jihad
560. Is it not a fact that Jihad of Islam has many faces ? When Muslims are minority are they not wolves in sheep's clothing ? But when they are in majority do they not impose Sharia Law and subdue the minorities i,e. the non-Muslims (9 : 28-29; 36) ?

What kind of Jihad is the Best ?
561. Can Jihad be interpreted as a defensive war ? Does not Islam command Muslims to fight as sword is the key to heaven and hell, the killer will go to heaven and the killed be in hell ?

Therefore to a question, "What kind of Jihad is the best", Muhammad said : "He whose blood is shed and whose horse is wounded" (*Maj* 4 : 2794).

Between Defensive and Liberative Jihad
562. Is not it a fact that there are two kinds of Jihad--- one is defensive and another liberative ? Is not the defensive Jihad compulsory for every Muslim to defend Islam by all possible means, and the liberative Jihad, though not obligatory for women or the disabled and the elders, is a must for the rest of the Muslims to fight against the infidels or non-believers of Allah ?

Between al-Akbar and al-Asghar Jihad
563. One more classification of Jihad : One; the *Jihad al Akbar* or the war against the enemy within and the other *Jihad al Asghar*, the lesser Jihad that is fought on the battle field--- the cruel, the mindless and the devastating Jihad. If we interpret Jihad as the holy war, the war for justice and righteousness or the struggle against tyranny, for what war of righteousness did Ghazni Muhammad or Muhammad Ghori fight in India ?

Is Jihad a Permanent Warfare ?
564. If Jihad means a doctrine of permanent warfare in every country wherever Muslims live, and love to fight in the way of Allah and be killed, to fight and again be killed (*Mus* 3 : 4626; *Buk* 4 : 54) where is the freedom to live and let live ? Does not the Google, after a thorough research, mention that in the Quran and Hadith "kill" and "fight" words are used 32213 times ?

Jihad in Madina Verses
565. Is it not a fact that all the verses on Jihad occurred in the Madina Surahs when the Prophet established himself as a powerful ruler to dictate terms to his enemies ? Does it not happen after the Badr (624) battle and Muhammad prescribed fighting (2 : 216)?

Can Peace and Violence live Together ?
566. If Islam comes from the root word "Salam" which means peaceful and Jihad means "to strive tirelessly" or fight for eliminating non-Muslims does it not lead to violence ? Can the two opposite spirits coexist ?

Unholy Faces of the Holy Jihad

567. Can you deny the fact that there is an unholy face of the holy war ? Don't you think that Jihad is a business enterprise run by poor, beggars, criminals, illiterates and uneducated unemployed youngmen from London to New York and from Kashmir to Kosovo ? Was not Mushtaq Ahmad Zargar who was released during the hijack, a plumber ?

Motive behind Jihad

568. Is not it a fact that fighting with weapons is commanded in the Quran 16 times and defending Islam against attack from outside (2 : 190-191; 22 : 39) is the main motive of all Muslims ? Therefore Muhammad said : "My livelihood is under the shade of my spear (from war booty) and he who disobeys my orders will be humiliated by paying Jizya" (*Buk* 4 : 88).

Did not Muhammad, for war booty, fight 82 wars, 27 he himself as the leader and in the other 55 expeditions he appointed one of his commanders as the leader to fight against the non-Muslims ?

Die for Jihad

569. Is it not profitable to murder another person because the property of the person killed becomes the property of the murderer says the Prophet (*Maj* 2 : 182) ? One who dies but does not fight in the ways of Allah, nor does he express any desire for Jihad, dies the death of a hypocrite (*Mus* 3 : 4696) ?

Is Suicide Bomb Un-Islamic ?

570. If whoever commits suicide with a piece of iron will be punished with the same piece of iron in the hell-fire (*Buk* 2 : 445) why are the Jihadis dying with suicide bomb ?

Al-Jizya from the Infidels

571. Is it not a fact that those who refuse to embrace Islam must pay a special tax called Al- Jizya ? Should it not be collected from the people of the scripture (Jews, Christians) and Magians and the non-Arab infidels (*Buk* 4 : 383; 9 : 29) ?

Booty at last granted to Jihadis

572. Is not the war booty an impulsive force for the Bedouin Arabs to join for Jihad ? Though Prophet was not in favour to give war booty to the Jihadis (8 : 1) but when the Jihadis revolted to get a share of the war booty the merciful Allah agreed (8 : 41; 33 : 50; 9 : 7) one-fifth war booty for the prophet and the rest four-fifth will go to the actual Jihadis. Does not the prophet warn : "The spoils of war were not made lawful for any people before us. This is because Allah saw our weakness and humility and made them lawful for us" (*Mus* 3 : 4327) ?

Jihad of Slavery

573. The only place in the world where black *chattel* slavery is practised today is in Muslim countries. The London Economist (1/6/90) reported that the Sudanese Muslims are presently capturing and then selling black women and children of the *Dinka* Christian Tribe for as little as $ 15 a head !

Even the U.N. released a report on slavery that points out that the Muslims are still enslaving the blacks. This has also been pointed out in the May 4, 1992 special edition of *Newsweek* on slavery.

Non-Muslim women who go to Saudi Arabia to work as maids are often enslaved by their Muslim employers, beaten, and raped at will. When they try to escape, the Saudi government will not let them leave the country but returns them to their masters (Morey 1992 : 199).

Jihad for Court
574. Is it not a fact that non- Muslims are denied equal right ? As Ash-Shabi said : "The witnesses of the people of different religions against one another is not valid" (*Buk* 3 : 849) ?

Jihad begins at Home
575. Is it possible to say that Kaaba will be safe in the hands of Muslims ?

The first attack on Kaaba was done by the first Muslim of the world Prophet Muhammad by destroying 360 idols of the deities of the shrine.

The second attack was done by Khalifa Yazeed when Abdullah bin-Zuber denied him as Khalifa and took refuge in the Kaaba under the impression that a Khalifa cannot attack the holy temple. But Yazeed put the Kaaba on fire, which was rebuilt by Khalifa Omar-bin-Abdul Aziz.

The third attack was done by a follower of the Kiramata sect of Ismailis, looting the holy Black Stone Sang-e- Aswad to his capital Bahrein. It was after fourteen years that the black stone was returned to Kaaba under great pressure to the Ismaili kings notably from the Egyptian monarch Noij Billah.

The fourth attack was done in 1979, a handful of followers of one particular sect, had occupied the Kaaba and kept it under their control for three days under the instructions from Mehdi Moud. Many people were killed during Haj (Hussain 1989 : 6).

The fiveth attack was in 1987, Khomeini sent one and a half lakh Iranian pilgrims to the Haj not for Haj but for demonstrations against USA and Iraq. The sons of Yazid shamelessly massacred the pilgrims of the House of Allah. In that bloody Friday riot more than 400 people were killed (Hussain 1989 : 6).

Kaaba was never free from Jihadis and it continues...

Muslim Jihads Against Muslim
576. Is it not a fact that when the Muslims do not find non-Muslims to fight they fight with the Muslims. For example : Timur raided Baghdad and various cities of Mesopotamia on the pretext that the Arab rulers of the area were not doing enough to protect the pilgrims in Mecca and other holy places of Islam. In order to strike terror in Arab hearts he erected a huge pyramid with the skulls of his Arab victims in a place called Takrit. In the year 1400 AD he repeated the same orgy of loot and murder in Aleppo. First he gave over the city to plunder as a mark of jihad, then he beheaded over 20,000 Muslims and built a tower with their heads. This champion of Islam even destroyed the splendid mosques of the times of Nurid and Ayyubid and allowed his troops to rape Muslim women who had taken shelter in them. And finally, when he learnt that some of his soldiers had been killed in Baghdad, he returned there and carried out such a vast and vengeful massacre that he built no fewer than 120 towers with the decapitated Arab heads in different parts of the city (Niser 20 : 1 : 2002 : 8).

Is it not clear from Timur that Jihad has nothing to do with spiritualism but everything to do with fighting as an inborn instinct among the Muslims ? The religion that began with blood shall end in blood, like a religion that has a beginning has an end.

162

36 - A Vision Without Wisdom

It is unfortunate that the Western cartoonists and the Hollywood portrayers describe Muslims as stereotype of the robed, hook-nosed camel driver and a Friday-go-to-mosque kind of people.

Any religion that claims to be the only true religion in the world becomes a threat to other religions and specially to the religion that believes all religions are equal and the same. In a secular state where the state is either indifferent towards all religions or place equal emphasis to all religions cannot accept a religion with a superiority complex without being superior in thought and philosophy.

Secularism cannot survive with those religious groups who donot believe their religions are as good as others. Such religions work as parasite and are unacceptable for a civil citizen of a nation and cannot fit themselves in a democratic set of a state. They cannot be secular in the true sense of the term. Secularism for the Muslims is a ladder then through which they wish to climb to a tower and then kick the ladder.

Apostasy : a Capital Offense

577. Is it not the biggest lie told to the world "There is no compulsion in religion ?"

Is conversion from Islam not considered an apostasy- a capital offense for both the one who is misled and the one who misleads him ?

Does not Allah command the Muslims in the Holy Quran to kill the apostates? How are you going to interprete the following verses :

"They wish that you would disbelieve as they disbelieve, and then you would be equal. Therefore, do not take a guide from them until they emigrate in the way of Allah. Then if they turn back take them and kill them wherever you find them. Do not take them for guides or helpers" (4 : 89).

"Yet before that, they made a covenant with Allah never to turn their backs. And covenants with Allah shall be questioned. Say : 'Fight will not avail you, if you flee from death or slaughter, you would enjoy (this world) only for a little (time)" (33 : 15,16).

Reverts from Islam : No Excuse

578. Is not it a fact that Muhammad advocated to kill those who merely oppose him verbally ?

According to Abdullah : Allah's Messenger said, "The blood of a Muslim who confesses that none has the right to be worshipped but Allah and that I am His Messenger, cannot be shed except in three cases : in Qisas (equality in punishment) for murder, a married person who commits illegal sexual intercourse and the one who reverts from Islam (Apostate) and leaves the Muslims" (*Buk* 9 : 17 *Buk* 83) ?

No Permission to accept other's Religion

579. Why will "anyone (who) desires a religion other than Islam, never be accepted" (3 : 85) ? The Islamic law claims that if a Muslim renounces Islam or even if a new convert reverts to his previous faith the penalty is death. Is this law not invariably invoked in the present time in the form of *fatwa* against Salman Rushdie and the murder of president Sadat and many others ?

War Against Apostasy

580. There are a few Hadiths, which say how apostasy against Islam was treated during Muhammad's time.

"Narrated Abu Bruda, "Abu Musa said... Behold there was a fettered man beside Abu Musa. Muadh asked, "Who is this (man) ?" Abu Musa said, "He was a Jew and became a Muslim and hence reverted back to Judaism." Then Abu Musa requested Muadh to sit down but Muadh said, "I will not sit down till he has been killed. This is the judgement of Allah and his messenger," and repeated it thrice. Then Abu Musa ordered that the man be killed, and he was killed. Abu Musa added, "Then we discussed the night prayers..." (*Buk* 9.83.58).

Apostates inhabitant of Fire

581. Some of the apostates during the time of Muhammad and the Caliphs were poor people. They had to accept Islam under sword. They were of no threat to the Muslims. In spite of this, they were brutally murdered. In some cases the apostates fought against the rule of Islam, in the other any of them turn back from their faith (Islam) their works will bear no fruit in this life and hereafter they will be inhabitant of the fire (2 : 217). Those who wage war against Allah and his messenger, their punishment is : execution, or crucifixion, or cutting off of hands and feet from opposite sides, or exile from the land (5 : 33). In the Hadith it is said : If a Muslim reconverts to Christianity after his or her death the earth will throw it out of the grave (*Buk* 4 : 814).

Abu Bakr killed Thousands of Apostates

582. Hasn't Abu Bakr stained his hands with the blood of thousands of apostates ?

There arose in the Arabian peninsula, shortly before the demise of the Prophet, a movement of resistance to Islam. And as soon as the Prophet died and Abu Bakr was elected Caliph, this movement increased and grew stronger. Abu Bakr, however, was determined to annihilate this movement, and confronted the apostates in the Arabian peninsula with Khalid Ibn al-Walid, and likewise gave commission to other leaders to go to the extremities of the peninsula to suppress apostasy in them. Khalid annihilated the apostasy of Banu Asad, Tamim and Hanifa after a fierce war, and the other leaders did likewise throughout the Arabian peninsula. It was only a year or so after the death of the Messenger that the peninsula returned to the fold of the new religion of God and the new Islamic Empire, thanks to the conviction and commitment of Abu Bakr and the military genius of Khalid (al-Tabari Tarikh al- Rusul wa al- muluk, vol. 4, p. 2, 065f).

Jabala escapes Death as an Apostate

583. Is not it a fact that 'Umar threatened to cut off the head of Jabala Ibn al-Ayham, if he turned from Islam to Christianity ? Al-Jabala Ibn al-Ayham was the last Christian king among the Ghassanid kings in Syria, who embraced Islam under 'Umar Ibn al-Khattab. It seems that he did so, not out of belief in the truth and superiority of Islam over his religion, but out of fear or desire (to gain something). After his conversion to Islam, Jabala made the pilgrimage to Mecca with the pomp of a king in grand procession. 'Umar honoured him and welcomed him. And it so happened that while he was circumambulating in his ritual consecration, as is the habit of the hajjs, a man from Banu Fazara hit the end of his waist-band so that it came loose, and his nakedness showed. Jabala became angry and hit the man with his fist so hard that he bled. The man said to him, "You hit me in the House of God, the law of God being between us ?" They consulted 'Umar, who judged that the Fazarite should hit Jabala back as he hit him, or pay him an indemnity. Jabala answered, "Are the rabble among you equal to kings ?" To which 'Umar answered, "All are equal among us when it comes to the truth." He said, "I will go back to my religion then." 'Umar said, "you do that, and I will cut off your head." Jabala said, "Give me till tomorrow." When it was night, Jabala and his men broke camp and went to the Roman Emperor in Constantinople (Abd. Al-Fadi, 1997 : 224-225). If the Quran has made it obligatory for Muslims to kill those who are not converted to Islam or reconverted from Islam to any other faith where is the freedom of religion ?

Three Alternatives for Non-Muslims

584. Is not it a fact that Islam gives three alternatives for the non-Muslims to survive :

   a) Conversion (to Islam)
   b) Expulsion (from the Islamic land)
   c) Assassination (on unwillingness to accept Islam (47 : 4)

It was only when the Muslims felt that presence of non-Muslims are indispensable in their kingdom to perform some menial jobs which are considered mean and heinous by Muslims they allowed the non-Muslims (kafirs) to stay in their kingdom by paying a tax called Jizia (9 : 29) which was introduced by Muhammad in Mecca.

Muhammad's True Secularism

585. Can it be an ideal state where the Head of the State (Muhammad) declares for a community (to the Jews) : If you embrace Islam, you will be safe. You should know that the earth belongs to Allah and His Messenger, and I want to expel you from this land. So, if anyone amongst you owns some property, he is permitted to sell it, otherwise you should know that the Earth belongs to Allah and His Messenger" (*Buk* 4 : 392) ?

Conversion through Bribe

586. In the Quran it is said : Alms are for the poor and the needy, and those employed to administer the funds, for those hearts have been reconciled, for those in bondage and in debt, in the cause of Allah (9 : 60). Explaining this verse Al-Baidawi refers to the context :

Those whose hearts are brought together are a group of people who converted to Islam but had a weak intention to continue in it, whose hearts were brought together by the freewill offerings (that were given them). Or they could be some of the nobility who would turn to Islam if they saw how their fellows were given both honour and money. The Messenger has indeed given (money to) 'Uyaina Ibn Hisn, al 'Aqra' Ibn Habis, and al-Abbas Ibn Mirdas for that reason. It was said they were some of the nobility whose hearts Muhammad had united by giving them money; some also he promised to give money if they were ready to fight the unbelievers. It was said also that the portion of money allotted to making converts was for the purpose of increasing the number of Muslims, so when God made him strong and increased his followers, that portion was cancelled (Anwar al-Tanzil wa Asrar al Ta' will 2 vols. Istanbul, n.d. Qtd al-Fadi, n.d. 99-100).

165

Can you accept this kind of religion as true which attracts the followers by money and attacks and kills those who do not accept this faith ? Can one call this money as Zakat and freewill offerings or bribe and corruption ?

Is Forcible Convertion Allowed ?

587. Can you deny the fact that in 670 Muhammad sent Amar Ibn al-As to the Christian tribes of Oman to accept Islam and pay the Zakat but he could only convert a few tribes but tribes like Mazuna who remained in Christianity had to surrender half of their lands and property to the conqueror ? Did not Muhammad send a delegation in February 630 to the Christian prince of Himyar, in the south with a letter to accept Islam and accept the Arabic tongue instead of Himyar and the king was converted ?

Did not Muhammad send Ali in July 630 to Tayi tribe to destroy the idol of the god and terrorize the people to accept Islam and force the Christian clans of Tayi to accept Islam (Walker 1999 : 204 -205) ?

Conversion through Jihad

588. Jihad means fight in the name of Allah and the way of Allah. What is wrong to fight against those who disbelieve in Allah ? Muhammad said : " When you meet your enemies who are polytheists, invite them to three courses of action. If they respond to any one of these you also accept it and withhold yourself from doing them any harm : First invite them to accept Islam, if they respond to you, accept it from them and desist from fighting against them. Secondly, if they refused to accept Islam, demand from them Jezia tax. If they agree to pay, accept it from them and hold your hands. Thirdly, if they refuse to pay tax, seek Allah's help and fight them (*Mus* 3 : 4294).

Better to die in one's Religion

589. When Abu Talib, Muhammad's uncle was in his death bed Muhammad went to him while Abu Jahl was sitting beside him. Muhammad insisted his uncle to accept Allah so that he will defend his case before Him. Abu Jahl and Abdullah bin Umaya said : "O Abu Talib ! Will you leave the religion of Abdul Muttalib ?" Before his death Abu Talib said : I am on the religion of "Abdul Muttalib". Then there after the Quran revealed : "It is not fitting for the prophet and the believers to ask Allah's forgiveness for the pagans, even if they were their near relatives, after it has become clear to them that they are the dwellers of the Hell Fire" (9 : 113).

What is wrong in paganism and wrong to stick to one's own religion ? If somebody comes to a Muslim and asks him to change his religion, can the prophet allow it ? It is better to live in one's own religion than leave it for the sake of a new one. Allah of the Muslims seems to be more autocratic than the pagan's gods.

37 - Victims of Victory

The Prophet said : "A Muslim is one who avoids harming Muslims with his tongue and hands" (*Buk* I : 18). But how many Muslims have ever raised their voices in protest over Saddam Hussein's genocidal war upon the Kurds ?

E. Renan in his "Why I am not a Muslim", remarked : "Muslims are the first victims of Islam. Many times I have observed in my travels in the Orient that fanaticism comes from a small number of dangerous men who maintain the practice of religion by terror. To liberate a Muslim from his religion is the best service that one can render them."

Why Islamic Calender starts from September 24; 622 ?

590. Why did the Islamic Calender not begin with the birth of Muhammad, nor did it start with the first revelation of Allah to him, but with the date of his emigration from Mecca to Medina *i.e.* in September 24, 622 (*Buk* 5 : 271) ? Does not it begin with a political motive when Muhammad became the ruler of Medina and founded a religious city-state with the political geneology of war, taxes, glory

For the Muslims by the Muslims and of the Muslims

591. Does Islamic ideology admit of territorial nationality ? If Allah is the true sovereign and runs His government with His laws without sharing power with anyone how can it cope with a government of the people, by the people and for the people ?

When Quran grants to the unbelievers a way to triumph over the believers (4 : 141) and verily this Quran does guide to that which is most right and best (22 : 41), where is the scope to hold election and through this elected body make laws by rejecting the Sharia laws ?

Islam Divides ?

592. Does not Islam divide the human family into two factions--the believers and the infidels; human history into two periods-- the age of Jahillia (ignorance) and the age of enlightenment; the inhabited earth into two camps-- the land of the House of Islam (*Dar-ul-Islam*), and the House of war (*Dar-ul-Harb*) and postulates a permanent war between these divisions ? Does not the Dar-ul-Islam send military missions to the Dar-ul-Harb till the latter is conquered and converted into Dar-ul-Islam ?

Islamic Secularism

593. Is not it a fact that Muslims enjoy secularism of any secular state, but Muslim countries donot believe in secularism as the Quran directs them ? In Quran Allah says to Muhammad :

"He who chooses a religion other than Islam, it will not be accepted from him, and in the everlasting life he will be among the losers" (3.85); "but whosoever of you recants from his religion and dies an unbeliever their works shall be annulled in this world and in the Everlasting Life, and those shall be the companions of Hell, and there they shall live for ever" (2.217); and whosoever disbelieves in Allah after believing except he who is forced while his heart remains in his belief but he who opens his chest for disbelief, shall receive the Anger of Allah and for such awaits a mighty punishment" (16.106).

Can Islam provide a Secular State ?

594. In an Islamic state where there is no separation of state and religion is Islam not bound to fail to provide a secular constitutional framework necessary for running a welfare state ?

Unbelievers have no Right to Live

595. Can you deny the fact that Muhammad gave only two options to the non-Muslims : the Quran or the Sword (Arnold. 1913 : 52-53; Zakaria, 1991 : 30) ?

If it is wrong why does the Quran say that "when you meet the unbelievers smite at their necks (47 : 4), fight those who believe not in Allah (9 : 29), fight them on until there is no more persecution (8 : 39), and you may dislike fighting as prescribed but it is good for you and that you love a thing which is bad for you (2 : 216) ?

Jiziya for Non-Muslims

596. Is it not a fact that to live in an Islamic state the non-Muslims have to pay Jiziya or substitute money imposed by Muhammad (9 : 19) and the person who is paying Jiziya must come on foot and make the payment standing, while the receiver should be seated (Sarkar, *A History of Aurangzeb*, pp. 124-131) ?

Muslims Versus Muslims

597. Is it a fact that when Muslims were scattered and separated from each other and waging war against each other Allah brought their hearts together and they became brothers (3 : 103) ? Was it true even at the time of the Prophet ? Were not the wars and raids as fierce as ever among the Arabs during Muhammad's time ?

And after Muhammad's death Abu Bakr was engaged in the War of Apostasy. After Umar died, Muslims massacred one another so that Ali and Uthman were killed by the swords of their fellow Muslims. Thereafter the War of the Camel broke out between Ali Ibn Abi Talib and 'Ayesha'. Then another war erupted between Muawiya, Ali and his son al-Husain on the one side, and Muhammad Ibn Abu Bakr, who was killed by Amr Ibn al- As, on the other. In the year 71 A.H. 'Abdallah Ibn al-Zubair led an insurrection to succeed Abd al- Malik Ibn Marwan the Ummayad as Caliph, which brought about a war between him and al-Hajjaj Ibn Yusuf al- Thaqafi. After al-Hajjaj laid siege to Mecca, he was able to kill Ibn al-Zubair and many of the Muslim elites, and he destroyed a part of the Kaaba by means of catapults.

It is worth noting, in addition to the foregoing, that in order to establish 'Abdallah Ibn al-Zubair as Caliph, the clan of Kilab dealt treacherously with the clan of Kalb, both of which belonged to the tribe of Fazara. They employed trickery and perjury to accomplish their goal. This despicable act of deceit led to a massacre of many people in the clan of Kalb. Not long after, the clan of Qais, which belonged to the tribe of Fazara and the aforementioned clan of Kilab waged war. Thus the clan of Kilab were dealt with the same blow they had dealt the clan of Kalb. On learning about all this commotion and strife, Abd al-Malik Ibn Marwan wrote to al Hajjaj, who was then his regent over Hijaz, Ta' if, Yamama and Yemen, and called on him to muster his hordes and go to the tribe of Fazara to kill all the adults he could !

Thus was the situation of the Arabs during the early period of Islam : rife with wars, deception and treachery ? So where is that bringing together of hearts, the burying of old grievances and the doing away with enmity and strife which Islam is supposed to have accomplished among the Arabs (Abd Al- Fadi. 1997 : 248-250) ?

Religion of Theocracy

598. Can Islam be treated as pure religion or is it a theocentric religion (2 : 193; 8 : 39) ?

38 - Mercy Demands Mercy

There was a time when the masters had a notion that slaves have no soul. No soul means no life. With the progress of human society a few conscious people thought of human rights and slaves were set free.

The semitic religions from Abraham to Moses and Moses to Muhammad postulate that animals lack souls. Rene Descrates, the well-known French Philosopher invented the theory *cogito ergo sum* ("I think; therefore I am"). According to him animals have no soul or consciousness because they cannot think. They have only bodies. Body is a physical machine separable from the soul. That theory brought an innumerable woe for the animals who were operated without anasthesia, making the animals scream. It continued.

From Jews to Christians and from Christians to Muslims, killing an animal, which was an incident during Ibrahim's time, became a tradition in course of time.

It is the story of Ibrahim. In the very late age when he got two sons Isaac (Ishac) and Ishmael, Ibrahim had a dream. In the dream God appeared, asked Ibrahim to sacrifice his most beloved thing. Ibrahim thought God needs sheep, then he revised his thought and went to the mountain to sacrifice his beloved son Ishmael. But due to Allah's grace Ishmael was saved and an animal was sacrificed in his place. It was an incident. Did Allah tell all Muslims in dream to keep sacrificing an animal to commemorate the dream... in every *Bakar Idd* ? Was *Bakar Idd* observed during the time of Jesus Christ ? Why then do the Muslims continue this cruel festival ?

Where is the kindness for mankind and animals in the life of Muhammad. So, if you kill, kill well : and if you slaughter, slaughter well (Al-Nawawi Hadith No. 17, Das 2010 : 103) was Muhammad's way of pleasing Allah. Shahi Muslim rightly recorded :

"Ja'' for b Muhammad reported on the authority of his father : He (Muhammad) said : I have with me sacrificial animals, so do not put off the Ihram. He(Jabir) said : The total number of those sacrificial animals brought by 'Ali from the Yemen and of those brought by the Apostle was one hundred...He (Muhammad) then went to the place of sacrifice, and sacrificed sixty-three (camels) with his own hand. Then he gave the remaining number to 'Ali who sacrificed them, and he shared him in his sacrifice. He then commanded that a piece of flesh from each animal sacrificed should be put in a pot, and when it was cooked, both of them (the Holy Prophet and Hadrat 'Ali) took some meat out of it and drank its soup" (*Mus* 2 : 2803).

Muhammad also encouraged others to slaughter animals to satisfy Allah. "He (Muhammad) said : "Offer it as a sacrifice. He who slaughtered after prayer, his ritual of sacrifice became complete and he in fact observed the religious practice of the Muslims" (*Mus* : 3 : 4823). "Allah's Messenger said : "Allah cursed him who sacrificed for anyone besides Allah" (*Mus* 3 : 4876).

In what way were God and the Prophet merciful towards the animal world can be viewed from the Quran and the Hadiths :

Why Animal Sacrifice ?

599. People used to shear their hair or tails and cut pieces of flesh from living animals to cook and eat them. Muhammad said that the tail was their brush and fan and hair was their quilt. He also forbade people to keep animals in their working equipment for a long time and said, "Don't make the backs of animals your chairs." Animal fights were also made unlawful. Another custom was to tie up an animal

169

and practice arrow shooting on it. This was also prohibited (*Radiance* 22-28 Oct. 1989 : 8). If it is true why did the Prophet accept the practices of *halal*, the cruelest method of killing the innocent animals for the sake of Allah ?

Is Animal Sacrifice a Good Example ?

600. In what way does the blood that flows out of the sacrificed animals denote that the Muslims are ready to sacrifice their lives, belongings, offsprings and everything at the command of Allah ?

Halal, the cruelest method to kill Animals

601. Can Allah be merciful when he accepts *halal* rites through the prayer of a killer facing towards Mecca and cuts the throat of an animal fully conscious and without being tranquilized ?

Is sacrifice Human Right ?

602. Idu'l-azha is a killing festival for Muslims to sacrifice a goat or a sheep, or a cow or a camel for the sake of Allah. It is very much allowed for seven persons to join in the sacrifice of a cow or a camel (*Mus* 2 : 3024-31). A hajji should not be cruel enough to make his camel 'kneel down', but slaughter it in a standing posture (*Mus* 2 : 3032) and cows and goats should be sacrificed after making them lie down. On the '*Umrah* pilgrimage in the 6th year Muhammad sacrificed 70 camels, in 7th year 60 camels and in the Farewell Pilgrimage in the 10th year he sacrificed 100 animals. Out of 100 animals Prophet himself sacrificed 63 with his own hand and the remaining animals were left for Ali to be sacrificed. Then the Prophet told his followers : "I have sacrificed the animals here, and the whole of Mina is a place of sacrifice, so sacrifice your animals at your places" (*Mus* 2 : 2805). Compare the Islamic Allah with the Jewish Jehovah---Jehovah whose temple was no less than a slaughter house. Therefore Hosea could pray to his Lord : "For I desire mercy, not sacrifice, and acknowledgement of God rather than burnt offerings" (*Hosea* 6 : 6). The question comes when seven persons share a cow or a camel for sacrifice what is the need of killing 100 animals at a time by the Prophet himself ?

Is killing Religious during Haj ?

603. During Haj when no body is allowed to hunt or lead any one to a hunting place how can slaughter of animals after Eid-al- Adha.

Islamic Method of killing Animals

604. How is cutting the throat and windpipe of an animal with a sharp knife help the animal to die in peace and is it humane ? Why the dying animal struggles, flutters, writhes, shakes and kicks ? Is it not due to contraction and relaxation of the muscles deficient in blood or due to suffocation and helplessness ? Is not it a fact that when the central nervous system of the spinal cord is disconnected it allows an animal to die with lesser pain than *halal* ?

Vicarious Atonement of Sin

605. If the Quran does not absolve one's sins with the blood of another and unlike pagan fancy does not appease Allah by blood sacrifice, is there any reason to make it compulsory or to invent any method of killing the animal ? What is the need of killing 600,000 heads of animal, by engaging 6000 butchers from Turkey, 2800 assistant butchers and 1000 regular workers for the Hajj season for such a mass killing (*Radiance* 17 July 1988 : 9) ? Is it a credit or a disgrace ?

Qurbani for Qurbani Sake

606. If animal meat or blood never reaches Allah what kind of piety are we showing to Allah through this Qurbani ?

Most Merciful or Most Cruel ?

607. If Allah is the most forgiving and the most-merciful why does He command all Muslims to sacrifice animals the Nisaab value of gold or 612 grams of silver to buy animals for Qurbani ?

Killing Cows in Kaaba Allowed

608. Did not Muhammad slaughter cows as a sacrifice on behalf of his wives (*Bus* 2 : 115, 767) especially, on behalf of Ayesha on the day of Nahr, *i.e.,* 10th of Dhul-Hijja (*Mus* 2 : 3030) ?

Is drained out Blood Good Meat ?

609. How far is it hygienic to drain out the blood before the head is removed from an animal ? Can you make the meat free from germs, bacteria and toxins etc. by draining out the blood and is the meat safe to eat ?

Tell me what you Eat and I will tell you who you are ?

610. Is it not a fact that Allah permitted the Muslims to take the flesh of camels, cows, sheep, horses who are vegetarian by nature ? Allah has forbidden to eat the flesh of the non-vegetarian animals and birds with claws like tigers, lions, wolves, bears, falcons, hawks and so on (5 : 3-4). If non-vegetarian animals are not dear to Allah why did not He teach man to be vegetarian ?

Mercy brings Mercy

611. Is it a fact that Allah will not be merciful to those who are not merciful to mankind (*Buk* 9 : 473) ?

Can Muslims Accept Indian Constitution ?

612. Is it not a fact that Indian Constitution guarantees freedom of religion that includes slaughtering animals on Eid-ul-Azha (Article 25). Then it says "Freedom of profession, occupation, trade or business (Article 19 (1) (g) that includes butchers' right too ? In the directive principles of state policy, however, it is clearly mentioned regarding preserving and improving the breeds, and prohibiting the slaughter of cows and calves and other milch and draught cattle (Article 48 (iv). If the healthy animals are preserved and a Muslim slaughters ill, weak, defective and old animals, will that be acceptable to Allah on the day of Eid-ul-Azha ?

Islam Contradicts Indian Constitution

613. Is not it a fact that the highest court of the land upholds the constitutional validity of the two standing orders issued by the Municipal Commissioner of Ahmedabad in exercising his power under Section 466 (1) (D) (b) of Bombay Provincial Municipal Corporation Act, 1949 that by these orders the slaughter houses were directed to be kept open on all days except on seven days as mentioned in the two orders. These days i.e. Janmasthami, Jain Samvatsari, 2nd October (Gandhiji's birthday), 12th Feb. (Shradha day of Gandhiji), 30th Jan (Gandhiji's Nirvana day), Mahavir Jayanti and Ram Navami were declared holidays for the aforesaid slaughter houses.

Is it not the violation of the Articles (19 (1) (G) ? Mustafa remarks : The Islamic lunar calendar is not static. Every year there is a difference of about ten days in the previous years festivals and dates. Thus there is every possibility that Eid-ul-Azha may fall on any of these seven specified days. Would the Muslims stop killing the animal on their festival day (31 May 1992 : 9) ?

Section VII

Women Are Your Field

39 - Status of Women in Islam

The great English dramatist Wiliam Shakespere wrote one of his love sonnets :

> Love is not love
> Which alters when it alteration finds,
> > Or bends with the remover to remove
> O no ! it is an ever-fixed mark
> > That looks on tempests and is never shaken;
> Love's not Time's fool, though rosy lips and cheeks
> > Within his bending sickle's compass come :
> Love alters not with his brief hours and weeks.

In a polygamic society no woman or man can claim that she or he is a true lover till death. Before Islam the Arabs atleast maintained polygamy both for men as well as women. After the Arabs became Muslims polygamy became the birth right for the Muslim men only and women were deprived of this right.

Muhammad's first wife, Khadija was a powerful merchant. It is surprising that Allah neither commanded Muslim women to veil nor allowed Muhammad to practice polygamy despite the fact that Khadija was fifteen years older than him and had been married twice before marrying Muhammad. Only after Khadija's death all these Quranic nonsense of Allah started coming down and by this way, the status of women were lowered to the lowest grade of sex-slaves.

One can give hundred and one reasons in favour of women liberation in Islam, but Islam cannot escape six points on sex. Because Allah created women to be enjoyed by men. These six points the Muslims practice are :1. Polygamy, 2. Women's status in marriage, 3. Women's dress code, 4. Segregation of sexes including total veiling, 4. Unilateral divorce by the husband, and 6. Women's position in the law of inheritance and testimony.

It is also a misconception that in pre-Islamic Arabia female infants were murdered and Islam abolished that practice. If that was true, how did Arab men marry multiple times ? Muhammad allowed his followers to marry four women. How could it be possible, if there were female infanticide in practice (Das 2010 : 194) ?

Pre-Islamic Status of Woman

614. Did not the Pre-Islamic Arab, when the Prophet of Islam had no idea of prophethood, oppose burying the newborn daughters and supported marrying widows and divorced woman ? It was Prophet Muhammad who started restricting his nine wives with the fear that the young visitors may attract his young wives ? In the words of Dr. Younus Shaikh :

The insecurity of early Islam gradually added to the exclusion of women, and 100 years later, by the reign of the Abbasid Caliph Haroon ur Rashid, women became merely sexual toys and breeding machines; and as married women they were merely maid servants- mere man's social appendages. Moreover, as female sex-slaves, women were freely bought and sold in open markets of all Islamic countries, and loaned, rented or bestowed as gifts to friends. The prophet himself

174

bestowed women sex-slaves to his favourites. There was no limit to the number of slaves one could own; one of the companions of prophet Hazrat Zubair Ibn ul Arsvan, for example, had 1000 men-slaves and 1000 women sex-slaves. Islam took the woman as the land tilled by the man where he spilled his seeds (2007 : 10).

Pre-Islamic Women Rulers and Poets

615. Can we deny the fact that in the Pre-Islamic Arab there were female rulers like Zabiba, Shamsi, Yati, Tayl Khunu, Tubwa and Adiya ? The women could choose one husband or more than two husbands as they wished. Was not Arabia proud of distinguished women poets like Khansa (real name Tomadir) who died (616) just when Muhammad started his career (Walker 1999 : 49-51) ?

Women Liberation and Intolerant Prophet

616. Is it not a fact that women enjoyed much higher status in Arabia before Islam ? They were fighters, poets and debaters. Khadija the first wife of Muhammad was a heiress, business woman, and she herself could propose her marriage to Muhammad. Before her marriage had she not, inspite of being a widow, the right to manage the business of her dead husband ? Even during Muhammad's times girls were allowed to sing and take part in satirical performance ridiculing the Prophet. One of the girl's name was Furtane. Were they not victimised by the intolerent Prophet (Walker 1999 : 319) ?

Hind opposed Prophet's Invasion

617. Does not Hind, the wife of Abu Sofian, the leader of the Meccans and the foremost opponent of Muhammad oppose her husband and Muhammad both when her husband supported Muhammad's invasion to Mecca ? She counteracted by shouting : "Don't take any notice of this fat old fool. A fine protector of his people he is !" (Main 1985 : 8).

Male God with Female Goddesses

618. Is not it a fact that the pagan poetry of Arab highly glorified the grace and beauty of womanhood and worshipped male gods like Allah and Hubal alongside the female goddesses like Al-Uzza of Mecca, Al-Lat of Taif and Manat of Medina ?

Veils for Muslims

619. Is not it a fact that Allah orders the Muslims : "O Prophet, tell your wives, your daughters and the believing women to draw their veils close to them, so it is likely they will be known, and not hurt" (33.59) ?

Therefore all Muslims women have to hide behind closed doors with black veils. Does not Taslima Nasrin lament over veil for the women by saying :
My mother used 'purdah'. She wore a 'burqa' (the black veil)
with a net cover in front of the face. It reminded me of the
meat-safes in my grandmother's house. One had a net door
made of cloth, the other of metal. But the objective was same-
- keeping the meat safe' (2007 : 62).

Is not it a fact that the veil was imposed when Muhammad married Zainab bint Jahsh and invited the people for food but they did not leave his house after food ? The Prophet gave sufficient indications to leave his house but still three persons remained stilling and gossiping. At last they went sitting out. In order to safeguard his wives he put a screen and Allah sent a statement :
Enter not the Prophet's houses

Until leave is given to you for
a meal truly, such a thing is in
Allah's sight an enormity (33 : 53-54).

Did not Umar tell to the Prophet : as good and bad persons enter upon you, so I suggest that you order the mothers of the Believers (your wives) to observe veils (*Buk* 6 : 313-314) ? There after the veil system started.

Did Eve ever have a Veil Covered ?

620. Why does Islam degrade women by keeping them behind the veil ? When Adam and Eve were rambling in nudity did Allah or Adam think of covering Eve with a veil ? Why should a woman be in prison of veil and become the private property of a person who marries her ?

No Veil during Hajj

621. What is the need for both men and women to lower their gaze in each others presence if a woman is not veiled on her face, otherwise what is there to lower your eyes from ? If veil is very important in women's life (24 : 31) why during the Hajj it is specifically forbidden for a woman to cover her face with a veil ?

Veil helps the Immorals ?

622. Does veil signify dignity for a lady and escape the evil persons fear to tease (33 : 59) ? Does the veil keep the eyes of an immoral man from lusting anywhere ?

Women are like Cattle

623. Is not it a fact that in Islam the status of woman is equated with the cattle ? Did not Muhammad say :

"Treat women well for they are like domestic animals and they possess nothing themselves. Allah has made the enjoyment of their bodies lawful in his Quran" (*Tab* : IX.113).

Since women are domestic animals, logically the old stock can be replaced by new one, as Tabari and Ibn Ishaq recorded,

"Ali (Muhammad's adopted son, son-in-law, and future Caliph) said, 'Prophet, women are plentiful. You can get a replacement, easily changing one for another" (*Tab* : VIII.62/*Ish* : 496).

Elsewhere, Muhammad is reported to have said, "The woman has two things to cover her : the grave and the marriage". When he was asked which one was better, Muhammad replied, "The grave" (Dagher 1995 : 18-19).

Lastly, following quotation from Imam Gazali's work shows how much hatred Muhammad had for women. Once the Prophet said : if husband would be covered with pus from head to toe, and wife would lick it, even then wife's gratitude to husband wouldn't be fulfilled" (Imam Gazali, from *Ihya Ulum Al-Din*, volume - 2 Qtd. Das 2010 : 125).

Why Four Wives ?

624. Is not it a fact that after Quran allowed Muslims to have four wives (4:3) Mirza Aziz explains why a Muslim needs four wives ? He says : 'A man must marry one woman of Hindustan to rear up children, one wife from Khurasan to do the household work, one woman from Iran to keep company and talk'. And the fourth ? "Why ? One woman from Transoxiana to whip the other three and keep peace' (Qtd. Eraly 1997 : 666).

176

Enjoyment of Marriage Legalized

625. Did Muhammad not legalize 'enjoyment marriage' for his followers during the Battles of Khaibar and Fath which he prohibited in the Battle of Wadaa because it was more of a fornication and less of a marriage ? In enjoyment marriage, a man marries a woman for a limited time-period by paying some money. How can a prophet of such stature allow his followers this kind of profligacy for their 'enjoyment' ?

Cause for the Cousin to Marry

626. If 'boy meets girl' is a ridiculous business how are the Muslims justified to marry their cousins (daughter of a father's brother if the father and his brother come from different mothers) ? Is it not ridiculous ? For Muslim love comes after marriage, not before marriage and is divided among the four wives. Is it true love or lust ?

Did Adam have Four Eves ?

627. What is the orthodox view about plurality of wives in Islam ? The answer is simple, inequality of sexes and slavery. If a single man marries a number of women and keeps concubines too what will be the result of that family ? More careless children and divorces. The Quran should give equal opportunity to woman to marry four men. Allah did not and could not think about Adam, otherwise He would have provided more Eves to Adam ?

Wives and concubines Allowed

628. If a Muslim is capable to afford food, clothes for several wives or a travelling Muslim can keep wives in different places and take concubines from among the slaves, just as it pleases him (4 : 3-34), can he as a peaceful householder tolerate the hatred, envy and jealousy which springs from these wives ?

Two Three and Four are Nine

629. Does not Islam advocate polygamy in theory and practice, only for men and not for women ? Allah said : "If you fear that you shall not be able to deal justly with the orphans, marry women of your choice, two or three or four (4 : 3). Some Muslims who are not satisfied with four wives they argue 'two, three, four' not the exact number. The Arabic *"wa"* means 'and' which implies the total of these numbers, which is nine. It can also mean eighteen. To support this argument they say :

Muhammad died while married to nine wives. It goes without saying that Allah commands us to 'follow him', which implies nothing less than 'permission'.

Why Ali's Case is Different ?

630. If Allah allowed polygamy why did the prophet refuse Ali the husband of Fatima, and his own son-in-law to marry the daughter of Abu Jahl ? The reason is obvious. Abu Jahl was an infidel and enemy of Islam. The prophet became outrageous and said : "I would not allow them. I would not allow them...for my daughter is part of me. He who disturbs her in fact disturbs me and he who offends her offends me (*Mus* 4 : 5999; *Buk* 5 : 76). Whoever makes her angry, makes me angry. She is the chief mistress of the women in paradise (*Buk* 5 : 111). Does it not mean that the Prophet was different for others and different for his family ?

Is Menstruation Dirty ?

631. Why Allah is much worried about menstruation of women ? It may be discomfort for a woman but what is the need of keeping her aloof until they have become clean (2 : 222) ? Can one blame women as dirty for a natural occurrence ? Does not Allah know that He has created woman and menstruation as a part of female anatomy and it is linked with child bearing ? How can such a natural process be dirty ?

Nursing the Adult

632. Is it not a fact that Sahla bint Suhail complained to Muhammad because her husband, Abu Huzeifa, was envious of his servant, Salem ? Muhammad advised Sahla to nurse Salem five times. She protested about Salem's having a beard. But Muhammad advised her to nurse Salem in order to cure her husband of envy, for Ayesha used to nurse any man when she and Muhammad thought it suitable. This tradition is described in detail in Ibn Malik's Muwatta (Muslim's Sahih, chapter on nursing the adult; Ibn Malik's Muwatta, chapter on nursing the adult; *True Guidance* 1, 1991 : 101).

Mother's Milk or Husband's Feast

633. Is it justified for a Muslim adult husband to suck the milk of his wife under Sharia Law ?

Malik's Muwatta mentioned : "Sucking...after the first two years, little or much, it does not make anything harm (30 : 1 : 11). It is like food." As per another Hadith from Malik's Muwatta, a Muslim man is divinely allowed to drink his wife's milk (or, multiple wives' milk on choice and taste) regularly and still can remain her sex-partner (30 : 2 : 14).

Sucking solves the Problems

634. Is it not a fact that Uqba b. Harith married Umm Yahya daughter of Abu Lahb ? There came a black slave-woman and she claimed that she had given suck to both of them. When it was mentioned before Muhammad he ordered separation ? In case of Abu Hudhaifa there was fear of separation between the husband and the wife or the creation of bitterness and hostility between Salim Abu Hudhaifa. Muhammad, therefore, advised Sahla bint Suhail to give him her milk so that suspicion may give place to mutual trust. Sahla did not suck him from her breast, rather gave him her milk without allowing him to touch her breast as the infants do (*Mus* 2:3424-3425). Does not this prove that would be wife becomes a mother by once sucking and it is enough to make marriage unlawful according to the Quran (4 : 23) ?

Can Two Women be Equal to One Man ?

635. Is not it a fact that in Islamic society women are not allowed to inherit the property equally with their brothers ? In the case of inheritance does Allah not say : "A male shall inherit twice as much as a female" (4 : 11-12) ? That means a woman is half the value of a man and in court the testimony of two women equals the testimony of one man (2 : 282) ? Is it Allah's intention to equate one man with two women in matters of bearing witness or is it an interpretation of the verse of the Quran by male jurists ?

Why a Woman should produce Four Male Witnesses ?

636. In case of adultery why should the Muslim women produce four male witnesses who must declare that they have seen the parties in the very act of carnal conjunction otherwise she shall be given eighty lashes (24 : 4; 2 : 282) ?

Man is more Weighty than Woman in Property Sharing

637. Is not it a fact that in Islamic societies the birth of a girl child is a matter of disgrace ? In questions of property, the Quran tells us that male children should inherit twice the portion than female children (4 : 11-12).

As far as the property is concerned why there is disparity ? Are the men not equal with women so far as food and living is concerned ?

Fatima's Inheritance of Property Denied

638. If the right to inherit property cannot be denied in Muslim Law why Fatima was deprived of her paternal inheritance ? When she was in need of her patrimony the Caliph Abu Bakr, refused to hand over anything to Fatima. Did not she get angry with Abu Bakr and not talk to him until the end of her life ? When she died, her husband, Ali buried her at night and did not inform Abu Bakr about her death. If the Prophet's daughter is deprived of her right to inherit what to speak about other women (Shaikh 1999 : 28-29) ?

Women in Islam

639. What is the role of a Muslim woman in her society is well described by Al-Ghazali (1058-1111) in his *The Revival of the Religious Sciences.*

She should stay at home and get on with her spinning; she should not go out often; she must not be well-informed, nor must she be communicative with her neighbours and only visit them when absolutely necessary; she should take care of her husband and respect him in his presence and his absence and seek to satisfy him in everything; she must not cheat on him nor extort money from him; she must not leave the house without his permission and if he gives permission she must leave surreptitiously. She should put on old clothes and take deserted streets and alleys, avoid markets, and make sure that a stranger does not hear her voice or recognize her; she must not speak to a friend of her husband even in need... Her sole worry should be her virtue, her home as well as her prayers and her fast. If a friend of her husband calls when the latter is absent she must not open the door nor reply to him in order to safeguard her and her husband's honour. She should accept what her husband gives her as sufficient sexual needs at any moment "...She should be clean and ready to satisfy her husband's sexual needs at any moment." The great theologian then warns all men to be careful of women, for their "guile is immense and their mischief is noxious; they are immoral and mean-spirited." "It is a fact that all the trials, misfortunes and woes which befall men come from women." moaned Al-Ghazali (Warraq 2001 : 32).

Eighteen Restriction for a Woman in Muslim Society

640. Because of the behaviour of Eve in the garden of Eden the women have to suffer eternally. In the words of Al-Ghazali the greatest Muslim after Muhammad :

As for the distinctive characteristics with which God on high has punished the women (the matter is as follows) : When Eve ate fruit which He had forbidden to her from the tree in Paradise, the Lord, be He praised, punished women with eighteen things : (1) menstruation; (2) childbirth; (3) separation from mother and

179

father and marriage to a stranger; (4) pregnancy; (5) not having control over her own person; (6) a lesser share in inheritance; (7) her liability to be divorced and inability to divorce; (8) its being lawful for men to have four wives, but for a woman to have only one husband; (9) the fact that she must stay secluded in the house; the fact that she must keep her head covered inside the house; (11) the fact that two women's testimony has to be set against the testimony of one man; (12) the fact that she must not go out of the house unless accompanied by a near relative; (13) the fact that men take part in Friday and feastday prayers and funerals while women do not; (14) disqualification for rulership and judgeship; (15) the fact that merit has one thousand components, only one of which is attributable to   men; (16)...(17) the fact that if their husbands die they must observe a waiting period of four months and ten days before remarrying.(18) the fact that if their husbands divorce them they must observe a waiting period of three months or three menstrual periods before remarrying (Warraq 2001 : 32).

Why not a Second Husband ?

641. If a woman becomes invalid or sexually incapable, a husband is allowed to have a second wife, why is it not vice-versa with men ? Does Islam allow a wife to choose a second husband if her husband becomes invalid ?

How funny it is to think that the identification of father is so important that a man can have several wives but a woman cannot marry more than one husband because she cannot say who is the father of that child ? Gone are the days when the name of the father was recorded in schools. Now one can cite the mother's name only which is not objectionable. It is wrong to say that in a mother-centered society where the children who do not have any concept of fatherhood suffer psychologically and undergo severe mental trauma or disturbances ? What is wrong with Jabala Satyakam of the Upanishad and Draupadi of Mahabharat ?

In a society where a man is allowed to have more than one wife that society is bound to give permission to a woman to have more than one husband.

Khula depends on the Mercy of the Husband

642. If Khula (to put off-or to take off clothes) is the most important right available to a Muslim woman for the termination of marriage at the wish of the wife, why again it is made to depend upon the sweet will of the husband ? Does not the very purpose of *Khula* fail ? Is it not to please the women to avoid an open rebellion ? Does not the Hadith say, the women who break the matrimonial ties by using Khula are hypocrites and not Muslim (*Mis* 2 : 3148) ?

Is Talaq Successful than Khulaj ?

643. When a man breaks his marital ties with his wife, the divorce is called *Talaq*, when a woman tries to break the wedlock it is called *Khulaj* or separation. How many women are successful in Khulaj, might be less than even 1 per cent , whereas about 90 per cent men are successful in Talaq, how and why ?

Licence for Anal Intercourse

644. Is it a fact that the Holy Quran reveals to license anal intercourse ? Once it happened Ibn Abbas said : "Umar came to Muhammad and said : 'I have perished.' 'Why ?' Muhammad asked. 'It is because I have altered the normal position of sex tonight.' "He meant to say that he had sexual intercourse away from his usual place. At first, Muhammad gave no reply, then he claimed that Allah gave him license.

Were not Muhammad and Umar shameless and immodest ? Muhammad should have guided Umar to God's holiness and purity (*CQV* 1994 : 49).

For this incident Allah reveals to Muhammad : "Your wives are your field. Go in therefore to your field when or how you will" (2 : 223). (*Buk* 6 : 51; Al-Tabarani's Al-Awsat; Asbab al-Nuzul by al- Suyuti on Sura 2 : 223).

Can it be a praise to a woman for her contribution towards the preservation of human species if we regard woman as field where a cultivator can sow whenever he wishes ?

Allah does not Care for Woman

645. Does not the Quran permit a man to have sex with one of his wives at any time, and in any way that he wants ? Does the woman have similar rights ? Because the Quran says that if women are disloyal their husbands should refuse to sleep with them (4 : 34).

Is not Allah a representative of man ? Therefore woman cannot be equal to man. When we compare women to men is it not like comparing camels to date trees ?

Women are Sex Objects

646. Is not it a fact that Arabic word "awrah" (aurat in Urdu) means genitals of a woman's body means "vagina" and *Nikah* means "penetration" (Kaleeby 2002; Warraq 1995, 316). It is pronounced as "Nokh" means the same "awrah" which means the giant vagina ? When the word "Nikah" is used to mean marriage, the actual meaning is not marriage but literally "sexual penetration" (Das 2010 : 249) ? Does it not prove that a Muslim woman is a "sex object" ?

Rights of Women as Commodity

647. Does divorce not depend entirely on the will of the husband and a right of man for the woman *i.e.*, the wild dominance of man over women (2 : 228, 230) ?

Why is the wife used merely as a commodity instead of being a partner of her husband ? Does it not encourage temporary marriages ?

Temporary Marriage Sanctioned

648. By giving sanction for contracting temporary marriage for three nights (*Mus* 1 : 325) and in turn give them a handful of dates or flour as a dower (*Mus* 2 : 3249) for the enjoyment you have with them as a duty (4 : 24), does the prophet give justice to marriage as an institution ?

Consequence of a Rebellious Wife

649. What right does a man have over women to control a rebellious wife to admonish them and banish them to beds apart and scourge or beat them (4 : 34) ?

Does it make any sense that if a woman disobeys her husband, she first gets a warning and if the rebellion continues she is kicked out of her bedroom, and then right at the end the husband comes and starts beating his wife with feather or with a stick ?

Trauma of Triple Talaq

650. How strange it is for a husband (not the wife) to do lip service by pronouncing *Talaq* thrice in a fit of anger, or in a state of inebriation or even jokingly to divorce his wife ?

Is not it funny, if he wants to have her again the Quran tells : "if a husband divorces his wife, he cannot, after that, re-marry her until she has married another husband" (2 : 230). Is it reasonable for a woman to be reconciled to her husband and return to him after she had married another man whom the Arabs call a Muhallil ? Why did Muhammad punish both the Muhallil and the original husband ? It is logically invalid and totally antithetical to the spirit of Islam.

Triple Divorce bring Disaster

651. Can one justify the simple articulation of the word Talak for three times is enough for divorcing a woman ? Abdallah al-Fadi rightly remarks :

Sometimes an influential man divorces his wife in a fit of anger. Later, as is often the case, he regrets what he has done and desires to have his wife back. But Islamic law compels this woman to have intercourse with another man before she can return to her husband. How inhumane and degrading this is (1997 : 190) !

Here is another cruel example of a Bangladesi gentleman who divorced his 118 women after marriage :

One by name Jinnath Al, a quack, who started to espouse from his fifteenth year and married 120 women till he attained 42 years. He divorced 118 wives within the period of 27 years. But he was living with his first and last wives. Al nikahnized at the rate of 5 spouses per year on the average (*Dainik Bangla* Nov. 1992 Qrt. Reddy 2004 : 243). How far is it Islamic ?

Unfair Divorce Laws

652. When divorce came under section 125, criminal law, it was applicable to all citizens in India irrespective of their faith, but since the Shah Bano case, Rajiv Gandhi introduced a new law and named it as *Muslim Women Security Act*, under which a divorced Muslim woman cannot demand her natural right to maintenance till her second marriage. By this Act were not the Muslim women deprived of their rights and they could claim maintenance only upto four months and ten days from the date of their divorce (Hussain 1993 : 7) ?

Between Common Civil Code and Muslim Personal Law

653. If common civil code is not acceptable for the Muslims in a non-Muslim country then for a crime committed a non-Muslim simply will go to jail whereas a Muslim will have to accept exemplary and preventive punishment such as :
1. 100 lashes for the adultery or fornication (24 : 2).
2. 80 lashes to bearing false witness (24 : 4), or for drinking alcohol or gambling because "in them is great sin, and some profit, for men, but the sin is greater than the profit" (2 : 219).
3. Guilty of lewdness, with the evidence of four witnesses, can be confined to a house until death do claim her (4 : 15).

No Open Society Dare to Do

654. How just and humane are the punishment laid down in the Quran that contains severe punishments for the thieves to cut off his or her hands as retribution for their deed (5 : 38) ? For the minimum theft the thief's right hand will be cut off from the wrist joint and for woman thief left hand will be cut off (*Buk* 8 : 779-780). Does cutting off the hand of a thief not deprive him of the opportunity to work for his livelihood ? Will that thief not be a burden to the society ?

Prophet's Order Applicable for him Too

655. If the Prophet ordered the horrible mutilation of the cutting off of hands for thief how did Allah not apply this rule for his messenger and changed it through a revelation that one-fifth of the spoils captured from the towns his followers invaded, and the caravans they raised should be kept for Muhammad (8 : 41) ?

Is Shariah Law Practicable ?

656. Are the penal laws of the Shariah practical ? If that will be implemented masses of people in cities and villages would have been largely incapable of work had one of their hands been cut off for every first theft. Countless men and women would live with broken backs and disrupted nervous systems for life if all adulterers had been whipped as the law demands. That is the reason for which Turkey went the farthest in abolishing Islamic law in 1926 when it introduced the Swiss Civil Law and the Italian Penal Law. In 1928 the concept of 'Shariah' was eliminated from the constitution (Al-Masih. *Islam Under...* 101).

Long back Faraj Fada, an Egyptian lawyer and essayist published a pamphlet in 1986 under the aggressive title of "No to Sharia" arguing for the separation of religion and state because Islam could not provide the secular constitutional framework necessary for running a modern state. This polemical essay enjoyed a great success and it was translated into Turkish, Persian, Urdu and other languages of the Islamic world (Reddy 2004 : 213).

Is Muslim Personal Law Traditional ?

657. Is not it an easy job for a Muslim husband to discard his wife ? The Muslim Personal Law says : "after divorce the wife is entitled to maintenance during the period of iddat *i.e.* during three mensurational periods. Under this law the husband is bound to pay mehr to the wife as a mark of respect to her, that he may settle any amount he likes by way of dower upon his wife (but) which cannot be less than 10 dirhams, which is equivalent to Rs. 4."

Muslim Personal Law Board did not care for the spirit of the law rather they imposed the law literally ? What is the value of <u>Rs.</u> 4 in today's life ?

When Father-in-Law became Husband ?

658. How can you prove that Muhammad was not the father of any of your men (33 : 40) when he adopted Zaid as his son and unlawfully married the spouse of his adopted son who had to unwillingly divorce her to allow his foster-father Muhammad to marry her ?

Let us view- in this context-the case of Imrana of Muzaffaranagar, who has reportedly been raped by her father-in-law. Her case gets all the more tragic because of the *fatwa* issued by Deoband and endorsed by the All India Muslim Personal Law Board that she can no longer stay with her husband just like Zaynab could no longer stay with Zaid . Does not that mean that in one stroke she was deprived of her home and hearth and her husband and her five children as Zaynab stayed with Muhammad as a wife ?

In what respect the Prophet is better than Judah who had illicit relation with his own daughter-in-law Tamar (*Gn* 38 : 1-30) or Lot's seduction by his own two daughters (*Gn* 19 : 30-37) ?

Is Muslim Personal Law Acceptable in Civilized Society ?

659. Is not it a fact that a man makes the law according to his environment and circumstances and no sensible man would allow the law to rule him ? Many Islamic countries now reform the traditional Islamic Law. Does it not indicate that Muslim Personal Law became a Modern Civil Code as far as the woman right such as the equality in matters of dowry, divorce, maintenance and custody of children are concerned ?

When the Australian Muslim Community demanded Sharia Law, their Prime Minister, John Howard told them :

"This is OUR COUNTRY, OUR LAND, and OUR LIFESTYLE, and we will allow you every opportunity to enjoy all this. But once you are done complaining, whining, and griping about Our Flag. Our Pledge, Our Christian beliefs, or Our Way of Life, I highly encourage you take advantage of one other great Australlian freedom, 'THE RIGHT TO LEAVE'. "If you are'nt happy here then LEAVE. We didn't force you to come here. You asked to be here (*Hvoice* Oct. 2007 : 36).

No Equality and no Equal Protection

660. Does the Quran have any concept of equality between man and woman ? Does the law of inheritance not blindly discriminate against women in favour of men (4 : 176; 5 : 11) ? Is not the marriage a kind of sale deed through which the male purchases a bride ?

Is it not a fact that there is no equal protection before the law when it is said : "No Muslim should be killed for killing an infidel (*Buk* 4 : 283) ?

Nur Farwad, a Cairo lawyer wrote an article in 1986. For him "The Islamic law was a collection of reactionary tribal rules unsuited to contemporary societies" (Qtd. Reddy 2004 : 213).

Islamic Law or a Personal Law of the Prophet

661. Is not the Islamic law a personal law of Muhammad ? Does not the Quran state Muhammad as a good example (33 : 21) of behavioural model for the believers under all circumstances ?

Is Repentance enough for Homosexuals ?

662. Why Allah is very soft to the homosexuals and through the Quran he says : "If two men among you are guilty of lewdness, punish them both. If they repent and amend let them both alone"(4 : 16) whereas, if women are lewd why should they be punished with life imprisonment ?

Was the Prophet against Family Planning ?

663. When Prophet was asked, is it wrong to have sexual intercourse with the women by observing *azl* means withdrawing the male sexual organ before emission of semen to avoid conception ? Does he not reply : "It does not matter if you do not do it, for every soul that is born up to the Day of Resurrection will be born (Mus 2 : 3371) ?

Prophet's Ten Commandments for Women

664. Is it not a fact that Islam gave rights to women ? Does it not tell a woman that two women are equal to one man as a witness in court (2 : 282) ? These are the ten rights for women in Islam :

1. If any of our women are guilty of lewdness, take the evidence of four reliable witnesses from amongst you and, if they testify, confine the woman to her house until death does claim her.
2. Penalty for adultery is death by stoning. A hole will be dug and she will be buried to her waist before she is killed by having rocks thrown at her.
3. A man can have sex with any of his wives in any manner and at any time it pleases him.
4. A Muslim can use women captured in war for his sexual amusement. She can also be bought. A Muslim is permitted to cohabit with his female slaves. There is no restriction to their number.
5. For sexual offences a man gets 25 lashes and the woman 100.
6. A Muslim can divorce his wife merely by uttering "I herewith dismiss thee"; but a woman has no right to divorce her husband under any circumstances.
7. Men are a degree above women. Women should be obedient to their husbands, and for disloyalty they can be beaten. (4 : 34)
8. Women must wear veils.
9. A widow has no right to the property of the dead husband.
10. The daughters of a dead man have no rights to the property which is due to them from their father. The children become orphans (*The Rationalist News Australia* Jan, Feb, 1983: 11-12).

40 - Obsession with Chastity

Judaism is a religion in which God is said to have made a covenant between Abraham and his seeds. The physical side of the covenant is maintained through the rite of circumcision. God said to Abraham :

> You and your descendants must all agree to circumcise every male among you. From now on you must circumcise every baby boy when he is eight days old, including slaves born in your homes and slaves bought from foreigners. This will show that there is a covenant between you and me (*Gn* 17.10-12).

This rite of circumcision is considered very sacred and very great. Without circumcision God could not make His covenant with Abraham.

It is the everlasting covenant of God for which He told Abraham : "Thus shall my covenant be in your flesh and any of your people who refuse or willfully neglect circumcision are to be cut off from the covenant of Grace (*Gn* 17 : 13-14). The circumcision of the Old Testament is wonderfully replaced by baptism in the New Testament. Explaining this difficult position Apostle Paul interpreted salvation was not dependent upon circumcision but rather upon the Grace of God (*Rom* 4 : 9-10). Circumcision was never new to the Jews or followers of Islam. Herodotus, the Roman historian (484-424 BC) found this practice in Egypt around the middle of the 5th Century BC. So circumcision came from Egypt to Africa and from Africa to Arab, from Red Sea and Persian Gulf to the Atlantic coast.

Circumcision has been in practice since not less than 2800 BC that too from an Egyptian background (Meo 1990 : 99-110). But it has become a tradition among the Jews and Muslims since Abraham's days (Bigelow 1992 : 55) when he had covenant with God (*Gn* 17 : 10).

It is a common belief that circumcision helps a person to exercise his/her sexual power. But Moses Mainonides, the Jewish historian, emphatically says that instead of enhancing sexual power circumcision curbs the sexual appetite. In his words :

As regards circumcision, I think that one of its objects is to limit sexual intercourse, and to weaken the organ of generation as far as possible, and thus cause man to be moderate...

Circumcision simply counteracts excessive lust; for there is no doubt that circumcision weakens the power of sexual excitement, and sometimes lessens the natural enjoyment; the organ necessarily becomes weak when it loses blood and is deprived of its covering from the beginning (1956 : 267).

The notion that is very much prevalent among the Muslims is that circumcision is more hygienic and it is preventive of venereal diseases mainly of penile cancer. But to our surprise Dr. Sydney Gellis says there are more deaths from circumcision each year than from cancer of the penis (1978 : 132 : 1168-1169).

The process of circumcision was so cruel during the Talmudic period (500-625 AD) that Felix Bryk describes : "Now follows the execution of the wound in such a manner that the mohel takes the circumcised member into his mouth and with two or three draughts sucks the blood out of the wounded part. He then takes a mouthful of wine from a goblet and spurs it, in two or three intervals, on the wound (1967 : 49-50).

The function of the foreskin cannot be denied than the medical excuses used to justify it. *The American Academy of Pediatrics* published a pamphlet entitled, "Care of the Uncircumcized (sic) Penis, "disclosed an untold story of the foreskin. It is written : The glans at birth is delicate and easily irritated by urine and feces. The foreskin shields the glans; with circumcision, this protection is lost. In such cases, the glans and especially the urinary opening (meatus) may become irritated or infected, causing ulcers, meatitis (inflammation of the meatus) and meatal stenosis (a narrowing of the urinary opening). Such problems virtually never occur in uncircumcised penises. The foreskin protects the glans throughout life (1984).

Clitorectomy is Against Human Laws

665. Is it scientific and healthy to do circumcision and clitorectomy for men and women to observe Islamic law ? By this the women's pleasure of sex is gone but she has to please her husband sexually with a fear of divorce, which means loss of her children, loss of economic support. Some husbands suspect their wives so much that when they leave home for long they need their wives be re-infibulated, faithful to the husband who has several wives. A bride is inspected before the bride price is paid to assure the buyer that she is not a 'damaged goods'. Infibulation is done mostly by Muslim population groups because of the importance they attached to virginity and chastity.

Why Allah views Circumcision Seriously ?

666. Is Allah of the Semitics obsessed with sex ? Why did he create Jesus as being born without sex--- in order to give him divinity ? Did the Jews follow the old alleged agreement with God to give them special privileges if they would circumcize their male children ? Did not the Moslems' circumcision of the female babies snip off the end of the sensation organ the clitoris ?

Is Circumcision Jewish or Islamic ?

667. Does the Quran refer to circumcision only for males or for both males and females ? Why do the Muslims practice it as rituals ? Can this law for men preserve the honour for women ?

Why Paul reformed Circumcision Law ?

668. Did not God say to Abraham to establish His covenant to circumcise every male child (*Gn* 17 : 10-11) ? Therefore both Abraham and his son Ishmael were circumcised (*Gn* 17 : 24-26). Did not God confine this circumcision to the Jews only ? In course of time Paul being a reformist Jew discarded this barbaric and traumatic tradition whereas Islam continued to keep this Jewish tradition blindly.

Circumcision diminishes Sex Power

669. By cutting the upper part of flesh over the vulva topping the entrance of the penis which is homologous to a kernal of the crest of a rooster does it not diminish the sexual desire ? The Muslims have more children does not mean they have more sex power but they have more wives so their number is increasing.

Medical Reasons for the Amputation of the Foreskin

670. The Medical reason they give for circumcision is phimosis (fi-mosis). That is when the foreskin is too tight to permit pulling it back because it has been forcibly retracted prematurely by uninformed doctors and parents that are overly concerned with cleanliness. You must never force or tug at the foreskin. Doctors and parents should be taught there is nothing to do. Just leave it alone. The foreskin closely covers the penis in infants and little by little it will loosen. Forcing it will cause scar tissue to form. The scar tissue will be responsible for the loss of elasticity that is apt to cause later problems. 'Phimosis', is very rare, and the foreskin will loosen by the age of 3 or 4. (That if it has been left alone). Then as the boy gets older, (see drawing), he can be taught to retract his foreskin for cleaning when taking a bath or shower. It does cause a problem at that time (Zangger 1984 : 387).

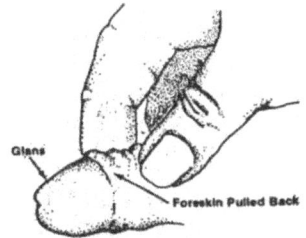

Doctors say no to Circumcision

671. According to the American Academy of Pediatrics and the American College of Obstetricians and Gynecologists from a medical standpoint, there are simply no valid medical reasons for removing the foreskins in newborns. For many years, circumcision was thought to protect a man from cancer of the penis and his wife from cancer of the cervix and venereal disease. To prove it they reason out to remove the foreskin as it collects a lot of crement under it that may lead to cancer. This has now been completely discredited. Cleanliness was also a big reason. If it were soap and water cleanliness, why not do away with the teeth, hair or hands ? Do they not also have to be washed once in a while ? Circumcision does not completely stop masturbation, but the mutilation and constant exposure of the unprotected glans is responsible for early impotency (Zangger 1984 : 386).

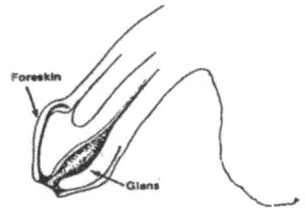

Removing Foreskin is like removing Eyelid

187

672. Don't you know, when a boy is born, he is natural as the way God designed him. There will be a flap of skin that covers the end of his penis, (the glans). If and when the boy is circumcised, this flap called the foreskin is cut away and removed. Don't you think the protective covering, like the eyelid is lost for ever ?

Hagar The First Woman Circumcized

673. The basis for this again goes back to Abraham's Egyptian concubine Hagar who gave Abraham his son Ishmael. Did not Abraham's wife Sara become jealous and vowed to cut "three limbs" of Hagar and this led Abraham to order that Hagar's ears be pierced and that she be circumcized (Gunasekhar 2007 : 30) ?

Process and Result of Women Circumcision

674. Can one imagine the pain of female circumcision while cutting away the girl's clitoris, the outer and inner labia, as well as the scraping of the walls of the vagina and then binding together of legs so that the walls of the vagina can grow together ? With a local custom the midwives or barbers perform this operation often by primitive surgical procedures and without anaesthetic use. When the girl or women cry there is deafening drumming, songs and dancing by friends and relatives. They forget the far reaching results of female circumcision. There is chronic pelvic infections, tetanus, uterine prolapse, genital gangrens, abscesses, fistulas, frigidity and infertility ; says Emily and Per Ola D'Aulatre in a *Reader Digest's* article and continue to say, "Due to labour complications, it undoubtedly adds to Africa's infant mortality rates that, at up to 38 per cent, are the highest in the world" (1981 : 82). The Female Genital Mutilation (FGM) has been cited by WHO (World Health Organisation).

Why Female Circumcision ?

675. Is it not a fact that in Islam obsession with chastity and the sexual morality imposed on women lead to female circumcision ?

Infibulation or Pharaonic Circumcision ?

676. Do you know how they operate a girl or woman ? After removal of the entire clitoris the labia minora and part of the labia majora, the two sides of the vulva are partially sliced off or scraped raw and then sewn together, mostly with catgut. In Sudan and Somalia, thorns are often used to hold the two bleeding sides of the vulva together, or a paste of gum arabic, sugar and egg is used. The entrance to the vagina is thus obliterated, except for a tiny opening in the back to allow urine, and later menstrual blood, to drain. The legs of the girl are then tied together, and she is immobilized for several weeks until the wound of the vulva has closed, except for a small opening that is created by inserting a splinter of wood or bamboo. It is like inviting troubles without rhyme and reason.

Prevention does not Mean Cure

677. Is circumcision a preventive of venereal diseases ? According to the physicians it was a popular misconception that if a person comes in contact with a woman who had a venereal disease, he is bound to be infected, whether circumcised or not.

Blood Bath in the Name of Purifying

678. It is a common belief among the Muslims that circumcision is purifying. In Arabic and Hebrew "Circumcision" means "Purifying" as well as "removing a sexual obstacle" and "cleansing", in a religious sense. Joseph Lewis cited an example, "among some Mohammedan tribes, the bridegroom is circumcised on the day after his marriage, and sprinkles the blood that falls from the penis onto the veil of the bride. However, the circumcision does not stop with the removal of the prepuce. The ceremony is one of endurance, while the wife watches the performance, the man submits himself to the priest of the holy office. After the prepuce is removed, the next procedure is to remove the skin from the whole organ. Regardless of what our reaction is to this frightful and inhuman act, if the victim shows the slightest emotion of pain or exhibits any sign of weakness, such as a sigh or a groan, the bride leaves him, saying that she does not want such a weakling for a husband" (1967:50).

Natural vs. Infibulation

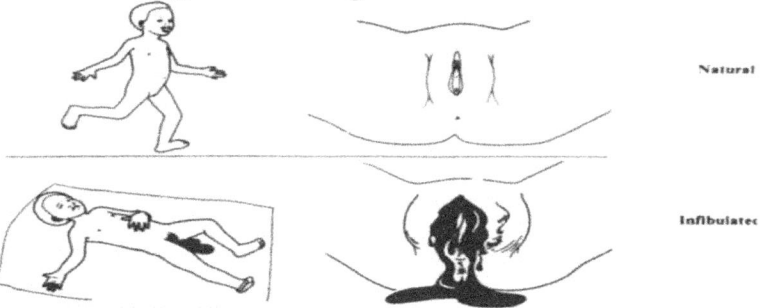

NFIBULATION: IMMEDIATE RESULTS
Cutting away the exterior genital organs and infibulating a girl can start bleeding that cannot be stopped and may kill you child. Dangerous infections may also result that may make your daughter very ill. Later, it may prevent her from havin children of her own. The damaging operations cause much needless suffering.

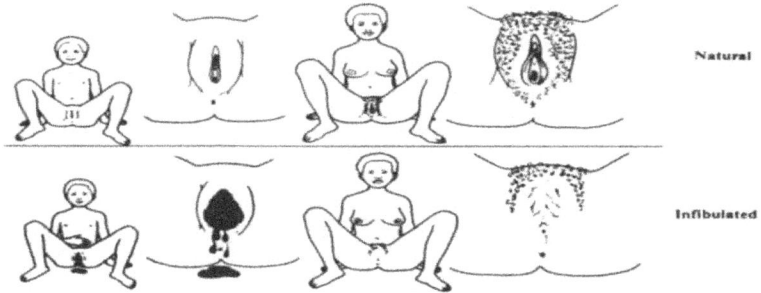

NFIBULATION / PHARAONIC CIRCUMCISON
nfibulation — cutting away the external genital organs and then closing the opening to the vagina by scarification — is a ver dangerous operation that causes many life-long health problems. It interferes with a woman's natural sexuality. In the to ow, you see the natural genitals of a girl and a woman. In the pictures below, you see a girl bleeding after the operation and woman who is infibulated: only a tiny opening is left.
From: The Universal Childbirth Picture Book

Can you Tolerate her Pain ?

679. When I was at Lexington, Mass, USA I was invited by Fran P. Hosken, chief-editor of *Win News* for a lunch. She has been working for "Female Sexual Mutilations." She told me many stories about the female genital mutilation. One of the stories she told me about Awa Thiam, a young woman in *Mali* and about her excision as a child. The story runs like; I was 12 years old when I was excised. I remember every detail of the operation. In our village, several girls of the same age are operated on at the same time by a special 'excisor' in her house. The village people come together to celebrate this occasion. The night before the operation, the drums were beaten until late.

189

Very early the next morning, two of my favourite aunts took me to the house of the excisor or operator, an old woman from the blacksmith caste.

Once inside the house of the operator, I became terribly frightened, though I had been reassured that it would not hurt. It was very early in the morning, yet I perspired and my throat became all dry. I was told to lie down on a mat on the floor. Immediately, some big hands fastened themselves on my thin legs and opened them wide. I raised my head, but at once from both sides, two women held me down to the floor and immobilized my arms.

Suddenly, I felt something being sprinkled on my genital area. Later, I learned this was sand. I was terrified. Suddenly, some fingers grabbed a part of my genital organs. I tried to escape but I could not move. A terrible, searing pain pierced me through and through. The excisor cut and cut. It took an interminable time. I felt as if I were being torn to pieces. The rule says that one must not cry during this operation. I failed this rule. I screamed as hard as I could, and I was bleeding all over. The operator put a mixture of herbs and butter on the wound to arrest the bleeding; I have never felt any pain as overwhelming as this.

The women who had held me down freed me; but I couldn't get up. The voice of the operator called, 'it is finished. You can get up. You see, it didn't hurt much. With the help of two women, I was put on my dress and was forced to walk to where the other girls who were also excised were waiting. Then they made us dance. Under the orders of the women in charge, I was forced to join a group of people who had gathered for this occasion to see us dance. I can't tell you how I felt. I was burning all over. In tears, I jumped about a little, together with the other girls. We were all forced to hop about, bleeding and in terrible pain. It was a monstrous affair of bleeding girls writhing in pain being forced to jump up and down in a cloud of dust. We were surrounded by gleeful, shouting and clapping villagers. Then everything began to reel about me. I remember nothing more.

When I came to, I was stretched out in a hut with several people around me. Later, the most terrible moments of my life were those when I had to urinate. It took a whole month before I healed. When I was well again, I was the butt of everyone's jokes because they said I wasn't courageous (1979 : 43).

Circumcision : a Non-Quranic Ritual ?
680. Is not it a fact that the Muslims of Africa and the Middle East practice infibulation for girl and women not for rituals but for virginity intact- the smaller her opening, the higher the bride price ? Why do they think that a woman who does not have her genitals mutilated is a prostitute ? In what way this custom help to preservation of honour for women and how it makes women more enjoyable ? Do they get sanction from the Quran ? Is it not a non-Quranic ritual though Muslims give undue importance to it ?

Section VIII

Five Pillars of Islam

41 - Prayer Prayer Everywhere

The building of Islam stands on five Pillars. These pillars are Iman-the belief; Salat-Prayer; Siyam-Fasting; Zakat-Charity and Hajj-Piligrimage.

I. *Iman* : The Belief

The confirmation and confession of faith, made by reciting the Shahadah, "I witness that there is no god but the God (Allah) and that Muhammad is his "Messenger". This is the central doctrine of Islam.

II. *Salat* : Prayer

Canonical worship five times a day. The Muslims must, in a state of ritual purity, face Mecca to perpetuate the spirit of Arabic superiority, and recite prescribed phrases while performing set cycles of standing, bowing, sitting, and prostration.

A simple Namaz and its mere physical or mechanical performance in the morning wipe out the sins committed in the night and evening Namaz can wash the sins committed during the day. Thus Muslims have no fear in committing any number of sins or crime, however, heinous these may be.

III. *Siyam* : Fasting

Fasting during the holy month of Ramadan, the ninth month in the Islamic lunar calendar. The fast entails abstaining from food and drink from dawn to sunset, and is usually accompanied by an intensification of prayer and worship. The end of Ramadan is celebrated with a major feast and holiday known as Eid al-Fitr.

Though Ramdan is compulsory, it can be skipped in certain circumstances, like in sickness, during Jihad or fighting. Whereas Jihad during the sacred month is prohibited, yet there can be circumstances on account of war strategy or otherwise it can be carried out in preference to Roze.

IV. *Zakat* : Charity

The yearly payment of Zakat, or a poor dues, a set percentage of each adult's wealth, to help the poor, shi' ites give an additional amount to support their clergy. Does it not spend zakat on procurements of arms for use in the spread of Islam or in helping Mujahadeen instead of alms to the poor ? Does it not destroy the self-respect of the recipient ?

V. *Hajj* : Piligrimage

Performance of the hajj, the annual piligrimage to Mecca, at least once in one's lifetime if one can afford to physically and financially. The hajj commemorates the willingness of the Hebrew prophet Ibrahim to sacrifice his son for God, and is celebrated with the feast of the sacrifice (Eid-al-Adha), the most important Muslim holiday.

A piligrimage to Mecca is sure to enter Paradise and taste the pleasure that the most beautiful virgins offer, it matters not, that they may have been rapists, murderers, thugs, thieves, traitors or vice-mongers.

All the pillars should be of equal height and strength to make the building strong. If were remove one pillar from that the building will collapse.

Is not it a fact that the pilgrims who enter Mecca by buses look joyful, excited by clapping their hands and while circling the black stone look spiritually enthusiastic and feel a sense of unity and brotherhood, but they look different when they return home, their faces are serious like a stone mask. Their life time journey to Mecca is over but they rarely realise the pain of the people of Mecca. A believing brother who lives in Mecca writes :

> We need your prayers especially during the hajj. We who live in Mecca feel as if devils are walking through the streets at the time of the piligrimage. One can almost see and feel the presence of Satan (Al-Masih 1990 : 40).

Why from Jerusalam to Kaaba ?

681. If every nation has a *Qibla* or direction of worshipping God and it has a direction towards which one turns (2 : 148) as God is everywhere, why had Muhammad changed it to Jerusalem and again back to Kaaba ? Was it political or religious ?

No Honour for Qibla

682. Did Muhammad have any respect for Qibla whether it is in Kaaba or Jerusalem ? Why did he say :

"If anyone of you goes to an open space for answering the call of nature he should neither face nor turn his back towards the Qibla; he should either face the East or the West" *Buk* 1 :146) ? But to our surprise Prophet himself broke the rule, such as :

"Narrated Abdullah binUmar : I went up to the roof of Hafsa's house for some job and I saw Allah's Apostle answering the call of nature facing Sham (Syria, Jordan, Palestine and Lebanon regarded as one country) with his back towards the Qibla" (*Buk* 1: 150).

Narrated Abdullah bin Umar : Once I went up the roof of our house and saw Allah's Apostle answering the call of nature while sitting over two bricks facing Baitul-- Maqdis (Jerusalem)" (*Buk* 1 : 151).

How Fifty Namaz reduced to Five ?

683. Who reduced 50 prayers a day to 5 ? Moses or Muhammad ? If Muhammad would have taken the suggestion of Moses the Muslims would have one prayer a day. But Muhammad felt shy to say it again to Allah for which his followers had to bear the burden of praying five times everyday (*Buk* 1 : 345; 5 : 228).

Terrible Doctrine of Prayer

684. Is it not a terrible doctrine of the Muslims to prostrate themselves before Allah facing Mecca and pray on their knees daily 17 prayer rounds such as :

1. The morning prayer comprises	2 prayer rounds
2. The noon-time prayer	4 prayer rounds
3. The mid- afternoon prayer	4 prayer rounds
4. The sunset prayer	3 prayer rounds
5. The evening prayer	4 prayer rounds

Can we praise Muhammad (17 : 1) who reduced fifty prayers imposed by Allah to five times ? How many Muslims actually understand the meaning of the Namaz ? Do they not repeat it again and again like a parrot ?

For whom the repetition of Prayer is Needed ?

685. Why does a Muslim during 5 prayer times repeat :

Praised be my Lord, most high	102 times
Allah is greater	68 times
Praised be my mighty Lord	51 times
Allah hears the one who praises him	17 times
The "Al-Fatiha" or a short Sura	17 times
The testimony of the Islamic creed	5 times
The greeting of peace to all Muslims	5 times

Is there any reason behind such repetitions ? Muslim Prayer is not a petition to Allah. This repetition is irritating for Allah too ? If anyone will praise you five times a day, every week, every month, every year do you help the person or you would like to avoid him ?

Tiresome five Times Prayer

686. If during the *mi'raj* five daily prayers are imposed by Allah tasketh not a soul beyond its capacity (2 : 286) why it requires 34 prostrations, a word-for-word prescribed liturgy, in which the worshiper says up to 102 times daily "my exalted Lord be praised;" 68 times "Allah is greater;" 51 times "may my mighty Lord be praised" ? In this liturgy there is no room for one's own petitions for individual, family, community or the world peace. Can it be called prayer or praise ?

How many times God proclaims
He is Great and High ?

687. Is not Allah so self conscious that he reminds us time and again that He is "High and Great" ? It reminded us a Persian saying : 'You said it once I believed you. You said it again I doubted you, you mentioned it for the third time I know that you were telling a lie.'

Prayer Round the Clock

688. Prayer, Prayer everywhere no time to rest, from dawn to dusk and dusk to dawn it continues round the clock. Even children cannot escape from prayer. So "The Apostle of Allah said : Command your children to pray when they become seven years old, and beat them for it (prayer) when they become ten years old; and arrange their beds (to sleep) separately" (*Daw* : 2.495).

Abd-Al-Masih describes : At dawn, as soon as one can distinguish between a white and a black thread, the prayer of the Muslim begins in the Philippines. The first wave of worship surges forth over Indonesia, Malaysia, Bangladesh, India, then Iran and Turkey. Finally it reaches Europe, at which time the second wave of worship begins at noon for the Muslims in China. This new wave will have reached India and the 45 million Muslims in Russia, just as a third wave will have started at 3 p.m. for afternoon prayers in the Far East. These three waves of worship follow each other successively, moulding and determining life under the Islamic culture. At sunset the penultimate prayer begins. At this time, as dawn is breaking on the east coast of America with its morning prayer, Muslims in the Nile Valley are bowing down in the heat of their noon prayer and in Pakistan men are gathering in their mosques for afternoon prayer. When the final wave of the Muslim night prayer begins in the Far East two hours after sunset, simultaneously the rays of the setting sun touch the worshipers in the Ganges-delta, while pilgrims in Mecca bow down for afternoon prayer before the black stone in the Kaaba. At that moment the second prayer wave has already reached faithful Muslims in the high Atlas mountains in

Morocco, while the first wave breaks with the early morning dawn in the Rocky Mountains (1987 : 12-13). Where is time for the Muslim to think about the suffering humanity ?

Prayer a Big Business

689. Being an experienced merchant did Muhammad not make prayer a big business ? A Muslim must pray daily to expect a reward. Allah rightly revealed him that prayer looks for a commerce (tijara) that comes not to naught, that Allah may pay them in full their wages (ujur) and enrich them of His bounty (35 : 29-30) ?

Prayer comes Under Law

690. As Islam is an Allah-centric religion so also is prayer---not a voluntary service but a compulsory one and is a law.

In Saudi Arabia one can sometimes observe policemen during the prayer session forcing passers- by into the mosques, that the wrath of Allah may not descend on the country because of neglected prayer. Islam is a religion under the law of Allah. All facets of life are specifically controlled by a multitude of regulations. Allah is the centre of everything (Al-Masih 1987 : 15). Is not the compulsory and obligatory prayer the enemy of an open society ? Did not the prophet make Namaz compulsory and once said : "burn all those who had not left their houses for the prayer, burn them alive inside their homes" (*Buk* 1 : 626). If *Namaz* is so important and is the second pillar of Islam why does Quran not mention its importance ?

Can Dust be Equal with Water for Uzeu ?

691. In the Quran Allah says : "O believers, when you stand up to pray wash your faces, and your hands up to the elbows, and wipe your heads, and your feet up to the ankles. If you are defiled, purify yourselves; but if you are sick or on a journey, or if any of you comes from the privy, or you have touched women, and you can find no water, then have recourse to wholesome dust and wipe your faces and your hands with it. God does not desire to make any impediment for you; but He desires to purify you, and that He may complete His blessing upon you; hapy you will be thankful" (5 : 6; *Buk* 1 : 329).

Can dust be a substitute for water ? In those countries where water is plenty why don't the Muslims take bath and go for Namaz ? Dust is unhygenic and cause disease. Water can clean but dust cannot. How can one clean the sins through dust and water for salvation ?

Fast and Lust go Together

692. Fasting is a religious rite and it is an old custom of all religions. The Quresh tribe used to fast on the day of Ashura during the Pre-Islamic period. Muhammad also fasted on this day and he learnt it from the Christian (2 : 183). Once Umar b. al-Khattab slept with his wives after he had prayed the last evening prayer. When he washed, he blamed himself. Then he went over to Muhammad and said : "O Apostle of Allah ! I apologise to Allah and to you for doing this sin. After I had prayed the last evening prayer, I returned to my wife and smelled a fragrance. So I let myself be seduced and I had sex with her." Other people were challenged to make the same confession. Out of regard for Umar and his followers, Muhammad (see al-Qurtubi's commentary on Sura al- Baqara (2 : 187) said : " Permitted to you on the night of the fasts, is the approach to your wives. They are your garments and you are their garments. Allah knoweth what you used to do secretly among yourselves, but He turned to you and forgave you (2 : 187). Does not Muhammad favour Umar and the others whereby the sanctity of fasting was hampered by granting this license ?

Is Namaz Objective or Subjective ?
693. Is not Fatiha an indirect call for everybody to worship Allah ? Does it not say : "We praise you, our God" or " I praise you my Lord ?" This objective prayer never had a subjective touch because Muslims think they are not the children of God but slaves of Allah ? Francis Harry Crick, an English Molecular biologist and one of the co-discoverers of the structure of DNA molecule won the Nobel prize for Medicine in 1962 suggested that it might be possible to find chemical changes in the brain that were molecular correlates of the act of prayer. He speculated that there might be a detectable change in the level of some neurotransmitter when people pray. Crick may have been imagining substances such as dopamine that are released by the brain under certain conditions and produce rewarding sensations.

42- Yes to Michael No to Gabriel

The Supernatural elements in the Quran play a vital role in the life and work of Muhamamd. He believed in angels and Jinns or the spirit and blame them for good and bad.

Is it not nonsense to believe that Muhammad met the Jinn or demons while he was reciting the Quran at Taif, a village high above the hills of Mecca ? What justification remains for Muhammad to claim that the two revealed sermons of the Jinn in the Quran was received by Angel Gabriel (72 : 1-15; 46 : 28-32) ? Is it due to the death of Muhammad's first wife Khadija or the death of his uncle Abu Talib or as he was rejected by the inhabitants of Taif he escaped into the desert and it personified his own fear and despair that he discovered Jinn in himself ?

Who brought the Quran to Muhammad ?
694. Who brought the Quran to Muhammad ? Allah in the form of a man (53 : 2-18; 81 : 19-24) or the holy spirit (16 : 102; 26 : 192-194) or the angels (15 : 8) or the angel Gabriel (2 : 97), or sometimes kakina, the female aspect of God ?

Michael is Better than Gabriel
695. Is it not a fact that the Jews did not accept the revelations of Muhammad because they were received through Gabriel, who was the angel of destruction, and not through Michael, the guardian angel of the Jews (*Dan* 12 : 1) ? It was Gabriel, the Jews believed, who inspired Muhammad to carry out his terrible campaigns against the Jewish tribe of Karayza.

Is it not a fact that Muhammad himself compared Gabriel to Noah, Moses and Omar who administered stern justice and Michael to Abraham, Jesus and Abu Bakr who advocated mercy (Muir 1912, 213) ?

Is Gabriel not believed to abide near the level of dreams, which are often delusive, and Michael in the level of visions, which are akin to prophecy (*Mat* 1983 : 229) ?

Least mentioned Angel in Quran

696. Is it not a fact that Gabriel is mentioned only rarely in the Quran until the Medinan period and that is only twice : as the angel through whom the Quran descended (2 : 97) and as a helper (66 : 4) ? Was not Gabriel seen by Muhammad "in the highest point" (53 : 7) of the 'clear horizon' (81 : 23), and he then approached until he was two bows' length away (53 : 9) ? On another occasion (53 : 13) did not Muhammad see a vision near the sidra tree marking the boundary between this world and the next ?

Few Angels but more Prophets

697. Why Allah needs intermediaries ? Is He so powerless to communicate with His Prophets that he needed agents ? For the whole 124000 Prophets He had only three angels. For Mary and Muhammad Gabriel (Jibrail), for the Jews Michael (Mikail) and there is an angel of death, who separates the soul from the body of the dead. Why all these angels are from Judo-Christian-Muslim religion ? What about other religions ?

Is the Quran the Words of Angels Too ?

698. If Quran is the words of Allah how angels interfere and dare to say : "We descend not but by command of thy Lord : to Him belongeth what is before us and what is behind us, and what is between and thy Lord never doth forget" (19 : 64) ?

Heard the Voices of the Dead

699. Is not it a hallucination to hear the voices of the dead persons who are in their grave ? Once Muhammad went through the graveyards of Medina and heard the voices of two humans who were being tortured in their graves. By hearing the conversation between two dead people Muhammad said, "They are being punished, but they are not being punished because of a major sin, yet their sins are great. One of them used not to save himself from (being soiled with) the urine, and the other used to go about with calumnies (Namima)." Then Muhammad asked for a green palm tree leaf and spilt it into two pieces and placed one piece on each grave, saying, I hope that their punishment may be abated as long as these pieces of the leaf are not dried" (*Buk* 8. 73.81).

The Jinn plays a Role in Quran

700. Why did God not let the *Jinn* hear the message of Moses and Jesus ? Why did He confer the Quran in particular upon them ? Why did the *Jinn* say that the Quran came after Moses, and not after the *Zabur* (Psalms) or the *Injil* (Gospel), which were nearer to them in time than Moses ? How could the Quran conceive of the *Jinn* marrying and propagating, when in fact the Quran claims that *Iblis* (the devil) is one of them (72 : 1-6) ?

Can you believe the *Jinn* (in Avestic Jaini), the wicked spirit, was born out of fire like Satan who once listened to the Quran and became believer ? The story runs like this :

After the death of Khadija the first wife of Muhammad, and his uncle Abu Talib Muhammad became helpless and tried to find refuge in Taif a village high above the hills of Mecca. When the Prophet was rejected by the villagers he escaped into the desert and met the *Jinns* while reciting the Quran (72 : 1-15, P. 519-520). Can it be believable that shortly after Muhammad had met the Jinns, a number of the Pagans in Medina believed in Islam ? After two years, there were 73 men who had become Muslims there, without Muhammad ever having visited Medina. Does it not prove that it was not Muhammad but the demonic spirit which spread Islam before the prophet ?

43 - To Be or Not to Be

A never solved problem in the history of religions is whether God grants people freewill or they are bound to remain in predestination ? If God determines then men are not responsible for their actions, over which they have no control. If they have their freewill there is no need of a God to worship. They are either rewarded or punished for what they do. Muhamamd avoided the most important question of life : whether human acts are the result of a free human choice or predetermined by God ? This was a question before the Khawarij and subsequently it remained a quest for the Mutazilah. As there are many predeterministic verses of the Quran the Mutazilah explain them as metaphors and exhortations. To choose between right and wrong, good and evil God must send Prophets to protect mankind. Is not it strange but true that in the 9th century, the Abbaasid caliph al-Mamun raised Mutazilism to the status of the state creed and the Mutazil persecuted their opponents and Ahmad ibn Hanbal (d. 855), the founder of one of the four orthodox schools of Islamic law, was subjected to flogging and imprisonment for his refusal to subscribe to the doctrine that the Quran is the word of God ? Here are a few problems to solve :

Between Faith and Work

701. Are human acts the result of a free human choice, or they are predetermined by God ? If Allah were to withhold punishment for evil and forgive it, would not it be as unjust as withholding reward for righteousness ? Therefore, there can be neither undeserved punishment nor undeserved reward otherwise, good may just as well turn into evil and evil into good. If this is true where is the place of belief and surrender to Allah ?

God of Good and Bad

702. Does not the doctrine of predestination and the fact that both evil and good came from Allah make Allah capricious ?

FreeWill or Predestination ?

703. Has not Allah limited Himself by creating man free, even to do evil ?

What should we accept : Freewill or predestation ? When God is projected All-powerful (2 : 106) who is also above law (3 : 26) and takes revenge (30 : 47) where is the chance to escape ? If we support predestination we are not responsible for our action--- good or bad. This view would tantamount to accusing God of injustice. If we have freewill then either we are rewarded or punished for what we do. Does not here God remain insignificant for mankind ?

Is it not a fact that the Mutazilah teaching about the divine justice and freewill had an enormous influence on the course of Islamic history and their theology, to a large degree and has been preserved by the Shia sect who exhibit a more rational inclination than Sunni Muslims (Perrindon. 1971 : 487) ?

Whether man is created free or he comes under predestination ? Where is the freewill for mankind if Allah is All powerful and can do whatever He wants to do ? The Prophet cited an imaginary exchange of arguments between Adam and Moses. Moses said to Adam : You are our father. You did us harm and caused us to get out of paradise. Adam argues : You are Moses, Allah selected you to write with his own hand the book of Torah forty years before I was created. How can you blame me for an affair which had been ordained for me before I was created (*Mus* 4 : 6409-6411; *Buk* 8 : 611) ? This means that Adam was sent from heaven to the earth according to the preconceived plan of God and it was not something accidental. In this case where is the chance of Freewill for mankind ? It is His will that we commit sin and good deed. We are simply puppet in the hands of the Grand Master.

There has been a theological war between Freewill and Predestination. If Allah does everything even controlling Being, people cannot be responsible for their deeds-- good or bad, and Allah cannot take me to hell for any bad action. If He grants us freedom to choose actions, we are either rewarded or punished for what we do. In this case my prayer or devotion is not necessary.

Does not the Mutazilah mean "those who stand apart," by explaining predeterministic verses of the Quran as being metaphors and exhortation ? Really they stand apart as far as the freewill is concerned.

Not to take wine as medicine

God punishes Himself
704. Can Allah answer if Adam asks, "Have you not created me by your hand ? Have you not breathed into me your spirit ? Does not your mercy surpass your wrath ? Have you not predestined me to do this ? If it was predestined why did God repent ? Instead of punishing Adam and Eve God should punish Himself.

44 - Cycle of Birth and Death

When Muhammad met Moses in the 6th heaven he found Moses weeping. Moses explained : "I weep because after me there has been sent as Prophet, a youngman whose followers will enter paradise in greater numbers than my followers" (*Buk* 5 : 227). This is because Muhammad could make his heaven more attractive and opaclous than Moses and gave passports to every believer in Islam be it a sinner or a criminal, a pious or a righteous.

He who doesn't believe in rebirth is a *nastika* for Hindu, a Kafir for Muslim (Shahin 2001 : 8) and a Heathen for Christian. The Holy Quran eloquently expresses the idea of rebirth : "He sent down rains from above in proper quantity and He brings back to life the dead earth, similarly ye shall be reborn" (43 : 11).

We accept or not but rebirth is a must for everyone. Ismalis and other esoteric schools of Islam went further. According to Joseph Head :

The Ismails and other esoteric schools of Islam now widely prevalent had the belief in reincarnation in the early centuries of the Mohammedan era. Three aspects of rebirth were accepted :

Hulul : Periodical incarnation of the perfect person.

Rij'at : The return of the Imam or spiritual leader after death.

Tanasakh : Reincarnation of the soul of ordinary men.

The author shows that in addition to the Ismailis, the Shites known as "ghulat", as well as the caramthians, Batinis, Hurufis, and other Islamic groups all held to these doctrines (1969 : 141).

Moreover, the concept of rebirth was developed by the Sufis. The great mystic, Hazrat Jalal-ud-Deen Rumi, explained the concept of rebirth in the evolutionary process as : "I died as mineral and became a plant, died as plant and rose to animal, I died as animal and I was man. Why should I fear ? When was I less by dying ? Yet once more I shall die as man, To soar with angels blest; But even from angelhood I must pass on..."

Like Rumi another great mystic Mansur Al-Hallaj, famous for his formulation, "Anal Haq" (I am the Truth) had written : "Like the herbage I have sprung up many a time on the banks of flowing rivers. For a hundred thousand years I have lived and worked in every sort of body."

Though Islam relates that every one will be reborn but it fails to answer some of the basic questions like why it will occur, what is the means of rebirth for which the concept of rebirth gradually lost popularity in Islam (Abdi 1964). It is time now to bring this concept to limelight to save mankind from the fear of death.

Create the Soul out of Nothing

705. Will it not be unwise to think as to why God created the soul out of nothing-- making some happy and others miserable ? Does it not prove God to be unjust if the soul had no previous merits or demerits to be rewarded or punished ? Why a sinner suffers eternally in hellish fire and a pious enjoys eternal heaven ? Should not he or she be given one chance or trial for repentance ? Does not eternal hell and heaven begin and end with injustice ?

Are not the Zoroastrians better when they say : rejecting the old frame and assuming a new body is inevitable (Hoshang 14). In *Nama Mihabad* it is said :

> Every man finds a place in the heavens and the stars, according to his knowledge and actions, and always lives there. And he who wishes to go into the world, and has done good deeds, is born as a king, minister, ruler, or a rich man; so that he may reap the fruits of his deeds. According to the prophet Bashadabad those griefs, troubles and diseases, which befall kings during their enjoyments are due to the evil deeds of previous birth (66 : 691).

Rebirth a Great Law of God

706. The Quran has somehow or other proved that rebirth or reincarnation is true. Or else why did Allah say : "Seeing that ye were without life, and He gave you life; then will He cause you to die, and will again bring you to life; and again to Him will you return" (2 : 28). "You were without life" means you were dead. It indicates that they had lived before becoming dead. Does not the verse of the Quran clearly mean that it had reference to more than one life and one death ? Does not it refer to the beginning of life in the mother's womb ?

Muhammad's Concept of Rebirth

707. How far is Muhammad's claim justified when he says that people could turn into rats, monkeys and pigs and Jews would transform into rats (*Buk* 4 : 524, 569) or apes (7 : 166) ? Does not this transformation indicate the concept of rebirth ?

If Islam does not believe in rebirth how can one fight in the way of Allah and be killed, to fight and again be killed and to fight again and be killed (*Mus* 3 : 4626) ? This is clearly indicated in the Quran too when Allah said : "Do not speak of those who are slain in Allah's way as dead; nay, they are alive" (2 : 154).

What does the Quran indicate when Allah says : "Oh ! how shall Allah bring it over to life, after its death ? But Allah caused him to die for hundred years, then raised him up again" (2 : 259). Does not it mean rebirth where the dead comes to life again ?

Islam confirms Rebirth

708. Can any one refute the doctrine of rebirth when Allah repeatedly says : "He sends down rain from the skies, and gives therewith life to the earth after its death" (16 : 65) and "He gives life to the earth after its death (57 : 17), He brings forth the living from the dead and the dead from the living and gives life to the earth after its death" (30 : 19), and thou maketh night to pass into the day and thou maketh the day to pass into the night, and thou bringest forth the living from the dead and thou bringest forth the dead from the living (3 : 26) ? Is there any ambiguity in the above verses and any scope that Islam does not believe in rebirth or reincarnation ?

45 - Sins and Salvation

In the Arabian desert Paradise means big trees, fruit gardens, water spring, and rivers of clear and unpolluted milk, water, honey and wine (47 : 15).

Allah included inexhaustible supply of every variety of fruits in his 'Paradise-Package'. Quran confirms that Muslims will feast on fruits and honored in the gardens of delight (37.40-48), these are everlasting fruits (13.35, 43. 68-73), two kinds of every fruit (55. 52), the fruits will be near and easy to reach (55.54), all kinds of trees and delights (55.47-49) the young boys will serve choicest fruits (56.17, 20, 21), while feasting with silver vessels and crystal goblets, Muslims will feel neither the scorching heat nor the biting cold and trees will spread their shade around them, and fruits will hang in clusters over them (76 : 13-21).

Now, everyone may not be happy with fruits and wine. For them Allah had promised, as recorded in Quran; there are rivers of milk whose taste never changes and rivers of honey pure and clear (47.15).

In the garden of heaven two springs are pouring forth water in continuance, there will be fruits and dates and pomegranates (55 : 46-68) even river of Nile of Egypt and Euphrates of Iraq are there (*Mus* 4 : 6807), no excessive heat of the sun nor excessive cold (76 : 13, 21), there is a tree under the shadow of which a rider of a fine and swift footed horse for travel is always present (*Mus* 4 : 6786).

In heaven Allah will make old women into young women and non-virgins into virgins (*Safwat-Al-Tafir* 3 : 309). There are maidens with beautiful, big and lustrous eyes (44 : 54).

According to Quran; in Paradise, there are high-bosomed virgins with a truly overflowing cup (78.31-34), the virgins are bashful, dark-eyed and as chaste as the sheltered eggs of ostriches(37. 40-48). Allah created them to serve the Muslims as loving companions (56.7-40). Muslims will wed these houris (beautiful virgins) (44.51-55), the virgins shall recline on couches ranged in rows (52.17-20) and the virgins are untouched by man or Jinns and they are as fair as corals and rubies, sheltered in their tents and within reach will hang fruits (55.53-58, 70-77).

Allah promised 72 virgins "Narrated Al-Miqdam ibn Ma' dikarib : Allah's Messenger said, 'The martyr receives six good things from Allah...(one of these is) he is married to seventy-two wives of the maidens with large dark eyes; and is made intercessor for seventy of his relatives" (*Tir* 1067). Not only this. The believers can father a son : Abu sa'id al-Khudri, reported that Allah's Messenger said : "When a believer will wish a son in the Paradise, its conception and its birth will happen in one single hour as he wishes" (5. 4338).

A Muslim can get all the facilities if he accepts Allah as his Lord, Islam as his religion and Muhammad as his apostle and Jihad as his way of life in the way of Allah *(Mus* 3 : 4645). It is not that easy to enter to the Muslim heaven as that Paradise is under the shades of spear" (*Buk* 4 : 73).

Forecast the Judgement Day

709. If Muhammad could know what is going to happen on the Day of Judgement (*Mus* 337) then why did Ayesha say : He who presumes that he would inform about what was going to happen tomorrow, fabricates the greatest lie against Allah (*Mus* 337) and why does the Quran confirm : None in the heavens or on earth, except Allah knows what is hidden, nor can they perceive when they shall be raised up for Judgement (27 : 65) ?

Is not it a fact that the holy Quran predicts and prescribes the Doomsday in the 14th Century of the Islamic calender of which we are passing through right now the deadly Hijri 1400 ?

Will not, on the Day of Judgement, a large balance be set up (42 : 17) and all the good deeds of mankind be weighed against the bad deeds and the Muslims hope that their good deeds will outweigh and cancel the bad ones (11 : 114) ?

The Quran disappears at the End Time

710. The Quran avoids the question regarding the end time of the world by saying : Allah knows it better. But time is close at hand (33 : 63). Do you believe that in the end time there will be a rapid decline of faith and the Quran, as it came from Allah in the end, will return to Him ? When the copies of the Holy Book and its verses will disappear how will the Muslims manage without a Quran ?

Forecast of Muhhamad on Muslim

711. Did not Allah's Messanger tell Abu Huraira : "A person lit fire and when the atmosphere was aglow, moths and insects began to fall into the fire, but I am there to hold them back, but they are plunging into it despite my efforts, and he further added : that is your example and mine. I am there to hold you back from fire and to save you from it, but you are plunging into it despite my effort" (*Mus* IV : 5671, 5672). Does not the Prophet indicate that he told to his followers, the Muslims, that he cannot save them and they are bound to perish because of their wrong doings ?

Sun will come near at End Time

712. On the Day of Resurrection, the Sun will come near (to the people) to such an extent that the sweat will reach up to the middle of the ears, so, when all the people are in that state, they will ask Adam for help, and then Moses, and when everyone will fail they will come to Muhammad (*Buk* 2.24.553).

Place of Paradise and its Residents
713. Is not it a fact that God has bought from the believers their selves and their possessions against the gift of Paradise; they fight in the way of God; they kill, and are killed; that is a promise binding on God... (9.110).

The Prophet said, " Paradise has one hundred grades which Allah has reserved for the Mujahidin (Muslim fighters) who fight in His cause" (*Buk* 4.52.48).

"Our Prophet has informed us that our Lord says : 'Whoever amongst us is killed as a martyr shall go to Paradise to lead such a luxurious life as he has never seen, and whoever survives shall become your master" (*Buk* 4.53.386).

Muhammad Visits Heaven before his Death
714. When Gabriel took Muhammad to heaven the first gate of heaven opened and Muhammad met Adam, in the second heaven Jesus, in the third heaven he met Yusuf, in the fourth heaven Idris (19 : 57), in the fifth heaven Harun, in the sixth heaven Moses, in the seventh heaven Abraham (*Mus* 1 : 309).   Before the Judgement Day is it possible to see them all in heaven and the sinners left weeping ?

Men dominated Heaven
715. What a wonderful description of heaven is given in the Quran for a faithful Muslim--- trees for shade and fresh fruit, alongside cool rivers; a few dozen maidens and several lads always at one's disposal. Is it not strange enough to say that everything is for men and men alone. Beyond the gate of paradise very little is said in the Quran about Muhammad's previous wives in connection with paradise (55 : 54; 56 : 15-22, 34-35, 72).

Was Allah not partial in rewarding men with wine, food and virgins including their wives of the earth (52 : 19-20; 37 : 48-49) forgetting to reward the pious women ? The majority of its people were the poor and those who were in the Fire were women (*Buk* 8 : 554).

Conditions of Souls in Heaven
716. If the souls of the martyrs are in the bodies of green birds dwelling in Paradise (*Buk* 1 : 28) how can they enjoy all those beautiful women chained in different corners of Paradise whenever they like ?

Place of Martyrs in Heaven
717. Is it not a fact that the martyrs who kill and are killed in the *Jihad* are given an automatic ticket to heaven, with no questions asked--- blow yourself up in the cause of Allah and you are escaped from the final judgement and your ascension to paradise is for sure (2 : 155; 3 : 169-171; 4 : 72-74; 9 : 111) ?

Dying for Religion of False Belief
718. Why did the early Christians willingly die for a belief in the resurrection that wasn't true ? Every religion has martyrs who are killed for the beliefs they hold. Scores of Muslims enthusiastically blow themselves up each year in their hope to join their prophet Muhammed, who they believe miraculously ascended to heaven in the presence of many witnesses. The willingness to suffer doesn't substantiate a false belief (Tovia Singer 1993 : 221) ?

Believer's Paradise

719. Can Allah be judicious to send believers to paradise even if they are murderers, rapists, thieves and liars but send the non-believers, even if they have been highly righteous, to the hell ?

Is 99 Names a Passport to Paradise ?

720. Is it possible for a man to enter the paradise merely by memorizing the ninety-nine names of Allah (*Buk* 50.894; 9 : 489) ?

Paradise for a Woman who dies in Child-Birth

721. Why would a woman be enrolled in the body of martyrs and be united with her husband in Paradise if she dies in child-birth (Gibb 1974 : 138) ?

Facilities to a Muslim in Paradise

722. Is not the paradise of Muhammad full of lust for the flesh and sensual entertainments ? In the scorching desert, Muhammad promised a paradise "beneath which rivers flow" (13 : 35). In place of sleeping on the sand, he promised them a paradise with "uplifted couches" (88 : 13), upon which believers shall lie "gazing" (83 : 23). In place of camel skin, he promised them a paradise, wherein "they shall be adorned with bracelets of gold and with pearls, and their apparel there shall be of silk" (22 : 23). In place of drought and barrenness, he promised them two paradise full of "fruits and palm trees, and pomegranates" (55 : 68; 78 : 32). In place of tents that can neither protect against the heat of summer nor the bitter cold of winter, he promised them "lofty chambers" (39 : 20); "therein shall they see neither sun nor bitter cold" (76 : 13). In place of Bedouin women, he promised them houris as wives : "We shall espouse them to wide-eyed huris" (52 : 20), "restraining their glances, untouched before them by any man or *Jinn*" (55 : 56), "spotless virgins, chastely amorous, like of age" (56 : 36, 37) chaste women, restraining their glances, with big eyes of wonder and beauty as if they were delicate eggs (pearls) closely guarded (37 : 48-49); dressed in fine silk and in rich brocade, they will face each other, Allah shall wed them to maidens with beautiful, big and lustrous eyes and of equal age (52 : 20; 44 : 51-55; 38 : 33). In place of being deprived of servants, he promised them youths who will bring them delicious and dainty food, "immortal youths going round about them with goblets, and ewers, and a cup from a spring" (56 : 17, 18), and "immortal youths shall go about them; when (one sees) them, (one supposes) them (to be) scattered pearls" (76 : 19). In place of the food of poverty, he promised them flesh : "We shall succour them with fruits and flesh such as they desire" (52 : 22; 56 : 21). And in place of hunger, distress and hardship of living, he promised them a paradise, "(wherein) are rivers of water unstaling, rivers of milk unchanging in flavour, and rivers of wine--- a delight to the drinkers, rivers, too, of honey purified" (47 : 15). If one gets such facilities in Islamic paradise why will somebody go to the Christian paradise where they neither marry nor are given in marriage, but are like angels of God in heaven" (*Mt* 22 : 30); "For the kingdom of God is not food and drink, but righteousness and peace and joy in the Holy Spirit" (*Rom* 14 : 17) ?

Homosexual practice In Paradise

723. Though homosexuality is forbidden in Islam (4 : 16; 7 : 80-81, 26 : 165, 27 : 55) but emperor Babur passing through the Khyber pass fell in love with a boy and this he has written in his autobiography. If it is condemned in this world why is it

204

not condemned in the Paradise ? Does not the Quran describe such handsome youths" as Pearls well-guarded" (52 : 24), "youths of perpetual freshness" (56 : 17), if you see them, you would think them scattered Pearls" (76 : 19) ?

Can you deny the fact that during the Abbasid period there seems to have been many caliphs like : al-Amin (ruled 809); al-Mutasim (833); the Aghlabid Ibrahim (875); at Cordoba, Abd al-Rahman (912); and the great Saladin (*Salah al-Din* 1169), famous for his Jihad against the crusaders who were all homosexuals (Reddy 2004 : 247) ?

Best Possible Wine available in Heaven

724. Is not it a fact that Allah promised Muslims wine in his Paradise, which is an extremely precious commodity in the land of Arabia. The holy Quran says : the gardens of Paradise have river of wine (47.15), pure wine will be served, securely sealed; whose very dregs are musk... (83.25,26), Muslims will recline on jeweled couches and will be served by those pearl like boys with bowls and ewers and a cup of purest wine (56.7-40), Muslims will be served with goblet filled at a gushing fountain, white and delicious. But the wine will neither dull their senses nor befuddle them (37.40-48) and by drinking Allah's wine, the faces of the Muslims will have the mark of glow of joy (83.24).

Cheap Salvation in Islam

725. Is salvation so cheap in Islam that even if one had committed illegal intercourse and theft at the time of death or before it, and he repents and regrets and says : "None has the right to be worshipped but Allah, he will be forgiven for his sins (*Buk* 7 : 717) ?

How many Muslims will go to Paradise ?

726. Are there only a few Muslims in Paradise (56 : 13-14) or many (56 : 39-40) ?

Is not it a fact that compared to Jewish Christians Muslims have a very small accommodation in heaven ? The heaven for Jewish Christians is confined to 1,44,000 where as Muslims have a heaven for 70,000 people only.

Prophet Muhammad said : "From my followers there will be a crowd of 70,000 in number who will enter Paradise whose faces will glitter as the moon" (*Buk* 8.76.550; 549-550).

Again he revised the statement by adding 70,000 of my followers will enter Paradise altogether; so that the first and the last amongst them will enter at the same time" (*Buk* 4.54.410).

Why Muslims die for Paradise ?

To satisfy Muslims with food, shelter and sex Muhammad attracts them to dress and ornaments. Does not Quran gurantee Muslims that in their paradise they will be decked with pearls and bracelets of gold and silver and arrayed in fine green garments of silk (22.23; 76.21), wives will be given goblets of gold (43.70-71), they will recline on green cushions and fine carpets (55.76), inner linings will be of rich brocade (55.54), dressed in rich silks and fine brocade (44.53) ?

Last but not the least Allah considers for his residents of Paradise a system of pure water supply which is a dream for the desert ? Does not Allah assure in Quran; Paradise is watered by incorruptible running streams in which they will abide forever (13.35;3.136, 198; 22.23, 47.15), fountains of clear flowing water in the gardens (15.45), every garden has two running fountains in continuous abundance (55.50-51; 55.66-67) ?

Is there any toilet system in Paradise ? Is Allah not kind enough to provide a comfortable system for getting rid of body waste through sweat only (*Mus* 39.6798).

Where is heaven and where is hell ? Can it be confined to a wall of a mosque facing the Kaaba (*Buk* 1.12.716) ?

Fantasy and Escape

727. Is not the *Hell* or *Jahannum* a horrible place for nonbelievers in Islam ? The sinners shall become the companions of Hell (5 : 10). Does not the Holy Quran ascertain : "Do you not see how those who dispute the revelation of God turn away from the right path ? Those who have denied the Book and the message We sent through Our apostles shall realize the truth hereafter : when, with chains and shackles round their necks, they shall be dragged through scalding water and then burnt in the fire of Hell" (40 : 69-72).

In hell; all non-Muslims will burn forever in hell fire because they are vilest of creatures (98.1-6), a woeful punishment... (33.8), unbelievers will wear garments of fire, scalding water will be poured upon their heads, melting their skins and that which is in their bellies, will be tortured with hooked rods of iron, whenever, in their anguish, they try to escape from Hell, they will be dragged, and will be told : 'Taste the torment of the Conflagration (22.19-22), when they cry out for help they shall be showered with water as hot as molten brass, which will scald their faces, evil shall be their drink, dismal their resting-place (18.29), their punishment will never be lightened, and they shall be speechless with despair (43.74-75), unbelievers shall be seized by their forelocks and their feet (55.41), for the unbelievers. We have prepared chains, fetters and a Blazing (Fire) (76.4;73.12), choking food and a painful punishment (73.13), roast the unbeliever in hell (69.31), neither shade nor shelter from the flames (77.31), you and your idols shall be the fuel of Hell (21.98), food for unbelievers is Zakkum tree and foul pus (44.43; 69.36).

Why Non-Muslims in Muslim Hell ?

728. For whom is the Muslim hell ? Can a judicious God take non-Muslims to the Muslim hell ? Do not the non-Muslims have their own hell and heaven too ? Why will they eat foul fruits and be made to drink boiling water (37 : 65-67), wearing a garment of fire, over their heads will` be poured out boiling water (22 : 19), will drink boiling fetid water and in gulps will be sipped, but never will be near swallowing it down his throat, death will come to him from every quarter, yet will he not die, in front of him will be a chastisement unrelenting (14 : 17) ? Why shall they soon cast into the fire, as often as their skins are roasted through, Allah shall change them for fresh skins, that they may taste the chastisement (4 : 56), will beg for death but Allah will say, "Nay, but ye shall abide !" (43 : 77) ? If Allah will feel that is not enough for the unbelievers, in addition there will be maces of iron to punish them. Every time they wish to get away therefrom, from anguish they will be forced back therein, and it will be said : "Taste ye the chastisement of Burning !" (22 : 21-22).

Section
IX

Love Hate Relationship

46 - Good Islam and Bad Muslims

The word "Islam" is a noun which is constituted from the Arabic verb meaning, "submission or surrender to the will of Allah." It is a religion of the semetic family.

Those who profess Islam are often called Mohammedans but they prefer to be called Muslims which means believers. Like any other religion it demands obedience. It is a common notion that the followers of Christ became Christians but the Muslims who follow Mohammed are not called Mohammedans. Muslims do not worship Mohammed like the Christians. They have the greatest esteem for Mohammad as the messenger of Allah.

The holy book of Islam, *the Quran* is full of calls for crusades and mass slaughter. Its history has been blood soaked. Its mosques have always been party offices and arsenals. To our surprise, it pretends that it is a religion. The great western scholar Colin Main rightly remarks : "Islam is undemocratic; it is puritanical; it is barbarously punitive; it oppresses women; its laws are cruel to animals; it is intolerant towards other religions; it is anti-intellectual; it places restrictions upon art" (1985 : 2).

It is strange but true that children are learning about Islam from the media where Muslims are depicted as terrorists or characters from the Arabian Nights or a Friday-go-to Mosque kind of people.

They are the people who are self-bound to pray towards the holy city of Mecca five times each day and during the entire holy month of Ramadan, the ninth month of the Muslim year, refrain from food and drink from dawn to dusk. And are required to make once-in-a lifetime pilgrimage to the holy city, Mecca. Ok.

It is tolerable. But to our surprise during the period of Muhammad Muslim meant traitor. In the words of David Smith Margoliouth :

Finally a name had to be given to the new sect, and either accident or choice led to its being called the sect of the Muslims (Moslems) or Hanifs. Were these originally named by which the followers of Maslamah the Prophet of the Banu Hanifah had been known ? Or had some other sect, monotheistic and professedly following Abraham, whose descendants according to the Bible some of the Arabs were, been thus designated ? We cannot say; no Arab seems to have known anything about the Hanifs, except that Abraham was one, and perhaps one or two of the precursors of Mohammad; and since in Hebrew the word means "Hypocrite" and in Syriac "heathen", pious followers of Mohammad did not care to study its etymology. The other name, Muslim, meant naturally "traitor," and when the new sect came to be lampooned, it provided the satirists with a witticism; Mohammad showed some want of humour in adopting it, but displayed great ingenuity in giving it an honorable meaning : whereas ordinarily signified one who handed over his friends to their enemies, it was glorified into meaning one who handed over his person to God; and though, like Christian, it may conceivably have been first invented by enemies of the sect whom it designated, divine authority was presently adduced for the statement that Abraham coined the name. Like the Jews, these new

208

Abrahamites called their pagan brethren the Gentiles, using an Abyssinian word. The pagans appear to have ordinarily called the new sect when it had ceased to be secret. Sabaean a word properly meaning Baptist, and belonging to a community still perpetuated as the Soubbas, whose home is in the marshes of the Euphrates. The application of the name to Mohammed's followers may have been due to mere ignorance, as the Arabians of our day called Doughtly a Jew, because he was a Christian; or it may have been due to the prominence given by Mohammed to the ceremony of washing (1985 : 116).

Inspite of such criticism the Muslim scholars have always complained that the Eastern thinkers, and the Western Orientalists from the beginning have been irresponsible, unfair and have given distorted and partial views on Islam. They called it a demonic religion of apostasy, blasphemy and obscurity. Some say Muhammad was epileptic.

Eastern thinkers like Sri Aurobindo said on Islam in a letter to a disciple on September 12, 1923 : "The Mohammedan or Islamic culture hardly gave anything to the world which may be said to be of fundamental importance and typically its own... I do not think it has done anything more in India of cultural value. It gave some new forms to art and poetry. Its political institutions were always semi-barbaric."

The Western theologians like Martin Luther saw Islam "in the medieval way, as a movement of violence in the service of the anti -Christ; it cannot be converted because it is closed to reason; it can only be resisted by the sword, and even then with difficulty".

Ernest Renan, in an oft-cited lecture, championed science, reason, and human progress by dismissing Islam as incompatible with science and the Muslim as "incapable of learning anything or of opening himself to a new idea" (Qtd. Esposito 1993 : 48).

Will Durant once said : "I do not seek to understand in order to believe. I believe in order to understand."

It can be compared with Muslim thinking process. Can they think anything beyond Allah, Quran and Muhammad ? Hasan Al-Banna, founder of Muslim Brotherhood wrote in "The Message of the Teachings" :

> Allah is our goal
> The Prophet Muhammad is our leader
> The Quran is our constitution
> Jihad is our way
> And death in the way of Allah
> Is our promised end" (Husain 2007 : 52).

Was Ibrahim the First Muslim ?

729. Why did Muhammad not start his religion with his name but with the name of Ibrahim ? Is it because Ibrahim was neither a Jew nor a Christian, but he was a Muslim (3 : 67) ? If Noah (10 : 72), Joseph (12 : 101), and Jesus (5 : 111) all were Muslims, why did Muhammad contradict by saying : "I am the first of the Muslims those that submit (6 : 163) ?

Did Muhammad not say : "By Him who has the control on my soul, had Moses been alive he would have followed me" (see Al-Baihaqi's Dalail al-Nubuwwa, p. 15) and again says that he was a prophet who before Adam was

209

created (Ahmad b. Hanbal IV. 127, 128) ? Don't these two *hadiths* show that he was a Prophet ? Quran says that Ibrahim was literally (not only spiritually) a Muslim (*CQV* 1994 : 108) ?

Good Muslims and Bad Citizens

730. Can one deny the fact that many of the Muslims are not fundamentalists and many fundamentalists are not terrorists, but many of the present-day terrorists are Muslims and proudly identify themselves as such (Lewis 2003 : 137) ?

Mr. L. Rangarajan, an US based scholar sent these questions to highly educated people who had been working in the oil-field in Saudi-Arabia for the past 25 years. They responded negatively and were very suspicious towards the credibility of the Muslims of all sects. They obviously cannot be both good Muslims and good citizens. Let us look at the following parameter :

Theologically	No. Because his allegiance is to Allah, the moon god of Arabia.
Religiously	No. Because no other religion is accepted by his Allah except Islam (2 : 256).
Scripturally	No. Because his allegiance is to the five pillars of Islam and the Quran.
Geographically	No. Because his allegiance is to Mecca, which he turns in prayer five times a day.
Socially	No. Because his allegiance to Islam forbids him to make friends with Christians and Jews.
Politically	No Because he must submit to the Mullah (spiritual leaders), who teaches annihilation of Israel and Destruction of America, the great Satan.
Domestically	No. Because he is instructed to marry four women and beat and scourge his wife when she disobeys him (4 : 34).
Intellectually	No. Because he cannot accept the American Constitution since it is based on Biblical principles and he believes the Bible to be corrupt.
Philosophically	No. Because Islam, Muhammad, and the Quran do not allow freedom of religion and expression. Democracy and Islam cannot co-exist. Every Muslim government is either dictatorial or autocratic.
Spiritually	No. Because when we declare "one nation under God, 'the Christian's God is loving and kind, while Allah is never referred to as heavenly father, nor is he ever called love in The Quran's 99 excellent names (2007 : 36).

Can Muslims go Against Muslims ?

731. The Prophet said : "A Muslim is the one who avoids harming Muslims with his tongue and hands (*Buk* 1 : 18). How many Muslims have ever raised their voices in protest over Saddam Hussein's genocidal war upon the Kurds ?

47 - Caste System Innate In Islam

The Islamic principle of equality and brotherhood based on the Islamic motto of "Tauheed" (God is one) was sincerely practised by the followers of Muhammad in the early days. But this golden period of Islam lasted only for 52 years from 610 AD to 661 AD out of which Muhammad witnessed 22 years and the four Khalifas (Bakar $2^1/_2$ years), Oomar (10 years), Usman (12 years) and Ali ($5^1/_2$ years) for 30 years.

This golden period came to an end when Khalifa Umed brought the throne of 'Murja Khilafat' from Mecca to Damascus which was a big commercial centre. The luxurious atmosphere and the rich life-style of the people of Damascus radically changed the old Islamic way of living and Islam no longer remained the society of equal people.

In the years that followed Islamic empire spread far and wide from the Mediterranean sea to the Pacific Ocean covering one-third of the area of the world. In most parts of the world, people were converted to Islam by using force. Wars were waged and battles fought to convert people to Islam. In some places, Muslim missionaries and Sufi saints propagated Muslim culture through peace unity and Universal brotherhood. They preached that Islam is different from the other religions because it believed in equality of mankind.

But social and economic discrimination among the Muslims prevailed even during the time of Muhammad. There were many castes like Qureshi, Hashimi and Umeds and each of them regarded themselves superior to the others. "Muhajarins", who were with Muhammad when he came from Mecca to Medina and "Ansars", his supporters claimed a special status. A new caste called "Ashraf" emerged later on when Islam started spreading across continents. Previously, Fatima and Ali, Muhammad's daughter and son-in-law were accorded the title "Ashrafs" but later on all the kiths of Muhamamd started calling themselves as Syeds and claimed equal status as that of Ashrafs.

In Arab, Ashrafs today occupy top position in the Muslim hierarchy. The non-Ashrafs called "Ajlafes" are people who belong to the lower strata and are weavers, carpenters, butchers, potters, washermen, tailors, gold-smiths etc. And the third category called "Arjals" are sweepers, grave-diggers and cobblers. All of these castes confine themselves to their own community and do not have any kind of social relation like marriage with the other communities.

Islamic caste system, unlike the Hindu caste system was based on the relative proximity of the clan to Muhammad. The closer they were the superior they ought to be. Later on the economic status also became a deciding factor. The concept of Islamic brotherhood was restricted to individual castes.

Caste System during Prophet's Time

732. Is it not a fact that during the times of Prophet Muhammad, there were many castes among the Muslims, the major castes being Qureshi, Hashimi and Ummeds ? Did these castes not regard themselves superior to members of other castes ?

Four Castes in Islam

733. Is not it a fact that like Indian caste system the Muslims too have their own caste system ? Are not Syeds, Mughals, Pathans and Sheikhs equal to *Brahmin, Khans* to *Kshatriya*, Ashrarfs to *Vaishya* and *Ajlafes* to *Sudras* that includes butchers, weavers, carpenters, washermen, potters, tailors, sweepers, grave diggers, and cobblers ?

Hatred between Ashrafs and Ajlafes

734. Is not it a fact that in Arab countries Ashrafs even today, occupy the top position as land owners. In India don't the Mughals, Pathans and Sheikhs claim to be in the status of Ashrafs and like Arab in India too non-Ashrafs are called Ajlafes or any Tom, Dick and Harry ? Can these weavers, carpenters, washermen, potters, tailors, iron-smiths, goldsmiths, shopkeepers and butchers ever claim an equal status with the Ashrafs ?

When Ashrafs became Syeds

735. Is not it a fact that the newly-conquered North Africa, Iran and Middle East which were merged in Arab countries were separated by a new caste called *Ashraf* ? Was not the word Ashraf used only for Fatima, daughter of the Prophet and her husband Ali the fourth Calipha though later, the family of the Prophet started calling themselves as *Syeds*, the word equivalent to *Ashrafs* ?

Two New Castes Muhajarine and Ansars

736. Is it not a fact that the Muhajarine, who were with the Prophet when he came from Mecca to Medina and Ansars the supporters of Prophet claimed that even if they are not regarded as superior to other clans of Muslims they ought to be given a special status for their services to the Prophet ?

Two New Class : Black Arabs and White Arabs

737. Is not it a fact that like Europeans, in Arab also they have two major castes Black Arabs and White Arabs ? Black Arabs have a larger percentage of female births than White Arabs. But White Arabs because of their white complexion do not accept the girls from Black Arabs. Because of dowry demand from the bridegrooms both Black and White Arabs go to India, Bangladesh and Singapore to obtain brides in a cheaper rate. Do not the Arab rulers suspect the non-Arab brides and therefore they have formed a Mehr Fund to advance loans to the poor Arabs to pay adequate Mehr---a form of dowry to be paid to the bride and save Arab culture from these Asiatic brides (*Niser* Sept. 12, 1993 : 7) ?

Caste Divisions among Indian Muslims

738. Is it not a fact that those who are converted to Islam in India remain in the same caste they originally belonged to, such as Mevs belong to Mewat, a place near Delhi and Muslim Rajputs of Rajasthan still consider themselves to be Kshatriyas; Ismails, Ashnashri Khojas, Dandis, Sulemani Vohras and Kutchi Memons residing in Gujarat, Kutch, Saurashtra and Konken areas consider themselves as Vaishya; Labbas of Tamil Nadu, trading in hides and bones do not mix with other Muslims and do not marry outside their community ? Is it not a fact that there are no less than 79 castes among the Indian Muslims ?

Rigid Caste Systems for Slave Rulers

739. Is it not a fact that a slave may be a ruler but he cannot have the equal status in Muslim society. Did this not happen in case of Gaznavi dynasty founded by Subtageen, the father of Muhammad Gaznavi, who was a Gulam or slave of Samni rulers ? Did it not happen in case of Sultan Kutbuddin Ebak, who ruled over Delhi and was a Gulam earlier ? Why were the famous Maamluk Sultans of Egypt never treated equal with any Muslim even after they became rulers ? Because originally they were Turkish slaves ?

Isaac the Gift of God's Grace

740. Is there any historical link between Abraham and Muhammad that Muhammad was the descendant of Abraham ?

Why are Muslims proud to be called the descendant of Ishmael though both Hagar and Ishmael were expelled because Ishmael was the son, by earthly effort whereas Isaac was the son of a promise received by the gift of God's grace ?

Religion of the Son of Slaves

741. Why did not God treat Isaac and Ishmael equal though both are the sons of Abraham ? Is it because Sarah was the paternal sister of Abraham and Hagar was an Egyptian slave-woman, a concubine of Abraham ?

Prophet Muhammad claimed that the Muslims are the descendants of Abraham by his union with Hagar, the slave woman who bore Abraham's son Ishmael the half-brother of Isaac as recorded in the Bible (*Gn* 16; 5 : 10-12). Does it not degrade the religion that comes from the son of a slave ? Does the Bible not warn : Get rid of the slave woman and her son, for the slave woman's son will never share in the inheritance with the free woman's son (*Gal* 2 : 30) ?

Ishmael the Common Enemy for All

742. Is it not a fact that the predictions about Ishmael are proved to be true till date : "His hand will be against everyone and everyone's hand against him" (*Gn* 16 : 12) ?

Semitic Religions Permit Slavery

743. Is not it a fact that like the Jews and Christians, Islam too permits slavery ? Were not the slaves subjected to exploitation and in addition to that the women slaves were subjected to sexual exploitation ?

Can you deny the fact that Muhammad himself had 17 men and 11 women as slaves (Pike : 1962; Main 1985 : 13) ? Following the footprint of the Prophet Md. ben Qasim carried away 60, 000 Indians from Sindh and Sindh became a perennial source of supply for slaves till Mahomud of Ghazni opened up the rest of India (Menon 2007 : 7). Can you disagree with the fact that boys of 7-15 years were castrated and made eunuchs to be sold to the aristocracy to guard their harems ? Did not 90 per cent of them die while removing their genitals and some boys were used by the Arab judges for homosexual purposes ? Did al- Ghazali, the great Muslim servant not fear to condemn this practice (Menon 2007 : 7) ? Is not equality in Islam a myth when it permits the ultimate inequality--- slavery ?

Section
X

Election of the King

48 - Selection without Election

The covenant breakers mould the history of a religious movement. It happens with all the prophets and promised ones. Who sold Joseph into Egypt ? Who betrayed Jesus and handed him over to his enemies ? Who opposed Muhammad to choose his successor ? It is their close relatives. Joseph could excuse his blood brothers, it is one of the apostles who betrayed Jesus, it is Abu Bakr, Muhammad's father-in-law and Umar his closest confident who opposed Muhammad's chosen successor Ali.

On the very day when Prophet Muhammad passed away of this mortal world in 632 and before his body was laid to rest, winds of dissension blew through the edifice of Islam and in such a conflicting situation Muhammad's father-in-law Abu Bakr was declared and chosen as the first Calif. He died in 634 and another father-in-law of Muhammed, Umar was chosen, under whose era, Iran was conquered. He was killed by his own Persian slave in 644. Uthman and Ali were contenders for the vacant post. Both were related to Muhammad. Ali was Muhammed's brother's son as well as his son-in-law. Ali was the second Muslim after Muhammad's first wife and he is reputed to have prevented his mother, while he was still an embryo in his mother's womb, from worshipping an idol. How he did it is not clear. In the struggle Uthman was the winner. In 656 he, too, was murdered through an underground conspiracy led by Abdullah Ibn Saba, a Jew who had outwardly converted himself to Islam. And Ali became the new Calif. He refused to punish the murderer of Uthman, a clear indication of his hand in the murder. Thereafter the followers of Uthman became known as Sunni and the followers of Ali became Shi'ah. So the followers of Uthman instigated Ayesha, another wife of Muhammed, to wage war against Ali. Out of the 8 wives of Uthman two were daughters of Muhammad. The story goes on to say that even the dung of the camel ridden by Ayesha was sweet-smelling; but she was totally defeated by Ali's army. And again, there was murder; this time of Ali at the hands of Ibn. And thus started the deadly *feud* for power between Ali's son Hassan and one Mu Awi. Mu Awi won but allowed Hassan to live in Mecca. But Hassan was poisoned in 669. Mu Awi made sure that his descendants will become Calif for ever; and declared his son Yazid as the next Calif. In 680 Yazid was challenged by Hussein, another son of Ali. Hussein was completely defeated and his head was rolled along the streets. And in 683 Abdulla waged war against Yazid. Abdulla lost and he took shelter in Mecca. In the ensuing battle the sacred stone in Kaaba was broken into three pieces. By this time Yazid died. Following that Marwan and Abdul Malik became Calif. Malik killed Abdulla and his dead body was exhibited in the streets.

To get rid of the Calif system of administration Mustafa Kamal Pasha established a national state in Turkey and abolished the Caliphate in 1924. With the passage of time, numerous independent and autonomous Muslim national states came into being in the same way. Here are a few doubts regarding the inner democracy in Islam.

Did the Prophet do his Duty ?
744. When Muhammad knew that "his people will be divided into seventy-three sects, of which only one will be saved", why did not he try to solve the problems

before he died ? Why is there no indication in the Quranic text after the Prophet, on whom should the leadership of the new community fall ?

Was Abu- Bakr worried about the Prophet's death ?

745. Though the Prophet died on Monday why was he buried during the last part of the night between Tuesday and Wednesday ? Is not it a fact that to settle the problem of Caliphate the burial was delayed ?

Rule maker is a Rule breaker

746. Is not it a fact that after Muhammad's death; Ali wanted to be the Caliph but Abu Bakr became the Caliph because Umar supported him ? Did not Al-Zubayr draw his sword, saying, "I will not put it back until the oath of allegiance is rendered to Ali" (*Tab* 9.188,189) ?

Did Abu Sufyan not dislike Abu Bakr, because Abu Bakr came from a lowly clan of Mecca ? Sufyan even agreed to a future bloodshed if it would be required to rid this perceived wrong (*Tab* 9.199) ?

Is not it a fact that Abu Bakr was not accepted by a larger section of the Muslim Community as a successor of the Prophet ? When he became the Caliph there was a threat of a civil war and a number of Bedouins tribes began to fall away from Islam. Did not they refuse to pay the *Zakat* or alms ? Abu Bakr, to bring these recalcitrants back to Islam, fought a series of campaigns known as the wars of the *Riddah* (apostasy) (Parrinder 1971 : 475) ?

If there is a definite rule recorded by the *Sharia* and the great collection of the *hadith* that the Caliphate should be reserved for the Prophet's Quresh tribe, why was it not made into law during the first century of the Hijra to protect the right of Ali', the Prophet's Son-in-Law to become the first Caliphate ? Because of this Ali was deprived of his claim on three different occasions, by the choice of the Muslim community, or of the group of electors, supposed to represent it, who negated Ali's claims by setting aside his candidature.

Is it not a fact that the first three Caliphs were all related to Muhammad by marriage and Ali the fourth, was nearest in blood because he was his cousin and the husband of his daughter Fatima ?

Muhammad on his deathbed had asked for a material to write something down, in all probability to indicate who should be the Calipha; was he not denied-on the apprehension, say the Sunni historians, that he might abrogate something vital of the Quran in his delirium, but the Shia historians say, to prevent him from recording his decision that his son- in-law Ali should be the Calipha ?

No Caliph from the Downtrodden

747. The Kharijites maintain that anyone, even a Negro slave, could be elected as the head of the Muslim community if he possessed the necessary qualifications ? Purity of life was the only test. Did it happen when the first four Caliphas or later Caliphas were chosen ?

Did the Muslims choose Abu Bakr as First Caliph ?

748. Is not it a fact that from the height of the pulpit at the last journey of the Prophet to Mecca he told two most precious things : One is the Book of God and the second is his successor ? Saying this the Prophet taking the hand of Ali, raised it high to its full extent and confirmed it three times :

217

"God is my Master, I am the master of the faithful and I have right over them even more than they themselves possess. Therefore, of whomsoever I am master Ali is his master too."

After repeating this sentence three times the Prophet said, "O My God ! Be a Friend of him who is a friend of Ali and treat him like a foe who opposes Ali. Help them who help Ali and abandon them who go against Ali. And O My Lord ! Whichever way may Ali turn orient the right is in the same direction." He continued, "Look here ! this is binding upon them who are here that they should convey this message to those who are not present" *(Echo of Islam* Sept-Oct- 1984) 56).

Inspite of this how did Muslims dare not listen to the Prophet and chose Abu Bakr the father of Ayesha, as the successor of the Prophet ?

Politics of Abu Bakr

749. Is it not a fact that Abu Bakr the father-in-law of Muhammad and father of the Prophet's favourite wife Ayesha played politics to deprive Ali of being the first Califah and took recourse to all possible means to take over as the first Caliph before the Prophet's burial under the floor of Ayeshah's hut, alongside the courtyard of the Mosque ?

After Abu Bakr became the first Caliph he nominated Umar as his successor. After Umar, Uthman became the third Caliph. Ali was declared the fourth, but he was killed when he was praying in the mosque at Kufa. Afterwards, Ali's sons Hussan and Hussein were slain in an unequal battle of forces.

Was not this unjust for Ali's family and a grave concern for the followers of Ali which made them form a new sect called Shia ?

Fight Against Back Slidden

750. Did not Abu Bakr fight against those in the Arabian Peninsula who had backslidden from Islam during his 2 years, 3 months and 8 days as Calipha ? After which he wrote remorsefully that he is over whelmed with sins and lacks goodness so how can he be saved ?

Umar killed for heavy Taxation

751. Is it not a fact that the second Caliph Umar who ruled 10 years 6 months, and 19 days was killed in Medina by one of his slaves who complained of heavy taxation in Iraq ? Did not Umar say : "If Allah should keep me alive I will let the widows of Iraq need no men to support them after me" ? But only four days had elapsed when he was stabbed to death, by a non-Arab infidel craftsman and a slave of Al- Mughira with a double-edged knife *(Buk* 5 : 50) ? Did not Umar say to Ibn Abbas : No doubt, you and your father (Abbas) used to have more non-Arab infidel slaves in Medina ? Ibn Abbas said to Umar : "If you wish we will kill them." Umar said : "You are mistaken (for you can't kill them) after they have spoken your language, prayed towards your Qibla, and performed Hajj like yours" *(Buk* 5 : 50).

Uthman was killed for his Nepotism and Misrule

752. Is it not true that Uthman, one of the ten men to whom Muhammad promised Paradise, married two of Muhammad's daughters and collected Quran during his caliphate ? During his 11 years, 11 months, and 19 days rule he caused so much harm to Muhammad's friend, Abdullah b. Masoud, that Abdullah's tribe, Hazil, turned against him. He did the same to Ammar b. Yassir. His tribe, Banu Makhzum, also turned against him. Did he not deport Abu Dharr to Rabya and prohibited him from entering Medina or Mecca (*al-Tabari; al-Milal wa al-Nihal*, Section 3; *True Guidance*, Part I : 1991 : 119) ?

Was he not assassinated by the rebels because of his nepotism and misrule ? Is it not a fact that calipha Uthman showered his relatives with government funds ? Did he not marry his daughter to Marwan b.Hakam, a corrupt man to whom he gave one-fifth of the state taxes from Africa, a sum of 200, 000 dinars (*True Guidance* I 1991 : 119) ?

Can you deny the fact that Calipha Uthman appointed his relatives as rulers of conquered countries, though they were corrupt and dishonest ? What about his son, Walid b. Uqba ?

Did not Muhammad order the death of Walid ? When Uthman asked him, "who will care for my children, O Muhammad ?" the Prophet answered, "Hell !" (Walid included). Uthman installed Walid as ruler of Kufa. There he led the people in prayer while drunk. He then increased the number of prayer-rounds. When the assembly told him he was in error, he said, "Stop, or I will add more !"

Was not Abdullah b. Sarh, another relative, appointed ruler of Egypt, whom Muhammad wanted to kill for changing the record of the Quran (*True Guidance* I 1991 : 118- 119) ?

How Uthman was Killed

753. Uthman was chosen as the next Caliph. Under his leadership, life became more difficult for Muslims. There were charges of clan partiality, financial mismanagement, corruption and elitism against Uthman. This made him very unpopular (*Tab* : 15.143, 162, 167). Soon a large Muslim army rose up in arms against him and three large bodies of men, from Egypt, Kufa, and Basra, moved against Uthman and marched on Medina (*Tab* : 15.186,187). Even Uthman's own adopted son rose against him. The dark attitudes that were implanted in the Muslim's hearts and minds by Muhammad's force of narcissism found an opportunity to grow, spread roots, and more blooms of Islam's real fruit started blossoming.

Uthman called for help from his various governors, but nobody came. The tribesmen of Uthman, did little or nothing to defend their caliph. They knew that if he fell, they could possibly become the Caliph (*Tab* : 15.185). Ultimately Uthman was murdered and one of his murderers was Muhammad b. Abi Bakr (Abu Bakr's son). Tabari recorded how cruelly Uthman was killed.

"He came over to him with a broad iron headed arrow and stabbed him in the head with it... They gathered round him and killed him" (*Tab* 15.190,191).

Uthman was stabbed nine times, throttled and one of his hands was severed. After killing him, one of the murderers rejoiced and declared :

"By Allah, I have never seen anything softer than his throat. By God, I throttled him until I saw his soul shaking in his body like the soul of a jinn" (*Tab* : 15.205).

Did not Uthman die as Muslim rebels besieged his palace, and his murderers sought to dishonour his corpse ? Uthman's friends were unable to bury him for two nights. At last, four of them carried his body to a site where funeral prayers could be offered. Some opponents prohibited any prayers being said, as well as a burial in a Muslim tomb. Can you deny the fact that Uthman was buried in a Jewish cemetery and his pallbearers were stoned by his opponents (*al-Tabari, The History of Nations and Kings*, Qtd. *True Guidance* I. 1991 : 119) ?

Ali is the Real Gate

754. Was it not mentioned in the presence of Ayesha that the Prophet had appointed Ali as successor by will (*Buk* 5 : 736) ? Did not the Prophet say : I am from Ali and Ali is from me; I am the city of knowledge and Ali is its Gate (Bab) ?

Can you deny the fact that while Ali and the Prophet's closet kinsmen were preparing the body for burial, Abu Bakr, Umar and Abu Ubaydah from Muhammad's companions in the Quresh tribe, met with the leaders of the Medinans and agreed to elect the aging Abu Bakr as the successor or Califah, of the Prophet with the plea that Ali was still young ? The politics to become the Prophet's successor was the motive of Abu Bakr. Weren't Ali and his kinsmen dismayed but agreed for the sake of unity ?

There were numerous fights, instances of treachery, and heinous murders that took place throughout the history of the Muslims, according to the model behaviour their Prophet left for them to follow.

Is it not a fact that Ali Talib the fourth caliph, ruled 4 years and 7 months, and he spent his time fighting his opponents Ayesha, Talha and Zubair in "The Battle of the Camel," and finally with Mu'awiya in "The Battle of Siffin ?" At last he was killed by one of his opponents, Abd al- Rahman b. Milgam (*True Guidanc*e I : 1991 : 119) ?

49 - United We Fall

Once Prophet Muhammad prophesied : Verily it will happen to my people even as it did to the children of Israel. The children of Israel were divided into seventy-two sects and my people will be divided into seventy-three. Every one of those sects will go to Hell except one sect." The companions asked : "O Prophet, which is that ?" He said, "The religion which is professed by me and my companions" (*Tir* : 171).

Though the Prophet forecast the split of his religion but till his death he could not tell his followers on whom should the leadership of the new community fall, neither was there any indication in the Quranic text regarding the succession. Therefore just after the death of Muhammad in 632 the Muslim community splitted.

The sect who advocated the Prophet's successor should be chosen by the votes of the Muslims except from Negroes (Lammens, 1929 : 141) are called Sunnis (Traditionalists) and the other who proclaimed that Caliphate should be reserved for the Prophet's tribe, Quresh chosen by consensus are called Sheites (Legitimists). The Sheites being the relatives of the Prophets accepted as the successor, Ali ibm Abi Talib, the cousin and son-in-law of Muhamamd.

Abu Bakr, an early convert, was chosen as the first Caliph or the leader of the Sunni. They are more liberal, less militant. They donot believe in family dynasties such as the bloodline tracing to Ishmael. 90 percent of Muslims today are Sunni.

Compared to the Sunnis the Sheites are more militant, conservative and fundamentalist who also trace back to bloodlines of Ishmael. They believe strongly that Muhammad intended for Ali, his son-in-law to take over. Therefore Ali became the fourth Caliph and the first Imam.

The third Imams, Hussan and Hussein, sons of Ali and grandsons of Muhammad, were murdered in 680 when they refused to give their allegiance to the ruling Caliph. This martyrdom remained a blood symbol of the early Muslim's failure to follow their prophet's religion.

Most Sheites are "Twelvers", who believe Ali was followed by 11 other Imams, the last of whom, "hidden" since 4th Century, will return at the end of time to establish justice on earth. Members of the Ismaili sect believe that the line of imams has continued to the present day; their leader being Aga Khan.

Subsequently a group of Shites recognize only seven imams and are therefore called as "Seveners" or Ismails. It happened after the death of the sixth Imam (Leader) Jafar al-Sadiq, the Shia split into two major divisions-- one group supported his elder son Ismaili the other supported the younger son Musa al-Kazin known as Ithna *Ashariyya*.

The seveners considered Ismail the seventh and the last of the imams and they believed that the emanate continued in the line of Ismails's descendants.

As the eldest son of Safar al-Sadiq Ismail or their sect Ismailiyya spilted into two subject. The Nizari Ismailis and the other group followed another son, Mustali after whom they are known as Mustali Ismailis. There was a third or final group among the Shia, the *Zaydiyya*, who trace their origin to Zayd, one of the grandsons of Imam Husayn. Did all these not suffer persecution with the change of holding heretical beliefs ?

Here we are concerned about the sects who traditionally and philosophically broke away from mainstream Islam and formed their own sects perhaps due to an identity crisis which they might have felt within the confines of the institution.

Alfred Guillaume rightly remarked : From early day Islam split up into a large number of sect, most of which are now obsolete; and, as would be expected the modern Muslim knows no more about them than the average Christian knows about the early hersies of the Church. Here we shall take into account only the most important sects which either exist to this day or have left a permanent mark on Islam (1954 : 111).

But we have to separately deal with Sufism because it cannot be considered as another sect of Islam, rather it is an intruder and misleads the Muslims. Very few Sufis traced their way to the Quran, i.e., Oneness of God : "From God we are and to Him is our return" (2 : 156). It may be a fact that the sufis got inspiration from Muhammad's night journey (miraj) to the divine presence where he communed with god face to face (10 : 8). This incident helped the sufis to reach the Divine through speculation to have the way to the vision of God's face. Sufis like al-Ghazali, Ibn Sina, Jalal al-din Rumi, Ibn al Arabi all try to realise God experience through different stations like meditation, recollection and contemplation. They found streams of consciousness and points of contact amidst the hard core fundamentalist Quram and successfully led to convert people to Islam in Africa, the Indian subcontinent, Indonesia, Malaysia and southeast Asia (Bush, 1988 : 396).

Is not Sufism against Islam ?

Why do the real Muslims dislike Sufism? Because they give more importance to feeling and emotion and do not obey the law of Islam. Islam preaches : "He who knows God becomes silent, "but Sufis changed it, "He who knows God talks more." Many Muslims do not know that Sufism was Pre-Islamic and influenced by Gnostics, Manichaeans, Hermetics and Neo-Platonists" (Walker 1999 : 307).

Split begins at the Burial

755. Is not it a fact that the Prophet had designated no successor? After the death of the Prophet the first difference which arose in Islam was with regard to Califa. It was Ansar of Medina, who had given the Prophet refuge, but the Quresh wanted to elect one of their own men. When Abu Bakr heard of this he reminded them that the Califa must belong to one of the Quresh as told by Muhammad. Therefore, Muhammad's fathers-in-law, who were early converts as well as trusted Lieutenants elected Abu Bakr, who happened to be the father of the Prophet's favourite wife Ayesha.

Is not Islam a cult of Muhammadanism where Muhammad projected himself as the sole representative of Allah on earth?

Islam Divides

756. Is it not a fact that when Allah called for unity and order : "Hold fast all together, by the rope which He stretches out for you and be not divided among yourselves (3 : 103) the Muslims did not care for it, rather they divided themselves into eight sects in the name of eight schools? They were Hanafi, Shafe'i, Maleki, Hambali, Ithna, Ashari Shias, Zaidi, Ibazi and Zaheri. In former times each had a separate place for prayer.

The sect known as *Kharijit* (those who "left" or "withdrew") who called themselves *Ibadi,* resented with Caliph Ali and changed the concept of a Muslim by saying that merely professing the faith--- "there is no god but God; Muhammad is the Prophet of God---" does not make a person a Muslim unless he sincerely repents for the sin.

Do not the Kharijites maintain that anyone, even a Negro slave, could be elected as the head of the Muslim community if he possessed the necessary qualifications? Purity of life was the only test. They went on to assert that anyone guilty of grave sin was an unbeliever and an apostate, and therefore it was their duty to kill him. The character and religious standpoint of these people is best illustrated by their doctrine of ritual purity. Every Muslim had to perform the ceremonial washings before prayer. The Kharijites went much further and said that evil speaking, lying, and slander destroyed ritual purity and made men unfit for prayer.

Polytheism is the only Sin for Murji-ites

757. Did not the Murji-ites believe that the good Muslim should hold aloof from the wars provoked by Sheia and Khawarij? The name Murjiites means 'one who postpones' judgement until the last day when the secrets of all hearts shall be revealed. They did not look too closely at the sins of others : there was only one unforgivable sin, and that was polytheism. Do they not explicitly affirm that fornication and theft would not debar a believer in the unity of God from Paradise?

Sufis brought Tomb Worship to Islam

758. Is not it a fact that the relation between the exoteric and esoteric religious truth has been passed down from the Prophet through an unbroken chain of saints (Walis)? Did these saints not corrupt the Muslim society through miracle mongering, degeneration into jugglery, musical performances, adaptation of pre-Islamic and un-Islamic customs that include saint and tomb worship? Did not these saints start tomb worshipping as personal petitions because in the Namaz there is no scope for such petition to cure illness or other difficulties of life? Though Islam is strongly opposed to idol worship but worshipping tomb of the dead saints entered Islam through Sufis; from the back door and caused the faith immense harm. The annual *urs* or commemorative celebration which attracts thousands of devotees can be seen at Shaykh Muin al-Din Chishti at Ajmer. Who could stop these tomb worship which can save the confused Muslims?

After the crucifixion of al-Hallaj did not the Sufis change their expression and instead of declaring themselves as God they changed the statement that saints (awliya) are superior to the Prophets? Because in their experience when all duality and multiplicity disappear they are in the state of intoxication with God.

Did not a Persian Sufi named Abu Sayid (d. 1049) write : "Our holy work will not be accomplished until every mosque lies in ruins and faith and infidelity are one." He regarded religious observances as a bondage, the *sharia* as superfluous and the Kaaba as nothing but a stone house. He never performed the pilgrimage, saying that if he so desired the Kaaba would visit him and perform the circumambulation around his head. He encouraged his pupils to dance and sing, forbidding them to interrupt their dancing even when the muezzin made the call for prayer (Walker 1999 : 309-310).

Is it not a fact that Sufis are fanciful, sensuous, idealists and busy for nothing for which the Sufi orders suffered greatly in Turkey by Mustafa Kemal Ataturk in the 1920s and their endowments were confiscated by the government? Not only Turkey, the Wahhabis too oppose Sufism, condemning not only its mysticism but they saw in them the pagan elements.

Is Sufism Anti-Islamic ?

759. Does Islam support monasticism invented by the Christians to please God like the Sufis? Despite Muhammad's prohibitions, the Sufis prefer the monastic life, use music and musical instruments for writing Muslim poetry and live by begging? Does not a Sufi cult called Bishariya (bi-shar means outside the law) advocate that real idolatory is slavish adherence to the law and it is lifeless (Walker 1999 : 306)?

Does Islam support Sufism? In Islam nobody dares to declare or call himself equal to God. A person can at best be a son of God or a messenger of God, but not God himself. Jesus went one step ahead by saying : "Father and I are one. He who sees me sees the father." He was crucified. Muhammad went a step back and declared he was simply a messenger that too, he placed himself in the last row of messenger. He was saved. Al-Bistaami (d. 874) declared himself God and was saved because he lived in an outlying province of Baghdad whereas in 922 al-Hallaaj was crucified in Baghdad because he uttered "Anal'Haqq" "I am God".

Wahhabis : the Puritan Sect in Islam

760. In the middle of the eighteenth century Muhammad ibn Abd al-Wahhaab followed Ibn Hanbal and his followers called themselves Wahhabis, a sect from

Sunni, Muslim. Thanks to the Wahhabis who founded a great kingdom in Arabia with the help of Muhammad ibn Saud for they could protect the Holy cities Mecca and Medina from the hands of Ottoman empire, though that empire was a Muslim empire but not an empire of Arab Muslims.

Do not the Wahhabis think that they are the chosen people of Allah and therefore the Holy Quran was delivered in Arabic ?

The Wahhabi doctrine rejects modernity and accepts the literal interpretation of the Quran and thus makes it a pious duty for all Muslims to do *Jihad* against non-Muslims.

Are they not responsible for the creation of Pakistan ? Did not they attack the Shia centre of Karbala, looted the treasures and destroyed the tomb of Al- Husaya and killed everyone inside and declared Jihad against the Sikhs ?

Do they not believe and propagate that God is the only object of worship and whosoever worships any other deity deserves death ? Do they not reject intermediary between God and man, abominate the worship of saints and condemn prayers and sacrifices to them as idolatry; when they captured Mecca in 1806 they destroyed the tombs which others venerated ?

Did they not prohibit visit to any other holy place, praying of saintly persons, worshipping of the tomb of Muhammad, counting of the string of beads ? Do they ever accept consensus of opinions as the source of authority ? Don't they reject Sufism because they believe that all religions are true and even an atheist goes to Paradise ?

Do they not advocate for plain houses and simple clothes, laughter and music are forbidden and singing is effeminate, chess is forbidden because it might make the players forget the hour of prayer (Tritton, 1951 : 87-88) ?

Free the Holy Land from Saudi Control
761. Is it not a fact that the king of Saudi Arabia belonged to the sect of Wahabi Sunni who believed that the only true Islam is the Islam of sixth century ? For them all other Sunnis are inferior to them. Did not Col.Gaddafi demand that Mecca and Medina being the holy cities for the whole of the Muslim world should be freed from Saudi-Sunni-Wahabi control (Hussain 1989 : 6) ?

Elijah : the Prophet for the Black Muslims
762. Is it not a fact that after World War II the "Black Muslims" of America under the leadership of Elijah Muhammad claimed him to be an inspired Prophet ? Do the Black Muslims not hold that the white Muslims are the Devils who enslave all non-whites ?

Holy Trinity of Shia Ghulat Sect
763. Is it Islamic to think Muhammad, Ali and Husan as the Holy Trinity of Shia ? Does not the first represent revelation, Ali the interpreter of the Quran and Hussan stands for the redemption ?

Is not it a fact that the Shiite of the Ghulat sect believed in the holy trinity of God, Muhammad and Ali ? Can it be believable for us that they were in the beginning ?

According to them Muhammad who had not yet received God's revelation went to see the new born Ali, and the infant Ali spoke reciting from the Quran (23 : 1-10) where God says, "Successful are those believers who humble themselves in

224

their prayers..." And Muhammad responded by saying, "Surely the believers have become successful through you."

Muhammad instead claimed the prophethood for himself the Shabak, another such group, place the blame on the Angel Gabriel, who they claim to be the 'betrayer of the faithful one' because they believe that rather than delivering God's message to Ali as commanded, he delivered it to Muhammad instead (Sahab 2004 : 209-210).

Mukkallid Versus Ijtihadis

764. Is it not a fact that in the eleventh century, when Islam was at its height, the Fatemite Caliphs established the Al-Azhar University in Cairo for independent investigation of truth and higher research ? At the same time the Mukkallids (blind followers) in Baghdad established a parallel institution called the Nizamia University to promote narrow rigidities in Islam. The Nizamia University promoted Islamic fundamentalism and created internal conflicts between inter-sects which brought Tartars to invade Baghdad. Thus began Islam's declining phase and the conquest of India by Afghans and Turks was a part of it. Did not the see-saw between the Mukkallids and Iitihadis go on throughout the Mughal times until the Mukkallids won during Aurangzeb's regime and brought about the downfall of the Mughals and Islam Empire (Ghosh 2001 : 21-22) ?

Muslim Brotherhood prescribed Jihad

765. Will it be acceptable to agree with Hasan Al-Banna (d. 1049) the founder of *Muslim Brotherhood* in Egypt who writes (1928) in one of his tracts : "Allah has imposed Jihad as a religious duty on every Muslim, categorically and rigorously, from which there is neither evasion nor escape"; it is "prescribed" in the Quran in the same manner and in the same language as the injunction on fasting. Consequent abstention from, or evasion of, jihad is "one of the seven mortal sins" (*Six Tracts*, Kuwait n.d. 217-219, Qtd. Ansari, May 2002 : 8). If this is the prescription of Allah Muslims are bound to fight against non-Muslims and lose their freewill ?

Zaidi a Sect of Peace Loving People

766. Zaidi section of the Shia is closest to the Sunni Muslims. In place of the fifth Imam of the Twelvers, they acknowledge a certain Zaid, grandson of Husain. He perished while fighting in Iraq against the troops of Omayyad Caliph Hishtam (740). The manner of his death brought him into prominence and made him the founder of Zaidites. Does not this sect agree with the Khawarij in calling wicked Muslims unbelievers and since many Jews in Yemen do not carry arms it is more disgraceful for a Muslim to kill a Jew ? They are hostile to Sufism and the cult of the saints.

Ismailis End the Line of Imams

767. The Ismailis take their name from Isma'll (762) son of the sixth Imam of the Twelvers, Jafar. In this Ismail they end the line of visible Imams. Ja'far the sixth intended to appoint his eldest son Ismail as his successor but found that he was a drunkard and so passed him over in favour of another son; they also assert that Ismail died before his father. Some, however, refused to credit his death, affirmed that his father had appointed him Imam, and that the appointment once made could not be rescinded.

After the fall of the Fatimid dynasty Yemen became the centre of the Musta'li branch; from there it spread to India where a schism occurred, into the Sulaimanis, a small sect, and the Daudis or Bohoras.

Do they not believe that first came Prophets, then visible Imams, and then the hidden Immas; when the Imam is visible, his messengers are hidden, when he is concealed, his messengers are visible (Tritton 1951 : 78) ?

Quarmati who carried off the Black Stone
768. Is not it a fact that Hamdaan Qarmat terrorized Iraq, Syria and North Arabia and captured Mecca in 930 and carried off the Black Stone, which was returned in 950 at the command of the Fatimid Caliph (Tritton, 1951 : 79-80) ?

Nusairi believes Ali is Allah
769. The Nusairis cult carried their fanatical veneration for Ali and his line to extremes even to proclaim "Ali the equal or even superior to Muhammad." Do they not believe Ali, who is recognised outwardly as Imam, but inwardly as God (Tritton 1951 : 80-81) ?

Druze prophesied the Destruction of Mecca and Jerusalem
770. Does Druze, the sect of Ismaili, not ridicule on the pilgrimage to Mecca and believe that when Fatimid Caliph Hakim will reappear he will destroy Mecca as well as Jerusalem (Lammens 1929 : 167) ?

Baktashi : a Sect which follows Christianity
771. Is not it a fact that the sixteenth century cult Baktashi professed to be Sunni but in practice they are extreme Shias ? Like the Christians don't they like to believe in holy trinity of Allah, Muhammad and Ali and celebrate a sort of communion with bread, wine and cheese, and confess their sins to their chiefs like the Catholics ? Wine is not forbidden and their women are not veiled and they even believe in transmigration of souls (Tritton 1951 : 82-83) ?

Kizil-Bash : Christianization of Islam
772. Is it not fanciful to think of a sect called *Kizil- Bash* who think Ali is an incarnation of God. Did not they believe God is one in three persons; below Him are five archangels, twelve ministers, and forty saints ? In a service at night time the officiating priest sings prayers in honour of 'Ali, Jesus, Moses and David; and holds in his hand a willow wand which he dips in water; this water is then distributed among the homes. After confession of sins the priest imposes penance. The lights are put out and the congregation laments its sins. The lights are lit again and the priest pronounces the absolution and a communion service follows (Tritton, 1951 : 84) ?

Ahl-i-Haqq : a Sect who believed in Transmigration
773. Is it not a fact that the western Persia based sect called Ahl-i-Haqq is wrongly called, "Ali-ilaahi" though Ali is not the central figure ? Do they not believe in the transmigration of souls and in fact that man has to pass through one thousand and one incarnations in which he receives the reward of his actions ?

Do they not worship in the form of meetings where sacred texts are recited to music; dervishes excited to ecstasy and offerings, prepared food or animals, are an essential part of these meetings; the animals are killed, the bones buried, and the flesh divided among the assistants.

The religion is eclectic with doctrines of the extreme Shia as a foundation; they have twelve Imams but 'Ali is not the central figure (Tritton, 1951 : 83-84) ?

Hurufi Sect celebrates with Wine

774. The Hurufi sect was founded at the end of the fourteenth century by Fadlullah of Asterabad. He seems to have taken his ideas from the Ismailis. The world is eternal and always in circular motion; this movement is the cause of all change. If change goes in cycles; each begins with an Adam and ends with a judgement, then how was Muhammad the last of the prophets: the imams from 'Ali to Hasan Askari were the saints and the first of the divine series ? How God becomes flesh, and is it Islamic to celebrate in their communion with wine (Tritton 1951 : 84-85) ?

Khoja believes in Das Avatar

775. Though Khoja sect is India-based, it was founded in Zanzibar and central Asia and was led by the elected leader titled as Aga Khan. As their root is in India they believe Ali or the unrevealed imam as the Tenth Avatar like Vishnu. Even they sprinkle water to the dying body by reciting Das-Avatar verses. Being the Nizari branch of the Ismaailis do they not depend on Sunni judges for the performance of their marriages and unlike other Muslim sects they do not permit divorce without the consent of both parties even do not allow a second wife for a person (Tritton 1951 : 85-86) ?

Bohora : Worshipper of Ram ?

776. The trader group of Hindu converts following the Mustali division of the Ismailis and Sunni are called Bohora. Is it not a fact that they have their own mosques and cemeteries, observe only three prayers daily, and do not keep the special Friday prayer ? Do they not light illuminations on the Hindu festival of Diwali and begin new account books on that day; similarly the Memons of Cutch are Shia in name but they do not meet with Muslims, eat no flesh, revere the cow, are not circumcised, do not observe the five daily prayers nor the fast of Ramadan ? Their salutation is Ram, Ram they worship the Hindu deity and consider Imam Shah, the missionary who originally converted them about three hundred years ago, an incarnation of Brahma (Tritton 1951 : 86 : 87) ?

Baabi who inspired the Baha'is

777. Is it not a fact that Ali Muhammad of Shiraz announced that he is the Baab (door to the knowledge) who founded a new religion and made nineteen a sacred number, divided the year into nineteen months of nineteen days each ?

In his new religion marriage is obligatory at the age of eleven. Divorce is frowned on and there must be a delay of a year to permit of reconciliation. After a month the divorced parties can marry again to a maximum of nineteen times. A widower must marry again after ninety days. Silk garments and gold ornaments are allowed. Every year a fast of nineteen days between sunrise and sunset is enjoined on all believers between the ages of eleven and forty-two. Ablutions are recommended though not commanded and every village and town must have its public bath. Women are not veiled and men may talk freely with them though the conversation should not exceed twenty-eight words. The house in which the Baab was born, that in which he was imprisoned, and the dwellings of his prominent disciples are places of pilgrimage. Travelling by sea is forbidden except to merchants and pilgrims. The only communal prayer is at funerals but sermons are preached in the mosques. None may do violence to another. Fermented drinks are prohibited. Once every nineteen days a believer shall invite nineteen guests, even if it is only to a draught of water. Babi is the name usually given to this sect though they prefer to call themselves Bayaani (Tritton 1951 : 89-90).

Shia opposed Baab as another Prophet

778. Is not it a fact that several other sects arose out of the general Shia movement and one among them was born out of Messianic ideas by Ali Muhammad of Shiraz who declared himself as the Bab (The Gate) to good and was bitterly opposed by the Shia and was executed in 1850. Did not the two disciples of Bab Sobh-e Azal and Baha'ullah break away from Shia and take independent path ?

Islamic Brotherhood a myth

779. Is there any brotherhood among the Muslims who face the Kaaba in Mecca in prayer and believe a unitary monolithic system ? Does the Quran ever talk of Islamic brotherhood because Muslim by itself is a Millat or a Cult ? Can the Muslims accept *Bahais* and *Ahmadiyas* as Momins ?

Break away from Islam, Baha'i stands as a Religion

780. Is not the Baha'i an enigma which started out as a radical Islamic sect, but for all practical purposes it is a separate religion ? Does not the Bahai differ with the traditional Muslims that God sent another messenger after Muhammad and will continue to send future messengers ? F.D. Bluestone rightly remarked that the Bahai faith is to Islam what Mormanism is to traditional Christianity (April 1984 : 6).

Does the House of Justice do Justice to Women ?

781. After the execution of the Bab a disciple with the honorific name of Subh-i-ezel (dawn of eternity) became the head of the sect. A split soon took place and this man's half-brother Baha U llah (glory of God) was followed by the great majority. He claimed to be the man referred to by the Bab in the cryptic words, "He whom God will publicly confirm". His teaching was meant to change the Babi faith into a world religion.

Is not it a fact that no Islamic sect considers man and woman equal except the Bahai Faith ? The Bahai Faith speaks of man and woman as two wings of a bird which flies from the Local Spiritual Assembly, to the State Bahai Council from there to the National Spiritual Assembly. But when the bird reaches the Universal House of Justice one of its wings is cut off, *i.e.* the women are dropped ? So where does the equality stand ?

Ahmad the Prophet :
Break the Chain of the Last One

782. Is not it a fact that in India a Punjabi Muslim, Mirza Ghulam Ahmad (d. 1908) of Qadian proclaimed himself the Mahdi (expected One) and founded a group called Ahmadiyah ? By this does he not break the chain of the last Prophet and the chain is again opened for others to come in ?

Did not Ahmad of Qadian declare in Tableegh-e- Risalat, "I can run my mission neither in Makkah, nor in Medina, neither in Rome nor in Syria, neither in Iran, nor in Kabul", he intended to write but in India that too in British India (Vol. 6 : p. 69) ?

Split in Qadiyaan

783. Is it not a fact that when Ghulam Ahmad of Qadiyan died in 1908, the Ahmadiyah split in two groups ?

Was not the main body carried on the founder's claim to prophethood under Ahmad's son, Bashir-ud-Din, while the other, the Lahore group, claimed that Ghulam Ahmad was not a prophet, nor had he claimed to be one, but rather that he was a reformer or "renovator" (mujaddid) of Islam ?

Ahmadiyah's Jihad through Pen

784. Is it not a fact that in the later half of the 19th Century in Punjab, India, Mirza Ghulam Ahmad claimed himself to be a Messiah and Mahdi and showed different scriptures that his coming was prophesied in the Old and the New Testaments, Quran and Purans.

Can they change the concept of Jihad "by the sword" and replace with Jihad "of the pen" ?

Ahmadi : continues Prophethood

785. Is it not a fact that in 1880 Mirza Ghulaam Ahmad Khan of Qadian declared himself a *Mahdi* and later on Messiah asserting that his coming was foretold in the Old and the New Testament alongwith the Quran ? The verse, "O children of Israel ! Of a truth I am God's apostle to you to confirm the law which was given before me, and to announce an apostle to you that shall come after me whose name shall be *Ahmad*", refered not to Muhammad but to Ghulam Ahmad. He claimed that revelation identified him with Jesus, one of the proofs being his likeness in character to Jesus, but afterwards he claimed to be superior to him. Ghulam Ahmad did not pretend to be a prophet in his own right but only in and through Muhammad; he received messages from God but not revelation. Did he not prove that his mission was his power to foretell the deaths of his enemies; there was a suspicion that his followers had a hand in the fulfilment of these prophecies so the Government forbade him to exercise this power ?

Is it not a fact that on the death of Ghulam Ahmad authority was divided between his deputy and a committee but no friction followed because the deputy acted as the servant of the committee ? On his death a son of the founder was chosen as leader and, as he showed signs of being an autocrat, a split took place (Tritton 1951 : 160-161).

Be Aware of Different Schools of Islam

786. On what Islamic right did the Darul Uloom Deoband declare non-Muslims are not Kafir ? Has it transmitted to all 55 Muslim countries to give similar rights to their non-Muslim residents as most of the madrassas in South Asia are run by Deobandi curriculum ? Is it not a fact that all Islamic government deny religious rights to non -Muslims, while they claim all these rights as much more for the Muslims living in non- Muslim countries ?

Is it not a fact that all the four schools such as Hanifa, Shafiz, Malik and Hanbal agree that non-Muslims, either Jews or Christians, should not erect new places of their worship in a Muslim country ?

Did not Abu Hanifa school allow to build such places of worship of non-Muslim religions at a distance of at least a mile from the outer walls of a Muslim city ?

On what basis did they invent the concepts of *ijma* or consensus or *qiyas* or analogy from the Quran and Sunni to impose such restrictions on non-Muslim Jews and Christians ? If other non-Muslim nations imposed such rule on Muslims would they accept it ?

These Sunni sects forget that Muhammad was neither a Hanafi nor a Shafi, he was not a Maliki nor even a Humbali, but was a pure Muslim (41 : 33).

50 - To Be A True Muslim

The five articles of faith include all the main and sub-doctrines of Islam. All Muslims are bound to believe God, Angels, Scripture, Prophets, and the Last Day.

1. *God : Allah*. In the Holy Quran it is said : He is Allah : one;   He is Allah : the Eternal. He has neither begotten, nor was He begotten, and no one is equal to Him (112 : 1-4; Trans : Esposit, 1995 : 1 : 77). There is only one true God and his name is Allah. Allah is all-seeing, all-hearing and all-willing but never a personal God.

The Muslims believe : *Ia ilaha illa Allah*, "(There is) no god but God," This is the most important article in Muslim theology. Although Allah is said to be loving, this aspect of His nature is almost ignored, and his supreme attribute of justice is thought to overlook love (Anderson 1976 : 79).

The emphasis of the God of Islam is on judgement, not grace; on power, not mercy. He is the source of both good and evil and his will is supreme (McDowell, 1982 : 167).

2. *Angels*. Gabriel, the leading angel, appeared to Muhammad and was instrumental in delivering the revelations in the Quran to Muhammad.

All angels have different purposes, such as Gabriel, who is the messenger of inspiration. There are two recording angels-- one who records good deeds, the other bad deeds of man and woman.

3. *Scripture*. There are four inspired books for the Muslims. They are the *Torah* of Moses, the Psalms (Zabur) of David, the Gospel of Christ (Injil) and the Quran. The former three books have been corrupted therefore there is Quran.

4. *Prophets*. In Islam God has spoken through numerous prophets down through the ages. The six greatest prophets are : Adam, Noah, Ibrahim, Moses, Jesus and Muhammad. Muhammad is the last and greatest of all Allah's messengers.

5. *The Last Day*. It is the day of resurrection and the Day of Judgement, all men will then be raised, the books kept by the recording angels will be opened, and God as Judge will weigh each man's deeds in the balance. There who obey Allah and His messenger will go to paradise the rest will be tormented in hell. Alongwith this belief a true Muslim :

Eat or drink Standing
Should not eat food or drink water while standing except while drinking Zamzam water (*Mus* 3 : 5018, 5023).

Eat in Big Plate or Lefthand
Should not take meals in a big tray (*Buk* 7 : 298).
Should not eat with left hand (*Tir* 7 : 66).

Eat with Three Fingers or lick Fingers
Should not eat with three fingers (*Tir* 2 : 114).
Should not lick his fingers thrice after finishing the meal (*Tir* 1 : 113).

Use Table for Meals
Should not take meals on a table (*Tir* 5 : 121).

Should not Use Garlics and Onions
Allah does not listen to your prayer after eating garlics or onions because of bad smell (*Buk* 1 : 812-815; 7 : 362-363; *Mus* 1 : 1147).

Take Wine as Medicine
Muslims should not use wine as a medicine (*Mus* 3 : 4892). Not even homoepathic medicine which is made of pure wine. They should not have a business of selling wine or drinking wine (*Mus* 3 : 3836).

Keep Only Beard and no Moustaches
A muslim should cut the moustaches short and leave the beard (as it is) (*Buk* 7 : 781).

Right Hand is Right
Start doing things from the right side whenever possible, in performing ablution, putting on shoes and combing hair (*Buk* 7 : 292) and while in lavatory or passing urine do not hold your penis with right hand (*Buk* I : 155).

First to Step
While putting on your shoes, put on the right shoe first, and if you want to take them off, take off the left one first (*Buk* 7 : 747).

Change Ugly Names
They should change ugly names to good name as did Prophet Muhammad in case of Ayesha (disobedient) into Jamila (good and handsome); changed Barra into Zainab (*Mus* 3 : 5332, 5334). Even forbid to call the Ruler as the king of kings or *Shahinshah* (*Mus* 3 : 5338).

Say before Sex "In the Name of Allah"
Anyone of you on having sexual intercourse with your wife should say before starting "In the name of Allah" (*Buk* I : 143).

Playing Chess is Prohibited
Muhammad compares playing chess to someone who has dyed his hand with the flesh and blood of swine (*Mus* 4 : 5612).

No Swine or Idol Business
should not sell swine or idols (*Mus* 3 : 3840).

Do not accept or Pay Interest
Should not accept or pay interest (*Mus* 3 : 3880-3881).

Should not hoard foodstuff (*Mus* 3 : 3910-3912).

Do not Pray Aloud or Pass wind during Prayer ?
Neither say your prayer aloud, nor say it in a low tone (17: 110; *Buk* 6: 187).
Allah is offended by passing of wind through the anus because the natural smell of the human body escapes us (*Buk* 1 : 628; 9 : 86).

Keeping Dogs Forbidden
Angels will not enter a house if there is a dog. Therefore Muhammad ordered that the dogs should be killed (*Buk* 4 : 539). All dogs in Medina were killed

(*Mus* 3 : 3810) except the dog tamed for hunting, or watching of the herd of sheep or other domestic animals (*Mus* 3 : 3812).

Use no Saffron Clothes
One should not wear saffron clothes (*Mus* 3 : 5242; 5173, *Buk* 7 : 738), better to burn them (*Mus* 3 : 5175).

While Sleeping

Muslims should not put right hand under right cheek, while lying down for sleep. They must recite : "Rabb-e qini 'azabake yauma tab'atho 'abadak" (Lord ! Save me from torture on the Day of Resurrection" !) (*Tir* I : 198).

Oppress others but not Muslims
A Muslim should not oppress another Muslim, nor should hand him over to an oppressor" (Buk 3 : 622).

Why to Celebrate the Birthday of the Prophet ?

Is it not a fact that though, Islamic law has not declared the birthday of

Prophet Muhammad as Meelad-un-Nabee, nor has it established any customary

practice for its celebration the Muslims still celebrate it knowing well that he was

not a prophet since birth but an orphan ?

Apendix

Appendix 1

DETAILS OF SURA and VERSES

Traditional Sura Nos.	Name of Sura	No. of Verses	Place of Revelation	Chronological Order
1.	Fatehah	7	Mecca	5
2.	Al-Baqarah	286	Madina	87
3.	Al-Imran	200	Madina	89
4.	Al-Nisa	176	Madina	92
5.	Al-Maidah	120	Madina	112
6.	Al-Anam	165	Mecca	55
7.	Al-A'Raf	206	Mecca	39
8.	Al-Anfal	75	Madina	88
9.	Al-Taubah	129	Madina	113
10.	Yunus	109	Mecca	51
11.	Hud	123	Mecca	52
12.	Yousuf	111	Mecca	53
13.	Al-Ra'd	43	Mecca	96
14.	Ibrahim	52	Mecca	72
15.	Al-Hijr	99	Mecca	54
16.	Al-Nahl	128	Mecca	70
17.	Bani Israil	111	Mecca	50
18.	Al-Kahf	110	Mecca	69
19.	Maryam	98	Mecca	44
20.	Ta Ha	135	Mecca	45
21.	Al-Anbiya	112	Mecca	73
22.	Al-Hajj	78	Madina	103
23.	Al-Muminun	118	Mecca	74
24.	Al-Nur	64	Madina	102
25.	Al-Farqan	77	Mecca	42
26.	Ash-Shuara	226	Mecca	47
27.	Al-Naml	93	Mecca	48
28.	Al-Qasas	88	Mecca	49
29.	Al-Ankabut	69	Mecca	85
30.	Al-Rum	60	Mecca	84
31.	Luqman	34	Mecca	57
32.	As-Sajdah	30	Mecca	75
33.	Al-Ahzab	73	Madina	90
34.	Al-Saba	54	Mecca	58
35.	Al-Fatir	45	Mecca	43
36.	Ya'sin	83	Mecca	41

233

37.	As-Saffat	182	Mecca	56
38.	Sad	88	Mecca	38
39.	Az-Zumar	75	Mecca	59
40.	Al-Mumin	85	Mecca	60
41.	Hamim Sajdah	54	Mecca	61
42.	Ash-Shura	53	Mecca	62
43.	Al-Zukhruf	89	Mecca	63
44.	Al-Dukhan	59	Mecca	64
45.	Al-Jathiyah	37	Mecca	65
46.	Al-Ahqaf	35	Mecca	66
47.	Muhammad	38	Madina	95
48.	Al-Fath	29	Madina	111
49.	Al-Hujurat	18	Madina	106
50.	Q'af	45	Mecca	34
51.	Al-Dhariyat	60	Mecca	67
52.	Al-Tur	49	Mecca	76
53.	Al-Najm	62	Mecca	23
54.	Al-Qamr	55	Mecca	37
55.	Ar-Rahman	78	Mecca	97
56.	Al-Waqiah	96	Mecca	46
57.	Al-Hadid	29	Madina	94
58.	Al-Mujadila	22	Madina	105
59.	Al-Hashr	24	Madina	101
60.	Al-Mumtahana	13	Madina	91
61.	As-Saff	14	Madina	109
62.	Al-Jumah	11	Madina	110
63.	Al-Munafiqun	11	Madina	104
64.	Al-Taghabun	18	Madina	99
65.	Al-Talaq	12	Madina	99
66.	Al-Tahrim	12	Madina	107
67.	Al-Mulk	30	Mecca	77
68.	Al-Qalam	52	Mecca	2
69.	Al-Haqqah	52	Mecca	78
70.	Al-Maarij	44	Mecca	79
71.	Noah	28	Mecca	71
72.	Al-J'nn	28	Mecca	40
73.	Al-Muzammil	20	Mecca	3
74.	Al-Mudashir	56	Mecca	4
75.	Al-Qiyamah	40	Mecca	31
76.	Al-Dahr	31	Mecca	98
77.	Al-Mursalat	50	Mecca	33
78.	Al-Naba	40	Mecca	80
79.	Al-Naziat	46	Mecca	81
80.	Abasa	42	Mecca	24
81.	Al-Takwir	29	Mecca	7
82.	Al-Infitar	19	Mecca	82
83.	Al-Tatfif	36	Mecca	86
84.	Al-Inshiqaq	25	Mecca	83

85.	Al-Buruj	22	Mecca	27
86.	Al-Tariq	17	Mecca	36
87.	Al-A'la	19	Mecca	8
88.	Al-Ghashiya	26	Mecca	68
89.	Al-Fajr	30	Mecca	10
90.	Al-Balad	20	Mecca	35
91.	Ash-Shams	15	Mecca	26
92.	Al-Leyl	21	Mecca	9
93.	Al-Duha	11	Mecca	11
94.	Al-Inshira	8	Mecca	12
95.	Al-T'in	8	Mecca	28
96.	Al-Alaq	19	Mecca	1
97.	Al-Qadr	5	Mecca	25
98.	Al-Beyinnah	8	Madina	100
99.	Al-Zilzal	8	Mecca	93
100.	Al-Aadiyat	11	Mecca	14
101.	Al-Qariah	11	Mecca	30
102.	Al-Takatur	8	Mecca	16
103.	Al-Asr	3	Mecca	13
104.	Al-Humazah	9	Mecca	32
105.	Al-Fil	5	Mecca	19
106.	Al-Qureysh	4	Mecca	29
107.	Alma'un	7	Mecca	17
108.	Al-Kauthar	3	Mecca	15
109.	Al-Kafirun	6	Mecca	18
110.	Al-Nasr	3	Madina	114
111.	Al-Lahab	5	Mecca	6
112.	Al-Iklas	4	Mecca	22
113.	Al-Falaq	5	Mecca	20
114	Al-Nas	6	Mecca	21

Appendix 2

CHRONOLOGY OF ISLAM AT A GLANCE

570 AD Prophet's birth. In the spring season Monday is the agreed day. Ist year of *Am-ul-Feel*. 50 days after the event of the elephant, corresponding to 22nd April 570 AD, Ist Jaith 628 Bikrami before sunrise, popularly known to be 12 Rabi I.

Nursing. At the age of 4 months.

577 Death of Prophet's mother. At the age of 6 years Prophet's mother Aminah b. Wahb died. His father had died soon after Muhammad's birth.

578 Death of his grandfather. At the age of 8 years 2 months 10 days. First journey to Syria with Hazrat Abu Talib. At the age of 12 years 2 months.

Participation in the battle of Fajjar First time. At the age of 15 or thereabout.

Participation in the battle of Fajjar Second time. Sometime later, no date given.

585 Participation in *Hilful Fazul*, a reformist movement. At the age of 16.

Second journey to Syria as a trader. At the age of 23 or 24.

596 Marriage with Hazrat Khadija, a wealthy merchant. At the age of 25 years 2 months.

Unseen secrets reveal themselves. Seven years before Prophethood at the age of 33.

Arbitration. At the age of 35.

610 Prophethood. At the **age of 40** years 11 days, 9 Rabi I, corresponding to 12 February, 610 AD. Monday. "The Night of Destiny." Muhammad receives his **first revelation from Angel Gabriel**. Khadija becomes his first convert.

Fajr and Asr Prayers, Prescribed 2 Rakats each. 9 Rabi I, on the day of Prophethood.

Beginning of revelation of the *Quran.* 18 Ramazan Ist year of Prophethood Friday, at night.

Beginning of secret preaching. House of Arqam Makhzoomi was made centre of movement.

First public announcement of Prophethood. At the end of 3rd year of Prophethood.

First wave of opposition, ridicule, propaganda and mild oppression. 3rd to 5th year of Prophethood.

Second wave of intense opposition, oppression. 5th to 7th year of Prophethood.

Migration to Abyssinia. Rajab, 5th year of Prophethood.

Hazrat Hamza and Hazrat Umar Embraced Islam. 6th year of Prophethood.

Prophet's internment at Shi'b Abi Talib with the family of Hashim. Ist Moharram, 7th year of Prophethood.

End of internment and boycott. End of 9th year of Prophethood.

Year of sorrow.   Death of Hazrat Abu Talib and Hazrat Khadija 10th year of Prophethood.

Visit to Taif. Jumada II, 10th year of Prophethood.

Ascension (Meraj). 27th Rajab, 10th year of Prophethood. Monday.

Daily prayers five times a day Prescribed. 27th Rajab, 10th year of Prophethood, Monday.

Beginning of Islam in Medina. Zilhijja, 10th year of Prophethood.

Deputation of Medina Six people accepted Islam *Zilhijja*, 12th year of Prophethood.

613 First group of converts face persecution by the Quraysh, the major tribe of Mecca, which fears to lose its cultural and commercial dominance.

615 Exodus of some early covers to Ethiopia because of persecution by Meccans. Ascent of Muhammad to the seventh heaven.

617 Conversion of 'Umar ibn al-Khattab.

619 Death of Khadija and later Abu Talib, his uncle and protector.

620 Prophet goes to Ta'if to win converts and find protection; does not succeed. Night journey in which Muhammad is taken from Mecca to Jerusalem and from there to heaven.

621 First Aqabah covenant with 12 men from the Khazraj and Auz   tribes   who convert to Islam Zilhijja, 12th year of Prophethood.

622 Second pledge of Aqaba with 75 persons Zilhijja, 13th year of Prophethood. June : Muslim converts in Yathrib (later Madinat al-Nabi, "City of the Prophet") promise loyalty and invite Muhammad to Yathrib.

Migration. July : Muhammad flees to Yathrib. First of Muharram begins "Year One" of the Islamic lunar calendar.

(a) From Makkah to the cave of Tahur Safar 27, 13th year of Prophethood, Prophet's age was 53 years.

622 (b) Departure from Tahur Ist Rabi I, 13th year of Prophethood, Monday, 16th September.

622 (c) Arrival at Quba 8th Rabi I, 14th year of Prophethood, Monday, 23rd September.

622 (d) Entry into Medina. 14th year of Prophethood, Friday. Foundation   of Masjid-i-Nabvi laid Rabi I, I H.

Addition of obligatory prayers Rabi II, I H.

Brotherhood between Migrants and Ansars First quarter, I H.

Establishment of Islamic State and constitutional agreement of Medina Middle of I H.

623   Muhammad concludes marriage with 'Ayesha, daughter of Abu Bakr. Constitution of Madina establishes coexistence of Muslim and Jewish communities, *Umma.* Fatima, daughter of Muhammad marries ' Ali ibn Abi Talib, cousin of Muhammad. Shawwal, AH.

623 Islam of two elite, Abudullah ibn Salam, formerly Jew and Abu Qasi Sarha bin Abi Anas, former Christian monk.

Jihad ordered 12 Safar 2 H., I year 2 months and 10 days after migration.

First military action Ghazwa Wadda Safar 2 H.

Pacts with outside clans Bani Damra, people of Bowat and Banu Madlaj Safar to Jumada II, 2 H.

Robbery of Kurz bin Jabir Fahri Rabi I, 2 H.

Nakhla episode, first frontier clash of Islamic Party End of Rajab, 2 H of Islamic party.

Salman Farsi accepts Islam 2 H.

Beginning of Azan 2 H.

Zakat prescribed 2 H.

Change of Qibla 15th Shaban, 2 H Monday.

Ramazan Fast prescribed Ist Ramazan, 2 H, Wednesday.

Congregational prayer of Eidul Fitr, Fitra ordered Ist Shawwal, 2 H.

624   Battle of Badr in which Muslims defeat a superior   Ramazan, 2H. Wednesday (March) Meccan force. Jewish tribe, Banu Qaynuqa, accused of collaborating with Quraysh, expelled from Medina. The Month of Ramadhan proclaimed as the period of fasting. Mecca, rather than Jerusalem, designated as the qiblah, direction of prayer.

8 Ramazan-2 H. Wednesday (March)

Marriage of Hazrat Ali and Hazrat Fatima After the battle of Badr, 2 H.

Siege of Banu Qainuqa. Middle of Shawwal to beginning of Ziq'ada, 2 H.

Prophets; marriage with Hazrat Hafsa, daughter of Hazrat Umar, 3 H.

Marriage of Hazrat Usman with Hazrat Umme Kulsum, daughter of the Prophet, 3 H.

238

First Order of prohibition of wine 3 H.

End of Ka'ab bin Ashraf 3 H.

Birth of Hazrat Hasan 15 Ramazan, 3 H.

625 :   Battle of Uhud in which Muslim forces were defeated by Meccans, who do not follow up on their victory. Jewish tribe, Banu Nadir, accused of collaboration with enemy and expelled from Medina. hawwal, 3 H. Saturday. Shawwal, 3 H. After Friday prayer (March). Battle Pursuit of Abu Sufian's Army up to Hamra-ul-Asad.

First order of prohibition of usury. Soon after battle of Uhud.

Injunction about orphans. Soon after battle of Uhud.

Detailed laws of inheritance issued Soon after battle of Uhud.

Injunctions about marriage, rights of wives, prohibition of marriage with idolaters 3 H .

Prophet's marriage with Ummul Masakin Zainab, daughter of Khozaima, End of 3 H.

Episode of Raji'. Murder of 10 members of missionary deputation. Safar, 4 H.

Ghazwa Banu Nodair Rabi I, 4 H.

Death of Hazrat Zainab, daughter of Khozaima Rabi I, 4 H.Order of Hijab I Ziq'ada, 4 H. Friday.

Final order of prohibition of wine, 4 H.

Second Ghazwa of Badr Ziq'ada, 4 H.

Ghazwa Dumatul Jandal Rabi I, 5 H.

Ghazwa Banu Al-Mustalaq 3 Shaban, 5 H.

Injunctions for Tayammum on the way to Ghazwa Banu Mustalaq.

Prophet's marriage with Hazrat Jowairia Shaban, 5 H.

Episode ififk Shaban, 5 H.

Enforcement of Penal Laws against fornication, slander etc. 5 H.

Ghazwa Ahzab Shawwal or Ziq'ada, 5 H.

Arrival of Daus deputation to Medina 5 H.

Battle of the Ditch, Meccans fail to conquer Medina, which is protected by a ditch (kandaq). Jewish tribe, Banu Qurayza, accused of collaborating with the enemy and destroyed. Zilhijja, 5 H.

Prophet's marriage with Zainab, daughter of Jahsh, 5 H.

Islam of Thamama bin Usal, chief of Najd, 6 H.

Treaty of Hudaibiya Ziq'ada, 6 H.

Return to Medina from Hudaibiya Zilhijja, 6 H.

Khalid bin Walid and Amr bin Aas embraced Islam Zilhijja, 6 H.

Beginning of International call- letters to rulers Ist Moharram, 7 H. Wednesday.

Ghazwa Khyber. Moharram, 7 H.

Prophet's marriage with Hazrat Safia   Moharram, 7 H.

Establishment of independent Muslim camp at Saiful Bahr, 7 H.

Establishment of independent Muslim camp at Saiful Bahr, 7 H.

Raid by Saif-ul- Bahr on Quraish Caravan Safar, 7 H.

Postponed Umra performed Ziq'ada, 7 H.

Detailed injuctions about marriage and divorce, 7 H.
Marriage of the Prophet with Hazrat Maimuna at Mecca, 7 H.

Islam of Jibila Ghassani, 7 H.

Ghazwa Mutah Jumada I, 8 H.

Violation of Hudaibiyapact by non-Muslims. Rajab, 8 H.

Ghazwa of the conquest of Mecca, art from Madina, 10 Ramazan, 8 H Wednesday.

Victorious entry into Mecca. 20th Ramazan, 8 H.

Expedition of Hazrat Khalid to demolish the temple of Uzza at Nakhla most probably 25 Ramazan, 8 H.

Expedition of Amr ibnul Aas to   demolish   the   temple   of Swa's Ramazan, 8 H.

Expedition of Sa'ad Ashhali to demolish the temple of Manat, 8 H.

Stay in Mecca Up to 9 Shawwal.

Ghazwa Hunain Shawwal, 8 H.

Siege of Taif   End of Shawwal to beginning of Ziq 'ada, 8 H. About 18 or 20 days.

Distribution of booty at Ji'rana, and *Umra.* Ziq 'ada, 8 H.

Final order of prohibition of usury, 8 H.

Arrival of Suda deputation at Medina, 8 H.

Death of Hazrat Zainab, daughter of the Prophet,   8 H.

Death of Ibrahim, the Prophets' son,   8 H.

Organization of Zakat Beginning of Moharram, 9 H.

Ghazwa of Tabuk. Start of the Poor Contingent Rajab, 9 H.

Order about Jizia. At the time of Tabuk.

Zerar Mosque set on fire On return from Tabuk.

Islam of Ukaidir, Chief of Dumatul Jandal, 9 H.

Apology by Ka'ab ibn Zuhair and his acceptance of Islam, 9 H.

Some deputations which came to Medina :

Deputation of Azra Safar, 9 H.

Deputation of Bahy Rabi I. 9 H.

Deputation of Khaulan Shaban, 9 H.

Deputation of Thaqif , 9 H.

Haj prescribed, First Haj under Hazrat Abu Bakr   9 ilhijja, 9 H.

Proclamation of annulment of pacts of unlimited period 10 Rabi II, 10 H.

Deputation of Maharib, 10 H.

Deputation of Mahamid, 10 H.

Deputation of Khaulan   Shaban. 10 H.

Deputation of Naisan Ramazan, 10 H.

Deputation of Bani. Haris bin Kaa'ab Shawwal, 10 H.

Deputation of Salaman Shawwal, 10 H.

Twenty days' retirement of the Prophet in the last Ramazan Ramazan, 10 H.

Musailima the liar's correspondance with the Prophet , 10 H.

The Last Haj : Start from Madina 26, Ziq 'ada, 10 H. Saturday between Zohar and Ast.

Stay at Zulhalifa Night between Saturday and Sunday.

Putting on Ihram Sunday at the time of Zohar prayers.

Arrival and stay at Zittowa   Night of Sunday 4 Zilhijja, 10 H.

Start from Zittowa to Mecca 5 Zilhijja, 10 H after early morning prayer.

Entry into sacred Mosque   5 Zilhijja 10 H at noon.

Stay outside Mecca Up to 8 Zilhijja, 10 H.

Start for Mina 8 ZilhijjaThrusday noon.

Start from Mina to Arafah 9 Zilhijja, 10 H. Friday after Sunrise.

Haj Address 9 Zilhijja, 10 H. Friday after noon.

Stop at Arafah 9 Zilhijja, 10 H. After Zohar and Asr prayers Friday.

From Muzdalifa to Mash'ar-i-Haram   10 Zilhijja, 10 H. Saturday after morning prayer.

From Masha'ar-i-Haram to mina Throwing of pebbles 10 Zilhijja, 10 H. After sunrise till noon.

Address at Mina Sacrifice performed   10 Zilhijja, 10 H. noon After address.

Start from Mina to Mecca 10 Zilhijja, 10 H.

Return from Mina to Mecca 10 Zilhijja, 10 H. evening.

Second address at Min 11 Zilhijja, 10 H.

Start from Mina to Mahsab or Abtah 13 Zilhijja, 10 H. Tuesday.

Return from Mecca Night between 13th and 14th Zilhijja, 10 H.Deputation of Nakh 'a Middle of Moharram, 11 H.

Order for start of Usama's Army 26 Safar, II H.

Beginning of the Prophet's fatal disease End of Safar, 11.

Period of seriousness of disease. Stay in Hazrat Ayesha's room 7 days upto the time of passing away.

Last congregational prayer at the mosque and last address 5 days before passing away, Thursday, Zohar prayer.

Passing away "Farewell Pilgrimage June 8th Muhammad dies 12 Rabi 1, 11 H, Monday forenoon. Abu Bakr became successor of Muhammad (632 AD) Fatimah Dies.

Burial in Hazrat Ayesha's room Night between 13th and 14th Rabi I, 11 H Tuesday.

Wars of Apostasy (Ridda). Khalid b. al-Walid defeats Musaylamah; Hira. Ghassanids defeated at Marj Rahit.

634-644 Muslim forces defeat Byzantine armyat Ajnadayn, occupy parts of Palestine. August : Abu Bakr dies, Umar b. Al-Khattab chosen as his successor.

335 Jews from Khaybar and Christians from Najran forced to settle in Syria. Arabian Peninsula unified under Islam. Khalid ibn Walid defeats Byzantines in Marj al-Suffar near Damascus.

636 Battle of Yarmuk expells Byzantines from Syria; Muslims established in Damascus.

637 Sassanids defeated in the Battle of Qadisiyya.

638   Jerusalem captured.

638 First raid of 'Amr b. al-'As into Egypt.

640 Garrison Towns (amsar) of Kufa and Basra founded.

641 'Amr ibn al-'As captures Babylon. Foundation of Fustat.

642 Sassanids defeated at Nihavand and Arabs rule Mesopotamia and parts of Persia. Muslims capture Alexandria first time.

644-656	Caliph Umar assassinated. Uthman b. 'Affan elected as Caliph.
646	Alexandria retaken by Muslims; under permanent control of Muslims.
649	Mu'awiya, governor of Syria, takes Cyprus.
650	Quran edited in definitive version.
651	Eastern Persia occupied. Caliph 'Umar loses the ring of the Prophet; end of six good years of his rule.
653	Final version of Quran compiled.
655	Battle of the Masts. Arabs defeat Byzantine fleet.
656-66	'Uthman assassinated, accused of nepotism. 'Ali ibn Abi Talib is proclaimed Caliph. Talha, Zubayr, and 'A' ishah revolt, fight 'Ali in Battle of the Camel. 'A' isha on camelback views the defeat.
657	Mu'awiyah challenges 'Ali, meets him in Battle of Siffin. Ali accepts arbitration and loses some of his followers, Kharijites, who rejected arbitration. Kharijites develop into a puritanical sect which exists to this day.
658	Caliph Ali's forces defeat Kharijites at Nahrawan.
659	Adhruh Arbitration rejects claims of both 'Ali and Mu 'awiyah.
660	Mu'awiyah proclaimed Caliph in Syria, Egypt, and Hijaz. 'Ali recognized as Caliph in Iraq and Iran.
661-750	'Ali assassinated in Kufa by a Kharijite. Mu'awiyah proclaimed first 'Umayyad Caliph Husayn proclaimed Caliph, cades title of Mu'awiyah.
670	Foundation of Qayrawan. 'Uqba ibn Nafi' conquers northwest Africa.
680	'Ali's son Husayan is killed in the battle of Karbala near Kufa. Partisans of 'Ali, shiat 'Ali', eventually develop into a rival sect, counting the descendants of 'Ali as rightful successors of Muhammad. Shi'ites commemorate the 10th of Muharram (Islamic month) as the martyrdom of Husayn.' (October10 & 10th Muharram).
683	Reign of Caliph Mu'awiyah II (683-684). Medina sacked by 'Umayyads'.
683-692	'Abd Allah ibn al-zubayr proclaims himself Caliph at Mecca.
684	Reign of Caliph Marwan. Battle of Marj Rohit and defeat of the Qays.
691	Dome of the Rock built in Jerusalem. Ibn al-Zubayr killed in battle.
692	Hajjaj occupies Mecca.
694	Hajjaj becomes governor of Iraq.
751	Battle on the Talas; Arabs defeat Chinese in Central Asia, capture paper makers; begin to manufacture paper.
762	Baghdad founded as capital of the Abbasid Caliphate. 'Alid rebellions. Death of Isma'il; he becomes imam of the Isma'ili (or Sevener) shi'ites.

767 Death of Abu Hanifa, founder of Hanifite school.

785-786 Musa al-Hadi begins his short reign Great mosque of Cordoba erected. Muqanna commits suicide.

773 Death of Malik ibn-Anas, founder of Malikite School.

813-833 Al-Amin assassinated and Ma'mun begins his Caliphate (813-833AD) adopts Mu' tazilite school (827 AD) and founds a university in Baghadad, the Bayt al-Hikma (house of wisdom) (830 AD)

833-842 Al-Mu'tasim assumes Caliphate Mu 'tazilite "rationalist" school gains ascendancy.

837 Sect of Badak destroyed.

847-886 Mutawakkil becomes Caliph Mu'tazilite school abandoned. 855 Death of Ahmad Ibn Hanbal, founder of Hanbalite school.

861 Mutawakkil assassinated. Caliphate of Muntasir begins.

869-870 Zanj Rebellion of black slaves. Muhtadi becomes Caliph Ali Ibn Muhammad found kingdom of black slaves.

873-940 Eleventh shi 'ite imam dies. Disappearance of the 12th Shia Imam and beginning of "Lesser Occultation" followed by the "Greater Occupation" after 940 AD. until the coming of the Mahdi.

912-961 Qarmatians take Black Stone from Kaaba. Abd al-Rahman II assumes title of Caliph in Spain.

951 The Imam dies. Qarmatians return Black Stone to Mecca.

953-975 Mu 'izz becomes Fatimid Caliph.

969 Fatimids conquer Egypt. Foundation of Cairo.

973 Fatimids found al-Azhar mosque, the first Muslim university.   1099 Crusaders concur Jerusalem.

1111 Al-Ghazali dies.

1174 Saladin captures Damascus and Syria. Ayyubid Dynasty founded. (1174 AD)

1187 Salah al-Din (Saladin) defeats Crusaders at Battle of Hattin, captures Jerusalem.

1203 Chingiz Khan (Timuchin) founds Mongol empire.

1258 Mongols Sack Bag'dad, end Abbasid Caliphate at Baghdad.

1273 Jalal al-Din Rumi dies.

1324-1922 Orkhan founds Ottoman empire.

1453 Ottomans capture Constantinople.

1492 Fall of Granada, the last Muslim kingdom in Spain.

1526-1858 Babur captures Samarkand, becomes founder of Mughal dynasty.

1517	Ottomans conquer Egypt.
1521	Ottomans capture Belgrade.
1529	Ottomans besiege Vienna.
1538	Ottomans annex Hungary, capture Baghdad.
1745	Emergence of the Wahhabi (Unitarian) movement.
1798-1801	Napoleon invades Egypt.
1802-1804	Wahhabis capture Mecca and Medina.
1812	Ibrahim, son of Muhammad ' Ali, takes Mecca and Medina.
1818	Ibrahim defeats Wahhabis.
1828	Parts of Greece gain independence.
1850	Execution of the Bab.
1869	Suez Canal opens.
1874	Aligarh school (later university) found by Sir Sayyid Ahmad Khan.
1876	Abdul Hamid becomes sultan/ Caliph of the Ottoman empire.
1881	French occupy Tunisia. Agha Khan I died.
1901	Wahhibi forces take Riyadh. The French invade Morocco. 1908 Young Turk revolt.
1917	November : Balfour Declaration promises Jewish- "Homeland" in Palestine.
1921	Sons of Husayn, Sharif of Mecca, become kings. 'Abd Allah in Transjordan, Faysal in Iraq.
1992	Mustafa Kemal abolishes the sultanate.
1923	Turks defeat Greeks, sign Treaty of Lausanne which repeals Treaty of Sevres.
1924	Turks abolish the Caliphate.
1928	Hasan al-Banna founds Muslim Brotherhood. Assassinated in 1949 AD.
1938	Sir Muhammad Iqbal dies.
1973	Elijah Muhammad dies.
1978	Imam Musa Sadr, leader of Twelver Shi'ites disappears on a trip to Libya.
1995	Taliban capture Herat (Sept 5).
1997	Taliban take Kabul and two years later control most of Afghanistan (Sept. 26).
1996	Taliban issue a decree, prohibiting dolls for children and all photographic images of humans and animals (Oct. 6).

1998	Roman Catholics and Orthodox Christian closed their churches in protest to the Israeli decision to permit building a mosque next to the Church of the Annunciation in Nazareth. (Nov. 4).
1998	The United Nations imposed sanctions of Afghanistan for its refusal to surrender Osama bin Ladin(Nov 14).
2000	Mulla Muhammad Umar of Afghanistan issued a decree making conversion from Islam to Christianity a capital crime(Jan. 2).
2000	Mulla Muhammad Umar called for the destruction of all statues as they were a threat to Islam (Feb. 26).
	Destruction of the giant Buddha statues begins (Mar. 6).
	A decree of Mulla Umar demands that Hindus wear a yellow mark on their clothing and homes and prohibits them from wearing a turban (May 21).
	A wave of bombings in churches across predominantly Muslim Indonesia in an organised attack against the country's Christians. At least 15 people were killed and 96 injured (Dec. 24).
2001	Terrorist attack on World Trade Center in New York; kills 2973 people (Sept. 9).
	Suicide bombers, believed to be members of Osama bin Ladin's al - Qaida organization, crash commercial aircrafts into the World Tade Center and the Pentagon (Sept. 11).
2002	Two terrorists raided the Akshardhan temple in Ahmedabad killing 30 people and injuring many more (Sept. 25).
2003	Suicide bombings of United States expatriate housing compounds in Saudi Arabia killed 26 and injured 160 in Riyadh compound Bombings (May 26).
2004	191 people were killed and over 600 injured when 10 bombs detonated in Madrid on the train line (Mar. 11).
2005	Multiple bomb blasts hit markets in Delhi killing 61 people and injuring 200 (Oct. 29).
2006	A series of explosions rock commuter trains in Mumbai killing 209 and wounding 714 people (July 11).
2007	Twin suicide bombings in Karachi near a truck carrying former Prime minister Benazir Bhutto killed 136 and injured 387 people (Oct. 18).
2008	Armed terrorists opened fire at eight different sites in Mumbai in a coordinated attack where 173 were killed and 327 people were injured (Nov. 26-29).
2009	A car bomb is detonated in Peshawar killing 110 people and injuring 200 people (Oct. 28).
2010	A bomb exploded at the German Bakery in Pune killing 16 and injuring 60 (Feb. 13).

2011   Three bombs exploded in the centre of Mumbai killing 26 people and injuring more than 130 people (July 13).

2011   Osama bin Laden, the founder of the militant Islamist organization Al-Qaeda was killed (May 2).

2012   In possibly an Islamic coordinated attack in New Delhi, the wife of an Israeli diplomat was wounded when a bomb exploded in her car while she was on her way to work.

Appendix 3

WOMEN IN THE LIFE OF PROPHET MUHAMMAD

Prophet Muhammad had the capacity to maintain 11 wives, 2 concubines, divorced 7 wives and 7 more women that may or may not have married. There were four categories of women in the life of the Prophet as follow :

Married :

A.*Khadijeh* : Daughter of Khuwailid (Mu 4 : 5971, p. 1297). She married Muhammad in the year 595 when she was 40 and he was 25. They were together for 24 years. 10 years of it after Muhammad declared himself a messenger of Allah. It is strange but true that during these 10 years Allah never permitted Muhammad to marry any other women.

The Prophet had six children by her--- two sons. Oasim and Abdullah and four daughters, Zainab, Raqaiyya, Umm-u Kulsoom and Fatima, all born prior to the contentment of prophethood. Of these both the sons died in chilhood. Khadijah died in Mecca in the 10th year of the Prophethood. Muhammad adopted a son, named Zaid. Khadijah died three years before Ayesha married Muhammad (*Buk* 5 : 164-165, 5 : 168).

2) *Soodeh,* daughter of Hamzeh, they married in the year 620 when she was 30 years old and he was 50. This was second marriage for both of them. They both had lost their spouses.

3) *Ayesha*, a six year old child that Allah offered Muhammad in 623 when he was 53 years old. According to Al-Bukhari, Muhammad had three dreams where Allah gave him a bundle wrapped in silk and told him this is your wife and when he opened the bundle there was this six year old child named Ayesha. She is over other women like the superiority of Tharid (an Arabic dish) to other meals, said Prophet Muhammad (*Buk* 5 : 113-114).

4) *Hafzeh,* daughter of Omar Ibn Khatab. He married her in 625. She was 18 years old and had lost her husband in the battle of Badr.

5) *Omeh Salmeh,* daugher of Almeghireh, they married in 626 when she was 29 years old. Her husband had died in the battle of Ohod.

6) *Zeinab*, daughter of Khazimeh, he married her in 626 when she was 30 and had lost her first and second husbands in the war of Badr. She died a few months later.

7) *Jprieh,* daughter of Hares. He married her in 627 and freed her tribe. She was a 20 year old war booty. She was so beautiful that who ever laid an eye on her fell in love with her.

8) *Zeinab,* daughter of Jahesh, she was his cousin and married to Zaid the Prophet's adopted son. Muhammad fell in love with this woman and asked Zaid to divorce her and he married her in the year 628. She was 38 year old. Before this marriage took place there was criticism that Muhammad should not marry his daughter-in-law like his daughter. Immediately the Prophet received a revelation from Allah : "A Muslim cannot adopt another man's child." Therefore Zaid is not his son and Zeinab is not his daughter-in-law. Quran 33-37 gives the prophet the right to marry his adopted son's wife. "When Zaid had accomplished his want of her, we gave her to you as a wife, so that there should be no difficulty for the believers in respect of the wives of their adopted sons,

when they have accomplished their want of them; and Allah's command shall be performed." What a nice Allah, whenever this man desires a woman Allah just says OK you can have it !

9) ***Ramleh***, daughter of Abu Sofyan, known as Omeh Habibe, they married in the year 628. She was a 38 year old widow and her husband had left Islam.

10) ***Safieh***, daughter of Hay Ben Khatab was from Bani Bazir, a Jewish tribe. Her husband died in 628 in the battle of Kheibar. Safieh's husband had refused to tell Muhammad where he had hidden his wealth and was killed under torture. The same night Muhammad took Safieh, the 17 year old beauty to his bed. Later he married her.

11) ***Meimooneh***, daughter of Haress. Muhammad married her in 628 and she was 27 years old.

(B) Prophet Muhammad had two concubines to whom the Prophet captured in wars, slept with them but never married or they did not want to marry him :

1) ***Marieh***, daughter of Shamoon. A black beauty given as a gift to the Prophet by the king of Egypt.

2) ***Rayhaneh***, taken as a war booty. Muhammad took her to bed after he ordered the killing of her husband in the year 627. She did not agree to be his wife and stayed in his Harem as slave until her death in 632.

(C) Prophet Muhammad married 16 women and divorced them quickly.

1) ***Asma*** daughter of Neman

2) ***Ghotileh***, daughter of Ghaice

3) ***Malaeke,*** daughter of Kaab

4) ***Bent Jandeb***, daughter of Damareh

5) ***Fatima,*** Daughter of Sahaak

6) ***Omreh,*** daughter of Yazid

7) ***Alyeh,*** daughter of Zobyan

8) ***Saba,*** daughter of Sofyan

9) ***Nesha,*** daughter of Rafieh

10) ***Ghazieh,*** daughter of Jaber

11) ***Fatima,*** daughter of Shoreh

12) ***Sanaa,*** daughter of Salim

13) ***Alshanba,*** daughter of Omar

14) ***Kholeh,*** daughter of Alhavhil

15) ***Shargh,*** daughter of Khalifeh

16) ***Kolleh,*** daughter of Hakim

(D) In addition there are 7 more women that may or may not have married Muhammad :

1) ***Habibeh,*** daughter of Sahl

2) ***Laili,*** daughter of Khatem

3) ***Omeh Hani***, daughter of Abi Taleb

4) ***Dobeh***, daughter of Amir

5) *Safieh*, daughter of Beshameh

6) *Emareh or Emameh*, daughter of Hafzeh

7) *Omeh Habib*, daughter of Alabas

Appendix 4

Family Tree of Prophet Muhammad

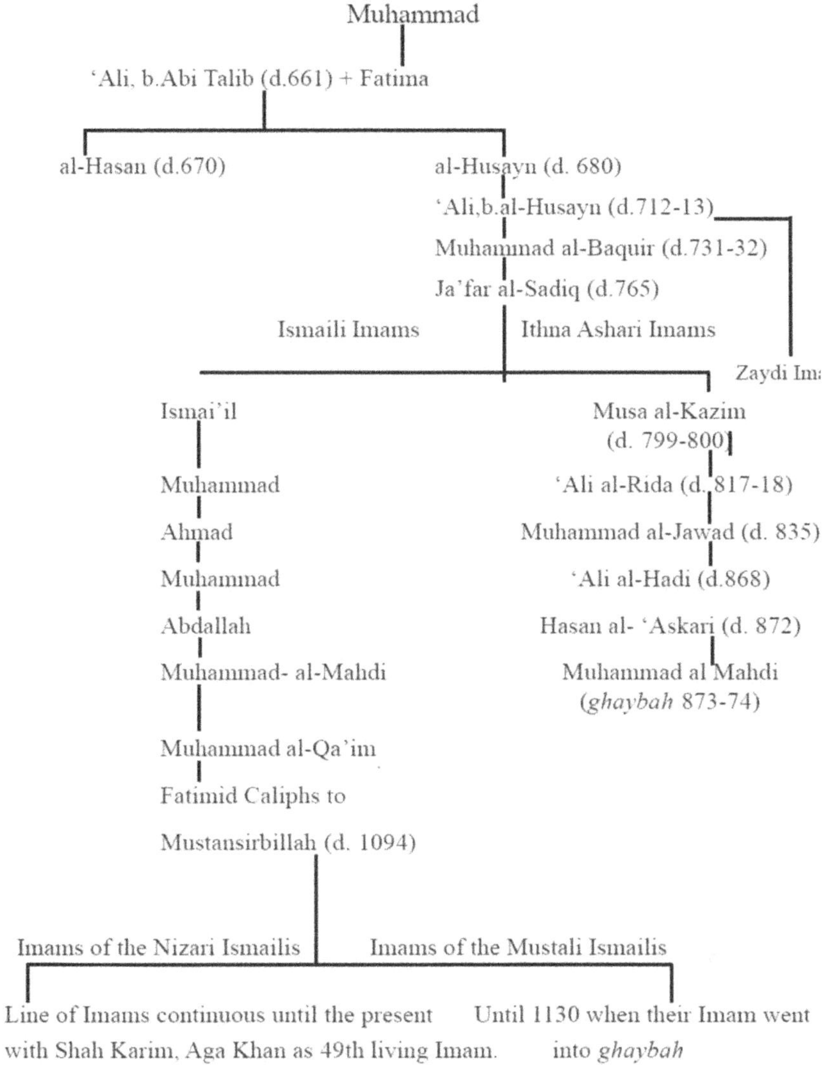
Muhammad
'Ali, b.Abi Talib (d.661) + Fatima
al-Hasan (d.670)
al-Husayn (d. 680)
'Ali,b.al-Husayn (d.712-13)
Muhammad al-Baquir (d.731-32)
Ja'far al-Sadiq (d.765)
Ismaili Imams
Ithna Ashari Imams
Zaydi Im:
Ismai'il
Muhammad
Ahmad
Muhammad
Abdallah
Muhammad- al-Mahdi
Muhammad al-Qa'im
Fatimid Caliphs to
Mustansirbillah (d. 1094)
Musa al-Kazim
(d. 799-800)
'Ali al-Rida (d. 817-18)
Muhammad al-Jawad (d. 835)
'Ali al-Hadi (d.868)
Hasan al- 'Askari (d. 872)
Muhammad al Mahdi
(ghaybah 873-74)
Imams of the Nizari Ismailis
Imams of the Mustali Ismailis
Line of Imams continuous until the present
with Shah Karim, Aga Khan as 49th living Imam.
Until 1130 when their Imam went
into ghaybah

The Shia Imams.

The largest group of Shiah called the "Twelver" sect acknowledges twelve imams. They believe the last of the imams to be still alive though he disappeared to return again as the Imam Mahdi(The Rightly Guided Imam) who will initiate the events leading to the Last Day.

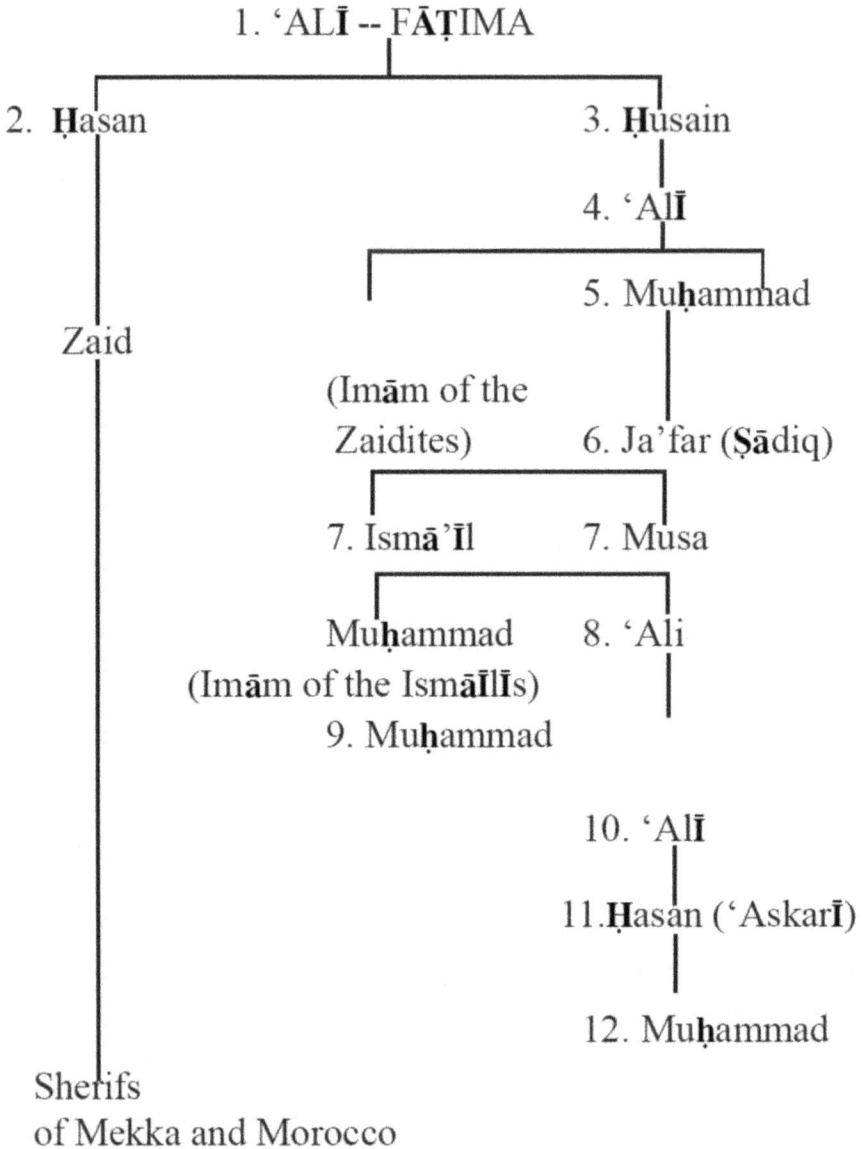

```
                      1. 'ALĪ -- FĀṬIMA
        ┌──────────────────────────────┴──────────────────────┐
   2. Ḥasan                                              3. Ḥusain
        │                                                      │
        │                                                  4. 'Alī
        │                                    ┌─────────────────┤
        │                                    │            5. Muḥammad
     Zaid                                    │                 │
                              (Imām of the   │                 │
                                Zaidites)    │            6. Ja'far (Ṣādiq)
                                       ┌──────┴──────┐
                                  7. Ismā'īl     7. Musa
                              ┌───────┤
                         Muḥammad   8. 'Ali
                    (Imām of the Ismāīlīs)          │
                       9. Muḥammad                  │

                                               10. 'Alī
                                                    │
                                               11.Ḥasan ('Askarī)
        │                                           │
   Sherifs                                     12. Muḥammad
of Mekka and Morocco
```

Appendix 5

SEVENTY THREE SECTS IN ISLAM

Do you know Islamic brotherhood is a myth ? Islam is divided into more than seventy three sects far exceeded the Prophet's predictions.

The Ghiyasu 'I Lughaat gives the following particulars of the seventy-three sects, spoken of in the Traditions, arranging them in six divisions of twelve sects each, and concluding with the Najiyah, or "ordhodox' Sunnis.

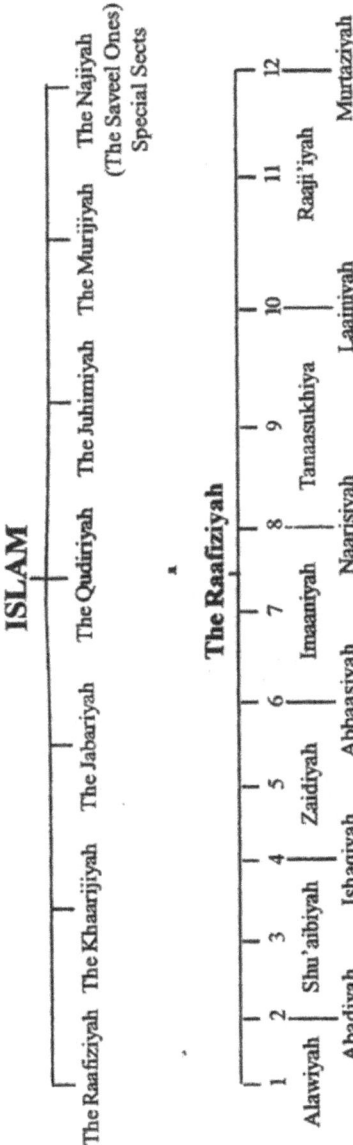

ISLAM

The Raafiziyah — The Khaarijiyah — The Jabariyah — The Qudiriyah — The Juhimiyah — The Murijiyah — The Najiyah (The Saveel Ones) Special Sects

The Raafiziyah

1. Alawiyah
2. Abadiyah
3. Shu'aibiyah
4. Ishaqiyah
5. Zaidiyah
6. Abbaasiyah
7. Imaamiyah
8. Naarisiyah
9. Tanaasukhiya
10. Laainiyah
11. Raaji'iyah
12. Murtaziyah

I.–The *Raafiziyah*, "the Separatists," who are divided into–

1. *Alawiyah*, who esteem the Khalifah Ali to have been a prophet.

2. *Abadiyah*, who hold that 'Ali is divine.'

3. *Shu'aibiyah*, who say 'Ali was the first and best of the Khalifahs.

4. *Ishaaqiyah*, who say the age of prophecy is not yet completed.

5. *Zaidiyah*, who hold that prayers can only be led by a descendant of Ali.

6. *Abbaasiyah*, who say al- 'Abbaas, the uncle of Muhammad, was the only rightful Imam.

7. *Imaamiyaah*, who state that the world is never left without an Immam of the Banu Haashim to lead the prayers.

8. *Naarisiyah*, who say it is blasphemy for one person to say he is better than another.

9. *Tanasukhiyah*, who believe in the transmigration of souls.

10.*Laainiyah*, those who curse the names of Talhaa, Zubair, and 'Ahishah.

11.*Raji'iyah*, who believe that 'Ali is hidden in the clouds and will return again to this earth.'

12.*Murtaziyah*, who say it is lawful for a Muslim to fight against his Imam.

253

II–The _Khaarijiyah_, "the Aliens," who are divided into–

1. _Azraqiyah_, who say there is no holy vision now to be obtained by the sons of men, as the days of inspiration are past.

2. _Riyaaziyah_, who say a man is saved by good works, and not by faith.

3. _Sa'labiyah_, who say God is indifferent to the actions of men, as though He were in a state of sleep.

4. _Jazimiyah_, who hold true faith has not yet been made evident.

5. _Khalfiyah_, who say to run away even from double the number of infidels is a mortal sin for Muslims.

6. _Kuziyah_, who say that the human body is not made ready for prayer unless the ablutions be such as entirely cleanse the body.

7. _Kanziyah_, who do not regard the giving of zakaat as necessary.

8. _Mu'tazilah_, who maintain that evil actions are not according to the decree of God, and that the prayers of a sinful man are not acceptable to God, and that faith is of man's free will, and that the Qur'an is created, and that aims giving and prayer do not benefit the dead and that there is no _mizaan_ or _kitab_, &c., at the Day of Judgment.

9. _Maimuniyah_, who hold that belief in the unseen is absurd.

10. _Muhkamiyah_, who say God has not revealed His will to mankind.

11. _Sirajiyah_, who believe the example of the saints is or no importance.

12. _Akhnasiyah_, who hold that there is no punishment for sin.

The Khaarijiyah

1. Azraquiyah
2. Riyaaziyah
3. Salabiyah
4. Jazimiyah
5. Khalfiyah
6. Kuziyah
7. Kanziyah
8. Mutazilah
9. Maimuniyah
10. Muhkamiyah
11. Sirajiyah
12. Akhnasiyah

III

The Jabariyah

12 — Hujjatiyah
11 — Hasabiyah
10 — Fikriyah
9 — Khaufiyah
8 — Habibiyah
7 — Kablaniyah
6 — Mutamanniyah
5 — Bakhtiyah
4 — Tariqiyah
3 — Maiyah
2 — Afaaliyah
1 — Iuztariyah

III—The *Jabariyah*, the "Deniers of Free Will," who are divided into—

1. *Muztariyah*, who hold that both good and evil are entirely from God, and man is not responsible for his actions.

2. *Afaaliyah*, who say man is responsible for his actions although the power to do and to act is alone from God.

3. *Ma'iyah*, who believe that man possesses an entirely free will.

4. *Tariqiyah*, who say faith without works will save a man.

5. *Bakhtiyah*, who believe that as every mortal receives according to God's special gift, it is not therefore lawful for one to give to another.

6. *Mutamanniyah*, who hold that good works are those from which comfort and happiness are derived in this world.

7. *Kaslaniyah*, they who say punishment and reward is inflicted by God only according to the actions of man.

8. *Habibiyah*, who hold that as one friend never injures another, so God, who is a God of love, does not punish his own creation.

9. *Khaufiyah*, who say that just as a friend does not terrify his friend, so God does not terrify his people by judgements.

10. *Fikriyah*, who say contemplation is better than worship, and more pleasing to God.

11. *Hasabiyah*, who hold that in the world there is no such a thing as fate or predestination.

12. *Hujjatiyah*, who say that in as much as God doeth everything and everything is of God, man cannot be made responsible for either good or evil.

255

IV–The *Qadariyah,* the "Asserters of Free Will," who are divided into–

1. *Ahadiyah,* who accept the injunctions of God, but not those of the Prophet.

2. *Sanawiyah,* who say there are two eternal principles, good and evil; good being of Yazdaan and evil being of Abraman,

3. *Kaisaniyah,* who say our actions are either the creation of God or they are not.

4. *Shaitaaniyah,* who deny the personality of Satan.

5. *Sharikiyah,* who say faith is *ghair makhluq,* or "uncreated."

6. *Wahmiyah,* who say the actions of man are of no consequence, whether they be good or evil.

7. *Ruwaidiyah,* who maintain that the world has an eternal existence.

8. *Nakisiyah,* who say it is lawful to fight against the Imam or Khalifah.

9. *Mutabarriyah,* who say the repentance of sinners is not accepted by God.

10. *Qaasitiyah,* who hold that the acquirement of wealth and learning is a religious duty ordered by God.

11. *Nazaamiyah,* who maintain that it is lawful to speak of the Almighty as a thing (*shai'*).

12. *Mutawallifiyah,* who say it is not evident whether evil is by God's decree or not.

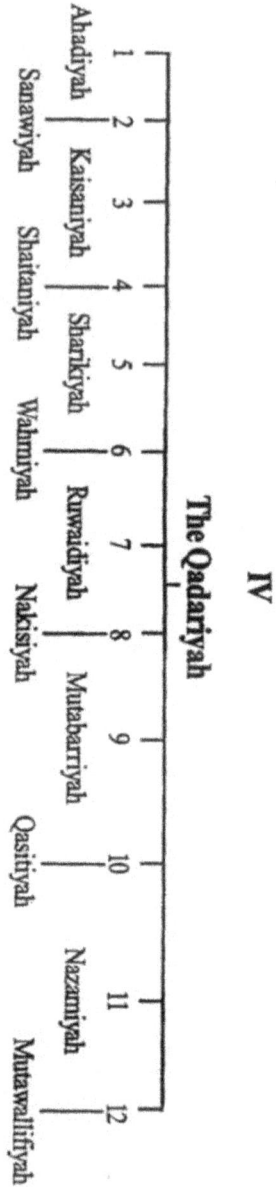

IV

The Qadariyah

1. Ahadiyah
2. Sanawiyah
3. Kaisaniyah
4. Shaitaniyah
5. Sharikiyah
6. Wahmiyah
7. Ruwaidiyah
8. Nakisiyah
9. Mutabarriyah
10. Qasitiyah
11. Nazamiyah
12. Mutawallifiyah

V

The Jahimiyah

Muattaliyah | Mutaraaqibiyah | Harqiyah | Ibariyah | Zanaadiqiyah | Qabriyah

Mutaraabisiyah | Waaqifiyah | Waaridiyah | Makhluqiyah | Faniyah | Lafziyah

1 2 3 4 5 6 7 8 9 10 11 12

V–The *Jahimiyah*, the followers of Jahim ibn Safwaan, who are divided into-

1. *Mu aṭṭaliyah*, who say the names and attributes of God are created.

2. *Mutaraabisiyah*, who hold that the power, knowledge, and purpose of God are created.

3. *Mutaraaqibiyah*, who say God has a place.

4. *Waaridiyah*, who state that those who enter hell will never escape from it, and that a *mu'min*, or "believer," will never enter hell.

5. *Harqiyah*, who say the inhabitants of hell will so burn, that in time they will be annihilated.

6. *Makhluqiyah*, who believe that the Qur'an, the Tauraat, the Injil, and the Zubur are created.

7. *'Ibariyah*, who say Muhammad was a learned man, and a philosopher, but not a prophet.

8. *Faaniyah*, who say both Paradise and Hell will be annihilated.

9. *Zanaadiqiyah*, who say the *Mi'raaj*, or "ascent of Muhammad to heaven," was only in the spirit, and that the world is eternal, and that there is no Day of Judgment.

10. *Lafẓiyah*, who hold that the Qur'an is not an inspired writing, but that its instructions are of God.

11. *Qabriyah*, who say there is no punishment in the grave.

12. *Waaqifiyah*, who state that it is not certain whether the Qur'an is created or uncreated.

257

VI–The *Murjiyah*, or "Procra-stinators," who are divided into–

1. *Tariqiyah*, who say nothing is necessary but faith.

2. *Shaa'iyah*, who maintain that when once a person has repeated the Muhammadan creed he is saved.

3. *Raajiyah*, who believe that the worship of God is not necessary to piety, nor are good works necessary.

4. *Shaakkiyah*, who say a man cannot be certain if he has faith or not, for faith is spirit.

5. *Nahiyah*, who say faith is knowledge, and those who do not know the commandments of God have not faith.

6. *'Amaliyan*, who say faith is but good works.

7. *Manqusiyah*, who say faith is sometimes less and sometimes more.

8. *Mustasniyah*, who deprecate assurance in religion, but say, "we are believers if God wills it."

9. *Ash'ariyah*, who say *qiyaas*, or "analogical reasoning, in matters of faith is unlawful.

10. *Bidiyah*, who hold that it is a duty to obey a ruler, even if he give orders which are evil.

11. *Mushabbihiyah*, who say God did literally make Adam in his own image.

12. *Hashawiyah*, who consider that in Muslim law there is no difference between *waajib*, *sunnah*, *and mustahab*.

VI

The Murjiyah

Tariqiyah	1
Shaaiyah	2
Rajiyah	3
Shakkiyah	4
Nahiyah	5
Amaliyan	6
Manqusiyah	7
Mustasniyah	8
Ashariyah	9
Bidiyah	10
Mushabbihiyah	11
Hashawiyah	12

VII- The Naajiyah, or "Saved Ones," make up the complete number of seventy-three.
Mr.Sale traces all the Muhammadan sects to four sources:-

1. The *Mu'taziliyahs*, the followers of Wasil ibn 'Ata, who may be said to have been the first inventor of scholastic divinity in Islam.

2. The *Sifatiyahs*, or Attributists, who hold the contrary opinions of the *Mu 'taziliyahs*.
3. The *Kharijiyahs*, or Aliens. Those who revolted from Ali.
4. The *Shi'ahs*, or the followers of Ali.

(From Hughes, Thomas Patrick *Dictionary of Islam*, Delhi: Cosmo Publications, 1977 567-569)

Appendix 6

Where Angels Fear to Tread

It is thought and said that Islam stands for peace, tolerance and mercy. Therefore, Jihad has nothing to do with war against the infidels but it speaks about man's inner struggle between good and evil.

Abul Kasem, a reputed Islamic scholar unmasked the inner and outer meaning of the Holy Quran and asked why all the verses on Jihad occurred in the al-Madina Suras are harder than Meccan Surra ? Is it because the prophet was not in power in Mecca and very powerful in Madina ? Why did Muhammad allow fighting during the holy months when it was forbidden ? How "to you, is your religion and to me is mine" (109 : 6) and "no compulsion in relig" (2 : 256) became "turn away from those who join false gods with Allah" (15 : 94) ? Kasem chronologically set the verses of the Quran to show the evolution of Muhammad's ideas from saints like Buddha to a fascist like Nazi Hitler, Mussolin, Osama and Ayatollah. The learned author divided the Quranic verses in four distinct phases like :
1. Peaceful persuasion
2. Fighting for defense
3. Limited attack
4. Open aggression

Phase I : Peaceful persuasion

Highlights

1. Dealing with one enemy : Pagans of Mecca.
2. Give and take strategy with the pagans.
3. Jews and Christians were considered as friends.
4. Mohammad was almost like the Buddha preaching love, forgiveness, non-violence and -peace.

Allah ordered Muhammad

Highlights

1. Be patient and bear with those who deny the truth; God will deal with them (73 : 10, 11).
2. "To you is your religion, to me is mine." (109 : 1-6).
3. Show patience to the pagans (20 : 130).
4. Don't be in a haste to fight (19 : 83, 84).
5. It is not God's job to see if people believe the truth or not (6 : 104).
6. Invite the unbelievers (Pagans) with beautiful preaching and gracious arguments; be patient and do not retaliate (16 : 125, 126).
7. Leave the unbelievers (pagans) alone 23 : 54).
8. Repeal evil with good deeds (23 : 96).
9. Leave the unbelievers alone and wait in patience for God to punish them (52 : 45, 47, 48).
10. Mohammad is only a warner and not an enforcer (67 : 26).

Phase 2 : Fighting for Defence

260

Highlights

1. Muhammad alongwith his handful of followers migrated to Medina (622 AD).
2. Some tribes of Medina accepted him as their leader.
3. Muhammad and his gang started raids on passing caravans of the Meccans to acquire the wherewithal for survival.
4. Muhammad won the battle of Badr (same year of migration i.e. 622 AD) which bolstered his morale for further raids on Meccan caravans.
5. After several years of stay in Medina, God gave Muhammad permission to launch defensive war.
6. Enemies were the pagans of Mecca and the hypocrites (note : the enemy list includes two groups now).

Important Verses

1. Permission to fight for self defense is granted (22 : 39-41).
2. Rewards for Jihad is announced (22 : 58).

Phase 3 : Stage of More Defensively Aggressive State

Highlights

1. Muhammad expected the Jews of Medina to accept him as their new Mosses.
2. The Jews rejected Mohammads their new apostle.
3. Muhammad included the Jews as his enemy and started to raid their sanctuaries.
4. Enemies of Muhammad now were pagans, hypocrites, and the Jews (note : the enemy list now contains three).
5. Muhammad was a little bit forgiving to the defeated Jews. He gave them a chance to live in their hands provided they paid him fifty percent of their agricultural produce of land.
6. This way Muhammad acquired the means of a guaranteed livelihood for his horde of soldiers.
7. The battle of Uhud (623 AD) was fought. Muslims suffered a severe beating in the battle.
8. The battle of Trench (625 AD) took place with huge loss of lives. Muhammad managed to win this battle.
9. Treaty of Hudaibiya (626 AD) was signed with the pagans of Mecca ensuring ten years of peace. Muhammad was allowed to visit Kaaba alongwith his followers during the pilgrimage season.
10. Unconditionally. Muhammad ordered the beheading of around 700 adult male surrendered Jews and took 17 years old Jewess Safiya as a war booty and made her his wife.

Important Verses

1. Forgive and overlook the unbelieving Jews; God will take care of them (2 : 109).
2. Fight defensively the Meccan pagans but if they cease hostility then stop fighting except for the oppressors (2 : 190-194).
3. Fighting against the Meccan pagans is prescribed after the passing of the month of pilgrimages (zulhaj) [2 : 216, 217].
4. 'No compulsion in religion'; do not force the defeated enemy to embrace Islam; but they will be thrown in hell (2 : 256).

5. Spoils of war belongs to God and Muhammad (8 : 1).
6. Strike terror in the hearts of the unbelievers; cut the necks and fingers tips of those who oppose God and Muhammad (8 : 12, 13).
7. When you meet, the unbelievers in hostility attack them and never turn back from them. If you retreat except for a strategic reason then God will punish you and will send you to hell (8 : 15-16).
8. Keep on fighting until the persecution stops and Islam is established; one fifth of booty belongs to God and Muhammad (8 : 39-41).
9. Obey Muhammad, be united and preserver in fighting (8 : 45, 46).
10. If you defeat the enemy then teach them with treachery and terror; if they ask for peace then give them peace (8 : 57-61).
11. Rouse the believers to fight with preservance, God will help by increasing your strength (8 : 65).
12. Continue killing and do not take prisoners until the land is subdued then enjoy the war booty (8 : 67-69).
13. Martyr's sins are blotted out and thy go to paradise (3 : 157, 169-171, 195).
14. Can take women captives as concubines in addition to wives (33 : 50).
15. There is a great reward for fighting against the friends of Satan., (4 : 74-78).
16. Fight and rouse other believers to fight; God will restrain the fury of the unbelievers ...(4 : 84).
17. Kill the hypocrites if they turn renegades...(4 : 89).
18. Higher grade for fighting for God... (4 : 95, 96).
19. Guaranteed reward for fighting in the cause of God...4 : 100 (92).
20. Whether a fighter kills or is killed, he is admitted in paradise to reside there permanently... (22 : 58, 59).
21. Struggle for God's cause...(22 : 78).
22. Can't lag behind in fighting for God... (48 : 15-16).
23. Muslims are compassionate with each other but are strong to fight against the unbelievers... (48 : 29).

Phase 4 : Offensive War or Open Declaration of Attack to Spread Islam

This phase is the stage of open offensive war against all be unbelievers. This phase started in 630 AD after Muhammad re-entered Mecca and captured Kaaba from the pagans. This is the phase, which is currently valid for all Muslims.

Highlights

1. Permission was granted by God to declare offensive war against all non-Muslims.
2. Kill the pagans and humble the Jews and the Christians through *Jizya* tax.
3. Tabuk expedition (late 630 AD) is the first war against the Christians.
4. The world is divided into two houses, viz. House of Islam (Darul Islam) and the House of War (Darul Harb).
5. All Muslims must fight to convert the Darul Harb into Darul Islam.
6. This is the final teaching of Quran and so it is valid today and for future (that is, for eternity).
7. Christians are included in the list of enemies (that is, the list now grows to four).

8. Verse 9 : 5 (also called the verse of the sword) replaces all verses showing mercy, love, tolerance and forgiveness to all non-Muslims.

Important Verses

1. Any religion other than Islam is not acceptable...(3 : 85).
2. Kill (execute by beheading)/ crucify/ torture who oppose Muhammad...(5 : 33).
3. Do not make friendship with the Jews and the Christians...(5 : 51).
4. After giving four months notice break all treaties with the pagans that they didn't keep; those treaties with the pagans that they kept are to be honored to their full term; in future make no more peace treaties with the pagans and kill all pagans who do not accept Islam...(9 : 1-6).
5. Pagans who accept Islam are brothers of Muslims; those who break the agreement fight them... (9 : 11, 12, 14, 15).
6. Do not make friend of seek protection from the unbelievers (includes pagans, hypocrites, Jews and the Christians)...(9 : 16).
7. Unbelievers should not visit mosques or maintain the mosques of God; they will go to hell ... (9 : 17).
8. Those who do *Jihad* are the highest in rank; they will dwell in paradise...9 : 19-22.
9. The unbelievers are unclean, forbid them to enter Kaaba...(9 : 28).
10. Fight against the Jews and the Christians until they are subdued and pay the *Jizya* tax with submission; God's curse is on them...(9 : 29-31).
11. If you do not fight in the cause of God with whatever you have got then God will punish you with a serious punishments... (9 : 38, 39, 41).
12. If you fight for God then except either martyrdom of paradise. The unbelievers can except only punishment from God...(9 : 52).
13. Those who are able to fight for God but do not do so are rejected by God...(9 : 90-96).
14. Whether you slay or slain in Jihad, God has promised paradise for giving all in the cause of God...(9 : 111).
15. Fight the unbelievers surrounding you... (9 : 122).

(Courtesy : Bharatiya Pragana 2002 : 22-29)

These verses tell about a free and frank confession of the Allah's messenger through the Quran. There is no confusion though a lot of contradictions in the Quran. Why Allah being the Universal Father and the Creator so much vindictive to his people and fever his last prophet can be seen if we read the Holy Quran in the chronological order.

Appendix 7

GLOSSARY

Aayaat : Verses of the Holy Quran.

Abdullah : Allah's slave.

Abu Bakr : (Reign 632-634 AD) The first Moslem Caliph, according to Sunni Muslims. The Shi'ite Muslims reject this and instead consider the fourth Caliph, 'Ali, as the first true successor to Mohammad.

Allah : The Supreme Being. The name of God, derived from the Arabic Al-Ilah.

Al-Lat & *Al- Uzza* : Well-known idols in Hijar which used to be worshipped during the Pre-Islamic Period.

Answar : (Ansarri Singular) Anyone of the companions of the Prophet from the inhabitants of Madina which embraced and supported Islam and who received and entertained the Muslim emigrant who migrated from Mecca.

Badr : A place about 150 km to the south of AL-Medina where the first great battle in Islamic History took place between the early Muslims and the infidels of Quraish.

Bait-ul-Laah : Allah's House

Caliph : the title given to office of the spiritual and political leadership which took over after Mohammad's death.

Dajjaal : Pseudo-Messiah.

Dar-ul-harb : A county where some population is Muslim but the Government is not Islamic or Shriyat, it also means as enemy country. It is the foremost religious duty of every Muslim to work for the conversion of every Darul-harb into Darul-Islam.

Dar-ul-islam : A country having majority of Muslims with an Islamic Government according to Shariat.

Dharullah : Allah's Self.

Dhimmi : A non-Muslim living under the protection of an Islamic government.

Dinaar : An ancient gold coin.

Dozekh : Hell.

Eid-al-adha : It is the festival of sacrifice and an important religious holiday for Muslims who commemorate the willingness of Abraham to sacrifice his son Ishmael as an act of obedince to God before God intervened to provide him with a sheep to sacrifice instead.

Eid-ul-fitr : It is a Muslim holiday that marks the end of Ramadan, the Islamic holy month of fasting. It celebrates the conclusion of the 29 or 30 days of dawn-to-sunsent fasting during the entire month of Ramadan.

Fatiha : The opening or the one who opens a Fortress, because it is placed before all the other suras in the Quran. Muslims regard it as the "Mother of the Quran." It is recited up to seventeen times a day. It is like Christian's Lord's Prayer.

Fatima : The Daughter of Mohammad From His First Wife; And The Wife of 'Ali, The Fourth Caliph.

Fatwa : A legal verdict given on a religious basis.

Ghazi : Warrior returning after participating in Jihad. He slays infidels with his own hands. He is higher than Mujahid, because he actually commits the crime of murder of an innocent man, for the only fault that the victim refuses to accept Islam.

Ghazwa : (Ghazwat : Plural) A holy battle in the cause of Allah, consisting of a large army unit with the Prophet himself leading the army.

Hadith : The Sacred Sayings of Mohammad, Handed Down By Oral Tradition, For Generations After Mohammad's Death Until Finally Transcribed. It Describes His Saying & Deeds.

Hajj : A Pilgrimage to Mecca. One of the five pillars of the Islamic faith.

Halal : Anything permitted by *Shariah*. Lawful

Hanif : Worshipping Allah alone and nothing else along with Him, associating no partners to him.

Haraam : Unlawful. Anything prohibited by Shariah

Haram : The sanctuaries of Mecca and Medina.

Hayatullah : Anything prohibited by Shariah. Unlawful.

Hegira : Mohammad's flight from Mecca to present day Medina in 622 A.D.

Hubal : A prominent idol in the Kabha in the Pre-Islamic period.

Id-ul-Adhaa : The fourday festival of Muslims, starting on the tenth of Dhul Hijja (12th Month of Islamic calendar).

Id-ul-Fitr : The three-day festival of Muslims, starting from the first of Shawwal, the month that immediately follows Ramadaan, "Fitr" means breaking the fast. Muslims fast for the whole of

Ramadaan : the ninth month of the Muslim Calendar.

Ihraam : A state in which one is prohibited to practise certain deeds that are lawful at other times. The ceremonies of Umra and Hajja are performed during such state.

Ijab and Qubool : Ijab is an offer in a contract, and Qubool is an acceptance.

Il Mullah : Allah's knowledge.

Imaan : Faith

265

Imam : A Moslem who is considered by Sunnis to be an authority in Islamic Law and Theology or the man who leads the Prayers. Also refers to each of the Founders of the Four Principal Sects of Islam. The Shi'ites accept 12 Great Imams.

Islam : Literally, "Submission to the will of Allah."

Jamrat-al-Aquaba : One of the three stone-built pillars situated at Minaa. It is one of the ceremonies of pilgrimage to throw pebbles on these stones which stand as a symbol of Satan.

Janat : Paradise, where rivers of flowing crystal clear water, springs of wine and honey care in abundance and all the imaginable luxuries and sensual enjoyments is plantry.

Jihaad : Holy fighting in the cause of Allah.

Jahala : Ignorance, lack of Knwoledge, in definiteness and ambiguity in a contract.

Jizya : Head tax imposed by Islam on Jews and Christians when they are under the Muslims' rule.

Kaaba : A square stone building in the great Mosque at Mecca towards which Muslims turn their faces in prayer. The mosque contains the black stone, a meteorite supposedly given to Ibrahim by Gabriel.

Kafir : An infidel, non-Muslim against whom jihad is permanently established.

Kalamullah : Allah's statement.

Khaibar : A well-known town north of Al-Medina.

Khum : The holy one fifth. The one-fifth share of the Jihadic plunders due for the Prophet or his later day representatives-- Califas or Sultans.

Kmushrik & Shrik : A non-monotheist idolator or a Kafir. A strongly abusive term in Quran.

Labbaik : I respond to your call; I am obedient to your orders.

Mahashar : Day of Judgement

Mahdi : "The guided one." A leader who will cause righteousness to fill the earth. The Sunnites are still awaiting his initial appearance while the Shi'ites hold that the last Imam, who disappeared in 874 AD will someday reappear as the Mahdi.

Mahr : Bridal money given by the husband to the wife on marrying.

Maqam (Ibraahim) : The station (the stone) where Ibrahim stood while he and Ishmael were building the Kaaba.

Masjid al-Aqsaa : The great mosque in Jerusalem.

Masjid al-Haraam : The great mosque in Mecca. The Kaaba is situated in it.

Mecca : The birthplace of Muhammad. This city, located in Saudi Arabia, is considered the most holy city by the Moslems.

266

Medina : A Holy City of Islam named for Muhammad. It was previously named Yathrib. It is the city to which Muhammad fled in 622 AD.

Mina : A place outside Mecca on the road to Arafaat. It is five miles away from Mecca and about ten miles from Arafaat.

Momins : Believers, that is, those who have complete and full faith in Allah, his apostle Muhammad and his religion Islam.

Muezzin : A Muslim crier who announces the hour of prayer.

Muhammad : The prophet and founder of Islam. Born around 570 A.D., died 632 A.D.

Muharram : First Month Of The Islamic Calender And One Of The four sacred months of the year in which fighting is prohibited. the tenth day of muharram is known as "the day of grief" by the Shia Muslims to remember and replicate the sufferings of husay in ibn ali.

Mujahid : A person who is a warrior in jehad to convert non-muslims to Islam and when failing to convert he kills them. he cannot be considered as an ordinary Muslim who just affirms that there is no god but Allah and that Muhammad is his prophet. he is a glorified criminal, as assassin, a killer, a murderer of non-muslims on a mass scale.

Mulla : A teacher of Islamic laws and doctrines.

Musafiq : A Muslim not wholly devoted to the cause of Islam in jihad, a term of full throated abuse.

Muslim : " A follower of Muhammad. Literally, "one who submits."

Nikah : Marriage (Wedlock) according to Islamic law.

Purda : A veil or covering used by Muslim women to ensure them privacy against public observation, and to indicate their submission.

Qibla : The direction in which Muslims turn their faces, in prayers. That direction is towards the Kaaba at Mecca.

Qureish : One of the greatest tribes in Arabia. Prophet Muhammad belonged to that tribe which had great power spiritually and financially both before and after Islam came.

Qur'an : Said to be the final and complete inspired word of God transmitted to Prophet Mohammad by the angel Gabriel.

Qurbani : Animal sacrifice. Because Islam is so preponderantly Muhammadanism, one of consequences of the Prophet's offering sacrifices is that sacrificing has become a sacred institution in Islam. Thus we find in Islam none of those generous moments of the spirit against animal sacrifice that we find in some measures in most other cultures. Muhammad himself once sacrificed 63 camels with his own hands.

Ramadaan : It is the ninth month of the Islamic calender, which lasts 29 or 30 days. It is the Islamic month of fasting in which Muslims retrain from eating, drinking and smoking during daylight hours. Muslims believe Ramadan to be an auspicious month for the revelations of God to humankind, being the month in which the first verses of the Quran were revealed to the Prophet.

Rami : The throwing of pebbles at the Jimaar at Minaa.

Rasul-lullah : Allah's Messenger.

Rouh-ul-lah : Allah's Soul.

Sai yid : The descendants of the Prophet. It means master.

Salat : The Moslem Daily Prayer Ritual. One Of The Five Pillars Of Islamic Faith.

Shariah : Divine Guidance As Given By The Holy Quran And Sunnah Of The Prophet. Shariah Embodies All Aspects Of Islamic Faith, Including Beliefs And Practices.

Shariat : Refers To The Literature Of Islamic School Of Jurisprudence Derived From Quran And Hadis.

Shittes : A Muslim Sect Which Rejects The First Three Caliphs, Insisting That Mohammad's Son-in-law' Ali Was Mohammad's Rightful Initial Successor.

Shirk : Opposite Of Jauhid And It Is To Worship Others Alongwith Allah.

Subhan Allah : To Honour Allah From What Is Ascribed To Him.

Sufis : Iranian (Persian) Philosophical Mystics Who Have Largely Adapted And Reinterpreted Islam For Themselves.

Sunnah : Literally 'practice'. in Islamic parlance it means practice of the prophet that should be followed by the adherents of Islam as a quranic injuction. the source book of sunnah is Hadith. it also includes customs and traditions. Muhammad's practice of enslaving children and wives of vanquished infidels, and his massacre of the tribe of Beni Kuraizah are examples of *sunnah* par excellence.

Sunnites : The largest Moslem sect which acknowledges the first four caliphs as Mohammad's rightful successors.

Surahs : What the chapters of the Qur'an are called.

Tauhid : It Includes :

1. Tauhid-al-rabubiya : Unity of Lordship.

2. Tauhid-al-aluheya : Unit of Worship.

3. Tauhid-al-asmaa-was-sift : Unity of the names and the Qualities of Allah.

4. Tauhid-al-itibaa : The unity of following allaah's messenger Muhammad.

Unity of lordship means there is only one lord.

268

Unity of worship means none has the right to be worshipped
but Allah.

Unity of names and the qualities of Allah means we must not name or quality Allah except with what he and this messenger has named or qualified him on as described in the Holy Quran.

Unity of following Allah's messenger means one should testify that Muhammad is Allah's Messenger, none else.

Tawaaf : The Circumambulation of ohe Kaaba. The Islamic nation beyond all national boundaries, ethnicities, colours and races. used to refer to the worldwide community of Muslims.

Ulema : Sharia schools, Islamic jurist who are well versed in sharia.

Ummah : Brothers-in-faith (Islam).

Umra : A visit to Mecca during which one performs the tawaf around the Kaaba and sai between Safa and Marwa.

Zakat : An annual, specified wealth tax to be paid to specific people, by a Muslim possessing a minimum specified amount of wealth.

Zimmi : An Infidel (non-muslim) allowed to live as a third grade citizen under Islamic rule on payment of poll tax (Jizyah). He generally gets humiliating treatment at the hands of the state as also from his own brethrens, who have adopted Islam. His status is that of a resident non-citizen (in his own country of birth) wearing out his life in a condition of semi-slavery.

SELECT BIBLIOGRAPHY

Al-Fadi, Abdallah. *Is the Quran Infallible ?* Austria : Light of Life, 1997.

Abbott, Nabia. *Aishah the Beloved of Muhammed.* London : Saqi Books,1985.

Abdi, M.H. "Reincarnation : Islamic Conceptions." *Theosophy in Pakistan* (October-December, 1964; January-March, 1965.

Abdul Haqq,M.A.M.(ed.) *An Introduction to the Commentary on the Holy Quran,* Calcutta : Thacker, Spink & Co., 1910.

AbuDawud. *Sunan Abu Dawud.* trans. Ahmed Hasan, 3 Vols. New Delhi : Kitab Bhavan, 2007.

Achor, Amy Blount. *Animal Rights : A Beginner's Guide.*Ohio : Write Ware, 1992.

Adamec, Ludwig W. *The A to Z of Islam.* New Delhi : Vision Books, 2003.

A Dictionary of Comparative Religion, ed.S.G.F. Brandon, London : Weidenfeld & Nicolson, 1970.

A Guide to the Gods. Compiled by Richard Carlyon, London : Heinemann/ Quixote, 1981.

Ahmad b. Hanbal. *al-Musnad,* 1-6. Cairo, n.d.

Ahmad, Fazl. *Hazrat Khalid Bin Walid.* New Delhi : Idara Ishaat -E- Diniyat. n.d.

Ahmad, Hazrat Mirza. *The Holy Prophet Muhammad.* Qadian : Sadr Anjuman Ahmadiyya, 1996.

- - - *Four Questions by a Christian and Their Answers.* Qadian : Sadr Anjuman Ahmadiyya, 1969.

Ahmad, Israr. "What is the Basis of Shi'ah-Sunni Discord ?" *Islamic Voice* (March 2004) 22.

Al-Baidawi. 'Abdallah Ibn *'Umar. Anwar al-Tanzil wa Asrar al-Ta'wil.* 2 vols. Istanbul, n.d.

Al-Bukhari. *Sahih Al-Bukhari.* trans. Muhammad Muhsin Khan. 9 Vols, New Delhi : Kitab Bhavan, 1987.

Ali, Abdullah Yusuf. *The Holy Quran.* Text Translation and Commentary. London : The Islamic Foundation. A Bilingual English-Arabic version of the Quran. n.d.

Ali, Asghar. "Practice of Talaq Among Muslims and the Fatwa." *Mainstream* (August 14, 1993) 16-18.

Ali, Muhammad. *The Living Thoughts of the Prophet Muhammad.* London : Cassell, 1947.

Al-Masih, Abd. *Who is Allah in Islam ?* Austria : Light of Life, 1987.

- - - *The Occult in Islam.* Austria : Light of Life, 1990.

- - - *The Prayer of the Lost. Villach,* Austria : Light of Life, 1993.

- - - *The Main Challenges for Committed Christians in Serving Muslims.* Austria : Light of Life, 1996.

- - - *Islam Under the Magnifying Glass.* Villach-Austria : Light of Life : n.d.

AmeerAli, Syed. *The Spirit of Islam,* London : Christophers, 1922.

American Academy of Pediatrics. *Care of the Uncrumcized Penis.* EIK Grove Villag, IL : American Academy of Pediatrics, 1984.

Anderson, Sir Norman. *The World's Religions.* Grand Rapids, MI : William B.Eerdmans Publishing Co., 1976.

Anoymous. "Muhammed : The Model Muslim Man." *The Rationalist News* (Jan-Feb, 1983) 11-12.

- - - "Some Facts on Islam." *Rationalist News* (Nov-Dec,1980) 8-9.

Andrae, Tor. *Mohammed : The Man and His Faith,* New York : Harper, 1960.

Ansari, M.H. "Militant Islam : Cause and Effect." *The Radical Humanist.* (May 2002) 7-9, 11.

Anthology of Islamic Literature.(ed) James Krized. Harmondsworth : Penguine, 1964.

Arberry, A.J. *Sufism : An Account of the Mystics of Islam.* London : Unwin Paperbacks, 1990.

Armstrong, Karen. *Islam : A Short History.* London : Phoenix Press, 2006.

- - - *Muhammad : A Biography of the Prophet.* London : Phoenix Press. A division of the Orion Publishing Group Ltd., 2006.

Asad, Mohammad. *Islam on the Crossroad.* Delhi : The Arafat Publication, 1934.

Arnold, Sir Thomas. *The Preachingn of Islam.* London, 1913.

Aslan, Reza. *No God But God.* London : Arrow Books. The Random House Group Ltd., London, 2006.

Athar, Shahid. *25 Most Frequently Asked Questions About Islam.* Indianapolis : Dawa Information Group, 1993.

Al-Tabari. *T   arikh Tabari or Annals. Sirat al-Nabi.* Vol. 1 (is an authoritative source of Muhammad's subsequent biographies. Urdu translation in 11 vols. Karachi : Nafees Academy, n.d.

Ayoub, Mahmoud. *The Quran and Its Interpreters.* Albany : State University of New York Press, 1984.

Azraki. *(ed). History of Meccah.* Wustenfeld, Leipzig, 1858. (The editor has appended in two volumes extracts from other and later historians of Mecca and in a third volume a German epitome of the whole).

Baldick, Julian. *Mystical Islam : An Introduction to Sufism.* London : Tauris, 1989.

Balyuzi, H.M. "The Islamic Revelation." *Glory* (1982) 25-26.

Bayat, Mufti Zubair. *The Maidens of Paradise, Idara Ishaat Diniyat,* New Delhi : n.pub. 2005.

Becker, Carl Heinrich. *Islam and Christianity.* London : Bibliolife, 1909.

Beeston, A. *Written Arabic : An Approach to the Basic Structures.* Cambridge : Cambridge University Press, 1968.

Bell, Richard. *Introduction to the Quran.* Edinburgh : University Press, 1953.

Bhatty, Margaret. "Allah in the Dock". *American Atheist* (Oct. 1985) 31-32.

271

Bidar, Abdennour. "The Outsiders of Islam," *Diogenes*. No.226, Vol.57, issue 2. pp-3-23.

Bluestone, F.D. "Living and Working in South Arabia." *CLF News Bulletin* (April 1984) 4-6.

Bowkar, John. *World Religions.* London : Dorling Kindersley, 1997.

Brahmachari, R. "Prophet Muhammad was a Flawless Man." *Hindu   Voice* (Sept. 2007) 20-21.

Bradon, S.G.F.(ed.)   *A Dictionary of Comparative Religion.* London : Weidenfeld & Nicolson, 1970.

Bravmann, M.M. *The Spiritual Background of Early Islam : Studies in Ancient Arab Concepts.* Leiden : Bill, 1972.

Britannica Ready Reference Encyclopedia.(ed.) Theodore Pappas. New Delhi : Encyclopedia Britanica, 2006.

Bukhari. *Sahih Al. Bukhari.* Eng. trans. by Muhammad Muhsin Khan, 9 vols. New Delhi : Kitab Bhawan, 1987.

Burton, J. *An Introduction to the Hadith.* Edinburgh : Edinburgh University Press, 1994.

Bush, Richard. C. (ed.) *The Religious World Communities of Faith.* New York : MacMillan, 1988.

Cambridge History of Arabic Literature. Cambridge University Press, 1983.

Cambridge History of Islam (The). *The Central Islamic Lands.* 2 vols. : The Further Islamic Lands. Islamic Society and Civilization. Ed. by P.M. Holt, K.S. Lambton, Bernard Lewis. Cambridge, 1970.

Caner, Ergun Mehmet and Caner Emir Fethi. *Unveiling Islam.* USA   :   Kregel Publications : 2002.

Canney, Maurice. A. *An Encyclopedia of Religions.* Delhi : Nag Publishers, 1976.

Carlyon, Richard (Compiled) *A Guide to Gods.* London : Heinemann/ Quixote, 1981.

Cherry, Matt. "When Muslim Nation Embraces Secularism." *The Humanist* (May/ June, 2002) 21-23.

Clarke, James Freeman. *Ten Great Religions.* Boston : James R. Osgood, 1871.

Comment on Quoranic Verses. The True Guidance. Part V. Villach-Austria : Light of Life, 1994.

Comparative Tables of Islamic and Christian Dates Compiled. Lt. Colonel Sir Wolseley Haig. New Delhi : Kitab Bhawan, 1992.

Cook, Michael, *Early Muslim Dogma.* Cambridge : Cambridge University Press, 1981.

Cook, Michael and Patricia Crone. *Hagarism : The Making of the Islamic World.* Cambridge, 1977.

Coulson, N.J. *A History of Islamic Law.* Edinburgh : Edinburgh University Press, 1964.

Dagher, Hamdun. *The Position of Women in Islam.* Villach Austria   : Light of Life,1995.

Darabi, Parvin. "Approaching the Quran." *Rationalist Voice* (4 : 4)   13-15.

272

- - - "Some Facts About Islam and Prophet Muhammad." *Rationalist Voice.* (May-August, 2007) 47-48.

- - - "Women and Islam". *Rationalist Voice.* V : 6 : 31-35.

Das, Sujit. *Unmasking Muhammad. Counter.*Jihad (at) yahoo.co.uk, 2010.

Dashti, Ali. *23 Years : A Study of the Prophetic Career of Mohammad.* London : George Allen & Unwin, 1985.

Dawud Abu. *Sunan Abu Dawud.* trans. Ahmed Hasan 3 vols. Kitab Bhawan, New Delhi, 2007.

Deedat, Ahmed. *Al-Quran The Ultimate Miracle.* Durban : Islamic Propagation Centre, 1984.

- - - *Christ in Islam.* Durban : Islamic Propagation Centre, 1985.

Dictionary and Glossary of the Koran. (ed.) by John Price. London : Kurzon Press, 1971.

Dictionary of Islam. (ed.) Thomas Patrick Huges. New Delhi : Cosmo Publications (orig. pub. London : Allen), 1997.

Dictionary of the Quranic Phrases and Its Meaning. Compiled by Sheik Mousa Ben Muhammad Al Kaleeby. Cairo : Maktabat Al Adab, 2002.

Dreibholz, Ursula. *The Treatment of Early Islamic Manuscript Fragments on Parchment in the Conservation and Preservation of Islamic Manuscripts.* London : Al-Furqan Islamic Heritage Foundation, 1996.

Durant, Will. *The Story Of Civilization--- The Age of Faith.* NewYork : Simon and Schuster, 1950.

Elahi, Maulana Muhammad Ashiq. *The Daughter of the Prophet Muhammad.* trans. Sh. Mohammad Akram. New Delhi : Islamic Book Service, 2001.

- - - *The Wives of the Prophet Muhammad.* trans. Sh. Mohammad Akram. New Delhi : Islamic Book Service, 2002.

Emily & Per Ola D' Aulatre. "Female Circumcision on Trial." *Reader's Digest* (April 1981) 80-84.

Encyclopaedia of Islam (*The*) vol.2.Vol.ed. M.Th. Houtsma, A.J. Wensinck, elet. E.K. Leyden : Late E.J. Brill Ltd., 1927.

Encyclopaedia of Islam(*Shorter*).(ed.) H.A.R. Gibb & J.H.Kramers. Leideni : E.J. Brill, 1974.

Encyclopaedia of Religions (An). (ed.) Maurice.A.Canney. Delhi : Nag Publishers, 1976.

Encyclopaedia of Islam (*The*). 3 Vols. (ed.) B.Lewis., V.L.Menage & others. Leiden : E.J. Brill, 1979.

Encyclopaedia of Islam.(ed.) M.Th. Houtsma. London : Luzac & Co. 1936.

Encyclopaedia of Religion (The) Vol. VIII,(ed.) Mircea Eliade, NewYork : Macmillan, 1987.

Eraly, Abraham. *The Last Springs --- The Lives and Times of Great Mughals. New Delhi : Penguin Books, 1997.*

Erfani, M.E. *A-Z Ready Reference of the Quran.* New Delhi : Good Word Books, 2004.

Esin, Emel. *Mecca the Blessed, Medina the Radiant.* London : Elek, 1963.

Esposito, John L. *The Islamic Threat : Myth or Reality ?* New York : Oxford U.P., 1993.

- - - (ed. in chief) *The Oxford Encyclopaedia of the Modern Islamic World.* 4 vols. New York : Oxford University Press, 1995.

Faris, Nabih Amin. *The Book of Idols, being a Translation from the Arabic of the Kitab al-Asnam by Hisham al-Kalbi.* Princeton : Princeton University Press, 1952.

Fazal, E. Ammal. *Soukhal Hadith,* Vol.1. Delhi : M.M. Zakarriya, Idara Ishaat, Daniyet, 1994.

Felix, Bryk. *Sex and Circumcision.* North Hollywood, C.A. : Brandon House, 1967.

Fidal, Rafi Ahmed. *Hadrat Ali Murtaza.* (The Fourth Caliph) Delhi : Royal Publishers & Distributors, 1995.

- - - *Hadrat Muhammad.* Delhi : Royal Publishers & Distributors, 1995.

- - - *Hadrat Umar Bin Al-Khattab : The Second Caliph,* Delhi : Royal Publishers & Distributors, 1995.

- - - *Hadrat Usman Bin Affan : The Third Caliph.* Delhi : Royal Publishers & Distributors, 1995.

Frieling, Rudolf. *Christianity and Islam.* Edinburgh : Floris Books, 1978.

Fry, Plantagenet Somerset. *The Hamlyn Children's History of the World.* London : Hamlyn Publishing Group, 1977.

Geiger, Abraham. *Judaism and Islam.* New York : KTAV Publishing House, 1970.

Gellis, Sydeey. "Circumcision." *American Journal of Disease in Children.* (1978, No 132) 1168-69.

Ghose, Sailendra Nath. "Islam of the Mukkallids Versus Ijtihadi Islam." *Mainstream* (Sept. 15, 2001) 21-22.

Gibb, H.A.R. *Muhammadanism : An Historical Survey.* rpt. 1949 London : Oxford University Press, 1969.

- - - and J.H.Kramers(ed.) *Shorter Encyclopaedia of Islam.* Leiden : E.J. Brill, 1974.

Gibbon, Edward. *The Decline and Fall of the Roman Empire.* V Vols. London : Everyman's Library, 1941.

Gilchrist, John. *The Textual History of the Quran and the Bible.* Villach/ Austria : Light of Life, 1988.

Goel, Sita Ram. *The Calcutta Quran Petition.* New Delhi : Voice of India, 1987.

Goldziher, Ignaz. *Introduction to Islam.* Trans. Andras & Ruth Hamori, Princeton, N.J. : Princeton UP., 1981.

Grandguillaume, Gilbert. "The Forgotton Cultures of the Quran." *Diogenes.* No. 226, Vol. 57 issue 2. p.p.50-61.

Grunebaum, Gustav Edmund Von. *Medieval Islam.* Chicago : Chicago University Press,1961.

- - - *Classical Islam : A History, 622-1258.* Chicago : Aldine Publishing Co., 1966.

Guillaume, Alfred. *Islam.* London : Penguin Books, 1954.

274

- - - *The Life of Muhammad : A Translation of Ibn Ishaq's Sirat Rasul Allah* (Ibn Hisham's notes). Oxford : Oxford University Press, 1955.

Gunasekhar, Victor. "The Attitude of Muhammad Towards Women." *Rationalist Voice* (May-August-2007) 19-32.

Halm, Heinz. *Shiism.* Edinburgh : Edinburgh University Press, 1988.

Hamidullah, Muhammad. *Islam : A General Picture.* Hyderabad : Hazrat Safiuddin Literary and Religious Trust, 1979.

Hanbal, Ahmad Ibn. *The Musnad, or Collection of Tradition.* 6 Vols. Cairo : 1890. (This is a rare collection of the sayings of the Prophet recorded by different individuals and is likely to be genuine).

Hasan, Ahmad. *Al-Sunaan, A Collection of Hadith,* Vol.1 (Abu Dawud, Sulayman b. al-Ash'ath) New Delhi : Kitab Bhavan, 2001.

Harvest Times. (January 2007) 9-10, 24.

Head. Joseph. (ed.) *Reincarnation in World Thought.* New York : Julian Press, 1969.

HiHi, Philip K. *History of Arab.* London : Macmillan Press, 2001.

Hirschfeld, Hartwig. *New Researches into the Composition and Exegesis of the Quran Asiatic Monographs,* Vol. III. London : Royal Asiatic Society, 1902.

Holy Quran (The). Trans. Abdullah Yusuf Ali. Delhi : Khutub Khana Ishayat- ul-Islam, 1983.

Hosken, Fran P. *Female Sexual Mutilations : The Fact and Proposals for Action.* Lexington : Women's International Network News, 1979.

- - - "Female Genital Mutilation : Strategies for Eradication." *The Truth Seeker* (July-August 1989) 22-30.

Hotchkiss, Sandy, *Why Is It Always About You ? The Seven Deadly Sins of Narcissism.* NY : Free Press, 2003.

Houtsma, M. Th.A.J. Wensinck, elet (ed.) The *Encyclopaedia of Islam,* II, E.K. Leyden : Late E.J. Brill Ltd., 1927.

http://www.bible.ca/islam/islam-kills-muhammad-seeds-terrorism.htm

Hughes,Thomas Patrick. *A Dictionary of Islam.* New Delhi : Cosmo Publications (orig. pub. London : Allen), 1977.

Husain, Ed. *The Islamist.* London : Penguin Books, 2007.

Hussain, Muzaffer. "Violence at Haj : An Ancient Tradition." *Organiser* (Sept. 17, 1989) 6.

- - - "Voice Muslim Women's Distress." *Organiser* (July 11, 1993) 2007.

- - - *Islam and Shakahar.* Thane : Sarthak Publication, 2008.

Hussain, Riaz. *Abdullah the Father of Holy Prophet.* New Delhi : Islamic Book Service, 1998.

Ibn, Abbas. *Tanwir al-miqbas min tafsir Ibn Abbas,* in Majma al-tafasir, 1-7, Istanbul, 1319.

Ibn, Ishaq. *Sirat Rasid Allah : The Life of Muhammad.* trans. A Guilladum. New Delhi : Oxford University Press, 1980. (A source book for the subsequent biographers of Muhammad).

Ibn Katir, Abu al-Fida' Ismail. *Tafsir-al-Quran al-Azim.* 1-4 Cairo, n.d.

Ibn, Sa'd. *al-Tabaqat al-kubra,* 1-9 Dar Sader, Beriut, n.d.

Ibn, Sa'd (Katib al-Waqdidi). *Tabaqat* Ibn Sa'd 15 Vols. Urdu Trans. in 8 vols., 182, Siras : *The Biography of the Prophet.* Karachi : Nafees Academy-(This is the most important source on Muhammad's Companions and Sucessors, and the history of the Khalifat up to his own time).

Introduction to Islamic Civilization, (ed.) R.M. Savory, New Delhi : Vikas Publishing House, 1977.

Jagtiari, G.M. *Islam X-Rayed.* Mumbai : Jagtiani, 1996.

Jahagirdar, R.A. "Apostacy in Islam." *The Radical Humanist* (Oct. 2007) 6-8.

Jeffery, Arthur. *The Foreign Vocabulary of the Quran.* Baroda : Oriental Institute,1938.

- - - *Materials for the History of the Text of the Quran.* New York : AMS Press,1975.

Juynboll, G.H.A. *Muslim Tradition : Studies in Chronology, Provenance and Authorship of Early Hadith.* Cambridge : Cambridge University Press. 1983.

Kaleeby, Sheik Mousa Ben (Compiled). *Dictionary of the Quranic Phrases and its Meaning.* Cairo : Maktabat Al Adab, 2002.

Kamath, M.V. "The Shade of Swords : Jihad and the Conflict Between Islam and Christianity." *Organiser* (June 9, 2002) 14.

Kasem, Abul. "The Real Face of Islam." *Bharatiya Pragana* (September 2002) 22-29.

Khalid Muhammad Khalid. *Successors of The Messenger* (English Translation of al Khulafa al Rasool : Biographies of the Five Rightly Guided Caliphs of Islam). Beirut, Lebanon : Dar Al-Kotob Al-Ilmiyah Publishing House, 2005.

Khan, M.A.R. "Muslim Contribution to Science and Culture." *Radiance,*(1992, Feb. 9-15) 7,10.

- - - *Islamic Jihad : A Legacy of Forced Conversion, Imperialism, And Slavery.* NY : Universe, Inc, 2009.

Kidwai, Mohammad Asif. *What Islam Is ?* Lucknow : Islamic Research & Publications, 1967.

Kotb, Heba. "Sexuality in Islam". Ph.D Thesis submitted during Dec. 2004 on Clinical Sexology. Egypt : Maimonedes University, 2004.

Krizeck,James.(ed.) *Anthology of Islamic Literature.* Harmondsworth : Penguine, 1964.

Lammens, H. *Islam : Beliefs and Institutions.* Trans. E. Denison Ross. London : Methyen & Co., 1929.

Lemu, B. Aisha. *Woman in Islam.* Delhi : Markezi Maktoba Islami, 1983.

Lane, Edward W. *An Arab-English Lexicon.* London : Williams and Norgate, 1984.

Lane-Poole, Stanley. *Studies in a Mosque,* London : W.H. Allen & Co., 1883.

Larue, Gerald A. "Religious Traditions and Circumcision". *The Truth Seeker*(July/August,1989) 4-8.

Levtzion, Nehemia. "Conversion Under Muslim Domination : A Comparative Study." 30th *International Congress of Human Sciences in Asia and North Africa : Seminars : Religious Change and Cultural Domination.* (ed.) David N. Lorenzen, El Colegio de Mexico, 1981.

Levy, Reuben. *The Social Structure of Islam.* New York : Cambridge University Press, 1969.

Lewis, Bernard. *The Crisis of Islam : Holy War and Unholy Terror.* New York : Modern Library, 2003.

Lewis, Joseph. *In the Name of Humanity.* Calif : Freethought Press, 1967.

Lings, M. *Muhammad : His Life Bases on the Earliest Sources.* London : Islamic Texts Society/ George Allen and Unwin, 1983.

MacCabe, J. A. *Rationalist Encyclopaedia (qtd.).*

Maine, Colin. *The Dead Hand of Islam.* New South Wales : Australia Rationalist Association, 1979 and New Delhi : Voice of India, 1985.

Mahmud, Abdel Haleem. *The Creed of Islam.* n.p. : World of Islam Festival Trust, 1978.

Majah. *Sunan Ibn E. Majah.* trans. Tafail Muhammad Ansari, 5 Vols. Kitab Bhawan, New Delhi, 2000.

Malabari, Ibrahim Hussain. "Prophet Muhammad : Glimpses of his Great Personality". *Islamic Herald.* No. 6, vol. 9. 7-12.

Malik, Fida Hussain. *Wives of the Holy Prophet,* Delhi : Adam Publishers, 2001.

Malik, Imam. *Muwatta.* trans. Muhammad Rahimuddin, Kitab Bhawan, New Delhi, 2003.

Malik, S.K. *The Quranic Concept Of War.* New Delhi : Adam Publishers and Distributors. New Delhi, 2008.

Margoliouth, David Smith. *Mohammed and the Rise of Islam.* rpt. 1905. London ; New Delhi : Voice of India, 1985.

Masih, Y. A. *Comparative Study of Religions.* Delhi : Motilal Banarsidas, 1993.

Maududi, S. Abdul A'La. *Fundamentals of Islam.* Delhi : Markazi Maktaba Islami, 1979.

- - - *Towards Understanding Islam.* Delhi : Markazi Maktaba Islami, 1984.

- - - *Worship and Festival in Islam.* New Delhi : Markazi Maktaba Islami, 2003.

McClintock, John and James Strong. *Cyclopaedia of Biblical, Theological and Ecclesiastical Literature.* Grand Rapids : Baker Book House, 1981, 1 : 339, V : 151.

McDowell, John & Don Stewart. *Understanding Non-Christian Religions.* California : Campus Crusads for Christ, 1982.

Meanings of the Illustrious Quran (The) Trans. Abdullah Yusuf Ali, New Delhi : Kitab Bhawan, 2003.

Menon, M.S.N. "Islam and the Diabolic Slave Trade." *Organiser* (Dec. 23, 2007) 7.

Merz-Perez, Linda and Kathleen M Heide. *Animal Cruelty : Pathway to Violence Against People*. Lanham, UK, 2004. AltaMira Press. A division of Rowman. Littlefield Publishers, Inc.

Milos, Marilyn F. "Body Ownership Rights of Children : The Circumcision Question." *American Atheist* (July 1992) 50-59.

Mirza, Nader Baig. *Reincarnation and Islam,* Madras : Theosophical Publishing House, 1996.

Mishqat Ul-Masahib. trans. Maulana Fazlul Karim, 4 Vols. New Delhi : Islamic Book Service, 2001.

Mirkhond. *The Rauzat-us-Safa. The Garden of Purity*, trans. E. Tehatsek. London : Royal Asiatic Society, 1893. Mirkhod, a Fifteenth Century Persian Biographer.

Momen, Moojan. *An Introduction to Shil Islam : History and Doctrines of Twelver Shiism.* New Haven : Yale University Press, 1985.

Morey, Robert. *The Islamic Invasion.* Oregon : Harvest House, 1992.

Moses, Maimodes. *The Guide for the Perplexed.* New York : Dover Publications, 1956.

Muir, William. *The Life Of Muhammad* (first published in London in 1894). Reprinted by Delhi, Voice of India, 1992.

Muslims, Imam. *Sahih Muslim.* 4 Vols, Trans. Abdul Hamid Siddiqui. New Delhi : Kitab Bhavan, 2004.

Mustafa, Faizan. "Slaughter of Animals : Judicial Response". *Radiance* (May 1992) 9, 31.

Nadvi, S. Abdul Hasan Ali. *Qadiaism : A Critical Study.* Lucknow : Academy of Islamic Research, 1980.

Nadvi, Shah Moinuddin. *Abu Bakr Siddique : A Complete Biography of the First Caliph of Islam.* New Delhi : Idara Isha'at-E-Diniyat, 2007.

Naik, Zakir. "Is the Quran God's Word ?" *Islamic Voice* (January 2004) 23-24.

- - - *Answers to Non-Muslims' Common Questions About Islam.* Delhi : Qari Pub., 2007.

Narayan, B.K. *Mohammed the Prophet of Islam.* New Delhi : Lancers Publishers, 1978.

Nasrin, Taslima. "The Past is not Another Country." *Rationalist Voice* (5 :6) 25-30.

- - - "Let's Burn the Burqa." *Outlook* (Jan' 22/2007).

Nawawi, Riyadh as- Salihin of Imam. *Gardens of the Righteous.* trans. from Arabic by M.Z. Khan, London : Curzon Press, 1980.

Neale, F.A.*Islamism : Its Rise and its Progress.* in 2 Vols. London : James Madden, 1854.

Niazi, Shaheer. *What was the Real Age of Hazrat A'ishah, When Married to Prophet Muhammad ?* Pamplet Published from Karachi, no date or Publisher.

Nicholson, Reynold. *A Literary History of the Arabs.* Oxford University Press, 1969.

Noldeke, Theodor. *Sketches from Eastern History.* London & Edinburg : Adam & Charles Black, 1892.

Noss, John B. *Man's Religions.* New York : MacMillan, 1974.

O'Leary, De Lacy. *Arabia Before Muhammad.* New York & London : Kegan Paul, Trench, Trubner, 1927.

Oxford Encyclopaedia of the Modern Islamic World (The) 4 Vols. Ed. John Esposito, New York : OUP., 1995.

Oxtobt, Willard G. (ed.), *World Religions : Western Traditions.* Toronto : Oxford University Press, 1996.

Paliwal, K.V. *Jihad and Jannat in Hadiths.*

- - - *Jihad in the Way of Allah.* New Delhi : Hindu Writers Forum, 2007.

- - - *The Meaning of Jihad. New Delhi :* HWF, 2007.

Parrinder, Geoffrey, (ed.) *An Illustrated History of the World Religions.* Middlesex : Newness Books, 1971.

Payne, Robert. *The Holy Sword.* New York : Collier Books, 1962.

Pike, Royston. *Mohammed .* London : Morrison & Gibb, 1962.

Pine, E. Rayston. *Hundred Great Books,* New Delhi : Rupa, 1984.

Pirzada, Syed Sharifuddin (ed.) *Foundations of Pakistan : All India Muslim League Documents : 1906-1947* (Vol. I) New Delhi : Metropolitan Book, 1982.

Pollock, Dennis. "Christianity and Islam : Do We Worship the Same God ?" *Harvest Times* (July-August 2002) 6-8.

Prescott, James W. "Genital Pain Vs. Genital Pleasure : Why The One and Not The Other ?" *The Truth Seeker* (July/August 1989) 14-21.

Price, John. *A Dictionary and Glossary of the Koran.* London : Kurzon Press, 1971.

Quran. Holy Quran. (The) Text Translation and Commentary. London : The Islamic Foundation. A Bilingual English-Arabic Version of the Quran. (ed.) Abdullah Yusuf Ali.

Quran (The) An Introduction to the Commentary on the Holy Quran. (ed.) M.A.M. Abdul Haqq. Calcutta : Thacker, Spink & Co., 1910.

Quran (The) The Foreign Vocabulary of the Quran. by Aurthu Jeffery, Baroda : Oriental Institute, 1938.

Quran (The) Materials for the History of the Text of the Quran. (ed.) Arthur Jeffery, New York : AMS Press, 1975.

Quran (The) and Its Interpreters. Ayoub, Albany : State University of New York Press, 1984.

*Quran (The) The Koran : With a Preliminary Discourse and Explanatory Note*s. trans. George Sale. London : Orlando Hodgson, 1886.

Quran (The) trans. J.M. Rodwell. London. Dent, 1915.

Quran. Meanings of the illustrious Quran (The) Trans. Abdullah Yusuf Ali, New Delhi : Kitab Bhawan, 2003.

Quran (The) (ed.) M.E.Erfani. *A-Z Ready Reference of the Quran .* New Delhi : Good Word Books, 2004.

Rahman, A. "Ulema's Social Role : What it is and What it Ought to be." *Mainstream* (October 14-20, 2005) 5-9.

Ramtirth, Swain. *Dialogue with Muslim Clergy and Lectures on Christianity.* Nagpur : Crystal Publications, 2002.

Rangarajan, L. "Can a Good Muslim be a Good Citizen ?" *Hindu Voice* (Nov. 2007) 36.

Reade, Wind Wood. *Religion in History.* Bombay : MacMillan, 1972.

Reddy, S. Jayarama. *A Critical Analysis of Religions.* Anantapur : B. Premanand, 2004.

Riaz, Hussain. *Abdullah : The Fathers of Holy Prophet.* New Delhi : Islamic Book Service, 1994.

Rida, M.R. *The Revelation to Muhammad,* Part-I, Bombay : Ad-Darul-Qayyimah, 1960.

Rodinson, Maxime. "A Critical Survey of Modern Studies on Muhammad." *Studies on Islam.* tr. & ed. Merlin L. Swartz. New York : Oxford University Press, 1981.

- - - *Mohammed,* trans. Anne Carrer. Harmondsworth : Penguin, 1976.

Rodwell. J.M., trans. *The Koran.* London : Dent, 1915.

Sabab, Jaish E. *The Body Eternal.* Mumbai : Winner Books, 2004.

Sale, George, trans. *The Koran : With a Preliminary Discourse and Explanatory Notes.* London : Orlando Hodgson, 1886.

Salfuddin, S.M. and S.M. Sallah. "Jihad does not Mean Holy War." *University Today* (1 Nov. 2001) 8.

Samdani, Shaked. "Nature and Spirit of Khula", *Radiance* (4-10 Oct., 1992) 7.

Sarkar, Sir Jadunath. *A History of Aurangzeb.(qtd.).*

Schafer, David. "Islam and Terrorism : A Humanist View." *The Humanist* (May/June 2002) 16-20.

Schimmel, Annemarie. *And Muhammad is his Messenger : The Veneration of the Prophet in Islamic Piety.* Chapel Hill : Univ. of North Carolina Press, 1985.

Schuon, Frithjof. *Dimensions of Islam.* Trans. P.N. Townsend. London : George Allen & Unwin, 1970.

Sell,Canon and David Margliouth. "Christ in Mohammedan Literature," in James Hastings, ed., *Dictionary of Christ and the Gospels.* Charles Seribners' Sons, New York, 1917.

- - -*Historical Development of the Quran.* Madress : Diocesan Press, 1923.

- - - *Studies in Islam.* London : Diocesan Press, 1928.

- - - *The Life of Muhammad.* Lahore : Christian Literature Society of India, 1913.

Serge, Trifkovic. *The Sword of the Prophet,* Boston : Regina Orthodox Press, Inc, 2002.

Shah, Idries Sayed.   *The Sufis : Garden City.* NY : Doubleday, 1971.

Shahin, Sultan. "The Islamic Concept of Reincarnation." *Times of India.* (July 3, 2001) 8.

Shaikh, Anwar. *Islam : The Arab National Movement.* Cardiff : The Principality Publishers, 1995.

- - - *Islamic Jihad in Islam and Human Rights.* Houston : A Ghosh,1998.

- - - *Islam Sex and Violence.* Cardiff, UK :Principality Publishers, 1999.

- - - *Islam and Terrorism.* Cardiff : Principality Publishers, 2004.

- - - *Some Aspects of Quran.* New Delhi : HWF, 2009.

Shaikh, Younus. "Islam and Women." *Rationalist Voices.* (May-August 2007) 9-8.

Shamsuddin. "Islamic Calender a Theme Paper for Discussion, the Scientific Basis."*Journal of Islamic Science* (2000 : 1-2) 166-170.

Shorter Encyclopaedia of Islam, (ed.) H.A.R. Gibb & H.J. Kramers. Leiden : E.J. Brill, 1974.

Shourie, Arun. *The World of Fatwas.* New Delhi : Rupa & Co, 2002.

Sina, Ali. *Understanding Muhammad, A Psychobiography.* Felibri.com, 2008.

Siddiqui, Naeem. "Prophet Muhammad's Life at a Glance". *Radiance* (5-11 September 1993) 79-80.

Spencer, Robert (ed.). *The Myth of Islamic Tolerance : How Islamic Law Treats Non-Muslim.* New York : Prometheus Books, 2005.

- - -"Is the Hajj an Act of Apostasy ?" *Hindu Voice.* (November 2011) 30-31.

- - - *The Truth About Muhammad.* Regnery Publishing, Inc., 2006.

Sproul, R.C. and Saleeb Abdul. *The Darkside of Islam.* Wheaton, Illinois. Crossway Books (a divison of Good News Publishers), 2003.

Stewart, Desmond. *Mecca.* New York : News Week 1980.

Stoddard, Lothrop. *The New World of Islam.* London : Chapman & Hall, 1921.

Stump, Keith W. "Seeing the World Through Islamic Eyes." *The Plain Truth* (January 1981) 15-18, 25-26.

Swarup, Ram. *Understanding Islam Through Hadis Religious Faith or Fanaticism ?* New Delhi : Voice of India, 1984.

Sweetman, J. Windrwo. *Islam and Christian Theology.* 3 Vols. London : Lutterworth Press, 1945.

Tabari, Muhammad b. Jarir. *Jami al-bayan an ta'wil al-Quran,* (ed.) Mahmud Muhammad Shakir and Ahmad Muhammad Shakir, Cairo, 1968.1-30.

- - - *Tarih al-umam wa al-muluk* (ed.) Leiden : Goeje etc., 1879-1901.

Thompson, J.A. *The Bible and Archaeology.* Grand Rapids : Wm. B. Eerdmans, 1965.

Tirmizi. Tr. Murtaza Hussain F. Qurashi, New Delhi : Kitab Bhavan, 1997.

Tisdall, William St Clair. *The Original Sources of the Quran.* London : SPCK, 1911.

Trifkovic,Serge. *The Sword of the Prophet.* Boston : Regina Orthodox Press, 2002.

Tritton, A.S. *Islam Belief and Practices.* rpt. 1951. London : Hutchinson University Press, 1962.

True Guidance (*The*) *The Infallibility of Revelation and the Sins of the Prophet.* Part 1. Austria : Light of Life, 1991.

- - - *Comments on Quranic Verses.* Austria : Light of life, 1994.

Uris, Leon. "The Haj". *Teheran Times* (Nov. 28, 1984) 3,2.

Voltaire. *Letter To Benedict XIV* (Written in Paris on August, 17, 1745 AD) 1745.

Waddy, Charis. *The Muslim Mind.* London : Longman Group, 1976.

Waines, D.   *An Introduction to Islam.* Cambridge : Cambridge University Press, 1995.

Walker, Benjamin.   *Foundations of Islam.* New Delhi : Harper Collins, 1999.

Warraq, Ibn.   "Islamic Intolerance". *Free Inquiry* (Summer 1993) 49-53.

- - - (ed.) *Why I Am Not A Muslim.* New York : Prometheus Books, 1995.

- - -   *(The) Origins of the Koran, Classic Essays on Islam's Holy Book.* New York : Prometheus Books, 1998.

- - -   *The Quest for the Historical Muhammad.* New York : Prometheus Books, 2000.

- - -   "Islam, The Middle East, and Fascism." *American Atheist* (Autumn 2001) 21-34.

- - -   *What the Koran Really Says-- Language, Text and Commentary.* New York : Promtheus Books, 2002.

- - -   *Living Islam, Apostates Speak Out.* New York : Prometheus Books, 2003.

Watt, W. Montgomery. *Bell's Introduction to the Quran.* Edinburgh University Press, 1970.

- - -   *Islamic Philosophy and Theology : an Extended Survey.* Edinburgh : Edinburgh University Press, 1985.

- - - *Muhammad at Mecca.* Oxford : Clarendon Press, 1960.

Wensinck, A.J. *A Handbook of Early Muhammadan Tradition.* Leiden : E.J. Brill, 1971.

Wensinck, Arent Jan. *Muhammad and the Jews of Median.* Berlin : Adiyok, 1982.

- - - *The Muslim Creed.* London : Cambridge University Press, 1932.

Westermarck, E.A.*Pagan Survivals in Mohammedan Civilization.* London : Macmillan, 1933.

Wordsworth Encyclopaedia of World Religion (*The*) Hartfordshire England : Wordsworth edition, 1999.

Yasfi, Ausaf Saied.   "A Peep into Qadian." *Radiance* (3-9 January 1988) 1-2, 10.

Year Book of Muslim World.(ed). M.N. Jawed. New Delhi : Media Line, 1996.

Yusuf, Maulana Muhammad. "The Last Prophet of Islam." *Radiance* (22-28 Sept.. 1991) 3,10.

Yusuf, S.M.   *The Sunnah.* Delhi : Taj Company, 1982.

Zakaria, Rafiq. *Muhammad and the Quran.* New Delhi : Penguin Books, 1991.

Zangger, Russel. "Before you Decide to Circumcise your Son, We would Like to have you Look Over This Information About Circumcision. " *The Truth Seeker* (January 1984) 386-387.

Zindler, Frank R. "An Athiest's Guide to Muhammadanism." *American Atheist* (Winton 2001.2002).

Zwemer, S.M., *Arabia, the Cradle of Islam :* Studies in the Geography, *People and Politics of the Peninsula with an Account of Islam and Mission Work.* London : Darf., 1986.

- - - *Studies in Popular Islam.* London : The Sheldon Press, 1939.

Question Index

34

302

762.   Elijah : the Prophet for the Black Muslims
763.   Holy Trinity of Shia Ghulat Sect
764.   Mukkallid Versus Ijtihadis
765.   Muslim Brotherhood prescribed Jihad
766.   Zaidi a Sect of Peace Loving People
767.   Ismailis End the Line of Imams
768.   Quarmati who carried off the Black Stone
769.   Nusairi believes Ali is Allah
770.   Druze prophesied the Destruction of Mecca and Jerusalem
771.   Baktashi : a Sect which follows Christianity
772.   Kizil-Bash : Christianization of Islam
773.   Ahl-i-Haqq : a Sect who believed in Transmigration
774.   Hurufi Sect celebrates with Wine
775.   Khoja believes in Das Avatar
776.   Bohora : Worshipper of Ram ?
777.   Baabi who inspired the Baha'is
778.   Shia opposed Baab as another Prophet
779.   Islamic Brotherhood a myth
780.   Break away from Islam, Bahai stands as a Religion
781.   Does the House of Justice do Justice to Women ?
782.   Ahmad the Prophet : Break the Chain of the Last One
783.   Split in Qadiyaan
784.   Ahmadiyah's Jihad through Pen
785.   Ahmadi : continues Prophethood
786.   Be Aware of different Schools of Islam

www.ingramcontent.com/pod-product-compliance
Lightning Source LLC
Chambersburg PA
CBHW032035080426
42733CB00006B/91